# Early Yorkshire Bladens

First Published in Great Britain in 2015
by Karen & Graham Proudler
Forge Cottage, Field Farm, Aston Lane, Shardlow
Derbys DE72 2GX
Copyright ©Karen & Graham Proudler, 2015
ISBN 978-0-9566831-6-8

All rights reserved. No part of this book may be reproduced or transmitted in any form or by any means, electronic or mechanical including photocopying, recording or by any information storage and retrieval system, without permission from the Publisher in writing. No guarantee is made or implied that the information contained herein is without error. Information is for readers' convenience and reference only, anyone requiring accurate information should verify same by seeking professional assistance and conducting their own further research.

Email: proudlers@gmail.com
Privately Printed

## Abbreviations

| | |
|---|---|
| Abp | Archbishop |
| CSP | Calendar of State Papers |
| CTB | Calendar of Treasury Books |
| CUL | Cambridge University Library |
| NUL: DMSC | Nottingham University Library: Department of Manuscripts and Special Collections |
| DNB | Dictionary of National Biography |
| EIC | East India Company |
| HoC | House of Commons |
| HoL | House of Lords |
| JBoT | Journals of the Board of Trade and Plantations |
| LRS | London Record Society |
| MHS | Maryland Historical Society |
| MSA | Maryland State Archives |
| WYAS | West Yorkshire Archive Service |
| YAJ | Yorkshire Archaeological Journal |
| YAS | Yorkshire Archaeological Society |

*All dates prior to 1752 are old style unless stated otherwise*

## Acknowledgements

With thanks to the Earl of Rosse, the Hawke family, Lord Savile and other portrait owners for permission to use images. Special thanks to Kirsty McHugh, Archivist, Yorkshire Archaeological Society, also the Board of Trinity College Dublin, Barnsley Archives and Local Studies, the Borthwick Institute for Archives at the University of York, Doncaster Archives, West Yorkshire Archive Service, Nottingham University's Manuscripts and Special Collections Library, British Library, Dr Andrew Hopper - Centre for English Local History at the University of Leicester, Hull History Centre, Jenny Bussey and many others. Also thanks to Helena Coney for making trips to The National Archives possible.

**Two new books for 2015:**

**Martin Bladen: A Biography**   ISBN 978-0-9566831-5-1

**Early Yorkshire Bladens**   ISBN 978-0-9566831-6-8

Written by Karen Proudler

# WEST RIDING

```
                                                          YORK
                    Marston Moor

                                   Tadcaster
  DENTON    ASKWITH
                                              BOLTON PERCY
                                                    Nun Appleton
↕ 40 miles                     Towton   SCARTHINGWELL
                                              Church Fenton

                                              PONTEFRACT

             HALIFAX

          SOUTHOWRAM
              Cromwellbotham

                          WAKEFIELD
                          Thornhill

                                           Bullinger Wood (Hall)
                                         HEMSWORTH
                              CARLTON
                                                 South Kirkby
                       Barnsley
                                    DONCASTER
                  Wortley    Wentworth Woodhouse
```

Askwith, Harrogate (*North Yorkshire*) is 28 miles from Wakefield and 30 miles from York
Thornhill (*West Yorkshire*) is 6 miles from Wakefield and 35 miles from York
Hemsworth (*West Yorkshire*) is 7 miles from Wakefield and 29.5 from York
Wortley (*South Yorkshire*) is 20 miles from Wakefield and 50 miles from York

# Contents

| | Page No. |
|---|---|
| INTRODUCTION | 7 |
| BEGINNINGS | 9 |
| | |
| ROBERT BLADEN | 17 |
|     Sir George Radcliffe | 20 |
|     Dr Richard Berry | 28 |
|     Coney v Bladen | 33 |
|     Bladen v Wortley | 37 |
|     Savile Family | 38 |
|     Bullingshire Hall | 43 |
| | |
| JOHN BLADEN | 49 |
|     Letters to Lord Fairfax | 51 |
|     Treatise | 53 |
|     Birkheads | 56 |
|     Civil War | 61 |
|     Turncoat | 64 |
| | |
| NATHANIEL BLADEN | 67 |
|     Bladen v Watson | 68 |
|     Letters to Wrightson | 69 |
|     Fairfax Marriage | 74 |
|     Danby | 77 |
|     Popish Plot | 79 |
|     Paper Chase | 86 |
|     Duke and Duchess of Buckingham | 94 |
| | |
| FOURTH GENERATION | 109 |
|     Descendants of Nathaniel/Isabella: | 109 |
|     Isabella | 109 |
|     Catherine | 111 |
|     William | 114 |
|     Frances | 155 |
|     Elizabeth | 174 |
|     Martin | 193 |
| | |
| LEGACY | 197 |
| | |
| APPENDICES: | 199 |
|     Advice to a Son | 199 |
|     William Bladen, additional information | 202 |
|     Chronologies | 206 |
|     Wills | 225 |
|     Genealogy | 234 |
|     Additional Sources | 249 |
|     Name Index | 250 |

## CHARTS

| Chart | Page No. |
|---|---|
| Wortley - Radcliffe - Wentworth - Savile | 17 |
| Waterhouse - Lacy - Birkhead | 24 |
| Wortley - Radcliffe - Wentworth - Savile - Berry - Gargrave | 27 |
| Cavendish - Wortley - Coney | 33 |
| Birkhead - Lacy - Paslew | 59 |
| Birkhead - Rogers - Watson - Lindsey | 67 |
| Danby - Buckingham - Fairfax | 77 |
| Danby - Tongue - Bedloe - Titus Oates | 79 |
| Danby/Osborne Family | 90 |
| Danby/Osborne - Pembroke - Clarges | 97 |
| Walpole - Townshend - Pelham - Powlett | 103 |
| Court Circle | 123 |
| William's Descendants | 125 |
| Walpole - Townshend - Pelham - Bedford | 130 |
| Hamond - Brooke - Hawke - Pulleyne | 156 |
| Hawke | 175 |
| Elizabeth's Descendants | 179 |

# Introduction

Research into the earliest settled Bladen family in Yorkshire has produced two volumes: 'Early Yorkshire Bladens' and its companion book 'Martin Bladen: A Biography'. Although Martin is part of the same family discussed in this book, his career at the Board of Trade warranted more extensive detailed coverage than could be contained within this single volume. The two volumes taken together, therefore, complement each other and give a comprehensive account of these early Bladens in Yorkshire.

Their story begins in the beautiful West Riding just after the death of Queen Elizabeth I when James VI of Scotland arrived in London as the new King James I of England with a new message on the coinage 'I will make them one people'. Sadly, however, James would not live to see the union of the kingdoms as parliamentarians rejected the idea. Change was slow to take place and, in areas such as Yorkshire, a handful of ancient and noble families held control of the county in their hands. The earliest Bladens in Yorkshire prospered because they married into those families or became of service to them but, when Civil War came, they found their allegiances sharply divided and loyalties tested. Whilst living on Fairfax Manor land and being employed by the 1st Lord Fairfax and his Parliamentary supporting sons, the Bladens were also closely associated with two of Yorkshire's leading Royalists, which led to 'Black Tom' Fairfax challenging their trustworthiness.

After the war ended, Bladen descendants began to gradually fan out from Yorkshire. The ladies of generation four, who were called 'The Northern Stars' at Court, married and the trail of their descendants widened not just geographically but socially too and encompassed every level of society. There were descendants who became Earls, Lords, Governors, Secretaries of State, Members of Parliament, Lawyers, Army Majors, Colonels and Admirals of the Navy. Some would fight or work to maintain the Colonial Empire and supported, indeed promoted, the slave and sugar trades, or used their influence to encourage protectionism to benefit their self interests. Alongside those who achieved high office, success and even public adulation there were many who thrived happily in obscurity. Yorkshire Bladen descendants ran the gamut of less noble life experiences too, from clandestine marriages to theft, gambling and accusations of murder. But for every Bladen who was incarcerated in debtors' jail or, who died feeling bitter remorse at their abandonment by the world, there were tenfold more who were highly valued and served their country with distinction. Most major military engagements in the last 400 years have had a Yorkshire Bladen descendant involved somewhere, quite often several members of the same family and very often leading from the front.

These two volumes record some of their worthy life-stories but they are only a beginning, there are plenty of unseen sources and material still to be unearthed, and so the research will continue.

**Overview**

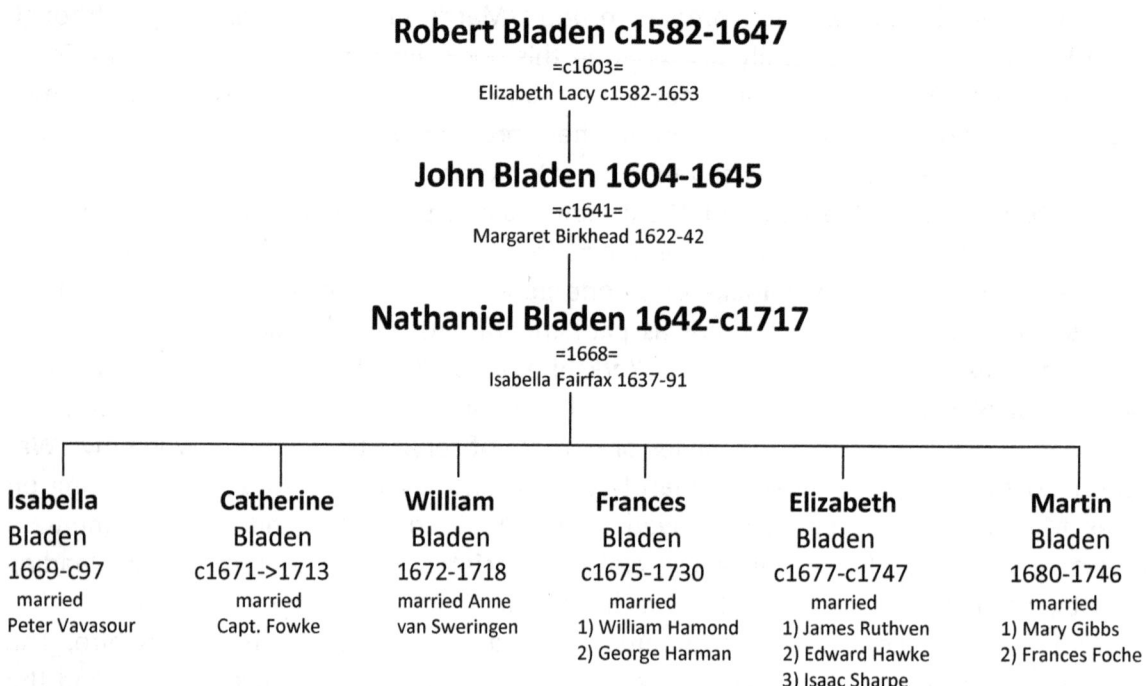

# Beginnings

Robert Bladen born about 1582 was probably the first of this family who settled in Yorkshire. It is difficult to be absolutely certain about this because of the difficulty of transcribing the parish registers and many early entries have been variously interpreted as Sladen or Bladen by different sources. Subsidy rolls (poll tax returns) show Sladens were in Yorkshire from 1379 and examination of the original early parish register entries by an independent palaeographer[1] confirmed entries as being 'Sladen'.[2] There is no evidence, therefore, of a settled family prior to Robert's arrival. The first event recorded for Robert was the baptism of his son John[3] in 1604 at Southowram in an area just to the southeast, but still within the parish, of Halifax and close to Cromwell Bottom (Cromwellbothom). The choice of this location was due to his wife Elizabeth Lacy, whose family had resided there for many generations and, indeed, contributed to the building of the very church where the baptism took place. The Bladen family's roots may ultimately have sprung from South Derbyshire in an area between Winshill and Newton Solney on the border with Staffordshire where there have been Bladens (with variations of spelling) as far back as the mid-1200s. A cluster of 'Bladon' field names[4] where the Rivers Trent and Dove converge may indicate that there was once a small settlement there from which the inhabitants took their name.[5]

Although nothing is known about Robert's circumstances prior to marriage, the fact that he was able to marry into one of the oldest and most influential families in Yorkshire indicates he must have been of some standing. As will be seen, the Lacys were well accustomed to making advantageous marriages which reinforced or, indeed, enhanced their own substantial status. Along with the Montagu, Savile, Waterhouse and Birkhead families, Lacys dominated the region, most of these families having been granted large areas of land spanning several counties in return for their support of William the Conqueror during the Norman Conquest. The Saviles were Marquis of Halifax, the Montagu family had been Viscounts and the de Lacy family (who had been granted 170 Lordships) held the Honour of Pontefract (of which Cromwellbothom was a part) and built a castle near Wakefield where many generations of Lacys lived. Through the centuries these ancient families married into other leading families in the area and individuals from these families were part of the early Bladen story. Elizabeth Bladen's Lacy family relations were to prove central to the prosperity of Robert and his family and so a few pages are devoted to them.

---

[1] David Bethell, FONS

[2] The West Yorkshire parish register for the year 1560 (20th March) has a baptism of a Henry Sladen (or Bladen), son of Edward of Warley. Sladens, however, were residents of Warley since 1379 (Poll tax returns)

[3] Court rolls examined: For the Manor of Wakefield 1274-97 - Vol. 1, YAS Record Series; 1297-1309 Vol. 2; 1313-1316 (and 1286), 1350 (21st & 26th October) Vol. 3; 1537-40 Vol. 9 and 1639-1640. Partial examination of the following: 1322-1331, 1331-33, 1338-40, 1443-36, 1550-52, 1583-85, 1608-9, 1664-65. Not all of the 670 parchments of court rolls, however, have been seen. Many Sladen entries have been mis-reported as Bladens

[4] Paget Family Estates: maps (1759) by William Wyatt; D(W)1734/2/3/139, D(W)1734/2/3/146, D(W)1734/2/3/152, Staffordshire Record Office

[5] Field-Names in South Derbyshire by William Fraser A.R.Hist.S., 1947, p101 (Newton Solney)

## Lacy Family

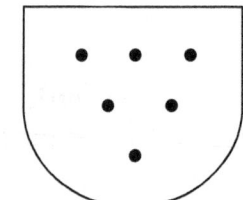

*Lacy Arms of Cromwellbothom*
*Argent, six ogresses: three, two, one[1]*

**John Lacy** 1395-1474 of Cromwellbotham
= Florence Molyneux b. 1398 of Lancashire in 1416 (*dau of Robert Molyneux of Lancashire*)

**William Lacy** 1417-44 of Cromwellbotham
= Joan Scargill in 1439 (*dau of Sir William Scargill of Thorpe Stapleton nr Leeds*)

**Thomas Lacy** 1440-99 of Cromwellbotham
= Ellen Neville (*dau of Robert Neville of Liversedge*)

**John Lacy** 1470-1531 of Cromwellbotham
= 1) Matilda (or Mary) Wortley (*dau of Sir Nicholas Wortley*)
= 2) Alice (or Joan) Leventhorpe 1477-1530 (*dau and heiress of Leventhorpe*)

**John Lacy** 1507-82 of Cromwellbotham
= 1) Ann Tempest d.1580 (*dau. of Sir Richard Tempest of Bracewell*)
= 2) Mary Gascoigne (*dau of Alveray Gascoigne of Garforth nr Leeds*)

**Richard Lacy*** 1530-91 of Cromwellbotham (*Tempest mother*)
= Alice Ellen Townley (*dau. of Laurence Townley of Barnside Lancaster*)
*Richard possibly took part in the Rebellion of the North

**John Lacy** of Cromwellbotham 1561-1638
= 1) Alice Birkhead (*dau. of Martin Birkhead*)
John Lacy = 2) Ellen Lister (*dau. of Michael Lister of Frierhead, Yorkshire*)

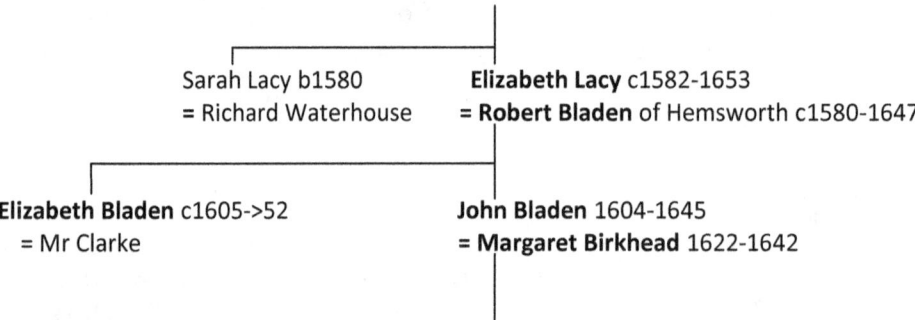

Sarah Lacy b1580
= Richard Waterhouse

**Elizabeth Lacy** c1582-1653
= **Robert Bladen** of Hemsworth c1580-1647

**Elizabeth Bladen** c1605->52
= Mr Clarke

**John Bladen** 1604-1645
= **Margaret Birkhead** 1622-1642

**Nathaniel Bladen** 1642-c1717
= **Isabella Fairfax**[1]

---

[1] Spencer Stanhope Manuscript Collection, West Yorkshire Archives SpSt/6/3/15

*Valley of the Sheep*
The area where Robert Bladen and wife Elizabeth first appear in records at Southowram, Halifax was surrounded by moorland which did not lend itself to premium grass or corn growing, so the dominant industry was wool and cloth-making and many big land owners used sheep farming to support their vast estates. Forty percent of the wool was sold to the colonies but the trade also provided much needed local jobs. In addition to owning the land which was rented out to farmers, Lacy's owned an ancient fulling mill (part of the wool-making process), water mills, corn mills and had mining rights to extract coal, stone and other minerals. They thereby had control of many of the natural resources and the staple industries of the area and they reinforced their status by strategic alliances both in business and by marriage.

Partnerships were forged with the Midgley and Ramsden families when, after the dissolution of the monasteries, land became available and the trio (Lacy/Midgley/ Ramsden) set about acquiring as much land as they could at this time. Midgleys were also an ancient family who held the Manor of Midgley and the Ramsdens had significant holdings in the cloth industry and land. One of the manors they purchased, Thornton, would in later times become home to Patrick Brontë, father of the novelists Charlotte, Emily and Anne and the Brontë connection continued to Southowram where, in 1837-38 Emily Brontë found herself in a teaching post at an exclusive boarding school - a post she only held for six months as she found the regime there too rigid.

Lacy family history stretches back a thousand years but, for the purpose of this book, has been restricted to highlight only those individuals of direct concern, though as maternal ancestors of the Bladens in Yorkshire, there is good reason to include them.[2] Robert's wife Elizabeth's great-great-grandfather, John Lacy, one of many of the same name, sets the scene for describing the family that Robert Bladen married into. His first marriage to Mary Wortley (of Wortley Hall, large landowners and iron masters) produced no children, but his second marriage to a Leventhorpe, saw him acquire the Manors of Leventhorpe[3] and Horton, which both had rich coal seams.

The next generation, Elizabeth's great-grandfather John, led a much more turbulent life than his father before him. He is doubly important to Bladen genealogy as two of his grandchildren married each other (Alice Birkhead and John Lacy) and were thereby direct Bladen ancestors. This John Lacy b1507 married Anne[4] daughter of Sir Richard Tempest of Bracewell and Bolling Hall near Bradford who was the Steward of the Manor of Wakefield. At least, that was only one of Tempest's titles as he was also Steward of the Duchy of Lancaster, Steward of Rochdale, Steward of Barnoldswick, Master Forester, Keeper of Quernmore Park, Justice of the Peace, High Sheriff of Yorkshire 1621, Receiver of the 3rd Earl of Derby (Lancashire estates) and many more titles as well as being in attendance at King Henry VII's funeral and Henry VIII's Field of Cloth of Gold.

---

[1] William Flower's Visitation of Yorkshire 1563/4; Sir William Dugdale's Visitation of Lancashire 1664/5, Vol. 85; Leventhorpes of Sawbridgeworth and Biographia Halifaxiensis by J Horsfall Turner. 1883
[2] South Yorkshire - The History and Topography of the Deanery of Doncaster in the Diocese and County of York by Rev. Joseph Hunter, Vol. 2, 1831, p200-203 for extensive Lacie history back to the Domesday Book
[3] The Leventhorpes of Sawbridgeworth by P.W. Kerr, 1935 p130 & 136; Also Harleian Manuscript 4630
[4] Some sources say he married Jane, daughter of Sir Richard Tempest

To have such a man, who was also Henry VIII's bodyguard, as your father-in-law could only be a good omen for John Lacy in an age where aligning yourself to someone more powerful and of a higher status than yourself was how to get advancement and, indeed, Tempest appointed his son-in-law to be his attorney and Bailiff of Halifax. Later, John Lacy would in turn appoint his own son-in-law James Stansfield to the same post, as Deputy Bailiff.[1]

As evidence of his status in the local community John, along with some neighbours, brought about the building (or rebuilding) of the small chapel, due east of Southowram called St Anne's, where Robert Bladen/Elizabeth would baptise their son 70 years later. A deed, dated 21st February 1530, stated *"John Lacy of Cromwellbothom, Esq, doth give to Thomas Savile of Exley, with others, as feoffees in trust, four closes of land in Southowram (in one of the which a chapel of St Anne, by him the said John Lacy, with his neighbours, is built) of intent that they the said feoffees shall be seized thereof to the use of the said John Lacy and his heirs forever...."*[2] The chapel already existed and had been part of an old manor house dating back to the mid-1400s (which is perhaps an explanation for what seems like its odd location, being some distance from villages or houses) but the group was responsible for saving and developing it and today it still survives as St Anne-in-the-Grove Church.[3] It appears in ancient records as sometimes called 'Lacies' chapel'.[4] Much later in 1793 it became a separate ecclesiastical parish quite detached from the main parish of St John the Baptist in Halifax.

At the time of the baptism of Robert's son, however, the two districts were shown in the same register; the infant John Bladen's record in St John the Baptist register for Halifax[5] has 'South' added to it, denoting the baptism took place at Southowram. The pattern of entries for the register was to write 'Hal' for those events that took place at St John the Baptist Parish Church itself in Halifax, but otherwise 'South' indicated the small Lacy chapel east of Southowram.[6]

John Lacy quickly became one of his powerful father-in-law's strongest supporters and, although Tempest had a high status role and an impressive list of posts, he seemed to have a weakness for quarelling with neighbours, in particular Sir Henry Savile of Thornhill who was Steward of the Honour of Pontefract (and who had been brought up in Henry VIII's court), Saviles being the other prominent family in the Halifax area. Tempest and Savile had fueded over stewardship of Wakefield which Tempest finally won. The fued between the men, however, continued for many years but it would be Savile who would ultimately prevail, with Tempest eventually being incarcerated in jail where he died.

---

[1] Yorkshire Deeds, Vol. 12 edited by William Brown and Glover's Visitation of Yorkshire 1563/64, p330
[2] Register of Halifax Church: endowment of St Anne's Chapel
[3] A Topographical Dictionary of Yorkshire, Thomas Langdale. 1822
[4] A Concise History of the Parish and Vicarage of Halifax, in the County of York by John Crabtree 1836
[5] Vicar at the time was Dr John Favour who was a popular Puritan, he was also a celebrated physician and lawyer and he founded Heath Grammar School in Halifax
[6] Not long after Robert and Elizabeth baptised their only son John, at the chapel her father sold St Anne's in Southowram in 1605 to Robert Lawe of Halifax for 5 Marks. The History of the Town and Parish of Halifax: Containing a Description of the Town etc by William Bentley, 1754

The hostility between the two men, if claims are to be believed, became known as the Wakefield-Pontefract fued, each man respectively owning those Manors and it was tribal with many lives being lost by those who got between the families. Some have speculated that it was actually a continuation of a 14th century dispute between the Lacy and Warren families - both families had been present at the Battle of Hastings and been rewarded with lands in the same area. Whatever the origin, a series of tit-for-tat murders took place and third-party attempts to end hostilities failed and those who attempted to intervene in the dispute usually paid a heavy price. After the murder of two men, including a priest, the Deputy Bailiff of Halifax (a Savile supporter) had challenged one of those involved to a duel which sadly led to both men dying of their wounds. Altogether some nine murders were attributed to the Tempest family generally, though not Sir Richard personally.[1] His younger brother Nicholas was considered one of the leaders behind the Pilgrimage of Grace, which is about to be discussed, and was executed for his part in it. Sir Richard was also accused of falsifying his records as Steward of Wakefield, submitting acreages of leased land that were lower than those actually leased and pocketing the difference.

*Pilgrimage of Grace*
Tempest and Savile, of course, took opposite sides in national issues too as in 1536 when Henry VIII broke away from the Roman Catholic church and began the dissolution of the smaller monasteries. The feuding families split between Savile who supported, and Tempest who was opposed to, the King's actions. John Lacy naturally took Tempest's side on the issue and was heard in the streets of Halifax inciting a group of men to go into Lancashire and *"raise the commons there"*. One of the group, Henry Farrer of Ewood Hall[2] said to Lacy *"who shall go with us into Lancashire"* to which Lacy replied *"your own self shall go and your company."* Farrer asked *"why will not Sir Richard Tempest go with us?"* to which Lacy said *"no, marry, but yourself,"*[3] though it was later said that Sir Richard Tempest's brother and servants did join the group in Lancashire.[4] The opposing side, supporting the King and headed by Savile gathered their forces to challenge the rebels but their numbers were insufficient and the Duke of Norfolk intervened to negotiate a truce. On 14th December 1536, the day before the truce, the King pardoned the rebels and the Royal Herald who delivered the message reported observing John Lacy in the crowd. This uprising became known as the Pilgrimage of Grace and spread throughout the north but was eventually suppressed.

The vicar of Halifax, Robert Holdsworth, not long after his appointment decided to side with Sir Henry Savile in the dispute[5] and, when his allegiance became known, found his vicarage being repeatedly ransacked.

---

[1] The fortunes of the Tempest family of Bracewell and Bowling in the sixteenth century, YAJ, 74 (2002), pp169–189; The History and Antiquities of the Deanery of Craven, 2 Vols (1878), Vol. 1, p96, T. D. Whitaker
[2] The Farrar/Lacy families were inter-married. John Lacy's own sister Margaret was married to Brian Farrar
[3] The Story of Old Halifax, by Thomas William Hanson, 1920
[4] Younger brother Nicholas Tempest (of Ackworth near Hemsworth) was one of the leaders of the Yorkshire Pilgrimage of Grace and was executed at Tyburn for his part
[5] The Story of Old Halifax, by T.W. Hanson, 1920 p96

Rev. Holdsworth, in the supposed privacy of his much-burgled vicarage, then had a casual discussion with a servant about events at the time .... *"By my troth! William, if the King reign any space he will take all from us of the church, all that we have and I therefore pray God send him short reign"*.[1] The conversation was divulged to the authorities and the priest was required to pay a heavy fine but at least he survived, initially that is. Leaders of the rebellion were not so fortunate and they were rounded up and hanged. Sir Richard Tempest[2] was incarcerated in Fleet Prison and died, probably of the plague, before his trial. As for John Lacy whose presence had already been noted, he further put himself in some danger after he wrote the following ditty:-

*"As for the King, an apple and a fair wench to dally withal, would please him very well"*[3]

and sent it to his son-in-law John Waterhouse (husband of daughter Dorothy). Seemingly harmless words sent to a relation were somehow brought to the attention of Thomas Cromwell, though in the retelling of the story there was confusion that the words were actually those of the Bishop of Canterbury, still Lacy was fortunate to escape with his life. With the popular revolt in the north quelled, Henry VIII continued his dissolution of the monasteries unabated, however the hostility between the Lacy/Tempest families and Savile/Rev Holdsworth continued and it was reported that yet again Rev Holdsworth's vicarage had been ransacked though, this time, John Lacy was named as the guilty party. The following year another Lacy relation, Thomas, with Tempest supporters again broke into the same vicarage which was empty at that time as the Reverend had gone to London to enlist help with the vindictive Lacy's. He had obtained 'Writs of Attachment' against them and subpoenas.

The latest break-in at the vicarage had yielded an impressive haul, and Thomas Lacy found a hidden stash of gold worth about £789-8s-9d - a fortune. Lacy then seemed to have had an attack of conscience and sought ways to return the gold and approached Holdsworth's parish priest Sir Alexander Emmet who agreed to take the gold and he returned it to Holdsworth when he returned from London, saying simply that it was handed in at Confession. Holdsworth took steps to have the subpeonas issued to the Lacy's and their servants but no one responded. John Lacy said: *"If they will have my head they will fetch it."*[4] He was later to admit that he had broken into the vicarage but that the gold was 'treasure-trove'. The Duke of Norfolk intervened to examine the matter and asked to see all involved, his thinking was that the fortune belonged to the King unless the priest could prove it was his.

---

[1] The Story of Old Halifax, by T.W. Hanson, 1920
[2] Tempests were connected with the great baronial house of Clifford - Earls of Cumberland
[3] The Story of Old Halifax, by T.W. Hanson, 1920, p99. Also, Letters & Papers, Foreign and Domestic, Henry VIII, Vol. 12, part 1 January - May 1537 pp323-354
[4] Ibid

An action was brought in the Star Chamber between Holdsworth and Lacy[1] and Holdsworth seems to have recovered his money. He may have lived longer, however, if he had lost his fortune as in May 1556 thieves broke into the vicarage, yet again, stole everything and murdered him. It is not known who the assailants were.[2]

After the death of Lacy's mother Alice Leventhorpe in 1530 and his father's death a year later, John inherited from both. From his mother he inherited the Manor of Horton and also Leventhorpe Hall[3] where he would later live. Not long after he came into his inheritance he got into a boundary dispute with neighbour William Rookes of Royds Hall. The bone of contention concerned the mining rights and an arbitrator in the form of John Tempest settled the matter. The arbitrator, however, could hardly have been classed as impartial as he was a relation of Sir Richard Tempest - Lacy's father-in-law. Lacy went through several successful law suits, such as in 1579 when the Duchy of Lancaster brought a suit against him for encroaching on Crown lands. In fact, it was said he had *'intruded into 34 messuages, four cottages, 183 acres of land, a water mill, corn mill and one coal mine in or near Horton - the Queen's possessions'*.[4] Lacy prevailed by producing court rolls which proved his case and the Queen's claim was set aside by decree and Lacy retained ownership.

So that was a brief outline of Elizabeth Lacy's ancestors, but to find out more about the immediate family Robert Bladen married into, we can now look at Elizabeth Lacy's father, another called John Lacy, and it is of interest to note that he made two exceptionally good matches for himself. His first marriage was to Alice, the daughter of Martin Birkhead, Attorney to Queen Elizabeth I,[5] the Birkheads being prominent merchants in the north of England. His second marriage was to Ellen, the daughter of Michael Lister of Frerehead (the Listers were an old, rich family of mill-owners and cloth merchants). John's daughter Sarah Lacy made a first-class marriage to a Waterhouse of Shibden Hall, the Waterhouse family holding the Manor of Halifax since 1545. So it is perhaps not too great a leap of faith to suspect that daughter Elizabeth's marriage to Robert Bladen should have been to a man of some standing.

Elizabeth's family were extremely wealthy and her father's new acquisitions by inheritance led to the family disposing of some of their older estates. In 1590 her father sold Old Syddall Hall to John Scolfield of Coley and in 1612 he then sold the Lacy's Manor House at Cromwelbothom to Thomas Gledhill.

---

[1] TNA: STAC 2/21/174 Holdsworth v Lacy. Plaintiff: Robert Holdsworth. Defendants: John Lacy, Thomas Savell, Richard Haldworth, Nicholas Brodley and others. Subject: Forcible entry into the vicarage of Halifax
[2] The Story of Old Halifax, by T.W. Hanson, 1920. Also, Letters & Papers, Foreign and Domestic, Henry VIII, Vol. 12, part 1 January - May 1537 pp323-354
[3] Yorkshire Deeds Vol. 2, edited by William Brown and Glover's Visitation p330
[4] The History and Topography of Bradford in the County of York by John James. 1841
[5] Martin Birkhead d1590 married Alice Lacy, daughter of John Lacy of Cromwellbotham. Steward to the Manor Court at Wakefield in the 1560s, Queen's Attorney in the North in 1574 and JP for the West Riding 1577, all other Ridings by 1584

If Robert Bladen's circle of contacts after marriage are any gauge, it can be surmised that his circumstances were greatly enhanced by the marriage, that he was the greater 'gainer' by the alliance. He made extensive use of his Lacy family contacts through the following years without there being a single mention of his Bladen relations.

All of which seems to point to his Bladen family originating outside of Yorkshire or were not of equal status to the new Lacy relations.

# Robert Bladen

Robert was born around 1581, probably outside of the county,[1] and was no doubt a gentleman, but not so high ranking that he was above being engaged in business or working as a Steward. He married Elizabeth Lacy and the couple had two children, though only one baptism of his son John on 24th March 1604 at Southowram,[2] has been found. There was also a daughter called Elizabeth as, many years later in a chancery case reference was made to John having a sister, Mrs Elizabeth Clarke,[3] who helped raise a grandson following the premature death of his parents.[4]

A few years after his son's baptism Robert was working, from around 1607, for the noble Wortley family (Lacy relations) at their estate at Wortley near Barnsley in South Yorkshire. How he came to obtain this post is a subject frequently considered in this book since it may reveal something about his earlier life, however his influential Lacy relations were probably behind the appointment.

It is doubtful that head of the family Sir Richard Wortley engaged Bladen as he died in 1603 although it may have been his death which necessitated the family requiring a steward as there is evidence that Robert was working for Sir Richard's widow Elizabeth shortly afterwards.[5]

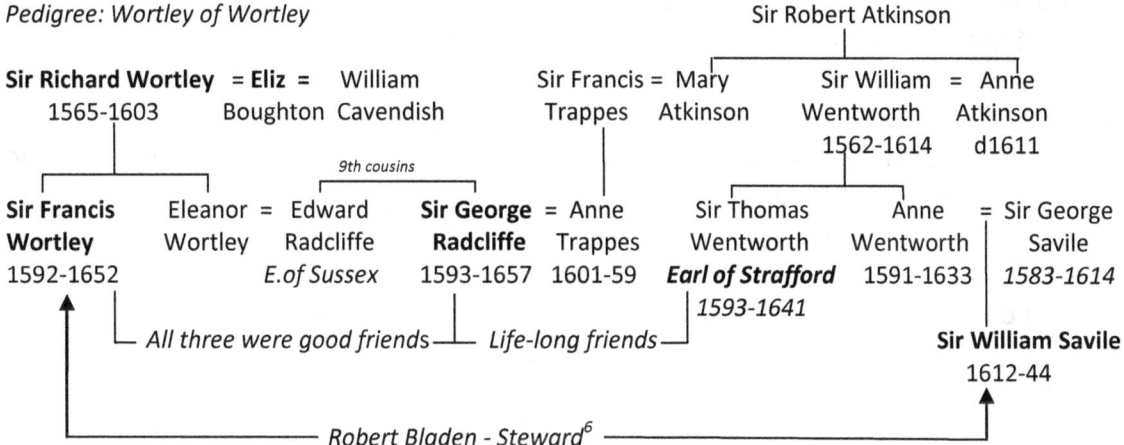

*Pedigree: Wortley of Wortley*

---

[1] https://archive.org/stream/parishregisterof37hali#page/362/mode/2up/; Parish Registers start 1538 and Bishops' Transcripts 1600
[2] Halifax Parish Register 1604
[3] TNA: C22/768/14, Bladen v Watson, 1654
[4] TNA: C10/142/2, Fairtax & Topham v Wrightson & Bladen. Robert Wrightson in his deposition said Nathaniel was "*under the care and protection by Mrs Clarke, his father's sister*" dated 1681
[5] TNA: C2/ChasI/C58/58 Con[e]y v Bladen, 1628
[6] *Sources for chart:* A Genealogical and Heraldic History of the Commoners of Great Britain and Ireland Vol. 3, by John Burke, p525, 1836;The Baronetage of England: being an historical and genealogical account of Baronets, Vol .1 by Arthur Collins 1720; Anne Radcliffe buried Westminster Abbey

The chart above shows the close-knit group of relations who would become part of Robert's world. Sir George Radcliffe in the centre of the chart was a close cousin to Elizabeth Bladen/Lacy and knew Robert very well. He will be referred to frequently in this book.

The family Bladen was engaged to serve was not very popular with the locals. Sir Richard Wortley had a reputation as a ruthless encloser and, just before he died, an alliance of some ninety tenants in Penistone (near Wortley) had grouped together to oppose his attempt to increase his profits by exacting tithes in kind[1] and they mounted a legal challenge. Emotions ran high and in 1591 a group, armed and with dogs, had forced their way into Sir Robert's estate at Wortley Park, shooting at the bull, killing deer[2] and damaging property. A gallows had been erected in the Park and a deer skin hung from it and a deer's head had been hung in the porch of the family's chapel with a note on it containing what was vaguely termed 'libel'. The Penistone tenants had a pact of secrecy amongst themselves and so the perpetrators of these crimes were never identified. In 1595 the tenants' legal action, which achieved some success, was brought into chancery and was still ongoing at the time of Sir Richard Wortley's death. After his death the widowed Lady Elizabeth Wortley[3] purchased her son's wardship and took over the running of the estates as Francis, the son and heir, was only aged 12 years at the time. As a young wealthy widow, Elizabeth immediately attracted prospective suitors and, as soon as 1604, there was a report that she was about to marry Sir John Harpur of Swarkestone.

Although the marriage never took place, the mention of Harpur raises the possibility that, if Robert Bladen's family originated in the South Derbyshire area, that John Harpur may have been the individual who connected Bladen with the Wortleys. Harpur was Deputy Lieutenant of Derbyshire as well as Governor of Repton School and Etwall Hospital. He was good friends with Gilbert Talbot, 7th Earl of Shrewsbury, indeed he was more than his good friend, more like his right-hand man[4] and, although Talbot failed to bring about the Harpur-Wortley marriage, he did end up having Elizabeth Wortley as a close relation when she married (around 1606) to William Cavendish (Talbot's brother-in-law). Cavendish became 1st Earl of Devonshire in 1618 and the couple resided in Derbyshire at 'Oldcotes', one of the houses built by Elizabeth's new mother-in-law 'Bess of Hardwick'.

With Elizabeth now residing in Derbyshire, the young son and heir Francis was sent away to school in Oldham where he was tutored by a Rev. Thomas Hunt. Newly appointed Steward, Robert Bladen, therefore had a free hand in running the Wortley estates in these early years.

---

[1] The History & Topography of the Parish of Kirkburton and the Graveship of Holme in the County of York by Henry James Morehouse. 1861
[2] West Riding Sessions Records: Orders, 1611-1642; Indictments, 1637-1642 edited by John Lister
[3] Visitation of the county of Warwick p421 showed her with the name Cavendish by 1619
[4] One of the largest branches of Bladen descendants in Shropshire originated at Longford-by-Newport where the Talbots had a large residence. There being a marriage in 1681 between Ralph Bladen and Margaret Talbot. Sir George Savile of Thornhill owned one-third of the nearby Wrockwardine parish

A chancery document of 1628, which will be discussed in detail later, referred back to this time and described Bladen as being employed by the widowed Elizabeth Wortley, she "...*employing in her affairs and retaining of money, one Robert Bladen of Hemsworth*".[1] The reference to Bladen being 'of Hemsworth' was probably after-the-fact, that is to say although he had close family in Thornhill about ten miles from Hemsworth and also purchased land and messuages there, it is not thought he actually lived there himself until much later, around 1620, as earlier records show him residing elsewhere. The Bladen family's movements, taken from deeds and other official documents, are as follows:-

*Early Places of Residence*
1604    Southowram nr Halifax & Cromwellbotham for birth of son - in wife's Lacy parish
1604-7  Possibly resided at Thornhill (with or near uncle Philip Waterhouse/aunt Helen Lacy)
1607-28 Steward at Wortley Hall
1614    Purchased land in Hemsworth (Bladen v Illingworth)
1615    Askwith (near Denton) Weston Parish - Named on deeds with Francis Wortley
1616    Lacy relations Uncle Philip and Aunt Nell (Helen) Waterhouse resided at Thornhill
1616    Askwith (near Denton) Weston Parish - Declaration with Richard Sunderland
1617    Purchased several estates in Hemsworth from the Gargraves
1619    Askwith (near Denton) Weston Parish - Profits of goods of felons
1619    Askwith (near Denton) Weston Parish - Wainwright Ward
1620    Purchased Hague Hall, South Kirkby, with Nathaniel Birkhead
1622    Son went to Cambridge University, then Gray's Inn
1622+   Hemsworth - Near to the Savile family's main residence at Thornhill
1647    Hemsworth

Early deeds co-signed by the young son and heir Francis Wortley and Robert Bladen refer to Robert as being of Askwith or Denton, some 30 miles north of Wortley Hall, both being part the Fairfax Manor and very close to the Fairfax seat of Denton Hall.[2] Over the years land in this area passed between different families, for instance sixteenth century Feet of Fines between the Fairfax and Wentworth families (Wortley neighbours) covering part of the area around Askwith and Denton,[3] show that Sir Thomas Wentworth and his wife Margaret Gascoigne were involved in land conveyances on the Fairfax Manor. The records also show that George Savile was involved in land conveyances in the same area. As a Lacy relation and a steward concerned with land management, Robert would have had dealings with all of these families.

At this point it is worth introducing someone who was an important figure in the lives of these early Bladens and played a pivotal role in connecting Robert Bladen with high ranking families and individuals. Sir George Radcliffe (shown in the centre of the small chart on page 17) was a cousin of Robert's wife Elizabeth Lacy (through the Waterhouse family) and referred to Philip Waterhouse and Elizabeth (née Lacy) as his aunt and uncle in his correspondence. The same two individuals who were also Elizabeth Bladen's aunt and uncle.

---

[1] TNA: C2/ChasI/C58/58 Thomas Cony [Coney] v Robert Bladen dated 1628
[2] Askwith is within the parish of Weston next to Denton and Ilkley between Skipton and Harrogate
[3] YAS Record Series, Vol. 8, Feet of Fines, Tudor Yorkshire, published by YAS, Leeds 1890

Radcliffe wrote a series of letters starting from around 1607 onwards when he was just 14 years of age from his school in Oldham to his mother at Thornhill, Yorkshire.[1] The Radcliffe family lived at Overthorpe Hall in Thornhill and were neighbours of Elizabeth Bladen's aunt and uncle Waterhouse. They were also very well connected with the most high profile residents of Thornhill, the Saviles.

*1616: Sir George Radcliffe*

Picture right:
Sir Thomas Wentworth (1593–1641), 1st Earl of Strafford, dictating to his secretary, Sir George Radcliffe (1593–1657) Anthony van Dyck.

*Reproduced with permission from The Trustees of The Capt. Christie Crawfurd's English Civil War Collection at St Edward's Hall, Stowe-on-the-Wold.*

**Earl of Strafford/Sir George Radcliffe**

Radcliffe had probably known Elizabeth Bladen his whole life and, from his letters, appears to know Robert Bladen very well by 1607 which might suggest that Robert and Elizabeth Bladen, in the early years of their marriage, had resided at Thornhill with Uncle Philip and Aunt Helen Waterhouse before moving to Askwith/Denton. Radcliffe often asked his mother to pass on regards to the Bladens, which indicates they were frequent visitors, or indeed resident at times, at Thornhill.

As can be seen in the above portrait Radcliffe, who trained as a lawyer, would later be in the service of Thomas Wentworth, the Earl of Strafford. The two became related when Radcliffe married in 1622 to Anne Trappes and the men became life-long close friends. Radcliffe's tutor at school was Mr Hunt, a respectable head school master who tutored a few privileged boys, including some from noble families. Indeed, alongside Radcliffe as a fellow student was the son and heir of Bladen's Wortley employer, Francis Wortley (yet to be knighted).

Francis and George were cousins and there were frequently references to Wortley in Radcliffe's letters home. The letters give some useful insight into the movements of various people, including Bladen, at a time when there are few other details to be found on him. Although only 14 years old when Bladen was appointed to the Wortley household, it is possible Radcliffe's influence with the Wortleys secured the appointment for his cousin's husband - though there are other possibilities which will be expanded on later.

---

[1] There are two portraits which look almost identical: one (as above) is by van Dyck, dictating to his secretary Sir George Radcliffe. The other is held by the V & A Museum and is "after" Van Dyck, by Henry Stone and is said to be Wentworth receiving his death warrant from secretary Sir Philip Mainwaring. John Wilson, Rare-books-in-Japan, has also given permission as holder of an out-of-copyright book where this picture was reproduced from, in addition to the portrait holders permission cited above

Radcliffe's first letter was written at Easter 1607[1] where he described Wortley as being about to go off to Oxford (Oxenforde) but, in fact, it was to be the following year on 18th April 1608 when Wortley did finally depart for Magdalen Hall, Oxford.[2]

In another letter, dated 10th November 1607, he told how his tutor Mr Hunt was about to pay a visit to Lady Cavendish (mother of Francis Wortley) at Oldcotes. Lady Cavendish appears in this volume under several names, depending on her status at a particular time: born Elizabeth Boughton, she married Sir Richard Wortley and became Lady Wortley and mother of Sir Francis, then after her first husband's death she married William Cavendish and became Lady Cavendish. Then, lastly, when her husband was made Earl of Devonshire, Elizabeth became known as the Countess of Devonshire.[3]

Some reports say that Bess of Hardwick's son William Cavendish and Elizabeth (née Wortley/Boughton) never left Hardwick Hall where they lived along with Bess, though Radcliffe's letter seems to refute that idea. Oldcotes was built specifically for William, the second and favourite son of Bess, during the 1590s and was just a few miles away from Hardwick. The fact that Elizabeth was residing in Derbyshire and her son Francis was away at school in Oldham, meant there was the need for a steward to take care of the Wortley estates as early as 1607 and, as Robert was known to have been engaged by Elizabeth in the period well before Francis was of full age, then his engagement with the family must have been from immediately Elizabeth remarried, around 1606 if not before.

Confirmation that Robert was engaged by the family prior to 1610 can be found in a later chancery case, Bladen v Wortley, where depositions stated that recently knighted son and heir 'Sir' Francis Wortley, who was still only 19 years old, approached Bladen just before Wortley's marriage to Grace Bouncker and they both asked Robert to continue working for the family and to be their steward. The relationship between Robert and the noble Wortley was good to begin with and, in fact, remained so for many years. Later depositions concerning Bladen's early service, stated:

*"And whether have you often heard the Defendant* [Wortley] *report well of him* [Bladen] *for his good behaviour and faithful service and hath acknowledged the Plaintiff* [Bladen] *to have been always fair for the preserving of the Defendant's* [Wortley] *credit and estate during his employment,"*[4] to which the answer was usually yes. One deponent added *"His Lordship* [Wortley] *did send unto the plaintiff Robert Bladen and request him to undertake the lettings and selling of his lands and managing of his said estate."*[5] Bladen agreed and the matter was settled.

---

[1] The Life and Original Correspondence of Sir George Radcliffe LL.D. The Friend of the Earl of Strafford by Thomas Dunham Whittaker, the Vicar of Whalley in Lancashire, 1810, p114

[2] The History and Topography of the Parish of Kirkburton and of the Graveship of Holme by Henry James Morehouse. 1861

[3] Aidan Haley, researcher at Chatsworth (Earl/Duke of Devonshire estate) confirmed that their papers contain no documentation for Elizabeth personally - either as a Wortley or Cavendish - and searched the 1st Earl of Devonshire's account books for references to Elizabeth and dealings with her stewards - though such payments were more likely to have been made with a personal steward and Robert was an estate steward. Sources consulted: 'The Cavendish Family' by Francis Bickley, 1911 and 'Oldcotes: Last Mansion Built by Bess of Hardwick' by Pamela Kettle, 2000

[4] TNA: C21/B19/16 and 23, Bladen v Wortley dated 1636

[5] Ibid

The Wortleys were not in residence for much of the time after Elizabeth's second marriage and, after the son Francis Wortley left university 1610-12, he was appointed Gentleman of the Privy Chamber to the Prince of Wales, heir to the throne. Prince Henry Stuart was just three years younger and Wortley's presence would have been required in the Prince's private chambers at Court. So, until 1612, when the heir to the throne died suddenly of typhoid fever, Bladen would have been free to manage the estate alone. For Sir Francis, however, despite his best efforts he failed to secure another position at Court.

Meanwhile, George Radcliffe's school days had also ended and he went off to London to study the law at Grays Inn where he continued to write to his mother. The following are extracts from his letters where names mentioned are relevant to the Bladens: Savile, Waterhouse and Wortley. Radcliffe's relation to the Wortleys and Saviles is depicted on the chart on page 17 and to the Waterhouse/Bladens on page 24.

10th October 1611
Radcliffe asked his mother, *"Remember me, I pray you, to my Uncle Phillipe and Aunt Nell with my thanks for their former love and also to Mrs Waterhouse of Shibden Hall".*[1]
The Mrs Waterhouse mentioned was Jane Bosvile, mother of Radcliffe and Elizabeth Bladen's Uncle Philip.

*"For Sir George I must and will ever acknowledge myself and what I have to be at his command"* From Grays Inn, 17th December 1613[2]
Radcliffe was even closer to the Savile family than the Wortleys and so mentions of Sir George Savile (1st Bt) were frequent. Sir George had taught Radcliffe rudimentary Latin and was both his godfather and his father's patron. In a later letter in the spring, 15th March 1616, Radcliffe told his mother that he saw Sir George Savile in London the previous day with *"My Lady and Mrs Mary"* going out of town with the King. This was a reference to George, his wife Lady Elizabeth Ayscough and perhaps one of their children. Radcliffe met up many times with the Saviles when they were in London and they, of course, all knew their Thornhill neighbour Aunt Nell Waterhouse (Helen Lacy) very well. Radcliffe even visited Sir George the following year 1617 when Savile was briefly imprisoned for contempt of court when Sir George became mired in a dispute over his deceased son's estate. Robert Bladen would later be engaged by the Saviles and given a life annuity and George Radcliffe's father was employed in managing the Savile estates.

In a further letter dated 3rd May 1616 Radcliffe wrote regarding the arrangements for his now deceased 'uncle' Philip Waterhouse. This letter, more than any other, shows just how close Radcliffe was to his Waterhouse/Bladen relations who resided next to his family home of Overthorpe Hall.[3]

---

[1] The Life and Original Correspondence of Sir George Radcliffe LL.D. The Friend of the Earl of Strafford by Thomas Dunham Whittaker, the Vicar of Whalley in Lancashire, 1810, p114
[2] Ibid
[3] Visitation of England and Wales, Notes: Volume 2. 1897. By Joseph Jackson Howard. In 1599 Richard Tempest sold for £100 the capital messuage of Overthorpe Hall in Thornhill, with 23 closes, 1 cottage and 2 crofts in Thornhill to George, son of Nicholas Radcliffe

Overthorpe would have been the largest house in Thornhill when George Radcliffe and his family lived there, except for the Savile's home at Thornhill Hall. Bladens would have been frequent visitors or may even have resided there, or nearby with their Waterhouse relations.

Overthorpe was demolished c1936.

**George Radcliffe's home, Overthorpe Hall, Thornhill**

Following the death of their uncle Philip Waterhouse in January 1614, in May 1616 Radcliffe was arranging a memorial stone, on which he consulted Robert Bladen (whose wife was Philip's niece). Radcliffe and Elizabeth Bladen/Lacy took the lead as next of kin to Philip and Helen Waterhouse.

On 23rd May, in a further letter to his mother, Radcliffe said: *"I have here sent you downe two very good hats, as I think, which Mr Bladen bought for myne aunt and you; he hath proferred me kindness about the lease at Haddersley: I pray you thank him."*[1]

On 31st May 1616 Radcliffe wrote to his mother again and said *"I consulted with Mr Bladen again about the farmes at Haddlesey, and we thought best that he should just speake to Parker, which he promised to do accordingly"*.[2]

Reference to Robert being asked to assist Radcliffe with a land lease in Haddersley also seems consistent with Bladen's activities on managing land interests.

On 14th June 1616, Radcliffe wrote *"I pray you thank my Aunt Nell for her kind token w'ch she sent me. I looked for her coate of armes to have come uppe, as Mr Bladen tould me it would be her[e]; but the workmen may leave room for it"*. This is a reference to the memorial plaque to Philip Waterhouse which Radcliffe was preparing and he wanted to include the Waterhouse and Lacy coats of arms - referred to elsewhere in this book - and the plaque still exists at Thornhill Church. It says:

*"Here lyeth the body of Philip Waterhouse,*
*3 sonne of John Waterhouse of Halifax esq,*
*Maister of Artes and sometimes Fellow of University Coll, Oxon.*
*He dyed the 16th of Januari 1614, the 57th yere of his age.*
*Hellen, daughter of Richard Lacye of Cromewelbotome esq,*
*his beloved wife, dedicated this monument to his memori"*.
Arms of Lacy and Cromwellbothom.

---

[1] The Life and Original Correspondence of Sir George Radcliffe LL.D. The Friend of the Earl of Strafford by Thomas Dunham Whittaker, the Vicar of Whalley in Lancashire, 1810, p114
[2] Ibid

*Waterhouse-Lacy Relations*

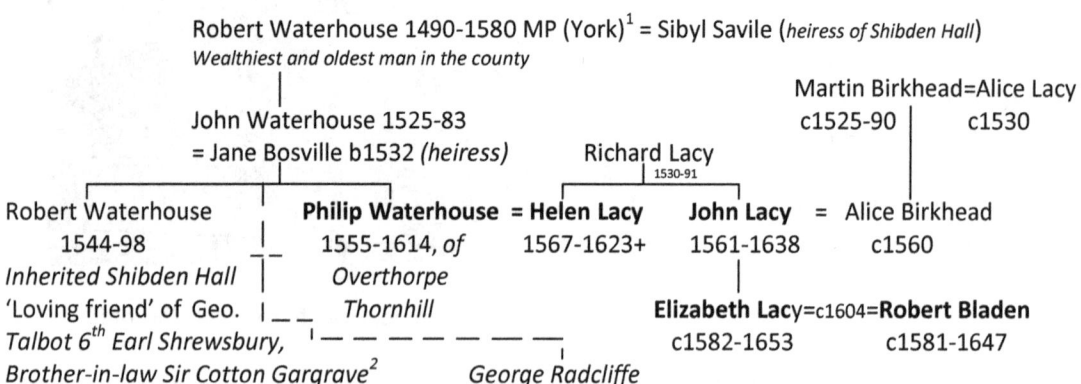

The real value of Radcliffe's letters is that they demonstrate just how closely involved Robert (through his wife's connections) was to all the leading, high status families in that part of Yorkshire at the time. It is perhaps also noticeable, however, that in all the documents and letters seen for Robert, it is only his wife's relations who are referred to, never anyone from his own family which, perhaps, reinforces both the suggestion that he was not native to Yorkshire and also that his own family connections were not of equal standing to his wife's.

We leave Sir George Radcliffe at this point, but only for a short while. He returns as part of the Bladens' story later.

Robert Bladen's employment by the Wortley family continued and, at some point in these early days as Steward, Robert had managed to resolve a difficult situation with a tenant. John Denton of Denton's Farm in Carlton[3] near Wortley, had held a tenancy on the estate since the time of Sir Richard but had fallen into arrears and Bladen had intervened by buying up Denton's remaining interest in his farm and acquiring the title. In recognition of him resolving what was perceived as a difficult situation, Sir Francis Wortley had given Denton's farm to Bladen, that is to say the lease on it for a peppercorn rent. This farm would later become the source of legal action between Wortley and Bladen.

In 1615 Lady Grace, wife of Sir Francis Wortley, died suddenly and Francis was distraught. For some reason Robert Bladen, at this time, questioned his willingness to continue in service to Sir Francis but, when news reached Wortley that Bladen was contemplating leaving his employ, he begged him to stay. A later deposition stated that: *"Shortly after the death of the Defendant's[Wortley] former Lady [Grace] that the Complainant [Bladen] had a purpose to be at the Defendant's [Wortley] service.*

---

[1] Connection between Birkhead and Waterhouse families: Richard Birkhead's Will of 1544 .... to my two eldest sonnes Richard and Martyne my lands at Crofton near Wakefield. To Elizabeth my wife and to my three younger sonnes Thomas, John and Robert my lands in Halifax. The rest to Anne, Sibyl, Elizabeth, Isabel and Margaret my daughters. Overseers of Will: Thomas Saville of Clifton, Robert Waterhouse of Halifax. Source Haworth Past and Present: A History of Haworth, Stanbury and Oxenhope by Joseph Horsfall Turner

[2] Robert Waterhouse's wife was Jane Waterton (daughter of Thomas Waterton), her sister Agnes married Sir Cotton Gargrave. Chart sources: Familiae Minorum Gentium and Biographia Halifaxiensis by J Horsfall Turner

[3] Carlton Manor was owned by the Wortleys. It was in the parish of Royston near Barnsley

*And that thereupon the Defendant* [Wortley] *did earnestly labour and entreat the Plaintiff* [Bladen] *still his servant and not to desert from him but to continue and do for him as formerly had, then saying and protesting unto the Plaintiff* [Bladen] *that he would forward him for his service."*[1]

Although the farm at Carlton given by Wortley was intended for him to reside in, being conveniently close to the Wortley estate, Bladen instead decided to sub-let it to generate an income for himself. The peppercorn rent seems never to have been paid but then neither did Sir Francis insist on payment and, given the trust Wortley placed in his Steward, Wortley bailiffs would have turned a 'blind eye' to the situation, that is, whilst ever Bladen continued to enjoy Wortley's support. Robert stayed with Wortley and was involved in nearly every transaction instigated during the period c1612-1630. He was responsible for all aspects of Wortley's land management, such as setting of rent levels, advising on manorial acquisitions, communicating with other estates and keeping the accounts and general business matters. In addition to their land-holdings and numerous Manors they owned, the Wortleys were renowned as iron-masters, having rich deposits of iron ore on their lands which had given their family financial strength for generations.

*Self-Aggrandizement*
Robert's service for Wortley continued without event for some years but, in the mean time, he sought to improve his own personal fortune. As Steward to one of the largest land owners in the area, Bladen was in an advantageous position with regard to land availability and acquisition as he would have had advance notice of any land disposals that were planned and it appears he took full advantage and acquired numerous properties at this time, many being in Hemsworth.

In 1616 Bladen, now 35 years old, was also involved with another nobleman, Richard Sunderland 1568-1634. Sunderland was a JP and owned estates at Coley Hall and High Sunderland. He was a Lacy relation through the Rishworths of Coley.

**Coley Hall**

Sunderland was also Treasurer for Lame Soldiers and married to Mary Saltonstall.[2] His other residence at High Sunderland, it has been said, was the house Emily Brontë based Wuthering Heights on - being only 1m from Southowram where Brontë also spent time.

The following document is a receipt by Robert Bladen, still living at Askwith, for £80 received from Richard Sunderland of Coley Hall regarding lands and tenements in nearby Barleby.

---

[1] TNA: C21/B19/16 and 23, Bladen v Wortley dated 1636
[2] Dugdale's Visitation of Yorkshire, Vol. 1, p76

On 11th January 1616 Robert completed an agreement between the following individuals: Mr Coney, Anthony Foxcroft of Halifax, Samuel Hoyle of Hoylehouse and Michael Bairstowe of Mirfield. He issued the following Declaration: *"Be it known unto all men by the said suit that I Robert Bladen of Askwith in the county of York, gent, have received and paid upon the day of the date hereof at the hand of Richard Sunderland of Coley Hall in the said County of York the sum of four score pounds of lawful money of England".*[1] Robert had entered into an agreement whereby he had sold land he had acquired in Barlby to Richard Sunderland and a Mr Coney - this is likely to be Sir Thomas Coney who subsequently brought legal action against Robert claiming Bladen refused to release him from a financial bond. Coney was closely related to the Wortleys, his son and heir having married the sister of Sir Francis. Coney's Bill of Complaint is useful as he explains Robert's connection with the Countess of Devonshire, even though Robert's own account of his dealings with the Countess differs somewhat - this will be discussed in detail later.[2]

Two more letters concerning Richard Sunderland, slightly out of chronological order, are worth mentioning. One dated four years later in 1620 was from Ro. Bixxon of Skircoat who was having difficulty getting money out of Robert and was appealing to Sunderland for assistance: *"Good Sir Sunderland, these are to request you to pursue your best endeavour to help me with my rent of Mr Bladen."*[3] The second was dated 20th August 1623, written in Robert's own hand, and was by way of a routine letter advising Sunderland that he was unable to attend an appointment as arranged but offering to re-arrange it the following week. It included a fleeting reference to his Aunt Helen (Nell) Waterhouse. Bladen wrote: *"...my friend whom should enter bond with and for the remainder of your money cannot that day be at Halifax by reason of some extraordinary occasion he hath to be done upon Friday and Saturday, besides my Aunt Waterhouse herself cannot be at home so to deliver your money."*[4]

## Richard Illingworth

The more Robert Bladen dabbled in his own land transactions the more involved he became in chancery proceedings as he was obliged to pursue tenants in court for non-payment of rents or other problems associated with the transactions. In this regard then in 1617 Robert instigated legal proceedings against Richard Illingworth of Allerton.[5] It would appear that a man called Edward Holdsworth,[6] who was probably a tenant of Bladen's in Hemsworth, became bonded to Richard Illingworth in respect of monies owed. When Holdsworth died, Illingworth claimed not to have received any monies from Holdsworth and so the purpose of Robert Bladen taking Illingworth to court was to address that issue as Bladen believed that Holdsworth had made payment and that Illingworth was withholding these funds - the sum involved being £11.

---

[1] WYAS: WDP53/15/5/5, Wakefield
[2] TNA: C2/ChasI/C58/58, Con[e]y v Bladen, dated 1628
[3] WYAS: WDP53/15/5/7, Wakefield
[4] WYAS: WDP53/15/5/7, Wakefield
[5] TNA: C2/Chas1/B166/78, Bladen v Illingworth, dated 1617
[6] This Edward Holdsworth may be related to the family that John Lacy had a feud with many years earlier

There is reference within the documentation to this matter covering a period of 2 or 3 years, therefore confirming that Bladen must have begun acquiring lands in Hemsworth as early as 1614. This is only one instance of numerous routine chancery cases he was involved in over money matters.

*1618: Profits of Goods of Outlaws and Felons*

Another area of business Bladen involved himself in was to jointly purchase the right to acquire the profits of goods of outlaws and felons. In any other county the Crown would have been the recipient of such property but, like the Duchy of Cornwall, the Duchy of Lancaster operated differently. The Lords of the Manors in this Duchy had the right to try felons and take the profits - a right which changed hands. A man called Dr Richard Berry, who featured large in Robert's life, acquired this right when only in his late teens and, by an Indenture of 1618, passed it to others including Bladen.[1] Bladen 'of Askwith' joined with Thomas Favell of Yorkshire and Thomas Shillito of Ulleskelf Old Hall in Aberford in the venture.

The following chart differs from the previous one on page 17 on the right-hand side, to show how Dr Berry's marriage to Prudence Gargrave propelled him up amongst the leading Yorkshire families:

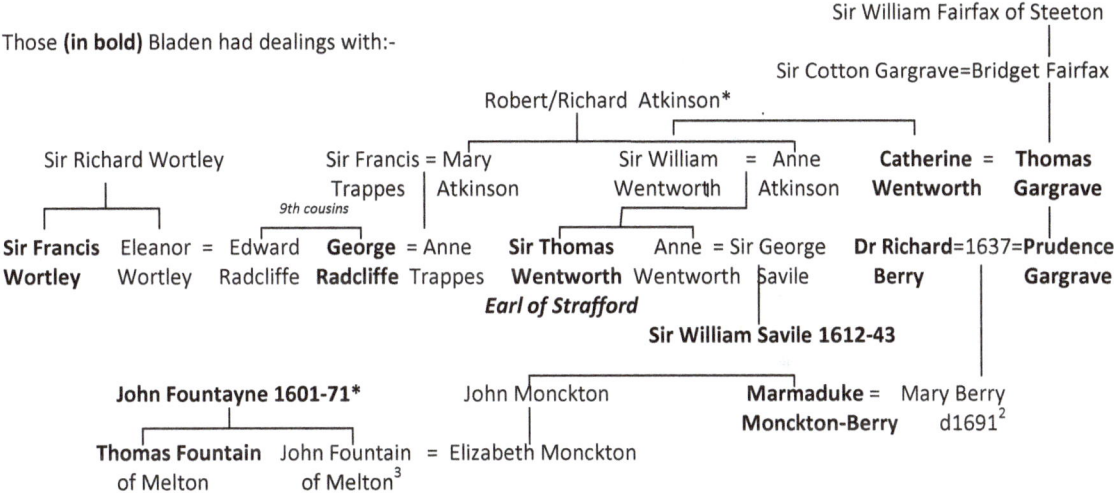

John Fountayne (business partner) became the heir of Dr Richard Berry, along with Marmaduke Monckton-Berry who was both Dr Richard Berry's nephew (through sister Susan) as well as being his son-in-law.

---

[1] Sheffield Archives, Wharncliffe Muniments: Wh M/D/65 - 14th January 1618

[2] South Yorkshire - The History and Topography of the Deanery of Doncaster in the Diocese and County of York by Rev. Joseph Hunter, Vol. 2, 1831, p426

[3] The Historic Lands of England by Sir J.B. Burke, Sir Bernard Burke, Vol. 1, 1848. Hunter's South Yorkshire pp89-90 Pedigree of Wentworth of Wentworth Woodhouse; Ga 12,281 (23 June 1651) Nottingham University Library, Department of Manuscripts and Special Collections www.westminster-abbey.org/our-history/people/anne-radcliffe STAC 8/18/1,f64; *Note: Hunter's South Yorkshire says Anne Atkinson was the daughter of Robert Atkinson, pp89-90 - Pedigree of Wentworth of Wentworth Woodhouse, other sources state his name was Richard

*Dr Richard Berry*

Berry's background was in medicine and he had gained a medical diploma from Padua,[1] the finest School of Medicine in Europe and had set up practice in Fleet Street, London for a while. Alongside the medical practice, he had a passion for wheeling and dealing in business ventures and property buying and selling. For him to be engaging in business transactions so early, he probably had inherited wealth which no doubt supported him during his medical training. Dr Richard Berry[2] was the man who Robert Bladen turned to for making deals, financing property transactions and arranging mortgages, a kind of 'one-man universal money-lender'. Berry's activities, however, were deemed to be 'sharp practice' by many he became involved with as he most often ended up acquiring those properties he loaned money against and tied up his clients in litigation for years.

Even before his advantageous marriage to a wealthy heiress, Prudence Gargrave, he had acquired the Manors of Hodroyd in 1625 and Havercroft (this estate, or part of it, was listed in his marriage settlement of 1637).[3] The purchase of Havercroft was done jointly with Thomas Levett of Lincoln's Inn, whose name will crop up again later.[4] Wife Prudence was the grand-daughter and heiress of Sir Cotton Gargrave who, like the Wortleys, had owned much of the Manor of Hemsworth, and Berry embarked on many years of property purchase and commercial dealings to the point where it seems difficult to imagine he would have found time to practice medicine at all, so the suggestion from some sources that he was physician to Oliver Cromwell needs to be considered with caution, especially since he had such difficulty holding on to his estates after the Civil War.

Robert's dealings with Berry dated from at least 1618 onwards, if not before and one of the men who connected to both Bladen and Berry was Nathaniel Birkhead, Elizabeth Bladen's uncle. Robert Bladen would join with Birkhead to jointly purchase Hague Hall (East Heage) in South Kirkby in 1620. Nathaniel Birkhead's father-in-law Roger Dale had married Margaret Brockett who later married Thomas Levett - Berry's business partner. When Margaret wrote her Will, probate 1648, she left some £7,000 and appointed Berry as her Executor. This, however, was challenged by her then forth husband (Levett) who put himself forward and was granted administration. So these men were all close business partners with family connections.

Both Berry and Bladen had acquired lands from the Gargrave family which, due to the family's mismanagement and unfortunate circumstances, were being sold off.

---

[1] Berry was a Member of the College of Physicians, Bachelor of Medicine MB, he was given a testimonial from Dr Thomas Clayton, Regius Professor of Medicine at Oxford to take to Padua, Doctor of Medicine MD of Padua (24 April, 1620) subscribed by Fonseca, an eminent professor, and licentiate in medicine of Oxford University. He was suspected of Popery whilst in Padua. Purchased Havercroft in 1623 (including South Hindeley, Hodroyd, Cold Hindley and Over Hindley and the capital messuage of Hemsworth High Hall, plus all Katherine Gargrave (née Wentworth)'s lands in Wakefield, Stanley, Horbury and Ossett)

[2] Dr Richard Berry 1570-1651

[3] South Yorkshire - The History and Topography of the Deanery of Doncaster in the Diocese and County of York by Rev. Joseph Hunter, Vol. 2, 1831, p410

[4] Elizabeth Levett (of the Levetts of Normanton, Wakefield) married Sir Thomas Gargrave (father of Cotton Gargrave) and purchaser of Nostell Priory

Berry bought the largest property in Hemsworth, High Hall, and Bladen acquired the neighbouring estate. Robert actually bought his land from Francis Gargrave whose mother (Bridget) was a Fairfax and daughter of Sir William Fairfax of Steeton.[1] Robert's grandson would, much later, unite the Fairfax and Bladen families by marrying a cousin of Lord Fairfax.

Head of the family, Sir Cotton Gargrave, was son of the famous Speaker of the House of Commons Sir Thomas Gargrave[2] who, in a speech on 6th February 1559, in front of the Privy Council and about thirty members of the House of Commons demanded that, in the name of the nation, the Queen should take a husband. Four days later she gave her 'Virgin Queen' response: if she would remain unmarried *"this should be me sufficient, that a marble stone shall declare that a Queen, having reigned such a time, lived and died a virgin"*. Sir Cotton's son, who also went by the name Sir Thomas Gargrave became equally renowned when he was accused of murder. A young servant boy in his employ, called Gardyner, was poisoned and his body was burned in an oven - and Sir Thomas Gargrave stood accused of his murder.[3] He was found guilty and sentenced to hanging at York in 1595; both his wife Catherine and later his daughter both attempted to clear his name posthumously but failed.

Following the execution of Sir Thomas, the estate, which comprised of 11 manors and lands, passed to his half-brother Sir Richard Gargrave[4] who, as his life progressed, developed some self-destructive habits. A weakness for drinking and gambling led, over a period of time, to him being forced to gradually sell off portions of the family's estate to fund his lifestyle. By 1634 *"everything was sold. He was living in low conditions"*.[5] At one time, it was said, he could ride from Wakefield to Doncaster entirely on his own land,[6] however, sadly by the time he died in 1638 he was a much reduced figure, travelling packhorse and died slumped over his horse's pack-saddle at a local inn[7] - or, in a London flophouse according to another source.

John Burke, the genealogical publisher, wrote of him *"The memory of his extravagance and his vices yet lingers about Kinsley"*.[8] The misfortunes of the Gargrave family therefore led to enforced sales of land in Hemsworth where Bladen and, in particular Berry, were well placed to take advantage of the opportunity to purchase at low prices.

---

[1] TNA: C22/624/18 Danby v Bladen. In a deposition by Cotton Horne of Wakefield it was stated that Robert Bladen bought his land from Francis Gargrave, half-brother of Sir Richard Gargrave. Gargraves were some relation to the Bladens, again through Elizabeth Lacy. Elizabeth's uncle Philip Waterhouse's brother Robert was married to Jane Waterton. Jane's sister was married to Cotton Gargrave. The Watertons were descended from Sir Robert Waterton (younger brother of the Lord of Waterton) who fought at Agincourt

[2] Sir Thomas Gargrave's mother was Elizabeth Levett - Levetts of Normanton, Wakefield

[3] http://www.parishofhemsworth.org.uk/ABriefHistoryoftheMonumentsandMemorials.pdf

[4] Sir Richard Gargrave 1575-1638: Inner Temple 1591, MP in 1597 and again in 1609, Justice of the Peace for the West Riding of Yorkshire, knighted in 1603 and he was High Sheriff of Yorkshire in 1604-5

[5] West Riding Sessions: 1611-42; Indictments 1637-42

[6] South Yorkshire - The History and Topography of the Deanery of Doncaster in the Diocese and County of York by Rev. Joseph Hunter, Vol. 2, 1831, p213

[7] The Historic Lands of England by Sir J B Burke, Sir Bernard Burke. Also in Hunter's S. Yorks Vol. 2, p214

[8] The Patrician, Vol. 2 by John Burke. 1846

*Danvers/Danby*

Bladen's acquisition of part of the Gargrave estate was challenged by the Earl of Danby. It is an unfortunate irony that the Bladens were taken to court not once, but twice, by the Danbys: first Robert faced proceedings around 1621-5 by Henry Danvers concerning an aspect of fee farms on the Gargrave estate.

Many years later his grandson Nathaniel, who was engaged by the Earl of Danby (2nd issue of the title) would also be taken to court by the same family. In respect of Robert's situation, complainant Danvers/Danby was brother-in-law to Sir Richard and Francis Gargrave (sons of Sir Cotton Gargrave) and in a deposition by Cotton Horne, it was stated that Robert Bladen had acquired *"a fourth part of the whole lands devised by Sir Cotton Gargrave to the said Francis his son"*. That one-quarter estate included three farms; Bullingshire Hall, Shurleys Farm and Lanes Farm and that Robert had held them for about seven years - which means the purchase took place about 1617. In other parts of the deposition there is reference to Robert having received monies for fees on tenanted properties and so he may have been engaged by Danvers/Danby as a land agent or in carrying out land extent assessments. As will be seen later, however, Robert's ability to acquire land and property was not matched by his ability to keep it.

*Wainwright Ward*

Land acquisition may have been behind Robert taking on a ward in 1619. In documents pertaining to the case, Robert and his family were stated to be living at Denton, a very short distance away from Askwith.[1] Wardship at this period of time, under the feudal system that operated, was often an oppressive (to the ward and his family) means of acquiring land. An Indenture of 1619[2] shows Robert took legal custody of Thomas Wainwright. Thomas was his father's heir but, because he was under the age of 21 when his father died, his family's estate, even the right to arrange his own marriage, automatically reverted to the Crown until that heir paid the Crown a sum of money. These matters were dealt with, on behalf of the Crown, by the Court of Wardship and Liveries who then arranged to 'sell' the Crown's wardship on to another person, usually a next of kin, but often to the highest bidder.

It is not known if Wainwright was any kind of blood relation to Bladen but, for the duration of his wardship, Bladen would have had control of Wainwright's estate, i.e. receiving rents. Wainwright's father had actually died in 1615 on 6th February when his son was just 9 years of age and it is thought that Bladen may have held the Wainwright wardship for some years.[3] Young Thomas Wainwright eventually married Agnes Smythe in 1631 and in 1633, when the young ward became of full age, he finally inherited his father's estate.

---

[1] It seems unlikely that Bladens moved between Askwith and Denton, rather that deeds were registered perhaps in different places

[2] Barnsley Archives: SpSt 60327/21 (145/21) dated 1619 Assignment of wardship of Thomas Wainwright to Mary Wainwright his mother by Robert Bladen. Sp.St/145/25 Sheffield Archives (now relocated to Barnsley Archives with the Spencer Stanhope Collection)

[3] Barnsley Archives: SpSt 60327 (146/2) Wardship of Thomas Wainwright. 1617/27

The estate consisted of one messuage at Cawthorne of 20 acres of land, 10 acres of meadowland and 30 acres of pasture. He raised a family and died in 1668 still possessed of his father's estate.[1]

## 1620s: Hemsworth

From 1614 Robert's movements can be traced through the various indentures, deeds and letters that were generated by his law suits and deeds of land transfers and, although the precise date of his going to live in Hemsworth is uncertain, it can be narrowed down to around 1620, perhaps when his son and heir John went off to university. Joseph Hunter, in reference to Hemsworth, in his authoritative book 'South Yorkshire' described the Bladens arriving in Hemsworth but gave no date: *"Some portions of the land of Hemsworth were sold by him [Gargrave] with the advowson to Robert Bladen, a gentleman who settled a family of some consideration here"*[2].

As well as land and a messuage, Robert also bought the advowson for Hemsworth church, which would have been a very desirable and valuable acquisition. It seems unlikely, however, that Robert personally ever had the chance to exercise his power of patronage as in 1636 it was the Crown's privilege and the King appointed Stephen Chapman who remained in post until after Robert's demise. Robert's grandson Nathaniel, however, did get the opportunity to make one or possibly two appointments until he sold the advowson to his friend Robert Wrightson in 1682 (or 1685, date of formal agreement).

The church of St Helens, Hemsworth dates back to about 1200 (not being mentioned in the Doomsday Book) and its advowson has been described, in Hunter's South Yorkshire as, by the 1800s, comprising: *"The manse [a house provided for the clergy], the ancient glebe [manor house or priest's house and land], on which are several houses, 204 acres of newly enclosed lands allotted to the rector at the enclosure of 1804, the surplice fees and a corn rent of £560 which was to be increased at the expiration of 21 years from the time of the enclosure. The presentation to this valuable rectory (and strange it is that, lying so near to the house of St Oswald of Nostel it escaped an appropriation) was regardent to the manor till the time of Sir Richard Gargrave. The Bladens seemed to have exercised the right only once or twice. They sold it, together with a good estate to Mr Robert Wrightson, the first of the name at Cusworth. He was patron at the time of his death in 1708, and the patronage is now enjoyed by his descendant and heir John Battie Wrightson Esq of Cusworth."*[3]

Though the above was written from a 19th century perspective, and there may have been changes in the interim, still it seems the Bladens' landholding was substantial and possession of the advowson would have given them some local power.

---

[1] Barnsley Archives: SpSt 60327/24 Marriage Settlement and Thomas Wainwright and Agnes Smith and 25 4th June 1631 and 24th November 1633
[2] South Yorkshire - The History and Topography of the Deanery of Doncaster in the Diocese and County of York by Rev. Joseph Hunter, Vol. 2, 1831, p426
[3] Ibid

North of the church was Hemsworth Hospital. Robert Holgate, a Hemsworth man and later Archbishop, the first Protestant Abp of York, in his Will dated 1555[1] established a grammar school and hospital in the village with a gift of land and money. Both Robert Bladen (in July 1637)[2] and Dr Berry (in 1642)[3] became involved in land and property disputes[4] with the trustees of Holgate's estate at Hemsworth hospital.

The advowson of Hemsworth Church will be discussed again later.

*1625: Renewal of lease on Carlton Farm*
Through the 1620s Bladen continued working for Wortley and enjoying good relations with the family. As evidence of those good relations, in 1625 the lease on his farm at Carlton came up for renewal and Sir Francis was happy to sign it in a moment, with no hesitation whatsoever. From later depositions, it was stated that he signed the farm lease renewal whilst sitting in the Red Room at Wortley Hall[5] and was observed by his bailiffs and other staff to sign it as a matter of routine, without discussion with Bladen[6] and was content to renew the lease for 21 years, until 1646. Of course no one in that room, however, engaged in their routine business could have anticipated just how much their world would change within that lease period, least of all Wortley himself. The status quo was not to be maintained for either Bladen or Wortley as, within five short years, Bladen had left (or been sacked) from Wortley's employ and had brought a Chancery Case against him and Wortley would be set on a path of dogged allegiance to the Crown that would see him locked up in the Tower for many years where he wrote poetry to pass the time.

Within months things began to change. In 1626 Bladen, it was alleged, gave Wortley investment advice concerning the acquisition of a manor which was then purchased for £500. It quickly became apparent that the advice was poor, that the manor was only worth a paltry £16 a year on an estate in person for life. At least, this was the allegation made by Wortley's counsel when Bladen eventually took Sir Francis to court.

It seems likely that this event was the beginning of the spiralling downwards of relations between Bladen and Wortley as, soon after, another event occurred concerning the Coney family which may have been smoothed over if Bladen had still enjoyed Wortley's support.

---

[1] Reports from Commissioners: Seven Vols (Third). Charities, (19) in England and Wales, session 29th Jan - 28th Jul 1828, Vol. XI, 1828, Bodleian Library, Oxford. Some detail in the Will ... *"that the brethren should wear gowns, all of one colour, white or white ruse, and the women wear long gowns of the same colour"*
[2] TNA: C 205/14/29 Commission to Inquire between Robert Bladen and Hemsworth Hospital. No return
[3] Nottingham University Library, DMSC, Ga 10,282 5th February 1642 'disputed messuages and lands'
[4] 1621: Bladen v Boyne - legal action against a Thomas Boyne: money matters, Yorkshire; 1622: Bladen v Parkin - legal action against Thomas and John Parkin: money matters, Yorkshire TNA: C3/337/48, C3/336/94 and C21/B27/13
[5] Old Wortley Hall was the predecessor of the current 18th century building
[6] TNA: C21/B19/23 Bladen v Wortley, 1636

*Coney v Bladen*

The Coney family were closely related to Lady Wortley with the marriage of her daughter Sarah to Sir Sutton Coney.

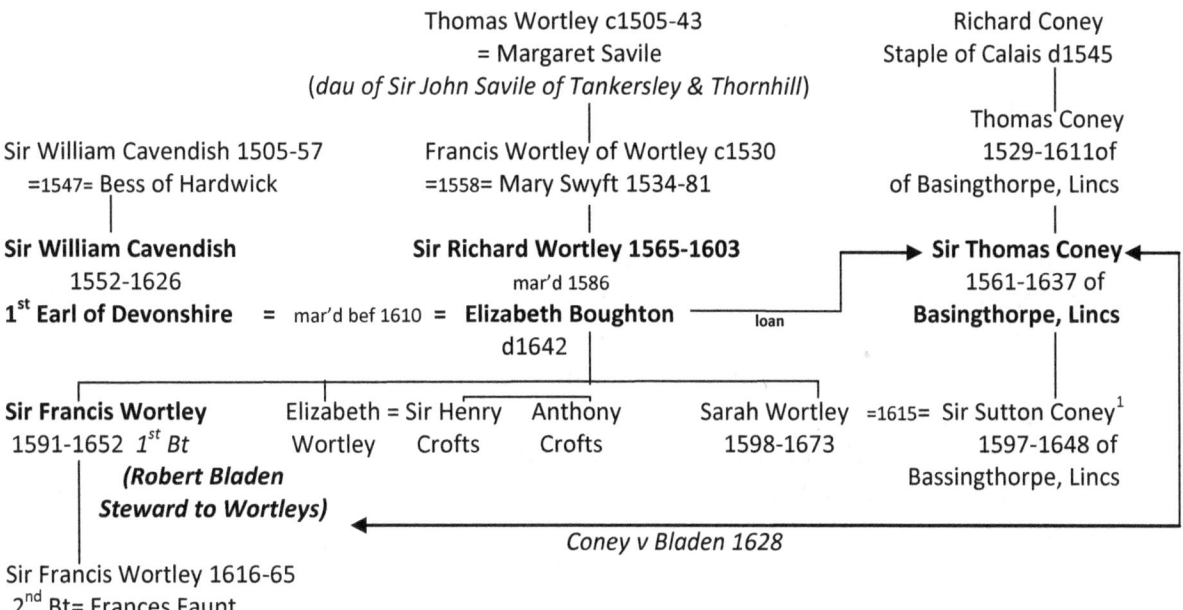

Like Sir Francis Wortley, Sutton Coney was a die-hard Royalist who would fight for the King in the Civil War. The very fact that his father Sir Thomas Coney brought legal action against Robert Bladen, the Wortley's steward, suggests that Bladen's break with Wortley had already taken place by 1628. In contrast, the Coneys' relationship with Wortley/Devonshire was steadfast, enduring until the end of the Countess's life when she assigned the Wortley estates over to a Robert Wolrich, George Cony [Coney] and Henry Houghton in trust for her grandson.[2] Anthony Crofts (on above chart) was also a Trustee.

So a Bill of Complaint was brought by Sir Thomas Coney of Lincolnshire as the Plaintiff and Robert Bladen being the Defendant[3] which stated that in 1617 Coney had reason to borrow money from the widowed Lady Wortley, then Countess of Devonshire. Sir Thomas Coney was the son of a Merchant of the Staple for Calais (then under English control) and, whatever his reasons for needing a loan, he did not keep up the repayments and became indebted to the Countess and, at that time, Coney stated that Robert Bladen of Hemsworth was her steward and this is how Sir Thomas came into contact with Bladen.

In his deposition he then listed various payments he made to Bladen through to 1621 and subsequent years but then, about 1623 a bond was set up for additional security against the debt through a man called Henry Potter. Coney continued to make payments for both rent of land and for the original loan. He said *"And your orator being likewise to pay unto the said Robert Bladen for certain rent which he pretended he had authority to recover and take by the direction of the said Countess"*.

---

[1] Alumni Cantabrigiensis by John Venn - son of Sir Thomas Coney of Basingthorpe
[2] Yorkshire Royalist Composition Papers, Proceedings of the Committee. Edited by John William Clay
[3] TNA: C2/Chas1/C58/58, Con[e]y v Bladen, dated 1628

Coney claimed to have made satisfactory payments but that Bladen would not release or discharge him from the bond and kept demanding more money.[1]

In Robert's reply to the Bill he made no mention of being in the employ of the Countess in this transaction or collecting rents on her behalf, but rather he claimed the Countess had devised land around Bassingthorpe in Lincolnshire to him for a period of time/rent and that he was, in effect, sub-letting portions and parcels of land. So, perhaps in the same way that he had sub-let the Carlton farm to under-tenants, Bladen was doing the same for the Basingthorpe land. The Countess's daughter Sarah Wortley had married Sir Sutton Coney whose family already had large landholdings in the area and Coney was therefore in debt to Bladen for rent but indebted to the Countess for the original loan.

Bondsman Henry Potter was required to sign a deposition as to the facts he was aware of and said that when the bond was in default by Coney's late or non-payment, Bladen *"did put the said Bond in suit at the Common Law"*. In the course of the law suit regarding the bond, Bladen also claimed that Coney's own wife had asked him for a loan of £5 and Bladen had obliged the lady, but Sir Coney denied all knowledge of this and would therefore take no responsibility for it. The bondsman, Henry Potter, in his answer confirmed Coney's non-payment and stated that he had freely and willingly entered into the bond in the first place.

The initial agreement concerning Bladen and Coney has already been briefly referred to in an earlier section, *1616: Sir Richard Sunderland*, where there is reference to the agreement that Bladen took out with Coney and it is clear from that document that he was acting on his own account and not on behalf of the Countess. The Coneys of Lincolnshire had a long history of land disputes with neighbours. Robert Bladen would later be in the employ of the Savile family who had land holdings in Barrowby in Lincolnshire close to Basingthorpe which had been inherited by the Saviles from the Vernon family. In the Will of Henry Savile, probate 1569 he said ... 'to my son George, the lease of a farm at Whissendine in the county of Rutland *"I have of the grant of Thomas Coney of Bassingthorpe Esq"*.' This Henry Savile was the great-grandfather of the William Savile who was Robert's next employer and who, along with a Maurice Berkley and George Sherrard, had a boundary dispute over land in Bassingthorpe with Coney.[2]

The fact that Robert was being sued by a Wortley relation over land Bladen had bought off the Countess for his own use and profit would not have gone down well with his employer or helped their deteriorating relationship. It is thought Wortley dismissed Bladen from his service in the late 1620s. Then, whilst Bladen would go on to secure employment with the Saviles, Francis Wortley's real difficulties were only just beginning. He had obtained a position at Court, being Gentleman of the Privy Chamber Extraordinary[3] to King Charles 1st just at the time when the King was set on a path of rigid defiance against Parliament.

---

[1] TNA: C2/Chas1/C58/58, Con[e]y v Bladen, dated 1628

[2] This Henry Savile also owned a manor at Southowram and his Will was witnessed by Thomas Gargrave and William Hamond

[3] Journals of the House of Lords Vol X, p672. 1836. Francis Wortley, Gentleman of His Majesty's Privy Chamber arrested. Wortley petitioned to be allowed 'the Privilege of Parliament'. 1643

Wortley's entrenched position as a die-hard royalist made his family uneasy for the security of the family estates and, in an attempt to protect themselves, they set about manoeuvring their assets to ensure survival. There may not have been a job for Bladen to do by this time if he had remained with Wortley because the estate was taken out of Sir Francis's hands and jointly held in trust by his brother Sir Edward Wortley[1] who sensibly showed more sympathy to the Parliamentary cause and near relation Anthony Crofts, in trust for the son of Sir Francis. Countess Elizabeth later bought out the entire estate from the trustees[2] and bequeathed it to her grandson Francis[3] after her demise and he subsequently applied to have the sequestered estates restored to the family by paying fines.

Bladen's timing of bringing a law suit against Wortley may have been calculated to inflict maximum damage as it was at the precise time when Wortley's fortunes were taking a turn for the worse. In 1629[4] Wortley had made a large loan to Thomas Bosvile of Newhall for which he had the Manor of Newhall as indemnity, then in 1633 he had lost a law suit over an inheritance of his wife's and was forced to pay £865 damages and, perhaps as a result of those damages, he found himself by 1635[5] stripped of control of his estate by his family. Few of his tenants or others who had dealings with Francis Wortley would have had much sympathy for any reduced circumstances he may have found himself in. He had a reputation, as his father did before him, of being a ruthless encloser and, as his steward, Bladen put his name to many deeds where tenants were refused renewal on their leases as Wortley sought to expand his land holdings and reduce the common land.[6] That is certainly what was done in 1629 when some of the tenants of Hoylandswaine were ejected and the Common was enclosed.[7] Wortley had petitioned the King to subpoena *"certain riotous persons breaking and inclosing Hoylandswaine Common"*.[1]

---

[1] The Countess of Devonshire assigned Manors of Wortley, Pilley, Hunself and Hoyland Swaine to Robert Wolrich and George Cony Esquire and Henry Houghton in trust for son Edward

[2] Wortley and the Wortleys: A Lecture delivered before the Sheffield Literary and Philosophical Society and also Rotherham Literary and Scientific Society by Revered Arthur Gatty D.D., Vicar of Ecclesfield and Sub-Dean of York in 1877, stated the Wortleys historically owned half of the Manor of Hemsworth and the advowson of the church. In 1635 after securing possession of the estate for 40 years and leasing the Wortley manors of Wortley, Pilley, Hunshelf and Hoylandswain to Anthony Crofts the Countess of Devonshire purchased it all back for £20,000 and put it in her grandson's name, according to Yorkshire Royalist Composition Papers

[3] Countess of Devonshire to Sir Francis Wortley on 14th January 1641. Sheffield Archives Wh M/D/108

[4] Sheffield Archives: Wh M/D/82, deed 3 September 1629 between Thomas Bosvile of Newhall and Sir Francis Wortley. Large sum loaned to Bosvile to assist his son. Manor of Newhall used as indemnity

[5] Sheffield Archives: Wh M/D/92, 93, 96, 97 and 98 Sir Francis Wortley devised various Manors to Elizabeth Countess of Devonshire

[6] Various Deeds have survived of transactions that were taking place at this time: Robert was stated to be *"of Askwith"* when they entered into a bargain/sale with a Robert Sotwell of Holylandswaine in Yorkshire regarding tithes for corn and grain from a messuage and a parcel of the rectory of Silkstone in Yorkshire. That same year, they had a similar bargain/sale in the same area to a Richard Kaye. Another transaction between Wortley and Bladen, dating from 1617, was a Final Concord between John Midgley, gent, plaintiff with Francis Wortley, Knight, and Robert Bladen, gent, deforciants regarding tithes of grain in Hoylandswayne in Silkstone. Consideration £100. Barnsley Archives: SpSt 60329 (147/34)

[7] An Indenture dated 1618, showed Wortley and Bladen with others: Thomas Hanson (gent), William Swifte (Clerk), Richard Sotwell, Nicholas Mokeson, John Cauldwell, Thomas Holme, Richard Hawkesworth, Godfrey Ellison, Henry Wood, Richard Haye, Christopher Ibotson, Thomas Gawnt, William Field, Nicholas Couldwell, George Gawthorpe and Agnes Catlin (widow) making an agreement with John Midgley regarding tithes of corn

Generations of Wortleys had been unpopular in the locality. Rev Oliver Heywood[2] wrote ....
*"Sir Francis Wortly's great-grandfather, being a man of great estate was owner of a town near unto him, only there were some freeholders in it, with whom he wrangled and sued until he had beggared them and cast them out of their inheritance and so the town was wholly his, which he quite pulled down and laid the buildings and town fields even as a common wherein his main design was to keep deer and to make a lodge to which he came at the time of the year and lay there, taking great delight to hear the deer bell, but it came to pass that, before he died, he belled like a deer, and was distracted"*.[3]

The end of the 1620s/early 1630s was a busy time for Bladen with litigation. Before resuming the story of his difficulties with Wortley, there was another case he was involved with concerning land at Hemsworth.

*1629: Hemsworth Land Dispute*
In 1629 Robert had some of his cattle depasturing on land in Hemsworth when not once, but three times, Elizabeth Redhead[4] who was a neighbouring farmer, or individuals working on her behalf, drove off his cattle and on the last occasion the cattle were seized and she demanded £5-3-4d be paid to her to secure their return. Redhead believed the cattle had no right to be on the land. The chancery case was actually in Dr Richard Berry's name as it seemed that the land Bladen was using was, in fact, owned by Berry: High Hall in Hemsworth had been passed down from Sir Cotton Gargrave to his son Thomas, then Thomas's wife Katherine acquired the Hall at her marriage and so sold on eventually to Dr Richard Berry. Bladen was his neighbour and friend and no doubt was grazing the cattle with Berry's agreement.

Elizabeth Redhead stated that the particular close, called 'Hempsyard' was not part of the title held by Berry (or Bladen) and the chancery bill was routed via the Duchy of Lancaster who had manorial rights in that part of Yorkshire.[5] Deponents were called, even Sir Richard from the Gargrave family, who all supported Berry and Bladen's right and title over Hempsyard Close. The outcome was successful for Berry/Bladen.

---

in Hoylandswaine. SpSt/228/2 dated 22nd April 1618 - Sheffield Archives (probably now relocated to Barnsley Archives though reference numbers are currently retained)
[1] Proceedings in the Star Chamber of 1633
[2] Rev. Oliver Heywood in 'Memoranda'. Diaries, Vol. iii, 81, edited by J Horsfall Turner
[3] West Riding Sessions Records: Orders 1611-42; Indictments, 1637-42 by John Lister. Also, in 1638, James Parkin, a yeoman of Mortomley nr Rotherham, was brought before the Assizes for publicly uttering ... *"I scorn Sir Francis Wortley's proposition with my arse, and I worship him with my arse"*
[4] In nearby Kinsley, Sir Richard Gargrave's estate had been sold and divided between Richard Berry and others, including Sir Thomas Monson whose daughter Anne had married Arthur Redhead of Howden
[5] TNA: DL4/79/5 Attorney General of Duchy of Lancaster v Redhead, or Berry v Redhead dated 1630

### 1630s: Bladen v Wortley

Once relations had been spoilt between Bladen and Wortley, the ensuing chancery case ensured every grievance over the preceding twenty years got an airing. Although only a proportion of the chancery papers have survived, they are sufficient to piece the story together.[1] The specific issue which brought Bladen to take Wortley to court was over his farm at Carlton which had many more years to run on its lease. His co-Plaintiff was Mary Holgate who had been sub-tenant of the farm with her husband and children. Subsequently her husband, Thomas Holgate, died a couple of years into his tenancy and his widow Mary and her children continued at the property until one day Wortley's bailiffs arrived and attempted to evict her for non-payment of rent. Mary described how a bailiff arrived at the house on a Saturday evening and, stooping to pick up a brick from a wall, entered the house trying to frighten her. He drew his sword, flourishing it up and down terrifying Mary and her young children. He stayed at the house all night trying to get her to vacate it but she steadfastly refused.

The following morning, the Sabbath, the bailiff forcibly ejected her from the farm with her young children. He locked the door and left all their possessions inside, telling her that the key would be delivered to a certain person but did not tell her who - the assumption being owner Sir Francis Wortley. Mary was found bewildered and weeping in distress near the church at Royston later that morning by one of the deponents in this case. For some time the house remained locked up until, at long last, the key was returned to her, or, as the deponent said, he thought it had been "sent to her little boy". Mary soon after joined with Robert to bring a Bill of Complaint against Sir Francis Wortley.

Other information to emerge from these depositions gives an interesting perspective on the individuals involved. Robert Bladen's depositions, perhaps not surprisingly, paint a picture of himself as a model employee to an ungrateful Wortley. He claimed that Wortley spoke well of him, calling him a 'faithful servant' who succeeded in preserving Wortley's good credit and estate but that Robert received insufficient money during his employment and that his duties involved him constantly travelling on behalf of the family into other counties and to London. He would claim that he received no payment for these journeys and that he had been forced to rely on his friends to put up bonds for him with interest for loans to pay, in particular for the continual need for horses and other necessary charges.

The Wortley lawyers' response was to attack Bladen with everything at their disposal. Firstly, as previously mentioned, a deponent claimed Robert had given poor advice to Sir Francis regarding the purchase of a worthless manor. Similarly Bladen was alleged to have persuaded Wortley to give £400 to freeholder Edmund Dandy for a lease which also proved worthless. It was also alleged that, in carrying out his duties as steward, Bladen took bribes for leasing Wortley property and lands and seriously neglected his duties. It was stated by more than one deponent that, in fact, Bladen had an allowance of 5 shillings per day when travelling away from home to cover his basic expenses and that the farm at Carlton he had been given by Wortley was in lieu of wages.

---

[1] TNA: C21/B19/16 & 23, Bladen v Wortley, dated 1636

Central to the Wortley's side of the argument was that the farm at Carlton should not have been sub-let to other tenants. They claimed Robert had done so without permission and that, not only had he allowed the property to fall into a state of disrepair but that he had never paid any rent whatsoever on it.

Mary Holgate, in her deposition, emphatically denied that there was any rent outstanding on the property, that she had paid (Bladen) and had relations who would stand surety for her in any event. Her father-in-law had volunteered to pay the rent if it should fall into arrears and Mary was able to produce a receipt for her payment. The question of what Bladen did with that rent payment is not satisfactorily explained in the documents. Perhaps if he had been used to not being required to pay it, he continued and just pocketed it. Wortley's bailiffs produced depositions stating that Bladen had never paid rent on the property, but neither had Wortley ever insisted on it. The Carlton farm was sub-let between three parties: Mary and her family resided in the house itself and two other farmers from nearby villages rented parcels of farm land for their use.

For his part, Bladen made no attempt to deny the sub-letting of the farm but stated that, in fact, it was Sir Francis Wortley himself who had sent for Thomas Holgate and pleaded with him to become his tenant saying that he would find him a 'kind and loving landlord'. It was claimed that the tenants renting the farm land had, by virtue of being tenants (or sub-tenants) in Carlton, exercised their rights to use the Common land for their cattle which, it was claimed, led to the area being overcrowded. In addition they took corn and hay from the Carlton Manor and carried it away to the use of their own farmsteads out of the area.

A large number of depositions concerned the condition of the farm, with Bladen stating it had been ruinous in parts from the start, others stating that he had allowed it to become so. Some deponents swore they had heard Wortley complain that Bladen spent too much time on other men's affairs instead of his own or that he had '*given up false accounts to the said Sir Francis Wortley*'[1] and that he had taken bribes over the lettings and under-valued them (on the books to Wortley) whilst pocketing the difference himself. There was even an allegation that Sir Francis Wortley himself had been put in difficulties when his accounts showed less than he had been expecting to cover funds he needed for the county and the city. The case left Bladen further encumbered by legal costs and in need of new employment.

*Savile Family*
By the late 1620s, when Robert's service to the Wortley family ended, he had been living in Hemsworth for some years and had leased (or mortgaged) many properties in that area as far back as 1615, no doubt some of the mortgages and refinancing he did were to pay for his various law suits. About ten miles away from Hemsworth was the village of Thornhill which had been home to the Savile family since 1370 and who were, at various times, administrators of the Manor of Wakefield and who held the Honour of Pontefract (along with the de Lacy family) and their seat at Thornhill Hall (Rectory Park) was well secured being surrounded by a moat.[2]

---

[1] TNA: C21/B19/16 & 23, Bladen v Wortley, dated 1636
[2] Ten miles as the crow flies

How the Savile family came to be Robert's next employers has already been hinted at in the examination of Sir George Radcliffe's letters. Radcliffe's family resided at Overthorpe Hall in Thornhill and his neighbours were Philip and Helen Waterhouse (Elizabeth Bladen's uncle and aunt). Radcliffe's life was closely tied to the Savile household as Sir George (1st Bt) Savile was his godfather and in 1618 had introduced Radcliffe to the man who would become his closest life-long friend, Thomas Wentworth (later Earl of Strafford). The closeness of these families was reinforced when Sir George's son, also called Sir George and who predeceased his father, married Lady Anne Wentworth, Strafford's sister.

Unfortunately Sir George 1st Bt had a loathing for his son Sir George and battled with his widowed daughter-in-law over the Thornhill estate. Both Sir George's, however, were deceased by 1622 and from 1624 the widowed Lady Savile (Wentworth) took occupation of Thornhill Hall for herself and her two sons, George (2nd Bt) aged 12 and William (3rd Bt) aged 11 years. No doubt through Radcliffe's strong influence, Lady Anne Savile who was running the estate as her son was not of full age, engaged the services of Robert Bladen around 1628-29 when her youngest son Sir William was at University/Inns of Court. She continued to run Thornhill until she died which was also the time when her son and heir William was of full age in 1633. The circumstances of Bladen's engagement to this family bear striking similarities to his earlier engagement to the Wortleys, where the widowed Lady Wortley had been left to run a vast estate whilst her son and heir was also a minor.

Lady Savile (Wentworth)'s occupation of the hall meant the Wentworth family spent a great deal of time at Thornhill and Robert Bladen would have known the Earl of Strafford (Radcliffe's closest friend) very well as he was a frequent visitor to the hall during Robert's employment, staying for some five days along with George Radcliffe in 1634-36 before both departed for Ireland. Strafford had also been appointed guardian to William 3rd Bt Savile who named Robert Bladen as a beneficiary in his Will.

Thornhill was quite an open house at the time with more than 59 people in residence.[1] Robert and his family did not, however, reside on the premises as their names are not on a list of those 43 residents in the household on 25th January 1624, nor one of 59 residents in 26th July 1637. Robert's son John (to be discussed later) who had completed his legal training at this time also knew both Radcliffe and Strafford well, indeed well enough to subsequently visit them both when they departed for Ireland.

When the young Sir William Savile (3rd Bt) reached full age he inherited estates spanning several counties and became one of the wealthiest men in Yorkshire. The family's main residences were at Thornhill, Rufford Abbey in Nottingham, with some 50,000 acres with an income of £7,000 pa and a house in York. He must have engaged Robert Bladen in a position of trust, perhaps as a land steward collecting rents etc because Savile was absent for much of the time. The death of William Savile's mother when he came of age meant he immediately acquired huge responsibilities domestically as well as being expected to assume a position of authority, which he did by becoming MP for Yorkshire and Old Sarum (rotten borough) and, through his guardian Strafford's patronage, he had a seat on the Council of the North.

---

[1] The Saviles of Thornhill: Life at Thornhill Hall in the Reign of Charles I by Barbara H Nuttall, 1986, p39

Savile's long absences from Thornhill would have necessitated him being dependent on a few key individuals to run his estates and, during the 1630s, the estates were run well. Like Wortley, Savile was an ardent Royalist and was with the King in 1642 at Nottingham when the Royal Standard was raised signalling the beginning of the Civil War. He took command of the Royalist Cavalry at the Battle of Winceby - he even used his own moated family home at Thornhill as a garrison for the King's forces.

Both portraits on the right were taken at the time when Robert Bladen was working for Sir William and Lady Anne Savile

Sir William's portrait dates from 1635-40 and Lady Savile's from 1643.

**Sir William & Lady Anne Savile (née Coventry)**[1]

The Saviles and Wortleys did not always get along, Sir Francis Wortley had a long-running feud with George 1st Bt Savile. There was an incident in 1626 where Francis Wortley and Sir Thomas Savile came to blows after a bitter political contest and a subsequent encounter right outside Parliament where they drew swords on each other. Wortley had been kicked by Savile whose footman then slashed his face. Certainly Robert's stewardship of the Wortley estates would have put him in direct contact with the Saviles who owned neighbouring estates. Indeed, George Savile was initially based in Lincoln where Robert also had dealings over land in Basingthorpe on behalf of the Countess of Devonshire (see Coney case) before moving to Thornhill in Yorkshire, so Bladen and the senior Savile's paths moved in the same direction.

As to what happened to Sir Francis Wortley after Bladen left his employ, Wortley steadfastly clung to the Royalist cause and was said to have been one of the first Knights to raise his sword for the King. It was said he was at the Siege of Hull where, on the opposing side, he would have encountered Robert Bladen's son John. His valiant attempts to rouse support for the King when Civil War came led to his capture by Sir Thomas Fairfax's forces and subsequent incarceration in the Tower of London. To pass the time away he wrote poetry and, when he did finally regain his freedom, his stature was greatly diminished. He never regained the power and authority he held before the war and died in relative poverty in London lodgings.[2]

---

[1] Cited in The Saviles of Thornhill: Life at Thornhill Hall in the Reign of Charles I by Barbara H Nuttall, 1986 with acknowledgement to Lord Savile of Gryce Hall for permission to print copies of the portraits of his ancestors but also with consent of the present 4th Baron Savile, John Anthony Thornhill Lumley-Savile

[2] Royalist Composition Papers, edited by John William Clay

At the outbreak of war in Nottingham, Rufford was too close to fighting and, initially the family retreated, along with their possessions to Thornhill but, within months, the King had fled London (where he had little support) and set up court at York and, initially the West Riding came under Royal control. The Battle of Winceby, however, saw a reversal of fortunes and not long after Savile had been appointed Governor of York he was dead.

The nine months pregnant Lady Savile had left Thornhill and was at Sheffield Castle when it was subsequently captured by parliamentarian forces. In time she was allowed to return to Thornhill but whether Robert continued in his employment there is not known because the Savile estate faced appropriation of its income by Parliament. Lady Savile remained defiantly loyal to the King to the bitter end.

Sir William Savile was only 32 years old when he died fighting for the King near York and in his Will he left a bequest to Robert Bladen and a few other gentlemen ..."*List of annuities to be paid out of my lands and milnes in Denby, Clayton and Ingbirchworth, co. York, John Batt of Okwell esquire £20; Thomas Farrar, gent, my servant £20, Joseph Sill of Thornhill, gent, £20, Robt Bladen, my servant 20 marks etc.*[1]"

It is possible that Robert Bladen's own death was attributable to the Civil War[2] although the specific year of his death in 1647 there was no fighting taking place in Yorkshire and his age and possible ill-health may have precluded him being involved in actual combat. Robert died before the destruction of Thornhill Hall which happened in 1648 when a parliamentary force took possession of it and razed it to the ground. The Savile family relocated to their other property at Rufford. Robert Bladen lived on for three years and, though some of his properties were lost through involvement with Berry, it is known that at least one or two Hemsworth properties did end up in his grandson's hands as well as the valuable advowson of the church. The principal property of Bullingshire Hall, however, was lost to Berry and Robert's descendants would fail in all attempts to recover it.

*1630s: Indebtedness to Berry*

Robert was enmeshed in complex financial arrangements with Berry which became increasingly messy as the years rolled by. An initial loan for £300 from Berry was followed, in 1629 by another for £450 and each time Bladen gave another of his properties over to Berry as security. On another occasion Bladen's request for further money was refused by Berry initially but later he was directed to the services of Joll and Talbotts who, Berry said, would loan Bladen more than he needed, leaving him some money in hand. A raft of Indentures was drawn up between Bladen and Berry showing that whenever Robert was in need of raising money it was his 'friend' Berry he turned to.

---

[1]YAJ, Vol. 5, pp1-47. 1920, by the Late J W Clay F.S.A. The other listed annuitants with Bladen were:- *John Batte* and his family of Oakwell Hall who were rent collectors for the Saville family; *Thomas Farrar* - probably a relation of the Henry Farrar who joined with Sir John Savile to purchase Manor of Ewood and Brearley from John Lacy, including the Manor and township of Midgley, water corn mill, Brearley Milne, a water mill in Cheswally and 9 messuages. Also related to William Farrar who went to Virginia in 1618; *Joseph Sill* d. 11 June 1645 of Thornhill and Skellow Grange - near to the Great Northern Road South Kirkby/Hemsworth. Sills were a Wakefield family, mercers, Governors of Wakefield Grammar School - as were many Birkheads. They owned estates in Wakefield, Stanley, Lofthouse and East Ardley

[2] Admon record for a Robert Bladen of Hemsworth on 30 October 1647 (Doncaster R.O., folio 501)

How many properties were involved in the 11 Indentures between them is hard to say, as some may have been for the same property at different times:

1) Indenture for messuage occupied by John Rosland
2) Indenture for messuage occupied by Richard Walker
3) Indenture for messuage occupied by Richard Forrest
4) Indenture for messuage occupied by Richard Abbot
5) Indenture re Bullingshire Hall in Hemsworth - later occupied by wife Elizabeth as her dower
6) Indenture for messuage occupied by Richard Green (Muro Inngs near farmer Henry Scholey's land)
7) Indenture for messuage occupied by Matthew Rawson
8) Indenture for messuage in Flithurst in the parish of Hemsworth
9) Indenture for messuage leased to John Oscliffe in 1641
10) Indenture for messuage leased to Thomas Thornton in 1641
11) Indenture for Hague Hall in South Kirkby in partnership with Nathaniel Birkhead

By 1632 yet again Bladen had need of money, most probably to fund the legal action he had instigated against Sir Francis Wortley over the loss of the Carlton farm house. Agreement was later reached and, in exchange for having security on Bladen's properties, Berry loaned him a further £450 at interest. Copies of two of the above indentures are held at Nottingham University's Manuscripts and Special Collections Department and both concern properties Bladen held in Hemsworth:-

* Counterpart lease by Richard Berry and Robert Bladen to Thomas Thornton, of a close of meadow of pasture called Redd Roydes containing 8 acres, for 21 years, paying £6 yearly. Location: Hemsworth, Yorkshire[1] (except woods, mines, quarries). Dated 1641

* Counterpart lease by Richard Berry and Robert Bladen to John Oscliffe, of a messuage, croft, 2 closes of meadow or pasture, and 18 acres of arable land, for 21 years, paying yearly £12.5s and 2 hens at Christmas. Location: Hemsworth[2] (except woods, mines, quarries). Dated 1641

After Bladen's death, Berry would claim that the purpose of the above deeds, both dated November 1641, was to safeguard the leaseholds by assigning new lives and thereby extending them. Bladen, perhaps like the Wortleys, could foresee looming turmoil as Civil War was approaching and sought to protect his assets and avoid confiscation. He may have been conscious that his strong adherence to Royalists leaders would make him particularly vulnerable if Parliament should prevail. How reliable Berry's claims were, however, is questionable as with the death of both Robert and his son John, Berry was free to make any claim he wished as the only surviving Bladen was the infant Nathaniel (John's son), so there was no one old enough to refute them.

---

[1] GA9471 Nottingham University Manuscripts and Special Collections
[2] GA9470 Nottingham University Manuscripts and Special Collections

If the Bladens felt cheated out of their property by Berry, then the Gargraves fared even worse. The family's acquisition of vast areas of lands acquired from the Abbeys of Yorkshire at the Dissolution, eventually devolved to a sole female heir Prudence who married the 'universal money lender' Dr Richard Berry, of whom it was said, he *"contrived to make himself master of their fortune, and the whole family sunk into obscurity"*.[1] Robert's grandson would later describe Berry as an *"injurious and designing man and having a covetous eye upon your orator's said grandfather's estate pretending that the farm and lands of the before recited deed enrolled would, in case of your orator's said grandfather's death without sufficient security to indemnify him against the debt due to Joll and Talbotts, and that he feared some settlement upon your orator's grandmother"*. In other words, Berry feared that if Robert Bladen was to die during his indebtedness to Berry that Elizabeth Bladen could legally claim her dower of one-third of Bladen's estate. So to cover that eventuality Berry sought Bladen's Bullingshire Hall property as security and further charged Bladen with £100 to enter into a bond - again for additional security. The grandson further stated *"the said Richard Berry designing to entangle your orator's said grandfather charged the said £450 upon Bullingshire Hall likewise. ..... Richard Berry discoursing together and accounting what was due from him the said Robert Bladen on the whole, upon the several securities, they did then compute them to the amount of £850"*.[2] Bladen never freed himself from indebtedness to Berry.

In 1648, shortly after Robert's death, a coverture agreement[3] was signed between the now widowed Elizabeth Bladen and Berry whereby Elizabeth would make use of her legal dower to live at Bullingshire Hall for the duration of *'40 years if Elizabeth Bladen should so long live'*.[4] As it happens she did not, she died just a few years later in 1653 and since it is known that the grandson Nathaniel lived with his grandmother until her death he would also have resided at the property until about the age of eleven years.

### 1647+: Bullingshire Hall

Robert Bladen had purchased Bullingshire Hall and surrounding woodland around 1617 and on 8th December of 1631 he devised the property to Dr Richard Berry in return for the sum of £300. Then at some later point, Bladen repaid Berry the sum. This became a bone of contention because Berry would dispute the sum was ever repaid and that he still had title to the property. Immediately after Robert's death, in fact the same year, the widowed Elizabeth Bladen found herself in a legal challenge over this property.[5] A Bill of Complaint was brought by William Baker of Windsor in Berkshire whose son Walter Baker had on his behalf, back in 1637, purchased the same Bullingshire Hall in Hemsworth for £500 from Robert Bladen, he claimed.

---

[1] Illustrations of British History 1: Biography and Manners in the Reigns of Henry VIII, Edward VI, Mary, Elizabeth and James I by Edmund Lodge, Vol. 1, 1791
[2] TNA: C6/264/15 Bladen v Fountaine, dated 1690
[3] Ibid
[4] Deed, dated 11th November 1648 allowed her to live there at a peppercorn rent until she died or for 40 years
[5] TNA: C10/12/16 Baker v Bladen, 1651

Yorkshire Subsidy Rolls (Poll Tax) for 1379 record a 'Thomas Bullyngschyr' in Hemsworth. The property thereby was associated with that family and thenlater became home of Francis Gargrave, a younger son of Cotton. No information beyond the above has been found on a Bullingshire Hall as it was probably pulled down many years ago, but there is on present maps of Hemsworth due east a Bullinger Wood and mention of 'Bullenshaw Villas' which would seem to be the likely location for Bullingshire Hall or Bullingshire Hall Farm, being located roughly between Hemsworth and north of South Kirkby and Hague Hall. The first Ordnance Survey map of 1841 refers to the area as Billing Wood and an 1854 map shows the same area as Bullingshaw Wood and so, with some migration of the name, it has survived though only the wood that surrounded the house remains.[1] A 1927 application to build a housing estate (which never materialised) named the site Bullinger Hall Estate with woods thereto belonging and 'Bullenshire Hall farm and greens'.

The legal action was brought because Baker had believed that Bladen held clear title to the property when he handed over £500 to him for the purchase of Bullingshire Hall but subsequently the dispute between Berry and Bladen had revealed that his title was in doubt, hence Elizabeth's residence being challenged. Baker, in his Bill of Complaint, called upon Elizabeth to make answer and many other Bladen family tenants of their other properties in Hemsworth.[2] Baker believed that Elizabeth, Berry, Fountain (Berry's heir) and others were conspiring against him and intent on producing deeds relating to other properties in Hemsworth for which there were deeds to support their case. In addition he called upon John Fountain to give evidence - as Fountain was the executor and principal beneficiary of Richard Berry's Will. Fountain painstakingly went through all the Indentures and Deeds he found amongst Berry's papers and denied he had any involvement in the deeds or collusion with Elizabeth Bladen. Fountain was to claim that when Bladen died he was indebted to Berry for the sum of £1,800.

*Widow Bladen*

Robert died intestate in 1647 and administration of his estate was granted to his wife Elizabeth.[3] Her name was frequently mentioned in correspondence of the late 1640s between Dr Richard Berry and his nephew Marmaduke Monckton-Berry - referred to earlier as living at Hodroyd House close to the Bladens at Hemsworth.

Original letters[4] have been preserved between Dr Berry and his nephew for the period 17th July 1649 to 20th May 1651 (days before his death) when Berry was fighting for his financial life in London against charges of delinquency. He was battling to rebut the charges that he had been a Royalist sympathiser in the Civil War and Colonel Bosvile of Gunthwaite had brought charges against him for delinquency at Goldsmith's Hall.

---

[1] TNA: SY/9/RD13/9R Bullinger Hall Estate, 1927 Hemsworth Rural District Council, LA Plans
[2] TNA: C10/12/16 Baker v Bladen, 1651: Those accused of colluding with Robert/Elizabeth Bladen to defraud Baker: John Ostercliffe, Richard Mond, Robert Andsley and Matthew Rawson and others. (John Ostercliffe is referred to elsewhere in this book as having a tenancy of Robert Bladen)
[3] On 30th October 1647 at Doncaster (fol. 501)
[4] 68 Letters between Dr Richard Berrye to nephew Marmaduke Monckton at Hodroyd Ga 12,768/1-70, Nottingham University Library, Department of Manuscripts and Special Collections

It was a two year long struggle for him to attend London and persuade the authorities that he had been 'reluctant' in the King's service and, eventually, he managed to escape without incurring loss of land or a large fine.[1] Writing to nephew Marmaduke in 1651 (who he addressed as Cousen Duke), he informed him that his troubles with delinquency were over, but was aggrieved against those who had brought charges against him and urged Marmaduke to make their characters known publicly. He said *"I bless God, my tedious delinquent business is finally determined, with much credit to myself and confusion to my adversaries, especially to Col. Bosvile, who prosecuted me spitefully"*. Berry firmly believed that some used the delinquency process to retaliate against their foes, or in Berry's case, it was those indebted to him who sought to take advantage of his predicament for their own ends. However, if indeed he had really been Cromwell's doctor, it surely would not have taken him the best part of two years to defend himself against Royalist sympathies after the war.

His letters were full of instructions and advice to his cousin on how Marmaduke should handle his affairs in his absence. Approximately twenty of these letters make very brief mention of the now widowed Mrs Bladen and it seemed that Berry was in control of her property and income from her tenants....

*18th January 1649: "... let not Mr Hurd's drunkenness hinder you getting monies of Mrs Bladen but press her to procure some sober friend to extract acquittances, these trifling delays I abhore".[2]*
*22nd January 1649: "yet you can return me Mrs Bladen's moneys and Cornforths".[3]*
*17th July 1649: "You forget to mention Mrs Bladen's debt for £20 of monies for which Mr Tho. Levett is able to give.... acquittances ....."[4]*
*No date: "Cousen Duke, ... I have got your acquittance signed and sealed and delivered for Mrs Bladen's use, before Roger Dodsworth, whom Mrs Bladen knew ..... if she can accept with reason she shall have another before whom she pleaseth, but let her not further delay, this money, let it be with the rest returned hither with all possible speed for though the tenants desire till the 20th day after Christmas, yet I hope your diligence will procure it sooner. Your loving uncle, Rich. Berry"[5]*

Roger Dodsworth (1585-1654) was an Antiquarian in Yorkshire - his father was the Registrar of York Minster and, as stated above, was known to Elizabeth Bladen. By his Will he left his historical manuscripts to Thomas Fairfax, 3rd Lord Fairfax of Cameron who, in turn, bequeathed them to the Bodleian Library, Oxford. Dodsworth was aided in his antiquary work by Thomas Levett (mentioned elsewhere in this book).

---

[1] South Yorkshire - The History and Topography of the Deanery of Doncaster in the Diocese and County of York by Rev. Joseph Hunter, Vol. 2, 1831, p411
[2] Ga 12.768/5 University of Nottingham Manuscripts and Special Collections
[3] DCO/1/8 Ga 12.768/8 University of Nottingham Manuscripts and Special Collections
[4] DCO/1/3 G12768/3 University of Nottingham Manuscripts and Special Collections
[5] DCO/1/7 Ga.768/7 University of Nottingham Manuscripts and Special Collections

*No date: " Cousen Duke, You can assure Mrs Bladen her attorney shall want no directions to find the Judgment in the Exchequer if she keep touch with us now at Candlemass,\* otherwise no penny ... nor favours in any kind of these monies with Cornworthy be not returned to me, I shall want for my journey homeward especially if my delinquency business be not easy in the conclusion - I mean for charges for I propose to buy a horse or come to Newark by coach and there purchase a horse to Melton..... Your loving uncle, Rich Berry."*[1]

\* Candlemass being February, it is possible that Cornworthy was a tenant of the Bladens and some kind of chancery suit had been gone through concerning him. Richard Berry's tone towards Elizabeth Bladen then seemed to become more urgent .....

*No date: "Let not Mrs Bladen delay you longer for the remainder of her monies ..... which every attorney can find if he knows the terms when Judgment was entered (Michaelmas term was the month her Judgment was acknowledged).*[2]
*19th February 1649: "Mrs Bladen to defray your charges which, I pray, exact of her. Otherwise, tell her you hereafter, at my insistence, to allow you for your care ....."*[3]

Fleeting reference is made to her in a further letter:
*April 1650: "When you have leave, I would wish Cornforth's common land leased to the Springwoods ..... I mean Ox Close Spring and Mrs Bladen's rood. Before you turn loose some cattle to the pasture, remember to burn mark them for me, best not let the bull 'scape if you can catch him" ..... "Lieutenant General Cromwell hath almost done all his benefit in Ireland as appeareth by his letters to the parliament published in print this day and is coming here to be in a head of an army into Scotland which is to rendezvous at the beginning of May."*[4]

One of Berry's letters touches on another Bladen relation:
*c1650: "Mr Linsey [Lindsey] hath prevailed with me to inquire of Mr Birkhead's Last Will and Testament which I pray do".*
Mr Robert Lindsey was married to Elizabeth Birkhead, sister to Margaret Birkhead, Robert Bladen's daughter-in-law, therefore the above is a reference to their father Nathaniel Birkhead's Will (he died on 20th Feb 1649 with probate on 24th April 1650). This undated letter was probably written therefore late 1649 or early 1650.

*1651- Death of Dr Berry*
Berry did not live long after returning from London where he had been defending his estate and he died in 1651. He left an annuity[5] to his daughter, on condition her husband adopted the surname Berry, but his principal beneficiary and executrix was his friend and business partner John Fountaine of Lincoln's Inn.[6] Some of Berry's Hemsworth property was devised to his daughter but the Bladen's property "called Bullingshire Hall Green Farm and the cow closes and mire ings and the 15 acres of field lands ..." appears to have ended up in the hands of the Fountaines.

---

[1] DCO/0/1/9 GA12.768/9 University of Nottingham Manuscripts and Special Collections
[2] DCO/1/11 Ga12.768/11 University of Nottingham Manuscripts and Special Collections
[3] DCO/1/2 GA12.768/12 University of Nottingham Manuscripts and Special Collections
[4] DCO/1/21 Ga 12.768/18,19,20,21 University of Nottingham Manuscripts and Special Collections
[5] TNA: PROB 11/217/545 - abstracted in the Appendices, p227
[6] John Fountain had married Elizabeth Monckton who was the grand-daughter of Dr Berry's sister Susanna Berry/Berrie. Hunter's South Yorkshire Vol. 1, p367 Pedigree of Fountayne of Melton

When Elizabeth Bladen died in 1653[1] the Bladen occupation of Bullingshire ended (as per the agreement with Berry) and John Fountain[e] duly took possession. After his demise, son Thomas Fountain continued the occupation.

It was to be 40 years, when the Bladen grandson was a mature lawyer, that the Fountain ownership of the property was challenged in court. In the meantime, however, the Fountains had taken the precaution of drawing up a conveyance on the property. Grandson Nathaniel (writing in 1691 to his friend Robert Wrightson) was filled with remorse over the fact that he never managed to regain title to Bullingshire Hall and said *"As to the possession so long in Dr Berry - I can only say the injury is still the greater"*.[2] In one of three codicils to his Will, Berry mentioned Dr [John] Levett and his wife claiming an injury regarding a land transaction with Berry and how Berry had promised to compensate Mrs Levett. Berry said *"although I do not remember any such promise or engagement yet my mynde and Will is that if she and her husband shall endeavour to advance the sale of Melton lands and that after the said lands sold and the debts and damage to me satisfied there shall not be sufficient left to make good £100 a year to her during her life then I will that my executor shall charge upon my other lands in Hemsworth and Kinsley Park £100 yearly to the said Mrs Levett during her life"*.

The Levetts, mentioned briefly in letters between Berry and Marmaduke Monckton about Elizabeth Bladen, were related to both the Birkheads and Berry families and a brief look at Berry's handling of the Levet(t) family shows remarkable similarities to his dealings with Robert Bladen. Berry had claimed great affection for the Levetts, Thomas in particular who he acknowledged had been instrumental in helping him amass a large part of his fortune. As previously discussed, Richard Berry jointly purchased the estate of Havercroft in 1626 with Thomas Levett, though Catherine Gargrave stated it was to be for Berry's sole use, so it seems Levett was a silent investor. Thomas Levett was married to Margaret Dale (step-mother to Nathaniel Birkhead's wife and Robert's son John had married Nathaniel Birkhead's daughter Margaret). Dr Berry loaned money to Dr John Levett (Thomas's brother) against Levett lands in Bentley, Cadeby and Melton and in a chancery bill of 1653 (Whitaker v Fitzwilliams Levett et al), which took place just after Berry's death, details emerge of what seems like another example of Berry's sharp practice. Berry's estate passed to his executor Fountaine after his death who, in turn, arranged for Fitzwilliams an attorney to collect the estate's rents. Whittaker, a tenant, was given what he would allege was an innocent piece of paper to sign - upon which he made his mark, as he was illiterate. The piece of paper later turned out to have been a bond and the tenant found himself threatened with being sued for recovery of the property. The two Levett brothers Dr John and Thomas, had borrowed heavily from Berry against their estates, and having failed to make a necessary payment ended up losing all their lands at Bentley, Cadeby and Melton to Berry.

Dr John Levett was the individual named in Berry's Will regarding an annuity to his wife - described by The Genealogist, page 87 thus *"it may be that these legacies to the Levets were an attempt on Dr Berry's part to atone for his too shrewd dealings with them.*

---

[1] D36/1 WYAS from the parish register entry
[2] Doncaster Archives DD/BW/F7/2, 26th September 1691

*Levet failed to pay his interest for the Melton estates which were fast in the hands of Dr Berry for he ordered them sold in his Will proved 4 July 1651.*[1] Berry was adept at seizing properties where his borrowers failed to keep their commitments and even more artful in being able to produce legal documents to justify his every transaction. Whether he 'conned' Robert Bladen's family out of their rightful estates cannot be proven, but certainly Robert's grandson Nathaniel would ardently believe Berry took full advantage of the parental vacuum for Bladens in the Civil War years.

*Children*

That concludes the story of Robert's life and now his son John, who predeceased him, will be looked at. Although Robert had a daughter Elizabeth, regrettably very little is known about her except for two mentions in chancery depositions. In Fairfax & Topham v Wrightson & Bladen, which will be discussed fully later, there is a reference to how a Mrs Clarke, 'sister to John Bladen', helped raise Robert's grandchild and then in Bladen v Watson in 1654[2] she is referred to as 'Elizabeth Clarke, Guardian to Nathaniel Bladen who was an infant at the time.' There was also a possible second daughter Sarah (of Haworth), who married John Pickles in 1634 but so far no supporting evidence has turned up to confirm this. Fortunately more is known about Robert's son John.

---

[1] Leavitt - by Emily Florence Leavitt Noyes, 1953 Vol. 4, p17
[2] TNA: C22/768/14 Bladon v Watson, 1654

# John Bladen

After John's baptism on 24th March 1604 in St Anne's Chapel in Southowram, his mother's Lacy family homeland,[1] the family resided possible for a few years at Thornhill and then at Askwith/Denton on land which formed part of the Fairfax Manor. John's formative years then were spent living in the shadow of Denton Hall and he was very well acquainted with his neighbours 1st, 2nd and 3rd Lords Fairfax.

What is known about John Bladen seems to suggest he led a simpler (less litigious) and shorter life than his father, or his son after him.

John attended St John's College at Cambridge University in 1622.[1] At least, there is some evidence to confirm his attendance there but nothing appears in Alumni Cantabrigiensis.

**St John's College, Cambridge, founded in 1511 by Lady Margaret Beaufort, mother of King Henry VII**

Fortunately, John left his mark in a book, as recorded by Arnold Davenport in 1939 in his 'The Elizabethan Period: Poetry and Prose'. Davenport wrote that within a copy of 'Polyolbion' dated 1622 there is an inscription of a poem written by "John Bladen of St John's College, Cambridge". His subsequent career as a lawyer would have necessitated his attendance at university and by 1624-25 John attended Grays Inn.[2]

*Relations with Fairfaxes*
The Bladen family's close proximity to the Fairfaxes brings their relationship to that family into question. Whether the family's reasons for being in Denton related to the Lacy family or Robert Bladen's employment in land stewardship is not known though it does seem likely Robert's activities would have brought him into frequent contact with other large landowners, including the Fairfaxes. Certainly John was closely involved with the family from at least 1621 onwards, just after the 1st Lord Fairfax had the dreadful loss of four sons killed in military action in just one year. Lord Fairfax's life was winding down throughout the 1630s yet he retained a keen interest in current events and political intriguing.

---

[1] WYAS: D53/1/4, Parish Register for Halifax
[2] Register of Gray's Inn 1625: "John Bladen, son and heir of Robert Bladen of Hemsworth, co. York, gent"

John was engaged by Lord Fairfax and, from John's letters to him (which have survived), it seems it was in the capacity of perhaps a personal secretary, conducting private business for him, advising on legal matters, liaising closely with family members and other friends and relations and keeping him up-to-date with current affairs. If Bladen was practising law at the Inns of Court in London at this time, that might have meant he was well placed to meet influential people and observe events and relay them back to Fairfax in Yorkshire who was keen for news.[1] As a 'servant' of 1st Lord Fairfax, John Bladen would have been well known to both his son Ferdinando and, in particular, to grandson Thomas who later became 3rd Lord Fairfax, who was closer to John's age and was living at Denton at the same time as John was there. Later labelled 'Black Tom' for his swarthy appearance, Thomas Fairfax also left Denton to attend St John's College in Cambridge and both men then subsequently attended Grays Inn to become acquainted with the law. Thereafter their paths diverged with Fairfax going straight into the army whilst Bladen remained in legal practice.

From information that emerged in the 1630s, it is evident that after John completed his legal training he divided his time between Yorkshire and London. He entered the service of the 1st Lord Fairfax, as mentioned above, but also fostered his relations with George Radcliffe and Thomas Wentworth (Strafford). Thornhill Hall was the point of contact after Wentworth's sister married Sir George Savile. Bladen was later to visit Radcliffe and Wentworth in Dublin in 1634 and sent a report of their progress back to 1st Lord Fairfax.[2] It is highly likely that the Bladen family's association with the Wentworths dates back to Robert Bladen's time working in South Yorkshire, as the Wortley estate abutted Wentworth Woodhouse and Francis Wortley was known to be an enthusiastic supporter of Strafford.

John Bladen's role allowed him close access to the Fairfaxes, as in 1631, in a letter to be discussed shortly, 'Black Tom' Fairfax was using Bladen's influence with his grandfather to try and get more money for himself. Thomas was in France at the time where he was later to contract smallpox which nearly killed him, and Bladen entreated the grandfather to allow Thomas a more generous allowance. In a letter dated 8th April of that year, John commented to Lord Fairfax that *"I have at this time no other news to commend to your Lordship than the health of your grandson and those letters"* and in a further letter of 28th May 1631 he said *"I have herewith sent your grandson's letters"*.

Fairfax engaged John, on a fee basis, to carry out certain business for him and, in return, Bladen kept him abreast of news and political developments. Parliament had been dismissed by King Charles and did not assemble until 1640 and the governing of the country was in the hands of the King personally, so Fairfax used his friends and servants to glean information and keep him in touch with events. There are six letters surviving of the correspondence between John and 1st Lord Fairfax, though only those written by Bladen have been preserved and their contents range from mundane matters to assessments of the current political situation.

---

[1] The Genealogy of the Existing British Peerage by Edmund Lodge
[2] The Fairfax Correspondence: Memoirs of the Reign of Charles I, edited by George W Johnson, Vol. II, 1848. Last of six letters from John Bladen to Lord Fairfax

*April 8th, 1631*

The earliest of the letters was written on 8th April in 1631 where Bladen was involved in procuring Fairfax a suitable litter and seemed to be having great difficulty in carrying out the task. Bladen also made a passing reference to some sort of *"a controversy betwixt my Uncle Birkhead, yourself and others"*. This seems likely to be a reference to Nathaniel Birkhead, who would actually be his great-uncle. John would later marry Nathaniel Birkhead's daughter, but at the time of the date of this letter, the marriage had not yet happened and so this would be a reference to his maternal relations and, of course, his father Robert had been in business partnership with Nathaniel Birkhead (son of Martin) in 1620 when the pair had purchased jointly the property of Hague Hall in South Kirkby.

Nathaniel Birkhead was considered a royalist sympathiser and in later years, after the Civil War, leased land to a royalist who was subsequently executed for his crimes against Parliament and had his land taken from him. Birkhead responded by immediately seizing the lease back for his land/property and this led to a dispute later when the new Commonwealth demanded he paid the remainder of the rent due from the lease. After his death, Birkhead's children squabbled about title and ownership of his property and, since John Bladen had married one of Nathaniel Birkhead's daughters, Bladens were involved too.

The detail in John's letters of 8th April gives an idea of the kind of business Fairfax had contracted him to do. Carrying of messages, conducting business for Fairfax and delivering money or instructions as directed. Various individuals were referred to in passing, such as Mr Bosvile sending his good wishes and this is likely to be Thomas Bosvile of Conisborough whose daughter Jane married John Waterhouse of Shibden Hall - father-in-law to Helen Lacy - the 'Aunt Waterhouse' referred to by Sir George Radcliffe. The rest of the letter was an update on the state of current affairs and a brief mention of the situation with the plague *"the fear of the sickness is not so great as it was, because the numbers do but continue at the same"*.

Towards the end of the letter the paid nature of Bladen's employment by Fairfax is clarified when he said: *"And now, my lord, I humbly return to my duty; and after the acknowledgement of your lordship's many favours, this last addition of your bounty of 2 l.[1] you sent me purchaseth more from me than I have to bestow; for, be your lordship assured, all I can do is due, and I have no other honour than to be your lordship's humble servant. J. Bladen"*[2]

*13th May, 1631*

Almost one month later, John wrote to confirm having attended the College of Arms, on Fairfax's behalf, to enquire about the addition of arms (supporters) to the Fairfax patent but, after a meeting with the Herald, Sir Richard St George,[3] John reported back that as the Fairfax Arms was granted in Scotland, then St George was not able to assist.

---

[1] The Mark never appeared as a coin in England, but only used as a unit of account, variously priced but perhaps roughly two-thirds the value of the pound

[2] The Fairfax Correspondence: Memoirs of the Reign of Charles I. Edited by George W Johnson, Vol. II, 1848 - all six letters from John Bladen to Lord Fairfax are from this same source

[3] Sir Richard St George 1550-1635, Officer of the College of Arms

An update on the long-awaited litter was included in the letter and an assurance that Fairfax's grandson was in good health. Mr Bellasis, Fairfax's cousin, was mentioned as learning that he had affronted the Lord President, Thomas Wentworth, 1st Earl of Strafford, President of the Council of the North, but had no idea how that happened.

*28th May 1631*
The third letter was dated just two weeks later. Still the saga of the litter was ongoing and John reported on progress. It contained an update on current affairs and reference to a scandalous story surrounding the death of Lord Audley which had taken place two weeks earlier. The story caused a sensation at the time when Castlehaven (Lord Audley) had charged his wife with adultery and, in return, she had accused him of ordering one of their servants to rape her and that he had committed sodomy with a servant. The trial concluded and Lord Audley was executed.

*9th June 1631*
A fortnight later and another letter demonstrated how close John's employment brought him to all those in the Fairfax family when John made an appeal for a greater allowance, on behalf of Fairfax's own grandson 'Black Tom' who was in France at the time. He forwarded the grandson's letters and added *"His present means only keeps him in meat and lodging with (scarce) an addition of clothes, much more of the chargeable exercise of parts, which is the end of his travel and your lordship's expectation. My humble suit, therefore, is that your lordship will be pleased to add a little more to this quarter, which may be abated at a more plentiful time. If not, at the best he can but be a wandering prisoner, debarred the enjoyment of the best of manners. This to your honourable consideration."*[1]

*6th July 1631*
The following month and in his fifth letter Bladen gave Lord Fairfax information of difficulties raising regiments for the 30-year-war: *"Likewise yesterday the Lord Marquis Hamilton commenced a press for the completing of his company, after three weeks' summons by the drum, which denotes a great deal of unwillingness of the common people to the Danish service"*.[2]

*2nd July 1634*
The sixth and final letter was written some three years later. He had last corresponded with Lord Fairfax in early June of 1634 and then, from mid-June Bladen was in Dublin where he stayed about one month. He was visiting his cousin Sir George Radcliffe who had travelled to Dublin with Thomas Wentworth.

---

[1] The Fairfax Correspondence: Memoirs of the Reign of Charles I. Edited by George W Johnson, Vol. II, 1848 - all six letters from John Bladen to Lord Fairfax are from this same source

[2] General Sir James Hamilton 1606-49 was attempting to raise an army of 6,000 to engage in the 30 year war, but his endeavours failed and his army returned home the following year. Hamilton, as a 15 year old, married Mary Fielding who was 9 years old at the time. The Fairfax Correspondence: Memoirs of the Reign of Charles I. Edited by George W Johnson, Vol. II. 1848

Before leaving Yorkshire, where he had been Lord President of the Council of the North and Privy Councillor, Wentworth had appointed Radcliffe to be the King's Attorney for the Council. Wentworth considered Radcliffe one of his closest confidents and took him to Dublin when Wentworth was appointed Lord Deputy of Ireland. In fact he sent Radcliffe ahead to prepare the way and made him a member of the Irish Privy Council. Wentworth arrived in Dublin by July 1633 and in a letter said, *"the Master of the Rolls (Sir Christopher Wandesford) and Mr (Sir George) Ratcliffe are those whom I only trust on this side [Ireland] and do humbly thank His Majesty that I have them here"*.[1]

Bladen's first opportunity to write to Fairfax was on 2nd July after he had been in Dublin for about three weeks and the topic of his letter concerned Wentworth's performance in post. The elderly Lord Fairfax had a particular interest in the family as his daughter Anne had married Sir George Wentworth of Woolley - cousin to the Earl of Strafford. John advised Fairfax of Wentworth's impact on the people and events in Dublin. The general consensus Bladen told him was that, though efficient as an organiser and administrator, Wentworth's high handed manner, as well as being ruthless and vindictive, was making him many enemies.

Bladen said there was, *"great expectation of this Parliament, which invites me to see a week's progress before I return for Yorkshire"* and which shows he took a keen interest in how the country was being run and, in contrast to Wentworth, he referred to Radcliffe as *"a man exceedingly improved in the state and the affection of officers"*.[2] The parliamentary session began on 14th July and, if Bladen remained the full week, that would take the duration of his visit to be about one full month.[3]

*"No Better Knowledge Than History"*
Not long after his final letter to Fairfax and still engaged in his service, Bladen wrote a long treatise which seemed to emanate from a consideration of the political difficulties that were manifesting themselves in the mid 1630s when King Charles I had dismissed Parliament and was governing the country himself. Although the country was some years away from the outbreak of Civil War, tensions between the King and Parliament had been rising for many years. Charles had entered into a secret pact with Philip IV of Spain to assist him against the Dutch and the massive ship-building project that ensued was costly. Charles enforced taxation by extracting Ship Money in 1634 from coastal residents, then extended it the following year to apply to all citizens, a move which was extremely unpopular. Written in August 1636, John Bladen's treatise came just weeks before the King's third levy of ship money in October of that year.

---

[1] Strafford's Letters, I, 99 and Fairfax Correspondence: Memoirs of the Reign of Charles I. Edited by George W Johnson, Vol II. 1848, p249

[2] The Fairfax Correspondence: Memoirs of the Reign of Charles I. Edited by George W Johnson, Vol. II. 1848

[3] The printer Strafford used during his time in Ireland was Alderman William Bladen (1585-1663). History of the King's Inns, or an account of the legal body in Ireland by Bartholomew T Duhigg, 1806

The treatise John wrote was called 'Miscellaneous Observations of the Principal Matters in this Court and State, as they consist at this present. August 1636. Abstracted and digested [by] John Bladen. Giving an Account of the Descent and Alliances of the King; a Catalogue of the Officers of State, Ambassadors etc and View of the Military and Naval Strength of the Kingdom.'[1]

It is hardly surprising that John should take such a sharp interest in the political situation at the time, since the Bladens were so well connected with many of those who would come to influence events or take command in the Civil War. For Bladen, who had a great interest in the workings of Parliament, the increasingly dictatorial activities of Charles I must have given him much room for thought and concern. Since John's visit to Dublin two years earlier, Strafford had made himself many powerful enemies in Ireland with his high-handed administration to the point where in July he was forced to return to London and justify himself to the King. Their presence in Ireland, however, did not prevent Strafford and John's cousin Radcliffe from retaining a firm grip on Yorkshire politics. Strafford appointed his brother-in-law Sir William Savile of Thornhill to the Council of the North and also made him Deputy Lieutenant of the West Riding and even the Fairfax's were still supporting the King at this time.

The widespread unease and anger caused by the King's unpopular imposition of Ship Money[2] taxation was probably the catalyst for Bladen's treatise. Those in the legal profession, like John, though faced with claims that the king's actions were illegal, had nonetheless supported the Crown not least because their own patronage depended on the Crown. Nonetheless, the increasingly dictatorial behaviour of the King and consequent growing discontent led Bladen to attempt a logical analysis of the balance of real power and, perhaps, to calculate a likely prognosis. The very fact that he wrote the treatise demonstrates Bladen was aware that the Monarchy was in some danger and its 'divine right' to govern might be challenged. It was an honest appraisal so *"that we may know our wealth and strength"* and, since Bladen later became a Captain in the Parliamentary army, then it is presumed that he was particularly interested in weighing up Parliament's prospects, its wealth and strengths against those of the King.

Part one of the manuscript was a royal genealogy of both King Charles and his Catholic wife. Bladen was, it seems, attempting to calculate where the King may look for support and listed those 'Allies of the Crown', both countries and noble individuals. *"Reasons why certain of the Nobility bear any part of ye Arms of the Crown in their Hatchments"*: families discussed were the Dukes of Norfolk, St Leger, Charles Somerset base son of Henry Beaufort (son of John of Gaunt, Duke of Lancaster), Henry Courtney - Earl of Devon, Edward Stafford, John Beaufort descended of Blanche of Artois, wife of John of Gaunt's son Edmund, Frances Stewart amongst many, many more.

---

[1] Add MS 18984 © The British Library Board, Manuscripts Department
[2] The King, in ruling without Parliament, was in constant need of finding new ways to raise money. His justification for the imposition of this direct taxation from the Crown was that the fleet needed to be increased to protect the seas around Britain against interference from the Dutch, French and Spanish was not readily accepted as being true

Part two of the manuscript was an extensive catalogue of the *'Principles: Officers, Vice-Governors and Ambassadors of State'* including those from whom the King selected his Privy Council. He compiled lists of *'Certain Officers and Ministers of State'*: Judges of the Admiralty, Officers of Trade, Kings at Arms etc and the *'Officers of ye King's household'* along with a host of nobles, spiritual and temporal. The purpose of this seems to have been to assess those people who had a dependence on the King and would be rigidly loyal to Charles. As an add-on to this list, Bladen highlighted three people he was particularly interested in. There was *Charles Neville* - who was living in Flanders after having been declared a Traitor by Parliament, had his estate seized and had been condemned to death. He was living there claiming the title Earl of Westmorland. The other two were *Robert Dudley* and *Sir Robert Shirley*.

Having concluded an assessment of where Charles I might look for support, part three of the manuscript looked at the other side of the equation and was an attempt to assess the country's strengths and assets: *"A View of the Strength of this Kingdom: both defensive and offensive (money, shipping and armour)"*. Against the King's 31 castles and forts along the coast that he funded from his exchequer, Bladen drew up a county by county breakdown showing the number of able men who were available, number of armaments and horses. Total figures he produced were: 296,131 able men, 1,413,105 armaments, and 6,777 horses. He stated the armour for both horse and foot was located in the Tower of London and described the country as having *"the best ..... facilities of any Army in Christendom"*.

The next issue Bladen examined was the level of ship building as of March 1636. He noted the name of each ship, number of men, ordinance and Captains but, as he was compiling his manuscript more ships were being built at a fast and furious pace and he said *"to this list there is yearly built new ships at whose calculation I dare not adventure upon more information of measuring"*. He later claimed that to his knowledge, upto August 1636, some 25 new ships had been built that year alone.

Lastly, Bladen ended his manuscript with a critical character outline of the two principal men of State:

*William Laud 1573-1645 - Abp of Canterbury*
Bladen's observations on both men suggests he knew them well - or knew 'of them' very well. Mention was made favourably of Laud's attempts to repair St Paul's Cathedral which had been partially restored only three years before the manuscript was written. Bladen praised Laud's wit and spirit but criticised: *"to ye King most faithful, studious of his profit and too resolute In the same"*.

*Lord Cottington* - Roman Catholic opposed completely to Laud but just as powerful. Of Cottington Bladen said *"Towards ye King as equally studious .... his garb habit and elegance denounces him dressed by ye Spanish"*.

Bladen concluded *"so are they* [Laud and Cottington] *ye instruments of ye King's indignation and revenge upon his subjects for their infractious behaviour in ye late Parliament"*.[1]

---
[1] Add MS 18984 - ©The British Library Board, Manuscripts Department

Although it is clear from these comments that Bladen's tolerance of King Charles had diminished he also seemed, like many others, to rather blame those advisors around the monarch, rather than Charles himself. John's part in the Civil War will be discussed further shortly.

*1637: Donation*
In 1637 John was called to the Bar and, still indulging in literary activity, his name cropped up in relation to a donation of books he made to the library of Gray's Inn:[1] *"1636: A further five benefactors were barristers including three future readers and the brothers Francis and Nathaniel Bacon, the veteran Oxfordshire JP Francis Gregory and young John Bladen, whose call to the bar in 1637 may have occasioned his gift of two books of that same year."* It is suspected that the above donation of books is a reference to the very earliest example that would, eventually, evolve to the principle of public lending libraries. Francis and Nathaniel Bacon, also mentioned, were nephews of the famous Sir Francis Bacon,[2] the philosopher statesman and scientist and in 1635 they presented the works of their famous uncle to the Library of Grays Inn.

*Birkheads*
Three years later 1st Lord Fairfax died and it is thought John Bladen must have spent some time in Yorkshire because by 1641 he married a local girl. He married at the age of 37 years to his 19-year-old cousin Margaret Birkhead on 2nd October 1641 at All Saints Church in South Kirkby. The marriage entry stated: *"Marriage of John Blayden Gen. to Mrs Margar. Birkhead".*[3] John and Margaret married without the consent, and against the wishes, of her father. A deponent in a chancery case was later to state *"that Margaret his daughter did marry Mr Bladen without consent of the said Mr Birkhead her father and that ... because the said daughter Margaret had married without the consent he would not look upon her. And saith he doth not know what debts the said Mr Birkhead pay or seemed to pay for the father or grandfather of the complainant but saith he hath heard the said Mr Birkhead say he hath paid much money for them the said father and grandfather of the complainant".*[4] Note: the above referred to chancery case, which will be discussed later, was brought on behalf of Nathaniel Bladen, so references to Mr Birkhead giving money to the father [meant John] and the grandfather [Robert Bladen].

Although Robert Bladen and Nathaniel Birkhead had combined to purchase property together, it may have been that Birkhead's objection to his daughter Margaret marrying John Bladen was based on the fact that the Bladens were Protestants. Unlike his father, Nathaniel may have had leanings to Catholicism. He was certainly considered a Royalist at the time of the Civil War when his estate faced Royalist Composition fines. In 1599 Birkhead was involved with the noted French recusant Ambrose Vaux where they co-signed a lease on Kirby Hall.

---

[1] Parergon, Vol. 14
[2] Sir Francis Bacon 1561-1626
[3] WYAS: D168/1/1/1, parish register of South Kirkby
[4] TNA: C22/768/14 Bladen v Watson, 1654

Described as *"a princely mansion in Northamptonshire which Eliza Vaux hoped to set up as a Jesuit stronghold"*.[1] Birkhead was also involved in the moated 13th Century Baddesley Clinton Manor House in Warwick, famed for its association with Roman Catholic recusants (Ferrers family) and which had an abundance of secret priest holes. It had so many of these hides that, during a 1591 conference of Jesuits, all were safely secreted away when the property was raided by the authorities. Also, on 13th July 1601 Birkhead, together with Thomas Tomlinson, co-signed documents on a moiety of the Manor of Isham, which had also been part of the Vaux family's possessions.[2]

**Hague Hall, South Kirkby, near Hemsworth[3]
purchased jointly by Robert Bladen and Nathaniel Birkhead**

Hague Hall was demolished in 1910[4] after suffering subsidence caused by local coal mining, indeed the above picture was taken as the building had started to buckle and fall apart.[5]

---

[1] NRO FH 3013; Gerard, Autobiography p149, cited in God's Traitors; Terror and Faith in Elizabethan England by Jessie Childs
[2] Shakespeare Centre, DR 3/349
[3] Reproduced with permission of Matthew of www.lostheritage.co.uk
[4] Hague Hall later passed into Watson descendants Green/Allot. Rev Henry Green d1738 who acquired ownership is not the same Rev Henry Green d1749 who was prebend of Ketton in Rutland who Martin Bladen held a lease from. It is not known if there was a family connection between the two Greens
[5] According to Hunter's South Yorkshire there used to be a monument to Nathaniel Birkhead 1579-1649 in South Kirkby Church, also daughter Alice d.1655

Birkhead's name was also closely associated with the Vaux's[1] when, following the failed Gunpowder Plot of 1605, a new 1609 Oath of Allegiance had to be sworn by Catholics; some members of the Vaux family were imprisoned for their refusal to take the oath.[2] As a lawyer, Birkhead may have felt the effect of the related Popish Recusants Act in 1605 which prevented Catholics from practising law.

Like the Lacys, the Birkheads feature large in the Bladen story, not just because of John's marriage to Margaret but because his mother, Elizabeth Lacy, was herself the daughter of Alice Birkhead (daughter of Martin Birkhead) and so there was already a cousin relationship. Margaret Birkhead was living at Hague Hall in South Kirkby close to Bullingshire Hall and Hemsworth, in an area where Robert Bladen had tenure or occupancy of several properties, at least until he mortgaged many to Dr Berry. Indeed, Robert had been joint purchaser of Hague Hall with Nathaniel Birkhead around 1620 when the property was conveyed to the two men from the previous owner Thomas Tempest[3] of the same Tempest family already mentioned in regard to John Lacy. At some point Bladen sold Birkhead his half of the property because later, when it came to Birkhead writing his Will, he was sole owner.

Although John's wife's name was recorded in the West Yorkshire Records[4] as 'Mrs Margar.' Birkhead, she was not already married. Margaret's baptism record in South Kirkby of 1622 was recorded as Mary. Fortunately, however, we can be certain of her credentials as a Birkhead, and called Margaret, because Nathaniel Birkhead's Will of 1650 referred to Nathaniel Bladen as being his grandson and the numerous depositions in chancery cases already mentioned from contemporaries who knew her as Margaret Birkhead, wife of John Bladen. Nathaniel Birkhead had received a large inheritance from his father Martin. When it came to writing his own Will, both his son-in-law and daughter Margaret Bladen had already died and, although he left grandson Nathaniel Bladen a generous portion, it was said that because Margaret had married against his wishes that it was a lesser portion than otherwise might have been due.

John and Margaret Bladen, however, were not left in peace for long to enjoy married life. In the year before their marriage, King Charles had taken 20,000 men up to Berwick-upon-Tweed to try to get the Presbyterian Church of Scotland under his control, only to fail and suffer a humiliating setback, this was also the escapade which was the catalyst for the Fairfax family's disillusionment with the King. Within months of the wedding, John would join the Parliamentary Army and wife Margaret would die in childbirth, or shortly after. They had one son, Nathaniel born in 1642 who became orphaned as an infant. John and Margaret were both descendants of Martin Birkhead and also John Lacy, see chart below.

---

[1] A cautionary note should be inserted here that George Salvin Birkhead 1533-1614 Arch Priest of England was a Roman Catholic who was also closely associated with the Vaux family at this time too
[2] McClure, 399 cited in Newsletters from the Archprebyterate of George Birkhead by Michael C. Questier
[3] Thomas Tempest 1530-78
[4] D 168/1/1/1

The reason for including the Paslew family in the following chart is to explain an inheritance that came to John's son:-

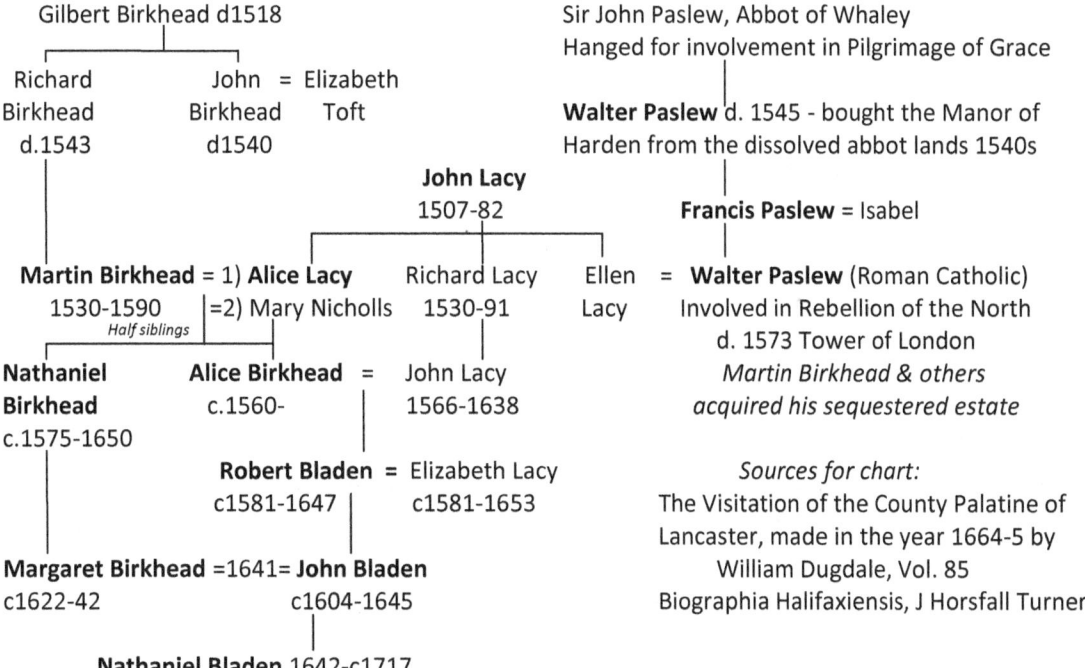

The Paslew family were Roman Catholics and when Walter Paslew (husband of Ellen Lacy) became involved in the Rebellion of the North in 1569, he was committed to the Tower of London and his lands were confiscated. He was incarcerated in the Lower Chamber of Beauchamp Tower, the same place that Robert Dudley, Earl of Leicester and favourite of Queen Elizabeth had languished; both Paslew and Dudley etched their names into the wall for the benefit of posterity. His grandfather, also called Walter Paslew of Riddlesden, had bought the Manor of Harden from the Rievaulx Abbey when Henry VIII's dissolution of the monasteries freed up large areas of monastic lands.

When the grandson who had inherited Paslew's lands found his lands sequestered, Martin Birkhead and a couple of others (including Rishworths who were Lacy relations) divided Paslew's land up between them and bought a section each. This is how Martin Birkhead[1] came to be in possession of the Manor of Harden which on his death[2] passed to his son Nathaniel Birkhead.

---

[1] *"Martin Birkhead became Lord of the Manor and bought 'The Grange' (now known as St. Ives) and Crossgate (pulled down in the twentieth century)."* The Bradford Antiquary, part XXIX, January 1938. By 1636 the Grange and Crossgate properties had been sold by Nathaniel Birkhead - the Grange being sold to Robert Ferrand, cloth merchant and Crossgate was sold to John Milner, clothier

[2] Martin Birkhead's Will bequeathed his lands at Southowram nr Halifax to Mary his wife for life. Harden Grange to Daniel his son, to Nathaniel Birkhead his eldest son he bequeathed armour, weapons, gold rings with seals of arms and the great book of Fitzherbert abridgements of the law. This Nathaniel Birkhead was Lord of the Manor of Haworth....Mr Bladen, in 1671, sold the manors of Haworth and Harden to Mr William Midgley, gent of Haworth and Joseph his son. Joseph Midgley, gent, the son, settled the manor in 1690 on himself for life, with remainder to his brothers Thomas and William and to the survivor of them. William

Nathaniel Birkhead, in turn, bequeathed[1] the manor to his grandson Nathaniel Bladen, along with Haworth.[2] The income from these manors supported Bladen for some time until he eventually sold the manors of Haworth and Harden in 1671 to William Midgley of Haworth and his son Joseph for £80.[3] Common ancestor to both John Bladen and Margaret Birkhead was Martin Birkhead,[4] who was an important figure in Yorkshire having been Steward of the Manor Court of Wakefield in the 1560s and Queen's Attorney in the North in 1574[5] and was a Justice of the Peace and Quorum by 1584. He was a Yorkshire lawyer (Gray's Inn) and a Parliamentarian, sitting on several Committees.

Martin owed his position of strength and success in part to the Lord President of the North being 3rd Earl of Sussex, also known as Thomas Radcliffe (related to the previously mentioned Sir George - cousin to Elizabeth Bladen). When Martin died on 6th July 1590[6] he had large land holdings in: Bingley, Bolton, Calverley, Fansley, Harden, Haworth, Keighley, Lofthouse, Marley and Wakefield. One of the supervisors named in his Will was William Savile, probably an uncle or great-uncle of the Sir William Savile who left Robert Bladen an annuity. Martin Birkhead's first wife was Alice Lacy, so he had himself married into the same Lacy family of Cromwellbothom that Robert Bladen would marry into, and had six sons and seven daughters. It seems likely that the use of the Christian names 'Martin' and 'Nathaniel' in the Bladen family stemmed from these Birkhead relations. Martin Birkhead's son Nathaniel, and his siblings, inherited great wealth from their father.[7]

---

Midgley died in September 1723 and is noticed in the Register of Burials as Lord of the Manor of Haworth. (A History of Haworth, Stanbury and Orenhope by J Horsfall Turner, 1879

[1] Ancient Bingley by Joseph Horsfall Turner
[2] Haworth Past and Present, A History of Haworth, Stanbury and Oxenhope by J Horsfall Turner. 1879
[3] Ibid
[4] Martin Birkhead lived in the *"Top house but one western side of Southgate where there is an excellent ceiling bearing the initials and arms of Martin Birkhead"* ceiling date 1584. Arms: 3 garbs. Crest, a goat's head erased and a garb. In Burke's General Armory: Sable three garbs or within a bordure argent (another the bordure or); Crest - a goat salient argent attired or, resting a dexter paw on a garb of the last. Source: Walks in Yorkshire: Wakefield and its Neighbourhood by William Stott Banks of Wakefield 1841. At the death in 1582 of John Lacy (Martin Birkhead's father-in-law), Lacy gave a chest with three locks with all his most valued documents contained in it and gave out three keys: one to Martin Birkhead, one to John Lacy and the last one to Richard Lacy with instructions that all three were to be present when it was opened
[5] Foster's Visitations of Yorkshire, p330
[6] Buried at Wakefield Church
[7] Martin Birkhead's father Richard: Wakefield Court Rolls of 9 August 1538, p56 state *"Richard Birkhede came into this court before the steward of the court and took from the Lord one parcel of land from the Lord's soil and waste containing 2 acres land called Smallclogh in Northourome just as they lay between peat pytts on the north, Sweremore on the south, Shepdenbroke on the east and Ovendenbroke on the west. Agreed. Entry fine 40s, new rent 8d."* Richard Birkhead's Will named Robert Waterhouse of Halifax as an overseer. Their grandchildren would marry through their Lacy relations. Martin's Uncle John Birkhead (brother of above Richard): Wakefield Court Rolls of 9 August 1538, p169 state *"John Birkehed by Brian Bradford, gen, tenant and sworn, surrendered into the Lord's hands one close called Syddalle with appurtenances: to the use of the same John Byrkehed and Elizabeth his wife and their assigns for a term of their lives and then longer liver of them. And after the death of the said John and Elizabeth that then the said close would remain to Gilbert Birkehed and his heirs forever, saving the right of any. Agreed. John and Elizabeth gave the Lord 12d as fine for entry and Gilbert gave the Lord 2s as fine for the remainder when it happened."* Martin Birkhead's son Richard: on 22 November 1583 - Court Rolls - he owned land abutting Wilcock on headland leading from Woodthorpe as far as the high road between Wakefield and Cheete

Nathaniel also received a generous marriage settlement from his father-in-law Roger Dale[1] which allowed him to purchase various manors and estates. On one such estate he had a tenant called Colonel Morrice of Pomfret Castle [Pontefract] a Royalist who was executed in 1645 for his part in the Civil War. When Morrice's assets were sequestered, including the land he leased, Birkhead must have felt in danger of losing his property and income and took steps to retrieve the man's lease after his death. However, a petition was brought by Thomas Brewster (for the State) that Birkhead owed rent for the remainder of the lease which he was required to pay. Birkhead also faced fines from the Commonwealth as he was suspected of having had Royalist sympathies during the war.[2]

*Civil War*

Despite his own, and his father's life-time of association with leading figures determined to support the King, the widowed John Bladen, with his many years close association with the Fairfax family, joined the Parliamentary Army. How difficult a decision that was can only be guessed at as when Civil War came, it must have become a tortuous process for those with Royalist sympathies but connected to the Fairfax family, who led the Parliamentarian cause. This may have been the situation that John found himself in.

Although it is known that John Bladen was a Captain in the Parliamentary Army, his name does not appear in the 1642 Army Lists of Roundheads and Cavaliers[3] - at least, not spelt as 'Bladen'. The Senior Archivist and Curator of Early Modern MSS at the Bodleian Libraries was able to locate some sources of Edward Peacock's papers at the University of Manchester Library and Lincolnshire Archives but was not confident that a further search of those papers would reveal anything further. He checked two different versions of the above work and all showed no Bladen entry, but all contained an entry for a 'Lt. John Bla**n**den' on page 39.[4] This John Bla(n)don was a Lieutenant in Colonel Thomas Grantham's Regiment which had been formed in the spring of 1642.

---

Sources: TNA Y034 Toft/Chibnall and Y0561 dated 1600; Memorials of the Order of the Garters: From its foundation to the present by George Frederick Beltz; The Visitation of the County Palatine of Lancaster 1664-5 William Dugdale, Vol. 85; The Pedigree Register, Vol.1, p322 Pedigree of Dale (Toft, Levett); Historical Sketches of the Parish Church, Wakefield by Joseph Lawson Sisson; Yorkshire Royalist Composition Papers by John William Clay 2013 (Birkhead); Hunter's South Yorkshire p451, also p365 Levett, Thomas and John (Hunter said Nathaniel Birkhead died aged 70 in 1640 which is incorrect as his Will TNA: PROB11/211 was written 12th February 1649 and probate was in 1650. Hunter p451 footnotes); E. Herts Arch. Soc., vii, p402 Brockett. Also Chancy's Herts, i, p32

[1] Nathaniel Birkhead witnessed the Will of his father-in-law, Roger Dale, of 1622-3 who left his estate to his third wife Margaret (Brocket) in which he was left £1,000 bond to provide a jointure for his wife Elizabeth Dale, this bond concerned the Manor of Ackworth and was the subject of chancery proceedings after his death

[2] Royalist Composition Papers No. 524 G141, p568, 17th October 1650

[3] The Army Lists of the Roundheads and Cavaliers: containing the names of the offices in the Royal and Parliamentary Armies of 1642, edited by Edward Peacock in 1863

[4] The National Archives catalogue has details of the records in Lincolnshire Archives, reference HILL 46 and for North Lincolnshire Museum 'Peacock Family Archive/Boxes 11-14' and Manchester University Library has 1860-82 Diaries, Antiquarian Collections Notes and Papers, references Eng MSS 125, 127-36, 216-86, 426 which may yield more information

In October of that year the Regiment was at Edgehill but arrived late, on 24th October, when the fighting had ended on the 23rd. It had been delayed arriving due to escorting heavy cannons. It was, in November of that year, also at the Battle of Aylesbury.

1643 was the year when Civil War raged around the Bladens in Yorkshire and John, if not before then most certainly by January 1643, was a Captain in Sir Thomas Fairfax's Parliamentary Army.[1] In 'The Fairfax Correspondence: Memorials of the Civil War', it was said: *"The Bladens had been servants of the first baron Fairfax, and Ferdinando had sent Captain Bladen to aid Sir Thomas in January 1643"*[2] The above quotation made reference to "the Bladens" being servants of the first baron Fairfax. Certainly John had been though, as previously mentioned, Robert's exact relationship to them is less clear. Ferdinando, the 2nd Lord Fairfax, sent Captain Bladen [John] to aid Sir Thomas [future 3rd Lord Fairfax]. The date mentioned is highly significant, so too is the context from which the above extract is taken. The Battle of Leeds took place on 23rd January 1643 and the reason that Captain John Bladen was sent to Sir Thomas 'Black Tom' was that Fairfax was amassing a force to attack Sir William Savile at Leeds. With over 3,000 men, Fairfax marched his men from Bradford to Leeds to engage the enemy in a battle that lasted three hours, the outcome of which was a decisive victory for Fairfax and Sir William Savile was forced to flee. Or, to view events entirely from a Bladen perspective, Robert Bladen's Royalist patron Savile of Thornhill was fighting at the head of the King's forces against his son John's Parliamentary patron Fairfax who quite likely had John Bladen amongst his officers on the opposing side. It is supposed that Robert Bladen himself was not involved in any actual combat, as he was aged mid-sixties and probably not in good health. There is no record of him having property sequestered after the war or facing delinquency charges, so he probably managed to avoid direct involvement. A short time later Thomas Fairfax responded to John Bladen's arrival. Writing from Wakefield on 27th January 1642 (n.s. 1643) to his father Ferdinando he said:- *"I thank your Lordship for thinking of sending Capt. Bladen to me. I have great need of one to assist me, having many things heavy upon me and being grown within these few days more unhealthful than I was".*[3]

Elsewhere, in Hull, a siege of that town in 1642 had been the first act of defiance against the King but had been marred when the Governor, Sir John Hotham, after his initial refusal to allow King Charles to enter the town, months later invited the Queen to take Hull when she arrived along the coast with troops from the Continent. Hotham was branded a traitor and a turncoat when news got out. As if to demonstrate the complexity of allegiances during the Civil War, Sir John Hotham's son[4] of the same name had initially joined Fairfax's Parliamentary Army, indeed, young Hotham had married Margaret Fairfax, daughter of Thomas Fairfax, 1st Viscount of the Gilling/Walton Fairfax line, cousin to Lord Fairfax. His brother-in-law was Matthew Boynton who had married Katherine, another daughter of Thomas 1st Viscount Fairfax and Matthew would, in time, be responsible for capturing the Hothams when they shifted allegiance towards the King.

---

[1] Black Tom: Sir Thomas Fairfax and the English Revolution. Andrew Hopper 2007
[2] Hull History Centre. BRS/7/53; Bod. MS Fairfax 30. Fol. 129: R. Bell (ed.)
[3] Memorials of the Civil War: Comprising the Correspondence of the Fairfax Family with the most distinguished personages engaged in that memorable contest. Vol. 1, edited by Robert Bell. 1849
[4] John Hotham (Jnr) 1610-45 son of John Hotham (Snr) 1589-1645 - both beheaded

Young Hotham did change sides and had begun negotiations with the Queen. For their actions both father and son were beheaded in 1645. Hull graphically demonstrated to the Fairfaxes just how dangerous it was to have the fate of a town in one man's hands and turncoats in their midst.

*Defence Committee for Hull*

By 1643, when Fairfax had based himself in Hull, it was felt safer to appoint a Committee of Defence to protect the town - so no one individual had the power to dictate a town's allegiance. The Committee comprised of the Mayor, Aldermen and other dignitaries and militia (including Captain John Bladen), four members of this committee had succeeded in seizing Hull for Parliament at the commencement of Civil War: i.e. Henry Darley (son of Richard), Sir William St Quintin, Matthew Boynton[1] and Mayor Thomas Raikes. Sir William St Quintin (Fairfax relation) is featured in the companion book to this one, 'Martin Bladen: A Biography'.

Writing on 27th August 1643[2] on the composition of the Committee to oversee the running of Hull, Lord Ferdinando (2nd Ld) Fairfax listed the names of those individuals he wanted to form the Commission to discover malignants:

| | |
|---|---|
| Ferdinand (2nd Lord Fairfax) | Commander in the North, Military Governor of Hull |
| Thomas (3rd Lord Fairfax) | Son of above |
| Sir Matthew Boynton | 1591-1647. Knighted 1618. MP, Sheriff of Yorkshire, Governor of Scarborough Castle. Seized the arsenal at Hull and arrested Hotham |
| Sir William Fairfax | Knighted 1630 but sided with Parliament in 1642. Served under Ferdinando Fairfax in 1643 at Leeds and Wakefield. Later at Hull and Marston Moor. Died 1644 at the Relief of Montgomery Castle |
| Colonel John Lambert | 1619-84 - Joined the Civil War in 1643 as Captain to Ferdinando Fairfax. Later, to become General John Lambert, Commander of the North. Lambert accompanied the Fairfaxes when they left Leeds to go to Hull - the sole parliamentary city in the north in 1643. 2nd in command to Cromwell in 1650. Sent to Scotland to negotiate with George Monck but his army disbanded and Lambert was Imprisoned and exiled |
| Sir Henry Fowlis | Sir Henry's father had been a courtier/agent to King James VI of Scotland, Elizabeth I, Prince Henry, Prince Charles - later King Charles I and served on the Council of the North. In 1632 King Charles made use of archaic legislation to compel gentlemen to pay a fine for not accepting the 'honour' of a knighthood. Sir Henry and his father Sir David Foulis (who had refused to attend Charles' Coronation) spoke out against that and against Wentworth for which they were censured and sentenced by the Star Chamber to imprisonment in the Fleet and such hefty fines that they were forced to sell off part of their estate to raise the money |
| Sir Thomas Mauleverer | 1599-1655 Knighted by King Charles in 1630, then declared a traitor in 1642, raised 2 regiments of foot and 1 regiment of horse for Parliament, Governor of Hull Castle, Regicide, Colonel in the Army |
| Sir Richard Darley | Appointed in 1627 by King Charles to the Council of the North, Justice of the Peace; his son Henry was one of four attributed with seizing Hull for Parliament |
| Sir William St Quintin | Knighted 1642, Sheriff 1648. Irish Privy Councillor, friend of Thomas Fairfax (Fairfax relations) |
| Sir John Bouchier | 1595-1660. Knighted in 1609 and was a Justice of the Peace in Yorkshire. He rebelled against the King in 1627 when Charles was trying to raise money by forced loans rather than recall parliament. Regicide. His great-grandmother (Countess of Salisbury) had been beheaded by order of Henry VIII |
| Sir William Allanson | Knighted 1633; on his way to Scotland to be Crowned Charles stayed with him and Allanson's first-born son was named Charles in the King's honour. 1622 Sheriff, Alderman, Lord Mayor in 1633, Clerk of the Hanaper and one of the Puritan Leaders. Merchant draper |
| Col. Francis Lascelles | Commissioner, High Court of Justice at King Charles I's trial - but not a regicide. Married Frances (dau of Sir William St Quintin above) |

---

[1] Sir Matthew Boynton c.1591-1647 married Catherine Fairfax, daughter of Thomas 1st Viscount Fairfax of Emmerley (Fairfax Gilton and Walton line) who had married firstly Robert Stapleton of Wighill

[2] C BRS/7/19 Hull History Centre 'A Commission of Ferdinando, Lord Fairfax, for the Discovering of Malignants in Hull and to seize their estates and also to compound with persons able to lend or contribute money or goods for the Parliamentary service'

| | |
|---|---|
| Alderman William Style | Puritan minister ordained 1620. Later spoke out against the King's murder |
| Alderman Henry Barnard | Mayor of Hull in 1642 |
| Alderman John Barnard | Mayor of Hull in 1640 |
| Alderman William Popple | Mayor of Hull in 1639 when King Charles I visited |
| Alderman Nicholas Denman | Mayor of Hull in 1644 |
| Richard Wood | Sheriff |

Sir John Lowther, Mayor Raikes, Capt Copley,[1] Capt Bright, Capt Waters, Capt Bladon, Mr Johnson and Mr Penrose.

*1643: Captain John Bladen*

His appointment to this Committee put Bladen right at the heart of the gathered Parliamentary forces of Yorkshire at that time. Hull was especially important to both sides in the Civil War as King Charles had deposited a large armoury there just outside the city and the location was chosen in case the King needed to get men and arms quickly to Scotland. At a major port it could be accessed via land or sea for rapid deployment. In setting up the Committee on 27th August 1643, Ferdinando had issued a Commission and Instructions to the Committee *"for the discovering of malignants in Hull and to seize their estates and also to compound any persons able to lend or contribute money or goods for the parliamentary service"*.[2] The committee was charged with examining any individuals within their town to ascertain their loyalties. Within a few months of being appointed to this Committee, however, Bladen himself faced charges of aiding the enemy. It is impossible to know if Bladen suffered from divided loyalties in the conflict, but others may have thought he did.

*1643: Turncoat*

The following is a summary of a document held by Hull History Centre which lists those charges brought against Bladen. Although it has an estimated date of 1645, the Duke of Newcastle was in self-imposed exile on the Continent after the Battle of Marston Moor in July of 1644, so it is more likely to date from late 1643 or early 1644.

The Delinquency Charges brought against Captain John Bladen were fourfold:[3]

### "Chardges Against Captain Bladen"

1) That he hath spoken dangerous words, that the Lord Fairfax had never a fairer time and, or reason, to make his peace with my Lord of Newcastle.
2) He being in hopes to be made Capt. of the Blockhouses, promised as soon as he got possession of them to delyver them upp to the enemy, or to that purpose.
3) He is a continuall retarder of all good means and endeavours that are made for safety and yoos of the Towne and Kingdome.
4) He is vehemently suspected to hold secret intelligence with the enemy."

---

[1] This is Christopher Copley d.1664 whose nephew Lionel travelled to Maryland with William Bladen (John's grandson) in 1691/2
[2] Hull History Centre C BRS 7/19
[3] Hull History Centre C BRS/7/53

What exactly happened to John after these charges were brought is not known but another who was charged with being a turncoat at the same time was Major John Gifford and the following comments were made by Andrew Hopper, author of 'Black Tom: Sir Thomas Fairfax and the English Revolution': *"Another prime concern of Fairfax's 'Short Memorials' was the preservation of his successful reputation as a successful general. In commemorating his first campaigns, Fairfax did this at the expense of others. In 1643 he became preoccupied with fear of treachery amongst his fellow officers. When Sir Thomas headed the committee at Hull to dig out traitors and turncoats he arrested one of its members, Captain Bladen, for giving intelligence to the enemy. Fears of treachery during the Fairfaxes' defence of Hull led to the arrest of Major John Gifford ..."*[1] In arresting Gifford and Bladen, Fairfax was doubting those close to him. John Bladen's close relationship to Thomas Fairfax and his family has already been mentioned, Major General John Gifford had led a force beside Fairfax at the Battle of Adwalton Moor in June of that year which had been lost when Gifford's left flank had been over-run by royalists, but the figures of that battle were quite stark: there were 10,000 royalists against 3-4,000 parliamentarians.

Royalist Composition Papers of March 1645 show that John Bladen was considered a delinquent and his estate had been sequestered and he had been obliged to compound for recovery: *"All ye Petitioners personal estate hath bin sequestered apprized to threescore and five pounds or thereabouts as by the Affidavit appeares and he forced to compound for ye same with ye sequestrators and hath paid xxx li as by accquittance doth and may appeare and security to pay xxij which with the 5 li pt being deducted amounts to ye sume of 65 $^{li}$. Out of so small an estate the petitioner in his true obedience to ye state did lend and pay at several payments these ensuing several sumes of money as by ye acquittances may appeare viz: to Mr Jno Bladen for ye use of ye King and Parliament 50 $^{li}$ and to Mr Tho Metcalfe and Mr Joseph Hillary for ye use of the Lo: Fairfax xx $^{li}$ besides other taxes and oppressions with souldiers on both sides".*[2] John's father-in-law Nathaniel Birkhead was also listed in the papers and it is possible that he assisted John Bladen pay the fee for compounding his estate. No record has yet been found of John facing a court martial which probably would have happened if the charges had been pursued.

It may also have been fortunate that John's father was still alive and in possession of his property and so assets listed in John's name were modest, meaning the fines he was required to pay were likewise smaller. Any inheritance from Robert the father would skip John's generation and fell to the infant grandchild Nathaniel in time; Robert managed to outlive his son to 1647, a couple of years after his son's death. Confirmation of John's date of death being around 1645 comes from a later chancery case where son Nathaniel b.1642 described his father as dying when he was about 2-3 years of age, i.e. 1645.[3]

---

[1] Andrew Hopper, 'Black Tom: Sir Thomas Fairfax and the English Revolution', 2007, p229
[2] Calendar of the Proceedings of the Committee for Compounding: Royalist Composition Papers, p157
[3] TNA: C6/264/15 Bladen v Fountaine, dated 1690

As to whether John was likely to be guilty of being a turncoat, no further record has been found but, as Dr Andrew Hopper of the University of Leicester pointed out *"Bladen may well have been innocent and a victim of the fevered anxiety that surrounded the looming siege of Hull as the Fairfaxes were very jumpy about traitors at that point"*.[1] Certainly John's relation to Radcliffe/Strafford and his father's close connection with both Wortley and Savile may have made Fairfax wonder where his loyalties lay. The other military officer, Major Gifford, arrested at the same time as Bladen, was imprisoned until 1646 in London but then exonerated and went on to serve the Parliamentarian cause as a Commander under Cromwell in Ireland. It is possible that, since no record of Bladen's death has been found, that he went there too. Other possibilities are that he died from injuries sustained in fighting or even the outbreak of plague that occurred in the Wakefield area around 1645.

Sadly, John and his wife had no chance to get to know their son Nathaniel. It is thought his wife died at their son's birth or soon after as later chancery documents show she took no part in her son's upbringing and there were no further children.

---

[1] Dr Andrew Hopper, Centre for English Local History, University of Leicester

# Nathaniel Bladen

Nathaniel's parents both died when he was an infant; his mother probably died at his birth in 1642 or shortly afterwards and his father was dead by 1645, swiftly followed by his Bladen grandfather in 1647 and grandmother in 1653/4. By the age of 11, he was without any parents, grandparents or siblings. On the maternal side, his Birkhead grandfather, for whom he was probably named, died in February 1649 and since his Will of that year made no mention of his wife, then it is thought she predeceased him. This is the immediate maternal family:

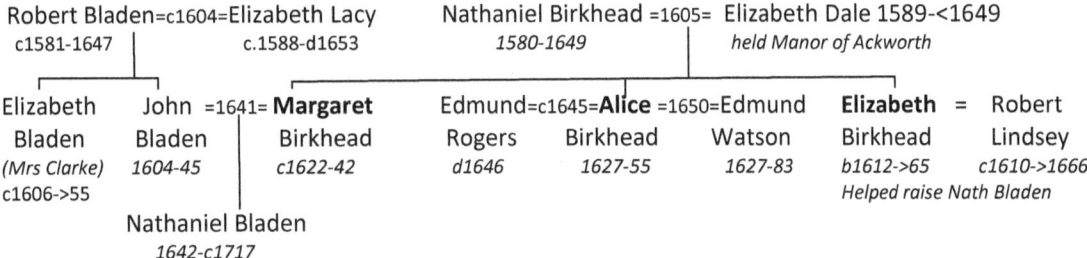

Grandmother Elizabeth Lacy was the longest lived of the immediate family and took care of Nathaniel from being a baby, as his widowed father was away serving with the army and she raised him at Bullingshire Hall until her own death in 1653. Grandfather Robert Bladen's complex legacy of property acquisitions and disposals has been discussed previously, but Nathaniel's maternal relations had their own share of difficulties over assets too.

Immediately his grandmother died, care of Nathaniel passed to Aunt Elizabeth Clarke, the sister of John Bladen, and straight away Mrs Clarke began a legal case - Bladen v Watson[1] - which seems to have been about securing a larger Birkhead inheritance for young Nathaniel. The case centred on the inheritance from Nathaniel Birkhead to his three daughters and so the defendants were their respective husbands Watson and Lindsey. Not all the chancery documents have survived, just some depositions which give a flavour of the grievances they had.

The estate of Nathaniel Birkhead had already produced one law suit between two of his daughters. In his Will, produced in the Appendices on p226, Nathaniel stated that daughter Alice was to receive the largest legacy as daughter Elizabeth had already received a marriage preferment of £1,500 from him, so Elizabeth was left just £50. That particular law suit arose because, in fact, although it may have been Nathaniel's intention to give his daughter £1,500 marriage settlement, he had not actually got around to doing it, so Elizabeth and husband Robert Lindsey sued fellow sibling Alice and her second husband Edmund Watson for that marriage portion itemised in the Will but which they claimed not to have received.[2]

---

[1] TNA: C22/768/14, Bladen v Watson, dated 1655
[2] TNA: C6/46/146 Linsey [Lindsey] v Watson (1652)

Thomas Hurst, Clerk, and Henry Harvey of Gawthorpe were appointed as arbitrators and a settlement was reached whereby the Watsons handed over a sum of £650 to the Lindseys plus some land.

*1655: Bladen v Watson*

The second chancery case was brought by Mrs Clarke (as Guardian to Nathaniel) for his share of the estate. The timing of this case being immediately after the death of the grandmother Elizabeth Bladen might suggest that Elizabeth had been reluctant to instigate proceedings during her lifetime. Mrs Clarke, however, had no such qualms. Although young Nathaniel had been well provided for in his grandfather's Will with land and manors in Yorkshire, it was felt by Mrs Clarke that as the sole male descendant on an estate with a male entail that he should have inherited it all. Only Margaret, of Birkhead's three daughters, had produced a male heir and depositions were given by several individuals who confirmed the presence of a document entailing the estate on a male descendant.

Interestingly, one deponent was Robert Wrightson, a 24-year-old lawyer who would later become a life-long friend and guardian to Nathaniel and his deposition was very supportive. Wrightson described meeting a man called John Bull who was related to Edmund Watson, one of the defendants, who told him that he had seen the deed of entail made by Nathaniel Birkhead but that John Bull claimed that Alice Watson (née Birkhead) had the deed of entail disposed of by getting John Bull and another man's daughters to throw the deed on the fire until it was burned. He also confirmed that the Birkhead's property at Hague Hall in East Hague South Kirkby had indeed between purchased by the two parties, Nathaniel Birkhead and Robert Bladen, from Thomas Gargrave. Another witness made a similar statement that he had also seen the deed.

The central complaint against Alice Birkhead was that she destroyed the Deed by having it burned and then she sent for Commissioners of Dedimus in her father's final days when he was sick. The Commissioners, however, did not arrive until three days after Nathaniel Birkhead's death when Alice was reputed to have said she would have given £300 for them to be three days earlier. Although the chancery case against the Watsons and Lindseys does not appear to have succeeded in full, as Alice Birkhead and the Watsons remained in situ at East Hague Hall and appeared to retain what parts of the estate they already had, there was some settlement later made in Nathaniel's favour. This will be discussed later in Nathaniel's correspondence with his friend Robert Wrightson.

An issue that did come to light in the depositions was that Nathaniel Birkhead was not entirely free to dispose of all his assets as his wife's jointure had to be considered. Wife Elizabeth Dale was co-heir to Roger Dale and, in Roger Dale's Will, Nathaniel Birkhead had been required to provide a jointure to support Elizabeth after his death and the Manor of Ackworth was acquired for that purpose, so he was not free to dispose of it. His father-in-law Roger Dale had made generous financial provision to Nathaniel Birkhead to ensure that this took place.[1]

---

[1] Records show that the Manor of Ackworth was sold by the Crown to Commissioners for the City of London in 1628 and therafter it was divided between the Park and Manor. The Manor was sold to T Harlaken and others before, by marriage, going to the Lambe family of Ackworth, one of whom was the heir of the four original grantees of the City of London

Even without inheriting the whole of the Birkhead estate, what Nathaniel Bladen was left with, however, should have been considered a healthy inheritance. His grandfather's bequest *"to my grandchild Nathaniel Bladen, son of John Bladen deceased, all those my manors of Harden and Haworth and lands in Wakefield with all and singular their rights rents...."* [1] was enhanced by those properties he inherited from his Bladen grandfather. Although Robert Bladen undoubtedly lost substantial properties to Berry, he managed to pass on at least two estates in Hemsworth to his grandson, in addition to the valuable advowson of Hemsworth Church.

*Robert Wrightson*
Shortly after this case, Aunt Elizabeth Clarke was no longer able to care for Nathaniel (or herself)[2] and arrangements were made for the young boy to go to school - he was probably about 14 by this time. It was claimed later by his friend Robert Wrightson that Nathaniel, as a youth, approached him to ask for assistance as he had no-one to care for him and Wrightson took pity on him and undertook to help him. Wrightson said Nathaniel *"importuned him for relief"*.[3] This was probably the time that Nathaniel was sent to Sheffield for his education with a Mr Potts and then went on to Cambridge University where his records state: [4] *'Nathaniel Bladen of Imsworth* [Hemsworth] *Yorkshire, son of John, deceased, bred at Sheffield (Mr Potts), admitted pensioner, tutor and surety Mr Morton, 6 May, aet 18. Bladen Nathaniel, 6 May 1661.* [5]

*Letters to Wrightson*
Robert Wrightson therefore knew Nathaniel, his Bladen family and the Birkheads very well. He was aware of Nathaniel's loss of family and also his assets and inheritances. He was an attorney and no relation to Bladen (though later through marriage, a very distant one) but stepped in to become guardian to the young man who, he would later claim, he *"in pity and charity cared for this hopeful man"*.

---

[1] TNA: PROB 11/211/845 24th April 1650 and TNA: PROB 11/214/608 3rd December 1650 Sentence
[2] TNA: C10/142/2 Fairfax & Topham v Wrightson & Bladen, date 1681 "Mrs Clarke, his father's sister, for long and until she was not able to maintain either him or herself"
[3] TNA: C10/142/2 Fairfax & Topham v Wrightson & Bladen, date 1681
[4] Admissions to the College of St John the Evangelist, Cambridge. Bladen John, father of Nathaniel Bladen p150, 1,35
[5] 1661: The Cockpit A small scrap of information from 1661 shows correspondence being addressed: *"For Mr Nath Bladen at the Cockpitt."* It is difficult to draw too many conclusions from such a small snippet, but there seem to be two possibilities. Close to the Inns of Court there was an area called the Cockpitt Steps (not too far away from Petty France and close to the Treasury and St James' Park) and Bladen may have been residing there prior to undertaking his legal training and his Uncle Lindsey was known to be at Petty France. Alternatively this may be a reference to the Cockpit Theatre. With the Restoration of King Charles II to the throne and the end of the Puritan era, theatres were at last re-opened to the public. Nathaniel Bladen certainly attended theatre and when he wrote 'Advice to a son' in the 1690s, he quoted from Shakepeare; he also wrote poetry which will be referred to later. The Cockpit, was in operation from 1616-65 (though prevented from performing 1642-60) and was the first theatre to be located in the Drury Lane area. It was small (52'x37') and similar in style to the much earlier Globe Theatre. Montaigne's English Journey: Reading the Essays in Shakespeare's Day by William M Hamlin, 2013

He paid for his clothing and arranged for Nathaniel's schooling for five years, then for another number of years he supported him at St John's College, Cambridge University. Thereafter, he arranged for him to attend the Inner Temple and continued to financially support him for years whilst Nathaniel studied to be a lawyer. The first letter between the two men dates from 1662 when Nathaniel was just 20 years old and at Cambridge University:

*1662*: 5th May, To Robert Wrightson from Nath Bladen at St John's College, Cambridge
*Worthy Sir, My cousin's kindness was something a trouble to me but when you assured me you were, as I have always found you, my most constant friend I had no longer place for grief.... I shall never esteem myself unhappy so long as I can assure myself rich in such a friend, assure yourself most worthy sir that, so far as any estate of interest that God hath lent me in this world will raise a farthing so long I may assure yourself you shall be no loser either in your great expense or fatherly care and pains, which I shall desire God above all pursue felicities I may live to requite. I have in my tutor's hands about eight pounds, I hope it will last till after the commencement though my tutor for sure will provide more about that time to be aforehand with me, besides the cost and trouble you have been at in sending to me and the like it has this year amounted to almost forty pounds, gown surplice and suit receive. Excuse, I pray you ... tell that pretender this is more than I expected, it hath taught me to expect naught till I can assure myself of it. I do not prize her kindness worthy to be rewarded with a letter. Sir, your obliged, Nath Bladen"* [1]

Since the Bladen v Watson case was still ongoing at this time, Bladen's animosity in the above letter was probably directed towards a Birkhead relation. In another letter he adopts the same hostile manner in talking about his Aunt Lindsey (née Elizabeth Birkhead) who *"doth not cease to prosecute me with her importunities."* Future mother-in-law Lady Fairfax would later claim in chancery that Wrightson took all the rents from Nathaniel's own property and used a small part of those rents to render Nathaniel financial support and pocketed the difference. That he took advantage of the young man and took his property, thereby depriving her grandchildren of their rightful inheritance. However, in Nathaniel's own words he heaped praise on his friend Wrightson who he regarded as a father-figure. He also explicitly stated that he would, one day, return the favours that Wrightson had done him so long as his estate 'could raise one farthing'. This, to a large extent, exonerates Wrightson from later claims that he only helped the boy because he wanted to seize his assets, as Bladen clearly indicates his willingness to see Wrightson repaid for his help. Whatever the truth of the matter, Nathaniel remained steadfastly supportive of Wrightson, who was about thirteen years older.

Shortly after he wrote the above letter, the young 21 year old Nathaniel found himself having to select the next vicar of Hemsworth Church. He inherited the advowson from his grandfather Robert and the vacancy had arisen when Rev Stephen Chapman, who had been appointed by King Charles I in 1636, was obliged to vacate the post following the Restoration of King Charles II in 1660.

---

[1] Doncaster Archives, Batty-Wrightson Collection DD/BW/F7/2

When the Act of Uniformity was introduced, which made the Book of Common Prayer compulsory, some 2,000 clergymen, including Stephen Chapman had refused to take an oath of compliance. They were subsequently expelled from the Church of England which led to a large section of non-conformity outside the Church of England which would develop into its own movement later.

Nathaniel appointed Mr Edward Mawson to the post and then, according to Nathaniel's version of events, he subsequently sold the advowson to his guardian and friend Robert Wrightson. This sale was to become a major bone of contention in the future as it appears to have been kept a private matter between Bladen and Wrightson and was not made common knowledge. This subject will be returned to in due course.

Two years later and well into his university studies Nathaniel wrote again to Wrightson, from Cambridge on 27th October 1664: *"Sir, I have received 10th of Mr Spencer which I beseech you to be pleased to repay him at Rotherham the 2nd November, he was unwilling to let me have any monies, he told me he had heard nothing of the last. I pray you so be pleased to keep this day with him and the next time I will give you greater notice at a more favourable time and not charge you with so great a sum. My Aunt Lindsey[1] doth not cease to prosecute me with her importunities but I intend she shall not reap any profit of them, I have satisfied her with a very plausible answer and it is now for Sir John Birkenhead.[2] But I have a fair respect to my promises and a greater for your friendship. She is at the White Hart in Newark. I wonder you have past thus much time in silence. I hope to be at Godmanchester[3] about the time you go up to London when I hope to hear what I so much desire the welfare of all my friends, in haste I rest, Sir, your humble servant, Nath Bladen"*[4]

The next letter was written two years later when he was nearing the end of his studies: *"From Nathaniel Bladen to Robert Wrightson April 3rd For my dear friend, ..... I pray write me word how you found good Mrs Wrightson at your return to London and how she is now. I hope God has decreed you many happy days together and how you got through your journey.....I received at Emsall[5] £20-6-0, which came very starkly from them, none paid any of it but Mr Hugh Wentworth who offered to lay down the other half with anyone and Holmes paid his share. I received of Mr Berry £47-09 and I paid your father £5-0-0, Mr Wrightson, if you would please to pay my Uncle Lindsey the remainder and mark it out so he has bespoke me a copper which was come to above that, but that is all I can hope to help him with and when I give a piece you. I will take what course you ask to secure you in payment or else pay you or a return of favour at London, whichever you choose. Pray Mr Wrightson oblige me in this and write to my uncle at Mrs How's house in St James at the upper end of Petty France to meet you at some place about The Temple Bar, for to receive it.*

---

[1] Aunt Lindsey was Elizabeth Birkhead (sister to Margaret, Nathaniel's mother)
[2] Sir John Birkenhead 1616-79 was Master of Requests from 1664-79 in the Minor Equity Court
[3] Godmanchester in Cambridge is the place, later referred to, where Robert Wrightson got Nathaniel to sign a deed giving him control of his property
[4] Doncaster Archives, Batty-Wrightson Collection, DD/BW/F7/2
[5] Ibid. South Emsall is a village just to the east of Hemsworth

*The copper holds 12 hogheads and will set out of London the 10th of April so the sooner you do this will be the greater kindness to you. Your affectionate friend and servant, Nath Bladen" Reverse: For Mr Robert Wrightson at the Blue Ball upon Wapping Wall, London.*[1] This letter contains confirmation, some ten years after commencement of the Bladen v Watson case, that at last Nathaniel received some kind of settlement from his Birkhead (Watson/Lindsey) relations. The mention of Hugh Wentworth[2] in the letter can be explained as him being a cousin of Edmund Watson. It would have been interesting to have seen the full chancery documents on this case as there was probably far more to the story.

Nathaniel stated that he had received sums of £20 and £47 of Dr Berry who was, of course, deceased by this time and had no male heir, so Dr Berry's estate making a payment to Nathaniel over this issue seems to tie together what had seemed like two separate issues. His Birkhead grandfather had bought Hague Hall originally with Robert Bladen and Dr Berry had numerous claims over Robert's estate when he died, therefore when Nathaniel pursued the Watson case, inheritors of the Berry estate must have become involved and, from the comments in Bladen's letter above, it seems like both sides (Watson and Berry) were made to make payments to Nathaniel. Though £67 is far short of the £500 Bladen would later claim his family was owed by Berry alone.

*1665*: 23rd, 1665 *"From N Bladen at the Inns of Court to Robert Wrightson:*
*Dear friend, I give you thanks for your care and pains in sending me the gifts which came very safe and also those sealed up. I pray if you have a convenience do me the favour and send me this enclosed by some of the Ld Strafford's, to my cousin Lacy at Knaresby [Knaresborough]. I do not intend to prolong the time above a fortnight longer as I see from Jackson Jarvice I wish it may prove a seasonable time for a Haworth journey. I have writ to my uncle to send his boy on horseback with a portmanteau to bring me a suit of clothes and nothing shall hinder my journey but death, sickness,\* or extreme bad weather. Your affectionate friend, Nath Bladen"*[3] *This letter was written at the height of the plague in London which does not seem to affected Bladen's presence there. The Great Fire of the following year was known to have been raging towards the Temple and Inns of Court on 4th September, just weeks before Bladen commenced his attendance at the Inner Temple.

Bladen's directions for his letters shows some interesting connections. He asks Wrightson (who was at Hemsworth or Cusworth) to direct enclosed letters via Lord Strafford (2nd Earl of the Wentworth family and son of the 1st Earl who was beheaded) for onward transmission to his Lacy cousin in Knaresby [Knaresborough].[4] Such were the lengths necessary for getting letters directed, via someone you knew! There is one final letter between Bladen and Wrightson, dated 1696, which will be discussed later.

---

[1] Doncaster Archives, Batty-Wrightson Collection, DD/BW/F7/4
[2] Hugh Wentworth 1608-80 of South Elmsall, son of Thomas Wentworth and Alice Watson, Alice being first cousin to Edmund Watson of the Watsons of Bolton-upon-Dearne branch
[3] Doncaster Archives, Batty-Wrightson Collection, DD/BW/F7/2
[4] These Lacy relations would have been descendants of Elizabeth's father's first marriage to Ellen Lister, from Thomas Lacy of Cromwellbothom=Anne Winckley. Thomas had a son Thomas Lacy (of Longworth, Lancaster) b.1628 who married Anne Hilton and they had six children: see Dugdale's Visitation of Lancashire 1664-65

*1666: Receiver of Arrears for the Treasury*
Nathaniel was admitted to the Inner Temple on 19th October 1666 and shortly afterwards, at just 24-years of age, he obtained an appointment at the Treasury as a Receiver of Arrears of Prize Ships, along with Charles Osborne. This was to be the beginning of a 25+ year relationship Nathaniel had with the Osborne family. His employment at the Treasury was of equal duration.

Wrightson's financial support of Bladen during his legal studies must have been minimal to say the least as he would later claim that he found Nathaniel in such a *"low condition"* financially, in May 1667 that the 25 year old was employed in a hazardous occupation and ... *"engaged about making gunpowder."*[1] Wrightson took pity on Bladen, who could not raise the necessary money to support himself and, purely as a means to assist Bladen, he offered to buy his Hemsworth property (both house and land) for £350. This was, Wrightson claimed, higher than the market price but he felt the time was right for Nathaniel to be financially solvent, that is to say solvent enough to consider marriage. Others (Fairfax) interpreted Wrightson's actions as him taking advantage of Bladen.

*Fairfaxes*
About 1666, if not before, Nathaniel had dealings with Lady Frances Fairfax of Steeton who had a great interest in the advowson of Hemsworth church which had formerly been in Nathaniel's possession. Her husband's grandfather, Sir William Fairfax of Steeton 1560-1603 had been buried at Hemsworth, along with other close family members. It seems, from Lady Fairfax's later depositions, that she was under the impression that the advowson was still in Bladen's hands and she remained under that impression for the following 12 years. There was an additional association between the Fairfaxes at Steeton and Trustees in Hemsworth, some distance away, in that the Trustees of Hemsworth School had ownership of land in Steeton. Lady Fairfax clearly felt she had some influence in that parish and wanted to hold patronage of the church. In 1680, she claimed to have paid Nathaniel Bladen (who, as it happens, would later become her son-in-law) a sum of money in 1666 in exchange for the advowson of the church. There is no way of knowing whether this was true, though it is clear from Wrightson's description above that Nathaniel was very short of money at the time. However the records do show that Nathaniel had already sold this patronage to his friend Wrightson in 1663.

Lady Fairfax's family chaplain was a man called Topham[2] and he was closely involved with her family's affairs, being an administrator and trustee of her late husband's Will. He had also been given the power, under the terms of that Will, to choose marriage partners for Lady Fairfax's children. It seems clear from what happened next that both Lady Fairfax and Topham were both in the dark as to who held the advowson at Hemsworth as the parties involved (Bladen/Topham) manoeuvred events to their own advantage.

---

[1] TNA: C10/142/2 Fairfax & Topham v Wrightson & Bladen 1681
[2] 1634-1712 William Topham

Everything revolved around Lady Fairfax's unmarried daughter Isabella. Isabella, like Nathaniel, had lost her father when she was a child. Sir William Fairfax, in 1642, was making preparations for the Civil War that was approaching and which would claim his life. He sent his wife and daughters Isabella and Catherine to London for their safety, arranging for them to stay with his sister-in-law Mrs Chaloner who lived near Charing Cross c/o Mr James Chaloner's house, Queen Street, near the Flower de luce Tavern.[1] His sons Thomas and William were given to the care of Lady Barwick at Toulston. Sadly, the children would never see their father again after he went off to war.[2] Fairfax died in 1644 at Montgomery.

An early letter from 1660 from sister Catherine (Mrs Lister) mentioned the 23 year old Isabella to their mother: *"I confes my sister Bell has reson to complain I have not writ to her, but my occasions have been something extraordinary, I have had two letters from her since I came from Steeton, but Betty Robinson has one every week. But I do but say this by the by, but to my knowledge I have not forgot to remember me to her in any letter. If I did I was either in troble or haste, and soe forgot ceremony, but I will doe it now therefore pray remember my kind love to her. I would write but it is late and Martin very ill tonight, soe I must subscribe me yr most obedient child." Kath Lister - 27th July 1660*[3] There are also several mentions of Isabella in the correspondence between Admiral Robert Fairfax and his mother, Robert being Isabella's nephew and he was extremely close to the Bladens throughout his life. In 1687 he mentioned his Aunts Bladen and Boynton being concerned that he had not yet got a commission in the Royal Navy. He said *"My Uncle Fairfax writ a letter to my Aunt Bladen [Isabella], most of it signifying how much he and my Aunt Boynton was concerned that I had got no employ"*.

Nathaniel Bladen wanted to marry Isabella Fairfax and Nathaniel (Lady Fairfax and Topham thought) held the advowson of Hemsworth church. Topham, on the other hand, had the power to choose Isabella's husband and he sought to be Rector of Hemsworth church. So it was quid pro quo. Wrightson, who actually had the power of patronage, had no interest in upsetting the applecart by interfering at this time as it suited him very well to have Nathaniel well married and off his hands after so many years 'supporting him'.

*Paver's Marriage License 1668*[4]
*Nathaniel Bladen gen., 23, London and Isabella Fairfax, spinster, 21, Steeton – there.*

In fact Nathaniel was 26 years and Isabella was 31 years of age.[5]

---

[1] The daughters may also have spent time staying with their Mulgrave relations. The Earl of Mulgrave 1564-1646 was first cousin to Queen Elizabeth I and, though his wife Ursula Thyrwhit was a staunch Catholic, Captain Edmund Sheffield (Mulgrave) fought on the parliamentary side in the Civil War and persecuted Catholics in his locale, to show support and loyalty to the Queen
[2] The Life of Admiral Robert Fairfax of Steeton by Clements R Markham - 1885
[3] Ibid
[4] Also in Boyd's Yorkshire Arch. Diocese Marriage Licenses. 1668
[5] One source says Isabella was baptised on 16th August 1637 at Steeton Chapel - 'The Life of Admiral Robert Fairfax of Steeton' by Clements R Markham 1885. Another source, the familysearch site, has her baptism at Bolton Percy Church. Given that the two places are 25 miles apart it is difficult to say which is correct. Isabella's family did live at Steeton, but Bolton Percy was the parish church for the Fairfaxes at Nun Appleton Hall. The Bolton Percy entry seems more likely, given what happened at Isabella's death. She died at her

It was to be some years before Topham got the opportunity to assume the incumbency of Hemsworth and only two years later before he was replaced. It is thought at this time Lady Fairfax exercised her right (or so she believed) to choose the next vicar, however, her choice of Ludlam seems to have immediately prompted Wrightson to come out of the shadows. Wrightson had no liking for the Puritan Stephen Ludlam and he immediately took steps to eject him and, instead, installed his own son-in-law to the post.

*Patronage of Hemsworth Church:*

|  | **VICAR** | **PATRON** |
|---|---|---|
| 1520s |  | Richard Wortley/ Lacys - then the Gargraves |
| 1636-62 | Stephen Chapman *Resigned at the Act of Uniformity* | Crown: King Charles |
| 1662 | Edward Mawson | Nathaniel Bladen |
| 1680 | William Topham - *Chaplain to Lady Fairfax* | Nathaniel Bladen (Wrightson) |
| 1682-85 | Stephen Ludlam - *Puritan, ejected* | Lady Fairfax?/Nathaniel Bladen (Wrightson) |
| 1685-1718 | Henry Farrer d. 1718 | Robert Wrightson d. 1708 |
| 1718-27 | William Lamplugh d. 1727 | Thomas Wrightson |
| 1730-46 | William Lamplugh d. 1776 | Robert Wrightson? Paid £35 p.a. stipend |
| 1749-63 | John Farrar d. 1763 (*son of above Henry*) | *Wrightson family held patronage of Hemsworth Church for 300 years from 1685* |

The battle over patronage as described, which began in 1666, took until 1680 to erupt into chancery proceedings and so will be discussed further later.

*1668: Declaration*
A couple of years after the appointments of Nathaniel Bladen and Charles Osborne at the Treasury Bladen's name crops up in records showing that he was now in the service of the wider Osborne family and, in this regard, he issued a Declaration concerning some financial arrangements in March 1667/8. First, however, the circumstances of this Declaration need some explaining: the Great Plague of London had devastated the population in 1665/6 shortly followed by the Great Fire 1666 and, whilst this was going on, the Anglo-Dutch Wars of 1665-7 were raging, all of which left Charles II desperate for money. The King tapped many sources for funds including the London goldsmiths, some of whom more correctly could be called goldsmith-bankers as they developed a wide remit which encompassed lending money to the Crown, government, merchants, livery companies etc. In addition many aristocratic families used them as personal bankers and used their vaults to safeguard their wealth.

---

mother's home in Steeton, but her body was interred at Bolton Percy Church, along with her mother who died shortly afterwards. Given her mother's preference for Bolton Percy at death, perhaps it was the same for the baptism

This had become necessary following Charles I's raiding of the gold deposits at the Tower of London prior to the Civil War, so wealthy families, including Nathaniel's employers the Osbornes, sought other safer locations for their valuable assets. These goldsmith-bankers would offer credit against items deposited with them and managed deposits in trust for their clients. The Declaration stated that King Charles had received the enormous sum of £248,866-3-shillings and 5-pence from Gilbert Whitehall (goldsmith-banker) and, in return, Gilbert Whitehall was to receive *"the perpetual interest for and in lieu and satisfaction of the sum"* which amounted to £14,931-19 shillings and 4-pence. So, what has this to do with Nathaniel Bladen? Well, the Declaration bearing Nathaniel's name further stated that the sum of £168 (of Whitehall's £14,931) was to be paid to Nathaniel yearly but, this is qualified by a statement from Nathaniel: *"NOW know ye that I the said Nathaniel Bladen do hereby acknowledge and declare that my name was only used in the said Indenture in Trust for Edward Lord Latimer and his heirs"*.[1] Latimer was Edward Osborne, son of Danby. This arrangement seems to suggest that Osbourne family money was brokered through Gilbert Whitehall to assist Charles II. Gilbert Whitehall was not alone in providing the service, a handful of other goldsmith-bankers such as Blackwells did the same thing. It is, therefore, no coincidence at all that the Osborne family should be looked on favourably by the King, nor should it be a surprise that Viscount Latimer's father, Danby, whose career had taken off at this time, should find himself appointed Treasurer of the Navy that same year.

Danby's appointments had included: Councillor of State in Cabinet Councils, Lord High Treasurer of England in 1673, Lord Lieutenant of the West Riding of Yorkshire, Lord President of the Privy Council, Lord Lieutenant of the whole of Yorkshire, Captain and Governor of Kingston-upon-Hull, Lord High Steward of England and High Steward of York and Hull. He would later become leader of the government before his enemies found a way to challenge his base of power when the Popish Plot brought about his downfall. Nathaniel's connections with the Osborne family (Latimer/Danby/Pembroke) would continue throughout this period and beyond.

*1668+: Employers/Patrons*
The handful of people who would employ Nathaniel Bladen was a tight-knit group, all known to each other or related. Basically he was employed for twenty years by the Osbornes (Danby) and then his wife's Fairfax relations, in addition to his work for the Treasury and some independent practice as a lawyer.

The following chart shows the small circle of related families who engaged Nathaniel's services. He was also, of course, conducting business transactions in his own right and, in later years, was involved in acquisitioning supplies for the army through his son's appointment as a Colonel of a Regiment.[2]

---

[1] Hull History Centre, DDFA2/25/2
[2] Engaging attorneys as stewards was commonplace - some would serve as steward to multiple estates

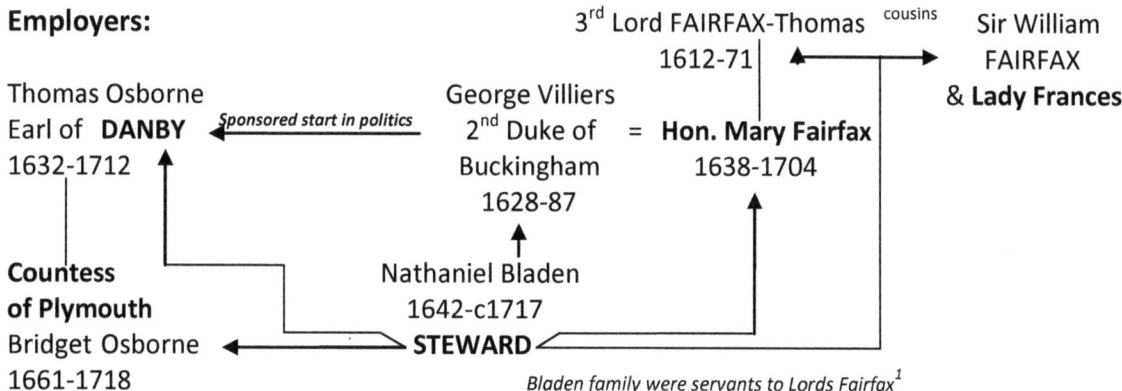

*Bladen family were servants to Lords Fairfax[1]*

*Earl of Danby (Osbourne family)*

After Nathaniel had been admitted to the Inner Temple he became associated with, first, Charles Osborne in a Treasury role in 1666 and then he became employed as Steward to Lord Danby, Sir Thomas Osborne, 1st Earl of Leeds and brother to Charles Osborne.[2] Nathaniel was called to the bar on 3rd November 1673 and, as a newly qualified lawyer in his twenties, the Osbornes were undoubtedly his first employers as steward. At the time he began his service to the family, Lord Danby was a rising star and Nathaniel was in post from the beginning to watch Danby's rise to become Treasurer and to then being on the Privy Council and eventually to his appointment as Lord High Treasurer and Chief Minister. In those days it was considered desirable for your advancement to 'hitch your star' to an important nobleman who may, if you were fortunate, become your patron and sponsor your progress. No doubt Nathaniel felt fortunate in being in Danby's household and hoped it would bring him personal advancement and fortune. In turn, Danby himself had found a sponsor in George Villiers, 2nd Duke of Buckingham, a royalist who had married Mary the daughter of the 3rd Lord Fairfax. Fairfax had acquired Villiers' estate after the civil war and so marriage to daughter Mary must have seemed an equitable arrangement for Buckingham to re-acquire his lands. This was how many men achieved advancement.

In 1678, no doubt at the bidding of his masters, Nathaniel wrote to Henry 4th Lord Fairfax, his wife's cousin, trying to get him to stand for Parliament with Viscount Latimer (Lord Danby's son) as his second. He urged him to *"take the opportunity of endearing yourself in a signal measure to the King and country by the representing your County in Parliament, a trust you will find them willing to confer on your Lordship for your own sake as also for the performance your family hath given them on the like occasion. And to encourage your Lordship's heart the more, I give you the assurance of a noble Second (who can contribute no inconsiderable share of interest to carry on the joint concern), my Lord Treasurer's eldest son, My Lord Latimer."*

---

[1] Sources for chart: Brian Fairfax's Life of the Duke of Buckingham, p39; Hunter's South Yorkshire: Pedigree of Osborne, Dukes of Leeds, Vol. 1, p143; A Biographical History of England, J. Grainger 1775

[2] CTB 1660-1667. Charles was Danby's younger brother 1633-1719, unmarried

And in case he was not inclined to accept the suggestion, Bladen hedged his bets by asking, in that eventuality, if Fairfax would be willing to *"give your interest for my sake to my Lord Latimer who will use that, and all other of his own and my Lord Treasurer's advantages to serve your Lordship and your family."* Bladen added, *"I serve a generous master and that it may turn to account in my fortune"*.[1]

Head of the family, Sir Thomas Osborne (the Earl of Danby) had been riding high as one of the most powerful men in England as Chief Minister to King Charles II. But with success he had acquired powerful enemies and, when apt circumstances arose, they seized the opportunity to bring about his downfall. Osborne was a Protestant and had been unhappy about King Charles II's decision to accept money from Catholic France at this time. France had wanted to keep England neutral and out of Louis XIV's wars, so when Osborne's enemies discovered money had been received from France they brought it to the attention of a furious House of Commons. Osborne's name was implicated, not the King's. Nothing Danby could say or do would lessen the anger he faced and calls for his impeachment. His detractors made repeated attempts to link him to the Popish Plot that was unfolding at the time. There was widespread alarm and fear of a conspiracy to return England to a Catholic country, a manifestation of which was a fictitious allegation by Dr Titus Oates and a Mr Bedloe that there was a 'Popish Plot' to assassinate the King. One prominent name after another was declared to be involved and it became a witch-hunt against those with supposed Catholic sympathies, some of the accused faced trial and some 22 people were executed. Oates's accusations, which were initially given credence, gave vent to that section of society fearful of the King's lack of legitimate heir which could lead to his Catholic brother succeeding to the throne.

Danby became a scapegoat for his numerous Jacobite enemies or those who personally did not like him (Halifax/Savile and Montagu), though in reality he had been simply obeying King Charles's directions and had excellent credentials as a Protestant. Brian Fairfax,[2] a cousin of Isabella Bladen, left an account of the Popish Plot ... *"Our first disturbance at Court, wch affected both the King and his honest servants, was the Popish Plot, wch was discovered September 1678 to a Justice of Peace in our parish of St Martin's and lest he should be active in prosecuting it he was barbarously murdered. This did rayse such violent passions in all sorts of men, some to conceale it, others to discover and punish it, that the whole nation was never after quiet."*[3] Although Danby's impeachment and arrest were for his actions as a Minister for the King, the facts centred on his opponents' allegations of his support for Catholic France and so fed directly into the growing widespread hysteria of a supposed Catholic plot to return England to Catholicism.

---

[1] The Fairfaxes of England and America in the 17th and 18th centuries by Edward Duffield Neill, 1868
[2] Brian Fairfax 1633-1711, literary uncle of 5th Lord Fairfax, lived at the Royal Mews near Charing Cross, London. Brian was the grandson (via Henry) of Sir Thomas 1st Lord Fairfax
[3] The Life of Robert Fairfax of Steeton by Clements R Markham - 1885

*1678: Popish Plot*

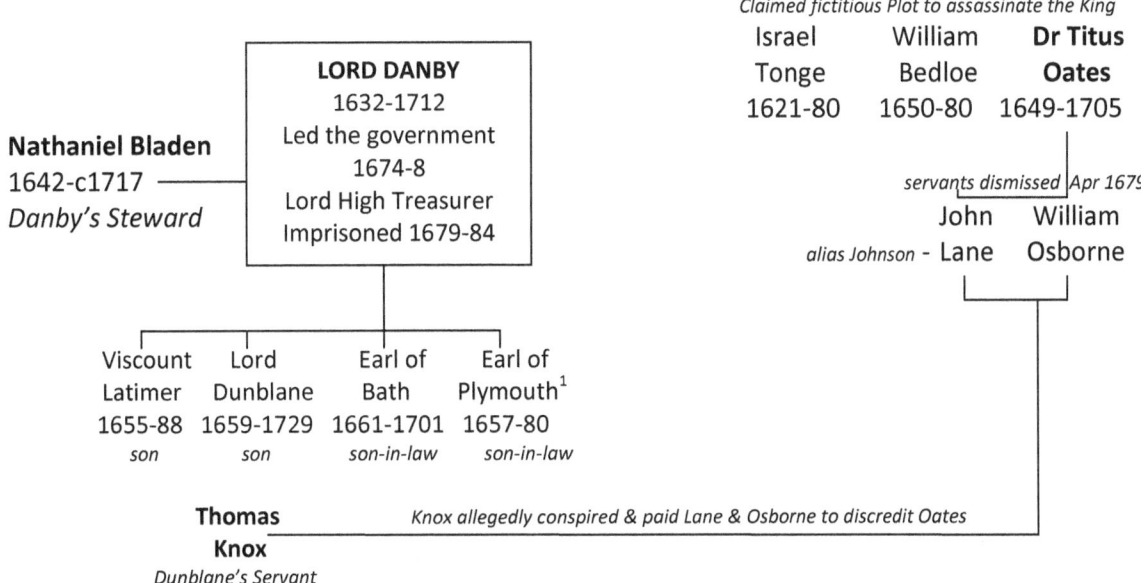

At this time, as a sub-plot to the main Popish Plot, three individuals emerged who, it was claimed, set out to undermine the testimony of Titus Oates and William Bedloe: Thomas Knox, William Osborne and John Lane.[2] Oates published an account of their conspiracy in 1679 against him[3] describing how he believed the men forged letters which had been dictated to them by Thomas Knox and swore an oath upon them before Justice Sir William Waller and Edmund Warcup to their veracity. Two of the men (Lane and Osborne) were recently dismissed servants of Dr Titus Oates and the third was a servant to Lord Dunblane (Danby's son Peregrine) and sometime Clerk to his being Justice of the Peace. In the trial of Thomas Knox and John Lane (son of Richard Lane, a Yeoman of the Guard) held at the Kings Bench for a Misdemeanour in 1679, at the height of the hysteria against Catholics, the servant of Dr Titus Oates, John Lane, made a lurid allegation about his former master, that Titus had attempted assault (intimate) with him on numerous occasions. The accusation was seen as an attempt to seriously discredit Oates and undermine his allegations of a Popish Plot.

The trial of the three men outlined how Lane had been paid by another man, Knox, to say whatever Knox asked him to. In addition to this allegation, the three men allegedly faked four letters - letters claiming that Oates had lied about a Catholic conspiracy. Two men (the third had run away and evaded court proceedings) were found guilty and sentenced to one year in jail plus fines.

---

[1] Sources for chart: Oxford DNB, Oxford University Press: Israel Tongue; Hunter's South Yorkshire p144: Osborne Pedigree

[2] The Tryal and Conviction of Thomas Knox and John Lane for a Conspiracy to Defame and Scandalize Dr Oates and Mr Bedloe thereby to discredit their evidence about the horrid Popish plot: at the King's Bench Bar at Westminster, on Tuesday the 25th of November 1679: whereupon full evidence they were found guilty of the offence aforesaid. Printed for Robert Pawlett, London, 1680 (Early English Books Online)

[3] Printed for Tho. Parkhurst, Thomas Cockerill and Benj. Allsop [8] pp33-36

During the trial Lane had expressed fear that he would end up in the pillory and so was expressly sent by the Judges to spend one hour in the pillory.

CHRONOLOGY - Danby

|  |  |
|---|---|
| 1632 | Born |
| 1661 | Sheriff |
| 1665 | MP York |
| 1668 | Navy Treasurer |
| 1671 | Treasurer |
| 1673 | Privy Councillor |
| 1673 | Chief Minister |
| 1678 | Impeachment - Popish Plot |
| 1679 | Royal Pardon |
| 1679 | Royal Pardon overturned |
| 1679 | Resigned |
| 1679 | House of Lords ordered him to The Tower |
| 1684 | Released from Imprisonment |
| 1688 | 1 of 7 signators to invite the Prince of Orange (wife niece of Charles II) to take the throne |
| 1689 | Lord President of the North |
| 1690 | Chief Minister |
| 1691 | Sidelined as a Tory as Whigs were in favour |
| 1694 | Impeached for allegedly taking a bribe from the EIC |
| 1694 | Political career over |
| 1712 | Died |

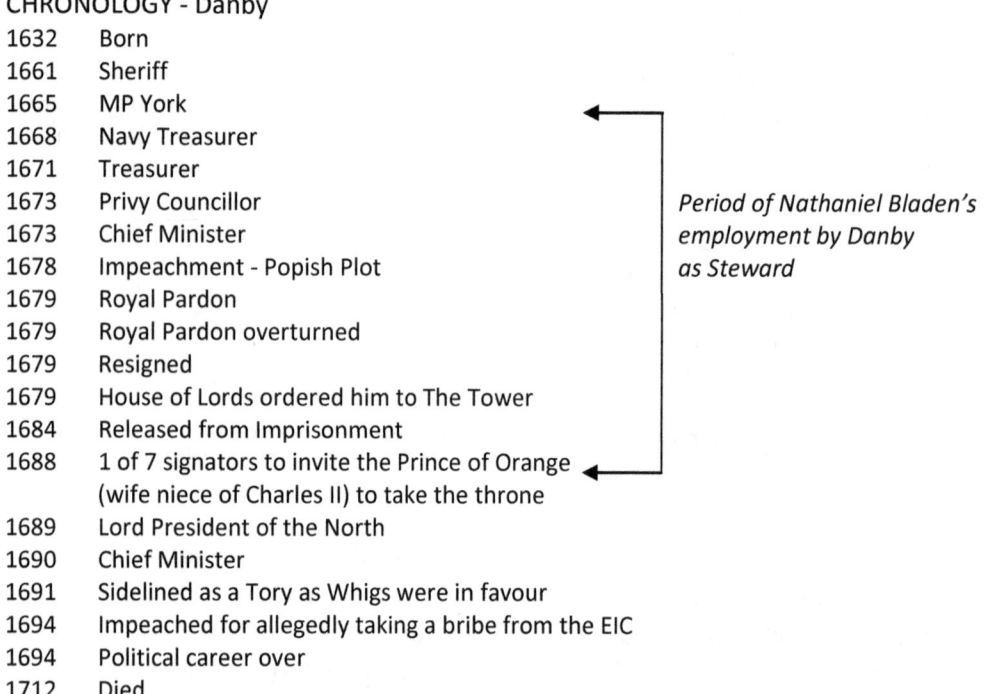

*Period of Nathaniel Bladen's employment by Danby as Steward*

What was Bladen's involvement in this? Well, the lead man in the conspiracy, Knox, was allegedly bribing the others to do his bidding and he was being bankrolled by his employer - Danby's son, Lord Dunblane - and as the family's Steward, Bladen did Danby and Latimer's bidding. Danby wrote: ... *"In the mean time let Bladen have 5 l. as money you lend him, but tell him you dare give no directions till you heare from me, which yet you cannot, and advise him that both he and Nox bee very cautious...."*[1] Viscount Latimer, Danby's son, had an interest in exposing the Popish Plot as a fabrication and had the financial means to 'buy' Knox who remained loyal to Danby throughout. Witnesses in the court proceedings described how Danby's representative came to see them on various missions. Some of them even named Nathaniel[2].....

| | |
|---|---|
| Mr Williams: | "Did ever anybody persuade you not to come to give evidence?" |
| Mrs Wiggins: | "No". |
| L.C.J. | "When was this you speak of?" |
| Mrs Wiggins: | "In February, the latter end" |
| Sergeant Maynard: | "Mr Dewy, who came in company with Mr Knox to you"? |
| Dewy: | "One Mr Blayden". |

---

[1] Thomas Osborne, Earl of Danby and Duke of Leeds 1632-1712, Vol. ii, Letters by Thomas Osborne; Andrew Browning. G.N. Clark, The English Historical Review, Vol. 60, No. 238 (Sep. 1945) pp408-410 published by Oxford University Press

[2] Cobbett's Complete Collection of State Trials and Proceedings, Vol. 7, by Thomas Bayly Howell, William Cobbett, David Jardine. 1810

| Sergeant Maynard: | "Who is that?" |
| --- | --- |
| Dewy: | "Steward to my Lord of Danby I think". |

On another occasion: "Wednesday the last of April Mr Bladen, the Earl of Danby's Steward, came to me at Whitehall, [Walter] Chetwynd present. We sent aside, he told me I had committed Mr Knox contrarye to law and threatened action of false imprisonment".[1]

The above was written by Israel Tonge (1621-80) who was living at Whitehall at the time and who was a confederate of Oates and one of the informers of the Popish Plot. It is evident that Bladen was heavily involved in trying to defend his master.

A series of letters has been preserved by the British Library dated April 1679 between Danby-Bladen-Knox.[2] Danby had been impeached in March of that year and, by 21st April 1679, he was incarcerated in the Tower of London and the letters date from the first two weeks prior to this. The first letter is from Thomas Knox to Lord Danby, dated 2nd April 1679, three weeks before Danby went to the Tower and seven months before Knox himself would face trial for his part in events. He described meeting up with fellow conspirator William Osborne (former servant to Titus Oates) and received an assurance from both Osborne and Lane that they would support Danby at his trial. He said *"I am confident I may persuade either of them to meet Mr Bladen"*. He added in reference to the informer William Osborne *"My Lord, the informer also told me that his name being Osborne, he thought he was oblig'd in conscience to serve your Lordship"*.

Two days later Knox wrote to Nathaniel Bladen relaying information he had gathered concerning the matter: *"It was this afternoon before I could get my friend to introduce me into the company of that woman who I told you I was informed could give so exact an account of several meetings of my Lord Danby with Mr Oates and Dr Tongue at Foxhall [Vauxhall]"*. The letter contains references to Lord Danby in his coach being seen in both Vauxhall and Wimbledon, both known to be addresses for Titus Oates and his cabal. Since Danby had been asked by the King to enquire into the Oates' allegations though, it is hardly surprising that such meetings took place but Knox questioned the woman (Mrs Downing) as to whether Danby had been in disguise at such meetings. The woman could not recall but described how a Mr Floyd would arrange to put the parties together *"he would cry to them - there comes my Lord and they would whip through the garden and meet him."* Mrs Downing also described how *"a Lady of great quality was with her who had a son with her, that was come from St Omers* [English Jesuits were educated at St Omers College in Normandy, France] *who was very inquisitive in this matter."*[3]

---

[1] Diaries of the Popish Plot: Being the Diaries of Israel Tonge, Sir Robert Scuthwell, Edmund Warcup, John Joyne and Thomas Dangerfield: including Titus Oates's A True Narrative of the Horrid Plot (1679)
[2] Add MS 28049: 1679-1684, f24, ff26,40, 109, 196 ©The British Library Board
[3] Add MS28049, ff40, ©The British Library Board

Another letter from Nathaniel Bladen to Lord Danby, dated April 1679, was probably written after Danby had been imprisoned as Bladen demonstrated support for Danby by saying *"It is not your absence, the infidelity and ingratitude of false friends, the malicious power of your enemies, nor all the disappointments and discouragement I have met since your Lordship's departure that can deter me a moment from performing the best services I can imagine to render your Lordship."* Bladen went on to praise Danby for his intention to appear personally to defend himself and offered Danby some encouragement saying *"this day hath brought to light something which may be of great service to your Lordship, I find there have been several consultations between Oates and Below to destroy your Lordship and this I thought I ought not to be concealed for one minute from your knowledge"*.

Bladen informed his master that the information has been passed to Lord Bath (Danby's son-in-law), the information having been sworn before a Justice and was to be retained to Danby's future use.[1] Interestingly, Bladen signed himself *"your Lordship's most faithful and humble and most obedient poor servant"*.

Danby himself was in the Tower of London for five years, not only had he been impeached, but he was accused of the murder of Sir Edmund Berry Godfrey. Godfrey was the magistrate who Titus Oates had made his deposition to regarding the veracity of his Popish Plot claims and who had been murdered by his own sword. The trial makes interesting reading in that full detail was allowed for the prosecution, but the defence attorneys for Knox and Lane were weak, short and ineffectual and, at the very end of proceedings when Knox tried to speak, the Judge would not allow him to utter a single word.

Extract from a letter from the Earl of Danby to his son Viscount Latimer ....."*I have only thought necessary to write three of the seven letters I Intended and I desire Bladen may carry those ....."*    Dated: 18th March 1680/1[2]

Two further letters from the British Library are dated two years later from Thomas Knox to Lord Danby. Danby was still in the Tower and Knox had been tried and convicted for his part of the sub-plot, spent one year in jail and had then been banished from the country. The first letter does not state his location but the second one was from Paris. In the first letter dated 6 April 1681 Knox said *"I little thought, when I went so legally to have those punish who durst to treat so villainously with majestie and conspire ye ruine to be first rewarded with a prison and now with a more cruel banishment"*. Then, in reference to Danby's opponents he said, *"if my blood could but atone their fury I do protest by all that's good I would yet sacrifice it all for your Lordship's service"*.[3]

In a final letter, dated 16th April 1681, some ten days later, Knox described to Danby how isolated he felt in France *"I am here lookt upon as a spy of your Lordship"*, yet whilst he was *"in London thought an agent of the Papists"* during the Exclusion Crisis.

---

[1] Add MS28049 ff24 & 25, ©The British Library Board
[2] Letter Earl of Danby to son Viscount Latimer refers to Bladen carrying letters for the Earl. Dated 18th March 1680/1. 29th April 1683. Nathaniel Bladen and Edward Osborne, Viscount Latimer (1655-1686) from The Danby Papers
[3] Add MS28049 ff196 ©The British Library Board

It is possible that Knox was making a veiled attempt to extract money from Danby in this letter when he said *"And since I had more courage than out of fear to turn villain so I hope I have more grace then for a pension to sell my Master"*. On appeal Danby was finally released.

Whilst Danby was incarcerated, Nathaniel had a different problem of his own to deal with when his mother-in-law, Lady Frances Fairfax, brought a Bill of Complaint entitled Fairfax & Topham v Wrightson & Bladen. That is to say, Lady Fairfax and William Topham (Fairfax family chaplain) versus Robert Wrightson (attorney and guardian) and son-in-law Nathaniel Bladen. The inspiration for this legal challenge was Lady Fairfax's discovery that her attempt to install a new vicar at Hemsworth had failed when she consulted the church diocesan records and found Wrightson's previously lodged claim. The cat was out of the bag!

Now that the truth was out in the open about the Hemsworth advowson, Lady Fairfax was livid. Whilst her anger stemmed from her belief that she was the owner and holder of the advowson, her deposition expanded to include everything that she felt aggrieved about, including the choice of Nathaniel to be her son-in-law. This would seem to confirm that the quid pro quo was between Bladen/Topham, with Lady Fairfax being sidelined regarding daughter Isabella's marriage. So she took the opportunity to also air her grievance on Bladen's financial status which, she claimed, had been misrepresented to her at the time. In fact, of course, her co-plaintiff Topham had sole jurisdiction in that matter and he had consented to the match. In addressing this specific issue, Nathaniel's friend Wrightson would later say *"the marriage took effect much to the surprise of the Defendant Bladen who never had, as he informed this Defendant* [Wrightson]*, but such promise in money"*.[1]

Her first accusation was that Nathaniel Bladen *"was but an infant"* when he sold the Hemsworth advowson to Wrightson. By that she meant he was not 21 years old, but that argument was successfully counteracted by evidence being produced from the parish registers to show that Nathaniel was over 21 years of age by some months at the time. The Lord Abp of York was consulted, as was the parish clerk who kept the register of births to obtain evidence of Nathaniel's birth date and this appeared to confirm to the Abp's satisfaction, that Nathaniel was in fact over 21 years at the time of both the exercise of the advowson and the Bladen-Wrightson deed of transfer of other property that Bladen held and they were therefore legal transactions.

Her second statement, that in 1666 she had paid Bladen a sum of money to pass over the advowson to her was denied and thirdly that Nathaniel's finances had been misrepresented to her, this was likewise refuted. The fourth issue she raised was that Wrightson's acquisition of Nathaniel's assets had denied her grandchildren their rightful inheritance. Wrightson's response to this was to claim that he had paid far more than the market price for those assets and had done so in order to render assistance to Bladen.

Whilst all these were issues that no doubt irked Lady Fairfax, none had in the past tempted her to bring legal action. It was the advowson that troubled her most as she most probably felt it impacted her own high status.

---

[1] TNA: C10/142/2 Fairfax & Topham v Wrightson & Bladen, 1681

Those with the power over advowsons were usually the Lords of the Manor, certainly the highest status individual in the area, which Lady Fairfax no doubt believed herself to be. Fairfax felt the loss of control for herself and her Bladen descendants. She claimed that Wrightson had exploited Bladen in his youth for his own advantage and that, as an Attorney at Law many years Nathaniel's senior, he only took on unofficial 'guardianship' of Nathaniel because he wanted something in return. He knew full well the value of Nathaniel's inherited assets, that he wished to obtain them for himself and that such support as he did give Nathaniel was sourced from the young man's own property rental income. Reference was made to an Indenture Wrightson had Bladen sign at Godmanchester, Huntingdon in Cambridge, by which Nathaniel acknowledged an indebtedness to Wrightson which would be repaid by Wrightson acquiring Bladen's property.

Lady Fairfax further claimed that Nathaniel had been told by Wrightson that Robert (Nathaniel's grandfather) had *"bound himself to the value of 500 Marks in bonds or feudal ties, and to avoid all fines had bound not just himself but his heirs too"*. This directly links back to the two leases that his grandfather Robert had entered into with Richard Berry and the allegation that Wrightson advised Nathaniel to convey away all the messuages lands and tenements he had in Wakefield to be free of this 'inherited' bond. To his credit, Nathaniel vehemently supported and was loyal to his friend Wrightson in direct opposition to his mother-in-law. Wrightson, in reply, muddied the waters by suggesting that the advowson was actually only given to Nathaniel's grandfather Robert Bladen in trust from Sir Richard Gargrave, Lord of the Manor of Hemsworth, and that the Gargraves themselves possibly had some claim to part of the title. Perhaps, like his grandfather Robert before him (with Berry), Nathaniel with Wrightson had put his faith in the wrong person.

The Answer to the Bill of Complaint referred to Nathaniel's property and lands in Wakefield having been inherited from his grandfather Bladen but also referred to property he inherited from his grandfather Birkhead (Birkett) at Haworth consisting of a lease for 44 years which expired about the time that Nathaniel came of age. The agreement for the sale of the advowson, between the two friends, was produced for the Court's consideration ..... "To produce to this Honourable Court, under the Defendant Bladen's hand and seal in these words .... *'know all men by these presents that I Nathaniel Bladen of the Inner Temple London, gent, hath made and before sealing hereof, at the hands of Robert Wrightson, gent, the sum of £10 in full satisfaction and payment of all sums of money to me payable for the sale of an advowson or right of patronage into the church of Hemsworth in the County of York, and I the said Nathaniel Bladen doth by these presents and my heirs devise for this quit claim to Robert Wrightson and his heirs all the right title interest claim demand whatsoever now and hereafter might or ought to have of in or to the said advowson or right of presentation. In witness whereof I have hereunto put by hand and seal the twentieth day of February in the twentieth year of Charles the Second of England, King, 1668'.*"[1] Curiously the formal agreement bears the date 1668, some years after Bladen and Wrightson claimed to have transferred patronage. Still the existence of the agreement made nonsense of Lady Fairfax's allegations of 1680 since she was unable to provide evidence of handing money over to Bladen in 1666.

---

[1] TNA: C10/142/2 Fairfax & Topham v Wrightson and Bladen, Yorkshire 1681

In his answers, Wrightson on the one hand stated that it was an act of charity to help the orphaned young man, but other answers seemed to hint at him expecting repayment at some time. He stated ..... *"this Defendant was not only well satisfied on the security of his money but did continue to pay and support the said Bladen until such time as the said Bladen would find some way to pay and discharge"* - which sounds like a loan with the expectation of repayment, rather than charity.[1]

So was Wrightson a generous benefactor, or slippery attorney? Would he have supported this young man for so long if Bladen had not such valuable assets is open to question, especially as Wrightson did eventually acquire those assets and, of course, Bladen's own promise to repay Wrightson for all the trouble he had gone to. Many years later the issue of the patronage of Hemsworth Church was again raised. In letters between Nathaniel's daughter Frances and her attorney Francis Taylor it appeared that Taylor and 'Mr Fairfax'[2] had gone through some papers and seen reference to the advowson. By this time only one of the individuals involved in the dispute was still alive, Topham now the parson of Bilborough. Colonel Martin Bladen, after his father's death, had taken hold of his father's papers at Hemsworth but by this time Martin's career was flourishing in Parliament and he was not present in Yorkshire to deal with matters, so Frances had sought her attorney's advice on the matter. Taylor briefly referred to Lady Fairfax's holding of the patronage and wrote to ask if Frances knew how that came into Bladen's hands and who had held the advowson prior to Lady Fairfax. A further letter asked *"What progress have you made about the advowson of Hemsworth? Remember Mr Topham is both old and infirm."* So the assumption is that Frances had been asked to look into the matter and, as Topham was the only party still alive, the attorney was urging caution considering the man's age.

Wrightson, it has to be said, became involved in numerous chancery cases all involving his acquisition of property and land:

1669    Naylor v Wrightson reference property in South Elmsall, Yorkshire
1681    Fairfax & Topham v Wrightson and Bladen, Yorkshire 1681
1690    Wentworth v Wrightson, reference property in Hemsworth, North Elmsall and South Kirkby
1699    Byfeild v Wrightson, reference moiety of the Rectory at Thorpe Arch, Yorkshire

The Wentworth v Wrightson case[3] was brought by Sir William Wentworth and Robert Monckton who were both descendants of Sir Thomas Wentworth and it was their claim that, through inheritance, they were co-heirs and entitled to a list of properties in Hemsworth, North Emsall and Kirkby which were held by Robert Wrightson. In his Answer to the Bill of Complaint, Robert claimed to have purchased the properties in 1656 for the sum of £228 with Indenture from Thomas Harper, gent, who held the title at that time. Very much like Berry, Wrightson took care of the paper trail for his property acquisitions.

---

[1] TNA: C10/142/2 Fairfax & Topham v Wrightson & Bladen 1681
[2] Cousin to the Bladens - possibly Bryan Fairfax 1676-1749, son of Bryan
[3] TNA: C5/194/49 Wentworth v Wrightson 1690

*1680: Funeral payment*
On 9th March 1680 Nathaniel's name appears in the official records (as Nath Bladon) as having received 120 Marks to pay the expenses for the funeral of the Earl of Plymouth. As previously mentioned, one of the illegitimate sons of King Charles was married to Danby's daughter (Countess of Plymouth) and, when the son died in 1680 at the age of just 23 years, the King paid Bladen for the cost of the funeral.[1] As part of his service to the Osborne family, Nathaniel carried out duties as the daughter's steward also.

*1681 - Treasury Receiver*
In February 1681 Nathaniel's appointment to the Treasury as Auditor of Imprests as a Receiver for arrears, concealments and embezzlements of prize ships and goods was renewed. This was covering the period of the two previous 17th century Dutch Wars and concerned goods taken into the ports of London, Portsmouth and Hull. He was joined in this appointment by Charles Osborne (Danby's brother), Henry Fanshawe (Danby's 'henchman'),[2] James Syms, Joseph Embreys and Henry Neville.[3] The connections Bladen made in the Treasury were to be useful to him in the ensuing years in using his influence to obtain lucrative posts for his two sons.

*1680 Paper Chase*
Nathaniel had a finger in many pies and, like his grandfather, was constantly on the look-out for opportunities to advance his personal fortune. One venture he got involved with was in purchasing from the King letters patent for the manufacture of white paper. Most paper in England, prior to 1675, was imported from abroad but a man called Eustace Barnaby had obtained a Royal Patent in 1675 for: *'the art and skill of making all sorts of white paper for the use of writing and printing, being a new manufacture never practised in any our Kingdom or dominions'*.[4] Nathaniel, along with a group of other investors in 1680, had obtained a similar patent for *'an engine method and mill whereby hemp, flax, lynnen, cotton, cordage, silk, woollen and all sorts of materials may be made into paper and pasteboard'*.[5] Barnaby had a paper mill at Stanwell in Middlesex and enjoyed some success with his venture, at least for a little while.

---

[1] 'Moneys Received and Paid for Secret Services of Charles II and James II from 30 March 1679 to 25 December 1688', by John Y Akerman, 1820. These funds were part of the Crown accounts called 'secret services' and which comprised of extraordinary expenses of the King's private estate or payments to private persons for services rendered to the Crown

[2] Henry Fanshawe 1634-85 was son of Thomas Fanshawe of Dengie Hall, Essex. He is described in 'The House of Commons 1660-90, Vol. 1, by Basil Duke Henning as Danby's 'Henchman' who visited Danby in the Tower during the Exclusion Crisis. Surveyor and Receiver of Greenwax fines 1677-9, commissioner for excise appeals -85, Registrar to King's remembrance in the Exchequer, MP Penryn

[3] CTB, 1681-85 Vol. 7

[4] The Educational Encyclopedia of Common Things by Richard Linthicum, 1903. Patent was dated 1675 for Eustace Barnaby

[5] Industries of Scotland: their rise progress and present condition by David Bremner. 1869

Then in 1682[1] Nathaniel[2] bought another patent from King James II, this time just in his own name, for *'the sole power, privilege and authority of making, sizing and complexly finishing all sorts of writing and print paper'* - a variation on Barnaby's original patent.

Nathaniel had been acquainted with a man called Henry Million,[3] a stationer in London who was overseer at Barnaby's mill and introduced him to Barnaby. Soon after, both Barnaby and Bladen were persuaded to sign over their patents to the (later infamous) Lady Theodosia Ivy (Barnaby being Ivy's agent).[4] Along with Nathaniel, Christopher Jackson bought another paper-related patent in 1684, this is the same Jackson mentioned elsewhere in this book who was related to Lady Frances Fairfax (Nathaniel's mother-in-law). Both Jackson and Bladen would later be co-defendants in a case brought by Mary Buckingham (daughter of 3rd Lord Fairfax) when they were jointly accused of mismanaging her affairs and defrauding her.

*Lady Theodosia Ivy (Ivie) 1623-1695*
Once again, Nathaniel Bladen managed to put his faith in the wrong person, in fact not just his faith but his money. Lady Theodosia Ivy's place in history is as a forger of legal documents. Thomas Neale, referred to elsewhere in this book, her opponent in chancery, called her "*The Late Lady Ivy, so many years famous for wit, beauty and cunning in law above any*".[5] The Lady in question was born Theodosia Stepkins[6] in 1623 and married three times. Firstly to Mr Garrett who died within a few years, at which point Theodosia's father arranged for her to meet Mr Anthony Browne of Weldhall in Essex who her father intended to be her second husband. Mr Browne, however, had consumed too much alcohol before their meeting and vomited in Theodosia's lap and his proposal was, not surprisingly, refused.

When the next suitor was presented by her father it was done so in terms of an ultimatum, that she accept him or her father would throw her out of the house.[7] Thomas Ivy (one time Governor of Madras and some twenty years her senior) was to become her third husband. They married and he settled a substantial sum on Theodosia's family, including, at his death, land in Wapping. The marriage quickly ran into difficulties as Theodosia went on a spending spree with Thomas's money and he was pursued by creditors. In an attempt to regain control of the finances, Thomas decided to relocate the family away from London but Theodosia resisted and the marriage began to fall apart. Both took steps to secure marital separation by petitioning Parliament for a private act to be passed, Thomas even corresponded in the 1650s with Cromwell on the matter, producing a pamphlet 'Alimony Arraign'd'.

---

[1] Patent No. 220 of 1682
[2] Company members: Nathaniel Bladen, John Dunston, Nicholas Dupin, John Briscoe, Adam de Cardonnel, Peter de Lanney, Elias de Grundy, Louise Gleurie, Richard Sprigg, Claude Bordiers, Henry Longueville, Paul Duplin, Robert Hill, Robert Shales and Abraham Wessell
[3] Henry Million, stationer, wrote his Will 1717, probate 1720
[4] Economic History Series Vol. 1, 1964
[5] Cited in: Early Modern Whale: The interesting Career of Lady Theodosia Ivy. http://roy25booth.blogspot.co.uk/2009_03_01_archive.html, Thursday 26th March 2009
[6] Ibid
[7] The Study of Six Criminal Women by Elizabeth Jenkins, 1949

Theodosia responded furiously and accused her husband of a host of appalling acts: that he made their servant pregnant, that he infected her with a disease, that he was violent to her, assaulted and deserted her. Theodosia was victorious in the chancery proceedings and Thomas was required to pay her £300 per year alimony. Thomas, for his part, still wished to have her back as his wife, even when she laughed mockingly at him in front of the Judge. A little later Thomas received a knighthood and Theodosia decided she liked the idea of being Lady Ivy and the couple got back together. He generously settled Malmesbury Abbey on her when Theodosia produced their daughter, but by 1669 his money had again been squandered and Sir Thomas attempted to retrench to London but, again, Theodosia refused to move. Thomas died in 1673 and so, then, began the battle for control of his estate. As per her marriage settlement, Theodosia claimed ownership of Thomas's land in Wapping which comprised of two leases: the other part being held by a Thomas Neale. Neale's lease included land owned by St Paul's but Lady Ivy disputed that ownership, saying that a portion of 7.5 acres belonged to her and she produced title deeds for it. Situated on this land was a Mill (thought to be a paper mill), and it was the use of the Mill that brought Lady Ivy into contact with Nathaniel Bladen in respect of his patent for the manufacture of white paper.[1]

The dispute between Ivy and Neale went to chancery and Ivy produced her title deeds - except, of course, they were not real - Lady Ivy had the deeds forged. Nathaniel Bladen and Eustace Barnaby had sold their white paper patents to Lady Ivy[2] and, in Nathaniel's case, this transaction involved Nathaniel acquiring Colnett's Mill from Ivy. Colnett being worth more than the transaction, Nathaniel made up the difference by giving Ivy £2,000. An Indenture Tripartite was drawn up in 1684:

Indenture Tripartite
Parties of the 1st Part:       Lady Theodosia Ivy
                               John Stepkins (the elder)
                               James Bryant's deceased estate (Lady Ivy's last husband)
Parties of the 2nd Part:       Thomas Coleman of St Andrew's Holborn - his widow
                               Sarah Coleman
Parties of the 3rd Part:       Nathaniel Bladen

Lady Ivy used the services of a man called Duffet to 'create' deeds for her. Duffet had produced documents for Sir Thomas Ivy in the past and used them as a template to produce fictitious title deeds for Lady Ivy. The initial chancery case found in her favour in 1683 after which she married for the third time to a Mr Bryan but by 1684 Mr Bryan was dead. That same year the chancery suit of 1683 was appealed.

---

[1] Mill for making paper and pasteboard. British Patent Number 220 published 10th July 1682 - Nathaniel Bladen

[2] A Chronology and Calendar of Documents Relating to the London Book Trade 1641-1700 by Donald Francis McKenzie and Maureen Bell, 2005. In 1690 on 28th March, the Governor and Company of White Paper Makers petitioned the Government for a Bill to Encourage Better Manufacturing of White Paper in England. On 31st March the Bill had its first reading. 3rd April was the 2nd reading, when it was referred to Committee. 15th April, Lady Ivy petitioned the Committee to be heard stating that she had purchased patents in 1682 from Eustace Barnaby and Nathaniel Bladen which were not expired. Existing paper makers (100 mills and 1,000 families) feared a new monopoly would put them out of business

The matter came before 'Hanging Judge' Justice George Jeffreys who ascertained the true title of the land as it became clear that Lady Ivy's papers were a forgery. The styling of the letters and form of legal address were not consistent with legal practise of the time. In order to make documents appear to be of the Tudor era Duffet added saffron to the ink, rubbed the document on a dirty old window, exposed it to strong sunlight and then carried it is his pocket for some time - to give the document 'age'. The Judge found against Lady Ivy in 1684[1] and ordered that she be prosecuted. All of which makes Bladen's dealings with her curious, as a lawyer himself he must have been aware that Judge Jeffreys had ordered her prosecution for falsifying Deeds. Ivy was again tried in the courts in 1686 but was acquitted and maintained till her death in 1695[2] that the Wapping land was hers by right.[3]

Some of Lady Ivy's other cases in Chancery:-

| 1673 | Ivy -v- Bateman, Sir Anthony |
| 1684 | Mossam -v- Dame Theodosia Ivy[4] |
| 1684 | Thomas Neale -v- Ivy (Attempts her greatest legal coup re lands in Wapping - Judge Jeffreys - took the case)[5] |

Bladen then spent the next 14 years trying to get his £2,000 back from different people. The first party Lady Ivy died, the second party Thomas Coleman died and interest then passed to his widow. When Sarah Coleman the widow died interest past to her relations and so on until finally in 1699 Nathaniel brought the matter to chancery in attempt to claim off Lady Ivy's personal estate. Although he did receive some income from Lady Ivy in the form of interest on the £2,000, it is unlikely he received one penny of the capital sum of £2,000. Those who had subsequently acquired an interest in the mortgaged Mill property, which included an attorney at law, were - according to Nathaniel's deposition in 1699 - attempting to impoverish the property to deliberately prevent him recouping anything from it.

---

[1] Study of Six Criminal Women by Elizabeth Jenkins, 1949
[2] The Lady Ivie's Trial: for the great part of Shadwell in the county of Middlesex before Lord Chief Justice Jeffreys in 1684 (Oxford 1929)
[3] http://www.mernick.org.uk/thhol/shadwell.html
[4] Cobbett's Complete Collection of State Trials and Proceedings, Vol. 7, by Thomas Bayly Howell, William Cobbett, David Jardine State Trials, p571
[5] "Between the years 1678 and 1684 the Lady Ivy, formerly Theodosia Bryan, was alternately Plaintiff and Defendant in a series of trials in which she was trying to establish a claim against the Dean and Chapter of St Paul's for a considerable and very valuable tract of land in Shadwell, how in the last of those trials, presided over by L.C.J. Jeffreys, it was proved up to the hilt that the deeds upon which she based her claim were forgeries executed under her orders; and how, after an information for perjury and forgery was issued against her, she disappeared completely". Transcript in Cobbett's Complete Collection of State Trials and Proceedings

*1686 - Countess of Plymouth*

Nathaniel continued to divide his time between Yorkshire and London[1] and had, for some time, been working for Danby's daughter Lady Bridget Osborne, the Countess of Plymouth. As previously mentioned, her young husband had died and the King had paid for his funeral. He had died of dysentery in Tangier where he had been head of a Regiment of Foot.[2] Nathaniel was now her Steward, probably in addition to his duties for Danby and Latimer, and had responsibility for keeping her accounts in order, receiving rents and paying her bills etc.

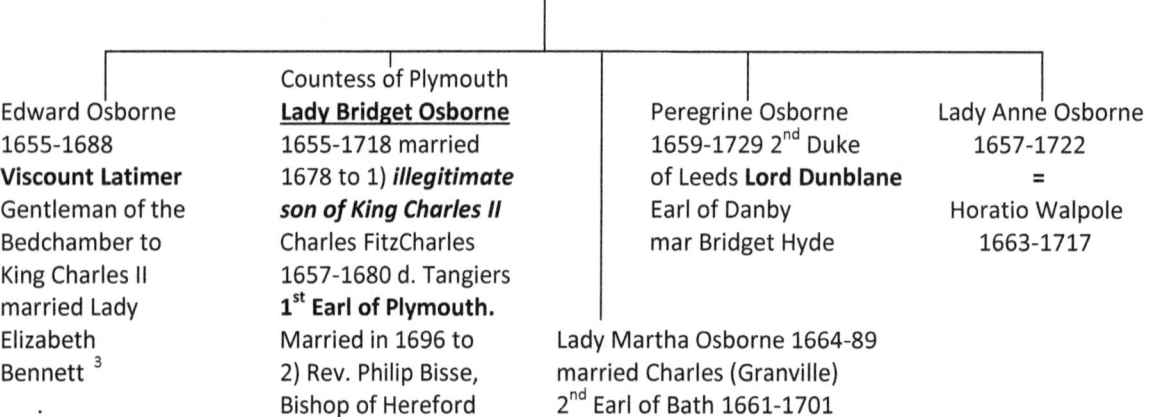

All appeared to be going well in the early years until 1686 when there was an incident which would lead to a series of dramatic events. As previously outlined, Bladen pursued his own interests in addition to acting as Steward to various members of the Osborne family but the two interests clashed on 20th August 1686. The Countess, on that particular day, had need of her Steward's services but he was absent. She wanted to see a reckoning of her accounts and had spotted a Deed amongst Bladen's papers at the desk he used at her house. The Deed was for a large sum of money, £2,000 to Lady Theodosia Ivy. On seeing this, the Countess jumped to the conclusion that Bladen, who was paid a modest stipend in her service, was stealing her money.

---

[1] The 1683 rate books for Westminster show him as residing at Duke Street, St James, Piccadilly Westminster (Highway Rates 1683-93, folio 11. He was at Gardiners Lane on 28 May 1684 and 25 March 1685) but, in addition, he had premises around the corner in Gardiner's Lane - this was probably where his lawyer's practice was based for which he paid 5 shillings per quarter. The annual assessment for 1683 shows him having 15 shillings but that he was 5 shillings in arrears. His domestic residence in Duke Street must have been of some style, if his neighbours were any measure, as he had the Right Honourable Lord Willoughby as an immediate neighbour and, a few houses along the street, the Countess of Plymouth, (Westminster Rate Books - Poor Rate and Oversears Account, 1683: 196, 201, 299-302. Folios 10, 18 and 19. Highway Rates, Folio 13 for 1686). By 1686 he was at the same address but only paying 2/- 6d and the Countess of Plymouth had gone

[2] CTB, Vol. 7, 1681-85. On 25th April 1681 Nathaniel was mentioned in Treasury documents whereby a George Beare and Thomas Thornton et al had presented a Petition regarding monies owed to them by the late Earl of Plymouth who, apparently before departing for Tangiers, had promised to pay Beare and Thornton 1,194 Marks and, after news of his death reached them, the men petitioned the Treasury and Nathaniel Bladen as Steward for restitution

[3] Marriage Settlement 29 September 1674, Hull University Archives UDDEV/21/47

She believed he was taking in her money from rents, not been keeping a proper tally and then used her money for his own investments, all without her knowledge. In other words, that he was an embezzler. When explanations were later made, Nathaniel would claim that on the 20th August he was away in Southampton conducting business for another of his clients and did not return home until 26th August and had never used her money for his own purposes, had always provided good accounts and denied any wrong-doing.

Both the Countess and the Bladens resided (in separate town houses) at Duke Street in London. Immediately Nathaniel returned home on the 26th, at 11 o'clock at night, visitors came knocking on his door with orders to take him to the Countess. Nathaniel later described how he was taken to a room in her house, locked inside and then the Countess and her brother Viscount Latimer entered the room and challenged him over her accounts. Not succeeding in getting him to admit to any embezzlement, they left the room which was locked behind them and Nathaniel was left there alone for hours. Sometime later a group of men, including Danby's son Latimer, entered the room to challenge Bladen once more and they threatened to cut his throat if he did not give them satisfactory answers. During the early hours of the next morning the same people went to Nathaniel's home and demanded from his family the locked secretaire and trunk containing all his papers, accounts letters etc to take to the Countess's house. That being done, the Countess presented the key to the locked cabinets to Nathaniel and asked him to unlock the same and show her the accounts. She was being careful not to break the law by forcibly breaking open his property or gaining access without his permission and was seeking to coerce him to do it himself. He refused.

Nathaniel was kept prisoner inside the Countess's house for many days until finally on 2nd September, he managed to escape and fled to Wallingford House (site of the present Admiralty building) nearby, where his Fairfax relation the Duchess of Buckingham lived, and asked for her protection. The Buckinghams were neighbours of the Osbornes/Countess of Plymouth in Yorkshire and the Duchess being at home at the time *"thought fit and did send to His Majesty's Guards for a file, or other party of Musqueteers or soldiers for the better security of her house"*.[1] Predictably and swiftly the Countess of Plymouth's people arrived and made a raucous noise outside Wallingford House demanding Bladen's return.

Frustrated in their attempts to get hold of Bladen they tried a different tactic. On the 9th September the Earl of Danby petitioned the King on the matter but no assistance was forthcoming from that quarter,[2] *"My Lord of Danby hath been here with the King to desire his protection towards his daughter, my Lady Plymouth, in a business between her and one that was her steward, one Bladen, whom she accuses to have run away with 2,000 l. of her money, and hath been sheltered since in Wallingford House by the Duchess of Buckingham, a relation of whose he had married"*. Finally, on 21st September, the Countess put a large notice in the London Gazette (one of the official journals of record for the British Government) in a move clearly designed to inflict the maximum possible embarrassment on Bladen.

---

[1] [Countess of] Plymouth v Bladen 3 Nov 1686. TNA: C9/117/25 and TNA: C6/258/78 dated 1687
[2] Also quoted in the Royal Commission on Historical Manuscripts, report Vol. 31, p455, 1912

**Advertisement**

*Whereas Nathaniel Bladen, Steward to the Countess Dowager of Plymouth, did on the 3rd of this Instant September, Run away from her Service with Two Thousand pounds of her Ladiships Mony in his Custody. These are to give Notice, That if any Body shall discover the said Bladen to the said Countess, who lives in Duke Street, West-Minster, so that he shall be arrested, and taken into Custody, they shall immediately receive a Reward of 100 l. from the said Countess, for their so doing.[1]*

The advertisement had an immediate effect because on that same day 21st September, Bladen found himself in Southwark Debtors' Prison and by 30th October he was in Court. Nathaniel was, however, defiant and asked the Court for time to prepare his defence, for which he was granted ten days, and also stated that he intended to bring counter-charges against the Countess for theft and trespass.

After Nathaniel had been locked up in the Marshalsea in Southwark for some time the Countess then sent one of her servants to him, inviting him to unlock the trunks so she could see his papers/vouchers and she would arrange his freedom, which he again refused to do. Nathaniel's length of imprisonment is not known exactly but may not have been too long as he was referred to as being at Appleton in Yorkshire [Nunappleton] by November when Admiral Robert Fairfax,[2] his wife's nephew, in a letter to a family member said Nathaniel has "absconded himself in Appleton House".[3] Admiral Fairfax was based in Wapping in the period 1686-7 receiving instruction on navigation from John Colson of Marsh Yard who was considered the best instructor in those days and may very well have been familiar with the trials of Lady Ivy and her claim of holding land in Wapping. Robert Fairfax is mentioned frequently in Nathaniel's letters and he was instrumental in assisting Frances Harman/Hamond when she was having difficulties with her Ham[m]ond husband and his family.

By 13th November Bladen was back in London, appearing before Judge Jeffreys, who was also a resident of Duke Street and would hold his cases in a room attached to the side of his house. The course of law proceeded with claim and counter-claim running into 1687 but the Countess was repeatedly non-suited and her cause was a lost one. The sums claimed by the Countess that were embezzled seemed to vary with each legal challenge, but in her last one she alleged that Nathaniel handled some £18,704 of her money of which £4,500 was never passed on to her. In relation to Bladen's torrid time, the following letter was written by Admiral Fairfax to his mother advising caution against his sisters' gossiping on the matter:- *"My dear Mother, I am very sorry to hear the news I hear tonight of my uncle Bladen. He has had a letter from my grandmother, being an account of his being fled from hence and absconding himself in Appleton House; wherein she writes that John Rennison (a farmer at Bilbrough) was the first raiser of the report, and brought it to your house, and that two of my sisters, which of them it was I do not know, being at Steeton, told my grandmother and put her into a great fright.*

---

[1] The London Gazette, Issue 2170, p2, dated 2nd September 1686 (though relates to 21st September)
[2] Had a house at Searle Street near to St Clement Dane Church and the Temple Church. The house was at the corner of Cook Court, facing Lincoln's Inn Law Court
[3] The Life Admiral Robert Fairfax of Steeton, Clements R. Markham, 1885

*Now my uncle is very much displeased, though I told him my sisters could not possibly be so ungrateful, much more my sister Betty (Elizabeth), who he hath been so kind to, and on that he hath spoke so kindly of her. It must be ignorance in them to relate such a thing, not knowing any certainty. Of it he saith he must use humanity to all people, and never expect any civility. Pray let my sisters know they must be cautious how they say anything at Steeton, for a hundred to one it is made twice as much of as it is. I love my sisters so much that I am concerned that they should be so indiscreet as be seen in such a thing as this. They must be very cautious as times are now, for the world is apt to relate any idle story again that they hear, for them that use it never want trouble. ....."*    Ro. Fairfax (London)[1]

It is curious that Plaintiff, Defendant and Judge should all be neighbours in Duke Street near St James's Park in London. The Judge's large property was added to and architect Sir Christopher Wren[2] was employed to do the work. Jeffreys extended his house to incorporate a wing which he used for chancery cases. Jekyl, Master of the Rolls, summarised this case in the register books viz: *"the defendant was the plaintiff's steward, and the bill was brought for an account.[3] Defendant pleaded that the plaintiff had imprisoned him, and upon promise of his liberty had got a trunk in which were all his vouchers, insisting that though he kept the key, yet it was easy to be opened and that it was to be presumed it had been so; and it was impossible for him to prove what the plaintiff had taken out, or to account without his vouchers. This plea was argued, and ordered to stand for an answer. Afterwards, by an interlocutory order, the trunk was directed to be delivered to the usher of the court, and upon hearing of the cause the then lords commissioners decreed the defendant to account, and ordered the trunk to be brought before the master, who was to open it in the presence of both parties, and they to have copies of the papers found in it, as they should think fit; in this case the court would not presume material papers, or even a suppression of any such, though it should seem that the trunk was got by the plaintiff in a very unwarrantable manner; and only took the best care they could, that the papers, whatever they were, should be produced."*[4] In February 1687, Hilary Term, the Countess again brought action against Bladen, despite having failed on the same charge previously. Her lawyer said, in response to Bladen's claim that he had been imprisoned ..... *"And touching the Plaintiff's imprisoning the Defendant, he may take his remedy by an action of 'False Imprisonment', but a man may surely justify the detaining of his servant, that was taking away his goods"*. The court found in Bladen's favour again.

Bladen argued that the Countess had no legal power to force him to open his own property and her agents acted illegally in imprisoning him against his will, threatening to cut his throat and take his property without his consent. He knew the Law had no power to force him to open his secretaire and trunk containing papers without his consent, which he repeatedly refused to give. In his answers Bladen indicated that after the Countess's actions were non-suited that he was about to commence counter proceedings against her.

---

[1] Life of Admiral Robert Fairfax of Steeton, Clements R. Markham, 1885
[2] 'Warrants etc.: May 1699, 1-10', *CTB, Vol. 14: 1698-1699* (1934), pp. 330-346. URL: http://www.british-history.ac.uk/report.aspx?compid=83015 Date accessed: 15 July 2012
[3] An Abridgement of the Modern Determinations of the Courts of Law Vol. 2
[4] 2 Wms's Rep. 681, 682. Also reported in 2 Vern. 32

This may have induced her to bring a halt to proceedings as her evidence never reached the required standard.[1] Final resolution of these actions by the Countess culminated in her seeking leave to dismiss her own Bill with costs ......."*Where there has been a proceeding in the cause which has given the defendant a right against the plaintiff*" to save herself from counter-action.[2]

### 1680s: Duke and Duchess of Buckingham

As mentioned earlier, when Nathaniel escaped from imprisonment by the Countess of Plymouth, he went straight to Wallingford House for refuge, the home of the Duke and Duchess of Buckingham, his wife's Fairfax relations who he also worked for. Precisely how long Bladen had worked for the Buckinghams is not known but it could have been any time from his marriage in 1668 over the next 19 years. The Duke engaged other near relations to work for him, such as Bryan Fairfax (1633-1711) who was Buckingham's agent. This is the same Bryan Fairfax who took the message to General George Monck (at Coldstream) which brought about the Restoration of Charles II. Bryan and his sons Bryan, Ferdinand and Charles were all particularly close to the Bladen family and are mentioned frequently in this book and the companion book Martin Bladen: A Biography.

After the Duke's death in 1687 Nathaniel was engaged to audit the Duchess's accounts for her estates in Bolton Percy, Hasleton, Nunappleton and Bilborough[3] and he attended the couple at Cleveden, their mansion house near Maidstone. Their Yorkshire estates would also have been managed by Bladen but their steward for collecting rents in Yorkshire was Christopher Jackson, who has already been mentioned in this book, as he was a Fairfax relation and was a tenant of Lady (Chaloner) Fairfax. He got involved in the same white paper patent fiasco as Nathaniel and, along with Bladen, was jointly accused later by the Duchess of mismanaging her business affairs and fraud.

The nature of Bladen's association with the Duke of Buckingham is far more mysterious if Nathaniel's comments are to be believed. In a deposition in 1694, when the widowed Duchess of Buckingham raised a bill of complaint against Nathaniel and Christopher Jackson, Bladen responded by stating that the "*the Duke made this defendant great acknowledgement and promises and that he owed his life and honour to this defendant*". This, together with Bladen's choice of language he subsequently used when describing how he helped Buckingham with his "*many incumbrances, obstructions and entanglements*", suggests Bladen may have also had some involvement in organising the Duke's complicated private life and extra-marital relations, maybe even some supporting role or involvement in the fatal duel that the Duke fought with the Earl of Shrewsbury.

---

[1] Federal Reports, Vol. 4
[2] 1687 Hillary Term: Case 24. Eq.Ca.Ab.11.pl.3.S.C. Eodem die. In Court: A dismission upon an election to proceed at law is not peremptory but the plaintiff may, after she has failed at law, bring a new Bill. Cases Argued and Adjudged in the High Court of Chancery, Vol. 1, Thomas Vernon, John Raithby
[3] TNA: C9/245/17 Buckingham v Bladen, dated 1694. Duchess of Buckingham v Nathaniel Bladen and Christopher Jackson

Although the Duke of Buckingham spent the final two years of his life in Yorkshire, the couple lived at Cliveden, near Maidstone, in the sprawling mansion that the Duke had commissioned and seemed not to have resided at Nunappleton, the Duchess's home that she inherited from her father, 3rd Lord Thomas Fairfax. Bladen observed that the Duchess had many times stated that she had no desire to ever reside there.

*Decline of the Fairfaxes*
Just a few years before Nathaniel married into the Fairfax family, Nunappleton had seemed to be at the very epicentre of national events. From this Fairfax residence letters were sent to General George Monck which put in motion events that would lead to the Restoration of the Monarchy. *"Messengers and petitions of all sorts were daily arriving"*[1] but Nunappleton's decline began in its owner's final years before he died in 1671. Nathaniel, marrying into the family in 1668, would have closely observed the changes as there was one set-back after another as the family barely had time to recover from one lot of death duties when another occurred in quick succession:-

- 1665 Death of 3rd Lord Fairfax's wife Anne
- 1671 Death of 3rd Lord Fairfax died on 12th November
- 1687 Death of Duke of Buckingham[2] (married to Lord Fairfax's daughter)
- 1688 Death of 4th Lord Fairfax
- 1691 Death of Isabella Bladen (née Fairfax)
- 1692 Death of Lady Frances Fairfax (Nathaniel's mother in law)
- 1704 Death of Mary, Duchess of Buckingham[3] 20th October 1704, aged 66 yrs[4]
- 1710 Death of 5th Lord Fairfax
- 1711 Nun Appleton (sale forced by creditors) sold to Alderman Milner of Leeds[5]

After his wife's death in 1665 (after 28 years of marriage) 3rd Lord Fairfax was confined to a wheelchair for the next five years (suffering from gout and war wounds). During these last years, his daughter and sole heir Mary, 'little Moll', would not visit him. Lord Fairfax was reported to have written to an unknown woman who advised him his daughter was residing in France.[6] His daughter's marriage to George Villiers, 2nd Duke of Buckingham in 1657 seems to have sealed the family's fate. It is hard to overstate just how far the power and influence of this branch of the Fairfax family declined after the years when Nathaniel Bladen married into the family.

---

[1] Lower Wharfedale: Being a Complete Account of the History, Antiquities and Scenery of the Picturesque Valley of the Wharfe, from Cawood to Arthington by Harry Speight, 1902
[2] The Duke of Buckingham (son-in-law to Lord Fairfax) had given King Charles II the white horse he used for his coronation
[3] Four Ainsty Townships: The history of Bolton Percy, Appleton Roebuck, Colton and Steeton 1066-1875
[4] Lower Wharfedale: Being a Complete Account of the History, Antiquities and Scenery of the Picturesque Valley of the Wharfe, from Cawood to Arthington by Harry Speight, 1902
[5] Ibid
[6] http://www.walter9.info/Fairfax/html/fairfax_family_-_part_5.html David Berryfell

The length of Nathaniel's association with the Duke of Buckingham is not known but, when the Duke died in 1687, Nathaniel claimed that the unexpected death came right in the middle of them setting up a life annuity. He stated that the Duke was appreciative of everything done for him and wanted to make sure Nathaniel and his family were taken care of[1] by granting him an annuity of £400 - in addition to the salary and expenses that Bladen received for auditing their accounts, the annuity to be raised out of the rental income of three farms in Bolton Percy. He further stated that, as the Duke and Duchess were childless and the Duchess being so closely related to Nathaniel's wife Isabella, they had wanted to give them an annuity for 99 years for the lives of Nathaniel, his wife and their daughters Isabella, Catherine, Frances and Elizabeth. He also stated that *"this defendant's wife Her Grace's near relation and true and faithful friend in all Her Grace's misfortunes and adversities, having often lent and supplied Her Grace with sums of money"* and that the annuity was in recognition of this kindness and the stoppage of the annuity would be to the *"utter ruin and undoing of the said Isabella, Catherine, Frances and Elizabeth, this defendant's children"*.

To back up his claim of the Duke's promises, he cited the names of various important individuals who were present at the time it was discussed: Lord O'Brien (Earl of Inchiquin) a Villiers relation of the Duke and the 1st Duke of Grafton and Mrs Mariane Braithwaite.[2] The Deed of Grant signed by the Duchess in 1688 providing an annuity came under scrutiny after the death of Nathaniel's wife Isabella, when the Duchess believed the annuity came to an end as she thought it had only been taken out in Isabella's name, so she claimed that had been her intention.[3] This case was actually brought by Nathaniel's daughters (Bladen v Ashe) but was unsuccessful as the Duchess's estate was in the hands of administrators at the time and bailiffs refused to sanction annuity payments.

During Nathaniel's employment he took responsibility for leasing the Duchess's property and land in Bolton Percy and Appleton Roebuck. It is possible that he occasionally acted outside of his remit because, following the Duke of Buckingham's death, his estate was tied up in the courts, with creditors and trustees being in control. Leeds Record Office has an undated document which states 'Particulars of the acres and of the yearly value of Non Appleton in the County of York' and which states that Nathaniel had arranged the leases without the knowledge of the trustees of that estate.[4] So, not for the first time, it is suggested that Nathaniel acted without authority.[5]

The previous dominance of the Fairfax family in this area can be amply demonstrated in the 1671 hearth tax returns which show that, out of 57 taxable houses in the district most had one single hearth whereas the Fairfax house had 35.

---

[1] TNA: C9/245/17 Buckingham v Bladen, dated 1694
[2] Reference was also made to Mr Levett of Hatfield in the counties of York and Lincoln
[3] TNA: C5/310/9 Bladen v Ash, 1700
[4] LCA DB/65/6 Milner Papers
[5] TNA: C9/117/25 and TNA: C6/258/78 Countess of Plymouth v Nathaniel Bladen

Nathaniel's role as Auditor and Steward to the Countess probably involved him in assisting her sell off or rent out those assets she had control over which were not already in the hands of creditors or the courts. Numerous loans had, over the years, been taken out against the estate but it had fallen into disrepair.[1] After the Duchess's death in 1704 it took seven years for the estate to be eventually sold off, probably quite cheaply, to clear the family's debts and by 1711 Alderman Milner of Leeds was the new owner.

## 1690: Bladen v Pembroke

Despite the enormous difficulties Nathaniel experienced with the Osborne family, he seems to have continued his association with them - certainly with at least one of them. A short while later, in 1690, he was involved in bringing legal action against the estate of the late Earl of Pembroke.[2] The Earl of Danby's daughter Catherine was married to James Herbert whose cousin was the 7th Earl of Pembroke and Nathaniel was called in to sort out the Earl's estate. Actually, if Philip Herbert, 7th Earl of Pembroke[3] had still been alive at the time then taking legal action against him would have been a dangerous thing to do.

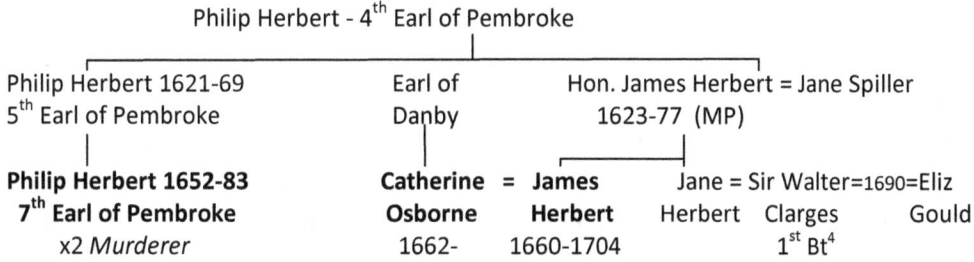

Pembroke was a convicted murderer, having violently killed Nathaniel Coney[5] in a tavern in 1678, Coney being a random passer-by who happened to be in the wrong place at the wrong time. At Pembroke's trial he was found not guilty of murder though guilty of manslaughter, but he escaped punishment by claiming privilege of peerage. The man who had prosecuted him was Edmund Godfrey who, it so happened, shortly after was found dead, impaled by his own sword and Pembroke was generally thought to be responsible. Godfrey has already been mentioned in this book as being the lawyer who took the deposition of Titus Oates in the Popish Plot. Conspiracy theorists at the time thought his murder evidence of a Catholic threat to the Establishment and charges were brought against Danby.

---

[1] Four Ainsty Townships: The history of Bolton Percy, Appleton Roebuck, Colton and Steeton 1066-1875
[2] Reports and Cases Argued and Decreed in the Court of Chancery in the Reigns of King Charles I., King Charles II and King William III (1652-93) pp164-9
[3] Philip Herbert 1652-83, 7th Earl of Pembroke
[4] Hunter's South Yorkshire, Pedigree of Osborne, p144
[5] Pembroke picked Nathaniel Coney at random to assault. Coney is likely related to the Coneys of Lincolnshire previously mentioned regarding grandfather Robert's law suit, Coney v Bladen

In 1680 Pembroke killed yet another man, but the privilege of peerage could only be utilised once, so a group of Lords was prevailed upon to ask the King for a Royal Pardon, and it was granted. Pembroke had friends/family in high places! So, yet again he got away with murder. Nathaniel Bladen, long after Pembroke was safely deceased, brought a legal challenge on behalf of the creditors of his estate. Pembroke had died leaving many debts and legal argument arose as to which creditors would have preference. The conclusion was that the heir was still entitled to receive rental income from the estate in financial preference to the executors or creditors.

### 1690: Bladen v Fountain[e]

Some 43 years after Robert Bladen's death, Nathaniel brought the issue of his grandfather's property, Bullingshire Hall, before the courts. Dr Richard Berry, of course, was long since dead and so was his heir John Fountaine, so Nathaniel brought a chancery suit against Berry's heir's son Thomas Fountaine. The timing of this law suit may perhaps have been related to the fact that Nathaniel had a 40 year reversion on the property, though the date when this ran from is not clear, whether it ran from his grandmother's death or date of occupancy of Bullingshire Hall.

The chancery documents provide a catalogue of the various indentures and deeds that existed between Bladen and Berry and the timeline against them and describe how the indebtedness of Robert Bladen increased. Most of the details have already been covered in Robert's section but the thrust of Nathaniel's case against the Fountaine[1] estate inherited from Berry concerned the fact that he believed his grandfather had repaid monies to Berry and that title to the Bullingshire Hall property should be his. However he must have failed in his attempt to recover the property as in 1696, in a letter to Robert Wrightson which is discussed shortly, he made reference to still holding a reversion to the property and not about to let it go in case his children could ever make use of it and was very bitter towards Berry's actions and, he claimed, Berry was a *"designing man."*[2] Some payout from Berry's estate, however, was subsequently made to Nathaniel.

The 1690s had not begun well for Nathaniel: first the case over his grandfather's estate did not totally succeed, an issue that had probably irked him his entire life. Quickly followed by the death of his wife Isabella in 1691 from typhus, she had been residing at Steeton with her mother at the time as it was reported that several of their servants also died of the same condition.[3] Then his mother-in-law Lady Fairfax died, although it is not known whether his mother-in-law's death was distressing to him or otherwise but he did relinquish his right to be one of her executors. Despite the legal action his mother-in-law took against him in 1680 relations were not permanently damaged between Nathaniel and Lady Fairfax.

---

[1] Fountayne/Fountains were business partners of Dr Berry and Berry's sister had married John Monckton (whose grand-daughter married John Fountayne) nephew of the John Fountayne 1601-71 that Berry left half of his estate to

[2] TNA: C6/264/15 Bladen v Fountaine - 29th July 1690

[3] Correspondence of the family of Hatton, being chiefly letters addressed to Christopher, 1st Viscount Hatton 1601-1704. From Isabella's sister's family, that is, Isabella's sister Catherine Fairfax and her second husband Littleton and, it is believed, the above correspondent is a sister of hers

Not only did she name him as an executor of her Will, which was not written until 1691, but she used his services to manage her own estate.

*Father's Influence to Secure Sons' Futures*
Through his wife's Fairfax relations and as Steward to Danby, Nathaniel had access to a wide range of influential people, but also in his own right, through his position at the Treasury and law courts, he was in contact with some key people who would make it possible for his sons to secure lucrative employment.

By the early 1690s his eldest son William, who was trained as a lawyer, was now seeking a suitable career/employment and Lionel Copley,[1] fellow Yorkshireman, protégé and right-hand man to Lord Danby, was one such contact Nathaniel made very good use of. Copley had been Lt. Governor at Hull, second to Lord Danby, and was rewarded for his service by being appointed Governor of Maryland. Nathaniel arranged for son William to go out to Maryland at the same time as Copley in the spring of 1692 where William initially was given the job of generally assisting the new governor with basic administration. Although Copley was dead within eighteen months of arriving in the Province, this was long enough for William to get settled and establish himself. A shortage of good Clerks in the colony meant there were multiple opportunities for William to work and he seized every opportunity for advancement.

Also emanating again from the circle that surrounded Danby, two other men became invaluable to Nathaniel: they were William Blathwayt and Edward Randolph. Both were close to Danby, both were connected with the Treasury[2] and both were involved with the colonial plantations. Blathwayt connected to Danby through being Secretary to Sir William Temple who was married to Dorothy Osborne and Randolph was Blathwayt's right-hand man. William Blathwayt knew Nathaniel Bladen well, both having attended the Inns of Court at about the same time and having posts at the Treasury and Blathwayt was responsible for at least one of William Bladen's appointments in Maryland as Deputy Surveyor General of Annapolis. Blathwayt was well placed to assist, having been appointed in 1696 as 'Commissioner for the promoting the trade of the Kingdom and for inspecting and improving the Plantations in America and elsewhere.'

It is also possible, in later years, that Nathaniel's relations with both Blathwayt and Edward Randolph paved the way for his youngest child and second son Martin to enter government. Indeed, Nathaniel was mentioned in Randolph's Will written 15th June 1702 when he stipulated that his daughter Sarah was not to marry without the approbation of Mrs Mary Fogg and Nathaniel Bladen of Lincolns Inn. Witness to the Will was Cath. Bladen - that is to say Nathaniel's unmarried daughter.

---

[1] Dugdale's Visitation of Yorkshire Vol. II, p54. Lionel Copley of Wadworth, Governor of Hull and MD
[2] English America and Imperial Inconstancy: the rise of provincial autonomy 1696-1715 by Jack M. Sosin, 1985 p83

Nathaniel continued to render son William assistance after he moved to Maryland by, for example, visiting Maryland Anglo-Americans when they touched base at Whitehall to promote William's advancement at every conceivable opportunity. He was, literally, William's eyes and ears this side of the Atlantic.

*1692: Lady Fairfax*

Lady Fairfax, in her final years, made use of Nathaniel Bladen as an attorney and he probably assisted as steward in some aspects of running her estate. Her eldest son Thomas, being cared for by Nathaniel's daughter Catherine in Dublin, was named joint executor (with Nathaniel) of Lady Fairfax's Will. All of her household goods were bequeathed to Nathaniel's children and Executors were named ..."*I make and appoint my son Thomas Fairfax and my son Nathaniel Bladen Sole Executors*". After the event, however, Nathaniel renounced his Executorship of the Will.

*Nathaniel's Statement Renouncing Joint Executorship*
"*Let this certify all persons whom it may concern that I do hereby refuse, release, quit claim and renounce all and all manner of right title claim order and into the executorship and administration of the Last Will Goods and Chattels of Dame Frances Fairfax late of Steeton in the County of the City of York deceased. Witness my hand seal this tenth day of January 1692. Signed: Nath Bladen. Sealed and delivered in the presence of ...Forsin, Wm Ashwood*"

Nathaniel's wife Isabella had died at Lady Fairfax's home at Steeton. A relation recorded the event .... "*the spotted feavour has bine in my mother Fairfax's family at Steeton, and carried of my sister Bladen and several of ye servants*". This correspondence was dated 19 Nov 1691 – the year Isabella Bladen died.[1] A wall monument was erected at Bolton Percy Church for both mother and daughter and can be seen below.

*Sacred to the memory of mother and daughter near this plaque lies interred the body of Isabella the wife of Nathaniel Bladen of Hemsworth. Daughter of Sir William Fairfax of Steeton knight and Dame Frances his wife. She departed this life October 25th 1691 leaving six children: Isabella, Katherina, William, Frances, Elizabeth, Martin. She was the most obedient child, a tender mother, supportive wife and faithful friend*
*And,*
*Likewise Dame Frances – her mother, relict of Sir William Fairfax aforesaid, daughter of Sir Thomas Challoner of Guisborough who was Governor and chaplain to Prince Henry, of their 10 children only 4 lived; viz William, Thomas, Catherine and Isabella named above. She lived mistress of Steeton above 60 years, an eminent example of piety and charity, born February 1610 and died January 1692.*

**Isabella Bladen and mother Frances Fairfax**
**Bolton Percy, All Saints Church, Monument**

---

[1] Bradfer-Lawrence, Harry 1887-1965 (Land Agent and Antiquary) Vol. II: West Riding MD335/13/2/2

*1694: Advice to a Son*
The early 1690s was a time of great change for Bladen. His wife and mother-in-law's deaths were followed by his eldest son William relocating to America. Daughter Isabella was married and living away from home, Elizabeth and Frances were approaching marriageable age, Catherine was about to go to Dublin to live with her uncle and youngest son Martin was preparing to go to board at Westminster School. Nathaniel must have felt the time was right to give his young son guidance, so he wrote a manuscript called 'Advice to a Son' in 1694. Some 20,000 words in length in his own hand-writing it gives an astonishing insight into his mind-set at that time; his thoughts on the monarchy, religion, business, education, career, government, money and marriage but, most of all, it was advice on how his youngest son Martin should live, how to handle people and warnings about difficult situations to avoid. It was based on Francis Osborne's treatise of the same name from the 1660s which had been hugely popular reading for some decades.

The Folger Shakespeare Library in Washington, USA purchased Nathaniel's 'Advice to a Son' in 1960 from the Seven Gables Antiquarian Bookshop in New York (which traded between 1930 and 1979) thereby saving it from obscurity and they have kindly given their permission for extracts to be cited, see the Appendices, p199-201. Even though Nathaniel based the outline of his huge edict on Osborne's earlier work, there is no doubting he adapted it to reflect his own personality and words of wisdom. The document is covered more fully in the accompanying book 'Martin Bladen: A Biography', since it was directed at Martin.[1]

One interesting anagram Nathaniel included at the end of the document was as follows: *'Sir Edmund Burie Godfrey, I find murdered by rogues'*. Sir Edmund Berry Godfrey is mentioned elsewhere in this book, at least twice. He was a Justice of the Peace who was given the task of taking a deposition from Titus Oates in relation to the Popish Plot. Bladen, being Danby's Steward, was closely involved in this matter and Godfrey's murder was a central event in escalating public fears of a Catholic uprising in England at the time when Danby was being linked both to the Popish Plot and murdering Godfrey; so an anagram that states "*I find murdered by rogues*" (rather than Danby) was highly significant and its meaning was not lost on Bladen. Another individual, the Earl of Pembroke, whose estate Nathaniel would later become involved with, was thought by many to have actually been the murderer, he had been found guilty of murder before and only escaped by using his peer's privilege to escape justice.

---

[1] In addition to the comprehensive 'Advice', Bladen included a few other items which were of interest to him as, for example, both Nathaniel and his son Martin shared a passion for poetry. He wrote about Claude Duval 1643-70 who was a contemporary of Nathaniel's, a French footman from Normandy who travelled to England and became a highwayman, though with a slight twist. Maybe it was his French charm, but he seems to have dazzled his lady victims by being gallant to them, whilst robbing their husbands, even dancing on the roadside with one of them whilst stealing from her husband. His fate, of course, like any other highwayman was at the end of a noose and his epitaph in Covent Garden Church says: "Here lies Du Vall, Reader if male, thou art look to thy purse, If female, to thy heart."

In 'An Answer to the Objections Against the Earl of Danby concerning his being accessory to the murder of Sir Edmundbury Godfrey' it was stated: *"that the same morning, that Sir Edmund was conjectured to have been murdered, he was at the said Earl's house, and that the Earl of Danby's gentleman that day went over the water with Sir Edmund; the which the Attestators of the Murder confute ...."*. It is possible that it was Nathaniel Bladen himself who dropped Edmund off on the other side of the river - hence his interest in the issue and this anagram.[1]

*1695: National Land Bank*
Another venture Nathaniel had an interest in was the National Land Bank, to which he was named as a subscriber in 1695: *"A list of the names of such of the subscribers of land and money towards a fund for the national land bank, who having paid in their subscription money, or subscribed the last instrument, are entitled to elect of be elected directors of the said bank."* There were four separate land banks set up at this time, one by John Asgill and Dr Nicholas Barbon[2] and another involved Thomas Neale (Nathaniel's colleague) but they were short-lived as by 1700 the projects had collapsed and were being wound up.[3]

*1696:* Some years after the previously cited letters Nathaniel wrote to his friend Robert Wrightson, there was one final letter from which it becomes clear that the outcome of Bladen v Fountain[4] was not entirely in Nathaniel's favour. This was the legal challenge he had brought against the Fountaines, who inherited property from Dr Berry, including Nathaniel's childhood home, Bullingshire Hall, which Nathaniel considered as belonging to the Bladen family:- *"Nathaniel Bladen to Robert Wrightson 26th September 1696:*
*Dear Friend, I have yours of the 24th for which I thank you kindly. As to the possession so long in Dr Berry - I can only say the injury is still the greater. It was an easy thing, for him, at the death of my Grandmother, and my minority, when I had no friends to look after me, nor any writings to instruct them, for him to do what he pleased, but if there were a Court of Conscience in all men's breasts t'would be easy to see the money was never pay'd. That money was at three percent till an act of parliament which determined the rate passed (I think about 1660), tis hard to pay them for which they neither payd nor lent but I think by a computation I made it hath overpayd them; but not for 550. Lastly as to the sale of the Revertion, I shall never agree to it: my children, it may please God, may outlive it, and I have lived hitherto without it, and I doubt not by the blessing of God to do so still and if it must go so, let it remain a moth and a curse to them that got it and keep it.*

---

[1] Nathaniel included in his notes a reference to Herbert Aubrey 1635-91 of The Blackfriars, Hereford. Aside from being a friend of Danby, it is probable that he was included as Bladen translated some writings or a poem of Aubrey. Aubrey was married to Joyce Brydges of the Priors Court branch who was distantly related to the Duke of Chandos line of Brydges and James Brydges became a good friend of son Martin
[2] The full name for Nicholas Barbon is .... Nicholas If-Jesus-Christ-had-not-died-for-thee-Thou-hadst-been damned Barbon, was the son of Puritans - hence the extraordinary middle name
[3] Document located at the National Library of Scotland
[4] TNA: C6/264/15 Bladen v Fountaine, dated 1690

*I am not sorry that I have spent some money upon it, and however it go, I shall own the reasons I have to be,   Your obliged friend, Nath Bladen*[1]

Note on page - written contemporaneously in the margin: *Robert Bladen, his grandfather, in 1631 mortgaged it to Berrie for 550; sold it to Baker for 500.  R.W. [Robert Wrightson]*[2] *purchased him Baker's Title for 11 guineas, the ____ upon Baker was forgot when this letter was writ.  Reverse:  To Mr Robert Wrightson at Cusworth near Doncaster."*

The subject of Nathaniel's letter has already been referred to in Robert's section, TNA: C10/12/16 Baker v Bladen of 1651 when, after Robert's death his widow Elizabeth was taken to court by William Baker father of Walter Baker over the title to this property (Bullingshire Hall) in Hemsworth.[3]

*1698: Green Wax Fines*

Nathaniel's association with the Treasury continued from the 1660s after he qualified as a lawyer.  He held various posts including in revenue collection and customs, such as from prize ships, and this association with the Treasury continued for the rest of his working life including with his associate Lord William Powlet whose family relationship to the government's central characters is shown as follows:

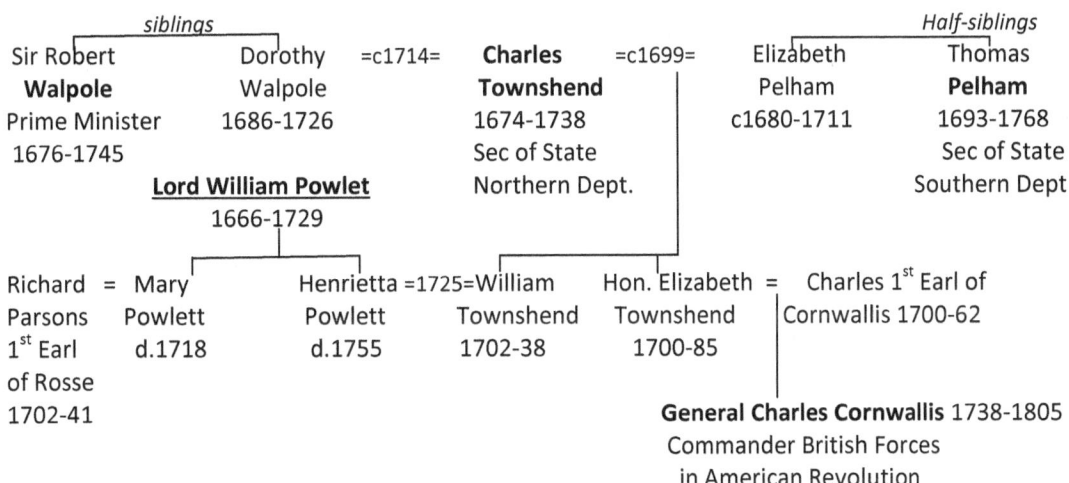

In 1698-99 Nathaniel, along with Arthur Robinson, was authorised by the Exchequer to inspect the records relating to Greenwax Revenue, which was income generated by various fines, including those imposed by courts.  Bladen and Robinson acted as nominees of Lord William Powlet who was a Whig MP and the Farmer or Manager of the said Greenwax Fines and Teller of the Exchequer from 1690 to 1706.[4]

---

[1] DD/BW/F7/11 Doncaster Archives, Batty-Wrightson Collection
[2] Will of Robert Wrightson DD/BW/W1/2 of 1 December 1707 bequests to children and grandchildren
[3] 1696: brought legal action against Francis Williamson and others regarding money matters - Middlesex
[4] Treasury Warrant to the Auditor of Imprests to the Keepers of the Records Relating to the Greenwax Revenue to Suffer Nathaniel Bladen and Arthur Robinson to inspect said records as the nominees of Lord William Pawlett, the farmer or manager of the said revenue.  CTB, Vol. 14, 1698-99 edited by William A Shaw, 1934, p169

Powlett was also the son of 1st Duke of Bolton who had taken over as Lord Lieutenant of Ireland from Townshend just as Martin Bladen returned to London. Powlett was another of Nathaniel's highly influential contacts and Powlett's family relations put him right at the heart of the British government of the day. Powlett's daughter Mary married Richard Parsons, 1st Earl of Rosse whose descendant would marry into the Hawke line and become Bladen descendants when Frances Harvey-Hawke[1] married the 4th Earl of Rosse.

*1700: Bladen v Ash*
To expand now on the previously mentioned case of Bladen v Ash regarding an annuity being paid to the Bladens (Nathaniel, wife Isabella until her death, daughters Isabella until her death, Catherine, Frances and Elizabeth). Eight years after the death of his wife Isabella, Nathaniel was still working for the Duchess of Buckingham but the annuity he believed himself entitled to was suddenly stopped by bailiffs on instructions from the Duchess herself, the last payment having been made on 25th March 1699. After a little while, with no resumption of annuity payments, it was Nathaniel's daughters who instigated legal proceedings on 16th October 1700 over the annuity. The defendant, however, was not the Duchess of Buckingham, rather the Bill was directed to a prospective purchaser of the Nun Appleton estate, Dame Mary Ash.

It is a mystery why it was left to the daughters of Nathaniel Bladen to bring this chancery case when Nathaniel was the central figure the case revolved around. It was the Bladen daughters' assertion that the annuity granted to Nathaniel and his wife for their lives had been also for their lives too. The plaintiffs were daughter Catherine, William Hamond (for daughter Frances) and the widowed Elizabeth Ruthven (who would later marry Edward Hawke), eldest daughter Isabella having died some time previously. They claimed to be in possession of a deed, draw up of course by their father, and signed by the Duchess allowing them 100 marks annuity for life. The Duchess claimed that she had been imposed upon by Nathaniel when the original agreement was drawn up because it was supposed to be only an annuity for his life and his wife. This is probably why Nathaniel did not wish to partake of the court proceedings in person as his drawing up such a deed 'apparently' against the Duchess's wishes and having her sign it could reflect badly on him and sour the relations he had enjoyed with the Duchess and her husband over the years.[2] Either that, or he feared his name on the court papers could expose him to the accusation of fraud in drawing up the deed in the first place, whereas his daughters had no responsibility for the creation of the document.

In his answer the bailiff/receiver Francis Colles, as servant to the Duchess Lady Mary, described how she felt *"very much abused and imposed upon"* by Nathaniel, *"that she intended not to make any grant but to Mr Nathaniel Bladen and his wife"* for a period of time not specified, that she was unaware that the children had been included in the grant and that it was for 99 years. The case the daughters put forward was that great arrears of the annuity had accrued since the bailiffs had refused to pay it and that they were facing ruin and starvation if the arrears were not paid to them.

---
[1] Hon. Frances Harvey-Hawke 1851-1921
[2] TNA: C5/310/9 Bladen v Ash, 1700

They also claimed that the expectation of such annuity had been used to support their portions of marriage settlements which would be in disarray if the annuity was not resumed. By this time two of Nathaniel's daughters had married: Isabella was married and deceased whilst Frances had married a Catholic. The marriage had taken place without the family's consent and Frances was facing ostracisation by an intensely hostile father-in-law. It is to be wondered if her lack of any financial prospects exacerbated the hostility she was already facing as a Protestant. The Bladen daughters informed the court that they had possession of the deed which they were happy to produce but, sadly, it would have been of no use. The Duchess's estate had been badly managed by her husband and was already in the hands of the courts. She was ruined and Lady Ash never did purchase Nunappleton. There was a complication for the Duchess in trying to dispose of the estate as the current Lord Fairfax, who had an interest in 'not' seeing the estate sold off, intervened to prevent the sale, he used legal means to 'sour the milk' and make the estate less attractive to a buyer.

*Early 1700s*
During the early 1700s Nathaniel became involved in a scheme involving his youngest son Martin who was in the army. In the period 1708-09 Martin moved extensively between Spain, Portugal and Gibraltar and, as Colonel of a Regiment, was allocated £15,497-4-9d for troop subsistence and uniforms. How that large sum was spent came under parliamentary scrutiny and Nathaniel Bladen was called to give evidence in a subsequent inquiry that took place. This matter is dealt with more fully in the separate biography for Martin Bladen which accompanies this volume, so is summarised briefly here.[1] The Duke of Marlborough and his wife had fallen out of favour with Queen Anne whose Tory ministers believed that only those profiteering from war wished to see a continuation of hostilities. From a desire to target Marlborough and have him removed from command, an inquiry was set up to examine irregularities in regimental spending. Martin Bladen was called to account for monies supplied to his regiment. Money had been drawn from the Treasury for uniforms and regimental supplies but there was no evidence of their allocation.

---

[1] *1709:* To briefly touch on the subject again of Nathaniel assisting his sons. Records show frequent transactions taking place involving both his Attorney-General son William in Maryland and Nathaniel in London. For example, many Wills for those in Maryland were proved in London via the Prerogative Court of Canterbury, and the two were well placed to arrange such matters. Not just Wills but an array of legal documents required authority and signatures from both places for the English judicial system. On 11th July 1709 documents from the Maryland Probate Court were presented at the London courts witnessed by Micajah Perry, N Blakiston, Nathaniel Bladen, Henry Darnall and Edward Diggs. Attested by said Puckle before Sir Charles Duncombe (Knt) Lord Mayor of London. The named witnesses here demonstrate how close the ties between London and Maryland were, as it is known Henry Darnall, for example, and his Diggs relations did not leave Maryland and Micajah Perry and Bladen were London-based. These documents are likely connected with Dunscombe's role as Receiver of Customs and Nathaniel's role in the Treasury regarding customs. Abstract of the Testamentary Proceedings of the Prerogative Court of Maryland by Vernon L Skinner, 2007: item 21:168, court session 11th July 1709. In 1706 there was a record of Nathaniel being in Wigan in Lancashire - at the sign of the Three Legs of Man in his legal capacity where he was involved in a case of the Attorney-General (Complainant) v Christopher Gradwell et al regarding rent arrears. This legal action may have been part of his Treasury duties

Nathaniel's name was mentioned by one of the deponents as being someone who had attended the Treasury and been advanced money for the regiment.[1] A captain of Martin Bladen's Regiment, Edward Strudwick, stated that Nathaniel had *"desired to make use of his name in an assignment made by Colonel Bladen bearing date 10th March 1709/10 of the off-reckonings of his Regiment, till the sum of £2,839-17s-6d should be paid, which he granted; but never furnished any clothing, or received any money, or gave any receipts on account of the said assignment, that he afterwards assigned over the said assignment, and thinks it was to Colonel Bladen's father."* Under oath, Nathaniel appeared and stated *"that he knew no more of the matter than that solicited at the Pay Office for the money and received tallies, all which he gave to his son"*. The Inquiry concluded *"Thus it appears that an Assignment was made, and the money paid by the Public, but we cannot find that any cloathing was ever provided in Consideration thereof"*.[2] There is good evidence that Martin did use regimental funds to enrich himself, as many other low-paid officers under Marlborough did, but neither Martin nor his father were ever in any danger of prosecution for their deeds as it was a widespread practice at the time.

Nathaniel's movements after 1713 are difficult to pin down. A death record has not been found but can be narrowed down to around 1717. He was obviously well enough in 1713 to attend the above Commission, though in a letter to his daughter Frances in early 1713 he described himself as being unwell and having difficulty reading. Later in 1713, youngest son Martin appeared to have taken over responsibility for legal matters in the family as in Plaxton v Bladen, referred to later in the section on Martin, a matter more closely associated with Nathaniel was dealt with by his son. One solitary mention of Nathaniel occurs on 9th June 1716 in a letter from Francis Taylor (attorney to Nathaniel's daughter Frances) to George Harman (her husband) at Scarthingwell which states: *"... as to the estate at Hemsworth I cannot tell what judgement to form therein, until Mr Bladen have looked over the writings left by his father relating to this matter. If Mrs Hamond will write to her brother for this purpose I'll carry up the deeds to London and there wee'l further consider of the title"*.

The above refers to Taylor being consulted over the future of the estate at Hemsworth (presumed to be Nathaniel's), but that he needed to wait until Martin Bladen went through his father's papers before Taylor advised the family how to proceed. The fact that the family needed to consult their attorney over the title to the property may be because it was not straightforward. This might suggest either the grandfather Robert may have assigned some part of the title to Dr Richard Berry or Nathaniel himself may have assigned some part to his friend and patron Robert Wrightson. It may be consistent with Nathaniel dying intestate that matters were unresolved so long after his demise. It is curious, however, given his life spent in the legal profession that Nathaniel appears to have left no Will. His later years were spent partly in Hemsworth Yorkshire but it is also known that he commuted to London no doubt to continue his legal practice, as letters addressed to his children do sometimes have the Inns of Court addresses on them.

---

[1] History and Proceedings of the HoC, Vol. 5, 1713-14
[2] Ibid

As daughter Frances was living at Scarthingwell relatively close to Nathaniel, it is possible he spent his final years living with her family, though he is not recorded in the Saxton parish registers as dying there. One final mention of Nathaniel is in a letter William Fairfax received in 1717. Some years before he died, daughter Frances wrote to Nathaniel saying that if she outlived him she would ensure he was buried near to her mother. In the event Frances did outlive her father but it is not yet known where he was buried. One possibility, which is yet to be explored, is that he travelled to Annapolis during 1718 when eldest son William was ill. William died in early August of that year and Nathaniel's whereabouts are unknown from this time.

## Heraldry[1]

On his son Martin's Inner Temple Admission Record, Nathaniel was stated to be an Armiger and, from original letters that have been seen to his children, he signed himself ... Nath. Bladen with[1] a wax seal of a lion rampant (Fairfax heraldry) over three inverted chevrons (Bladen heraldry - see right).

This symbolism has been noticed already at his wife's marble wall memorial at Bolton Percy Church in Yorkshire, see a close-up picture below. There is, however, no record at the English College of Arms of Nathaniel being officially granted a patent, so it is likely he merely adopted the arms under his own volition. An interpretation of the heraldic armory is given below. Given that the symbols appear on a monumental dedication to Isabella Bladen and her mother Lady Frances Fairfax, the two outside globes represent those two individuals:-

- The left-hand globe represents Nathaniel Bladen and Isabella Fairfax, being in two halves with the Bladen symbol to the left and Fairfax to the right.

- The right-hand globe represents Sir William Fairfax and Lady Frances Chaloner (Nathaniel's in-laws), being in two halves with Fairfax to the left and Chaloner to the right.

- The centre globe is a marriage of the four families' ancestral descent, being in quarters with the left side being Bladen above Lacy and the right side being Chaloner above Fairfax and may have been a dedication from Nathaniel's children, since they were the only ones who could claim descent from all four families.

---

[1] Description by Nicholas Maclean-Bristol who was in possession of the Hawke Papers until November 2009, at which point they were returned to Lord Hawke (deceased). Nicholas's wife is aunt to the current Lord Hawke

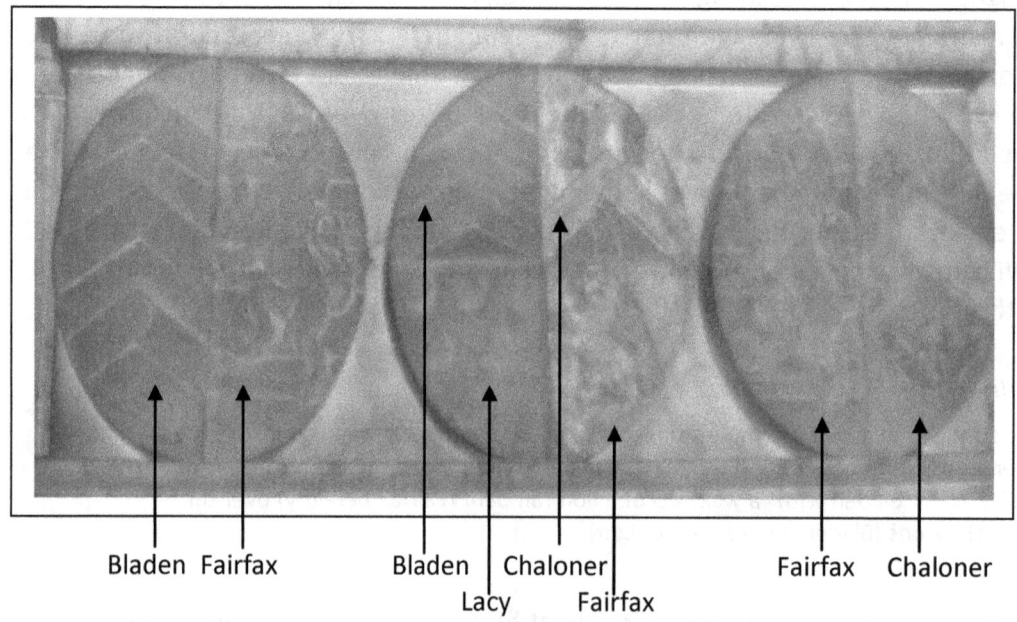

Bladen  Fairfax       Bladen | Chaloner      Fairfax  Chaloner
                      Lacy    Fairfax

In addition to the wall memorial to his wife and mother-in-law, Nathaniel had a separate memorial to his wife made:-

Plaque in All Saints Church, Bolton Percy
*In Latin:* Charae Memoriae Almae Coniugis, ciusque malris Nathaniel Bladen Superstes hue titulum Posuit Vixi et quem dederat Cuifum Jehova peregy.
*Translation:* In fond memory of (my) caring wife, to whom her husband Nathaniel Bladen has, in life been able to dedicate the above inscription. "I have lived and now passed on to God".

The next section outlines the lives of the six surviving children of Nathaniel Bladen and Isabella Fairfax and some of their descendants.[1]

---

[1] Bladens of Hemsworth Pedigree: MD335/13/2/2, West Riding, Vol. II - documents held by Bradfer-Lawrence, Harry 1887-1965, land agent and antiquary

# Fourth Generation

**Descendants of Nathaniel and Isabella Bladen**

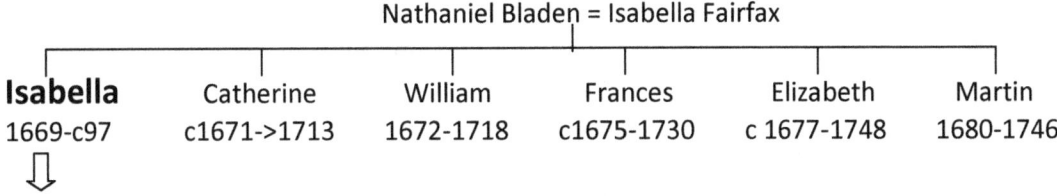

*The Northern Stars*

Nathaniel Bladen and Isabella Fairfax had six children and, although baptism records have only been found for half, it is possible to estimate the others with accuracy because they were listed chronologically on the monuments at Bolton Percy Church for their mother and grandmother. In addition, there was a record of a birth for a seventh child, Charles in 1685[1] who must have died in infancy. The daughters Isabella, Catherine, Frances and Elizabeth were known as the "Northern Stars" at court[2] which might suggest they had lovely Yorkshire accents.

*Isabella*
Eldest child Isabella was baptised on 2$^{nd}$ September 1669 in Wandsworth, a place where, just three years earlier, 99 people had died from the plague, but located a little distance from the Inns of Court where her father would have been working. She must have been married by 1692 when she is referred to as "Mrs Isabella" in her grandmother Lady Frances Fairfax's Will and she married a Catholic which, no doubt, did not please some of her relations:[3]

*"The Fairfaxes of Steeton were friendly, but whenever religion came up (as in the case of Isabella Bladen's mixed marriage) there is a strong undercurrent of hostility in their letters to each other – hostility to Catholicism as something alien and dangerous. Lord Fairfax of Cameron could correspond about genealogy and dine, but he was the same man, who with his father and Danby, conspired to overthrow the political power of Catholicism in Yorkshire in 1688 ….."*[4]

---

[1] Parish Register of St Margaret's Westminster 6$^{th}$ April 1685. Christening of Charles Bladon[Bladen] to Nathaniel and Isabella
[2] The Harleian Society Papers; Familiae Minorum Gentium, Vol. 3, Joseph Hunter
[3] Recusant History, Vol. 4, Catholic Society, 1958, p86
[4] In 'Familiae Minorum Gentium', Vol. 3, by Joseph Hunter, reference is made to the four daughters of Nathaniel/Isabella Bladen and how three were unmarried but that the fourth (Isabella) was presumed to have died young, which she did, in her twenties

Confirmation that Isabella was dead by 1700 came from Bladen v Ashe as the opening paragraph of that Bill of Complaint states:- *"Humbly Complaining show unto your Lordship your orator and oratrix Catherine Bladen, William Hamond, gent, and Frances his wife and Elizabeth Ruthven, widow, the <u>three surviving</u> daughters of Nathaniel Bladen of the Inner Temple ..."*. Isabella was later referred to as "<u>*late the wife of Peter Vavasour of Hazelwood*</u>[1] in the County of York". Further clarification on Isabella's date of death came in a letter her sister Frances wrote, in 1702, to their father Nathaniel where the marriage of Frances was being discussed. She said: *"Nor did we ever own our marriage till we heard ye writings were safe, which my sister Vavasour sent me word of."* Since Frances had married William Hamond about 1697 and Isabella had been alive after that event, then we can narrow her death down to 1697-1699. There are further references to her sister Frances staying at Hazlewood Castle after Isabella's death since Frances had, like Isabella, married into a Catholic family and would no doubt have gone there for support but it has not been possible to find a Peter Vavasour that had any children in the period when he was married to Isabella, so the assumption at present is that she died without issue.

Letters from Isabella's sister Frances Hamond at the time do make mention of Sir Walter and Lady Vavasour, the 3rd Bt (as the 4th was unmarried) and his mother was Ursula Belasyse,[2] a Fairfax who was already related to the Bladens, she was the grand-daughter of Ursula Fairfax, sister to Lord Fairfax. Information on the Peter Vavasour who was married to Isabella Bladen has been hard to find and it is not clear whether Peter's children had Isabella Bladen as their mother as he possibly remarried after Isabella's early death around the late 1690s. Peter was probably father to Walter Vavasour, 5th Baronet (who inherited the title from his uncle of the same name, Sir Walter Vavasour).

---

[1] Hazlewood Castle between Tadcaster and Aberford overlooking the Battlefield of the Battle of Towton 1461. Sir William Dugdale's Visitation of Yorkshire was conducted between 1665-66, just before the birth of Peter Vavasour c1667

[2] Her husband, Sir Walter Vavasour 1613-92 raised a Regiment of Horse for King Charles I in the Civil War, brother William was a Major in the King's service and third brother Thomas was killed fighting for the King at Marston Moor in 1644

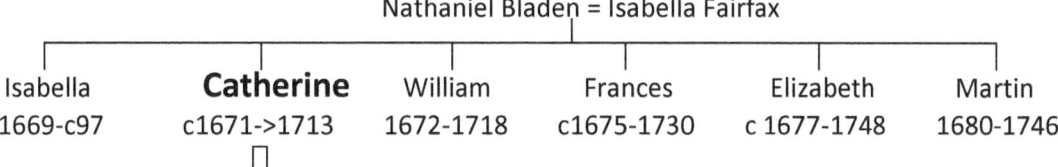

| Isabella | **Catherine** | William | Frances | Elizabeth | Martin |
| --- | --- | --- | --- | --- | --- |
| 1669-c97 | c1671->1713 | 1672-1718 | c1675-1730 | c 1677-1748 | 1680-1746 |

*Catherine (Kate, Katherina)*

Catherine devoted her early life to being a companion to her aging uncle General Thomas Fairfax and they resided in Dublin from around 1696 until his death in 1712. In 1702 Catherine briefly left Dublin in company with General Fairfax and was in London. Catherine and her uncle were very close and frequent visitors/correspondents of her cousin Admiral Robert Fairfax who, when not at sea, resided at Searle Street, Lincoln's Inn.[1] At this time she was known to have visited her father's legal chamber where she signed as a witness on 15th June 1702 the Will of Edward Randolph who was about to embark on his seventeenth and final voyage to America where he was Survey/Searcher of all the American plantations. Randolph had been very helpful to brother William in Maryland by assisting him obtaining appointments. It is thought Robert Fairfax named his two children Catherine and Tom after Catherine Bladen and her Uncle Thomas Fairfax.

*Maj.Gen. Thomas Fairfax 1633-1712*

1633   Born. Served in the army of the Protector in Ireland and was part of the West India Expedition that took the island of Jamaica
1694   Colonel on the Irish establishment, 4th Foot, Governor of Limerick (under Queen Anne)
1696   Brigadier General, Major-General, died at Dublin 11 March 1712. He was described, by someone called Evelyn, who travelled once with him as "a soldier, a traveller, an excellent musician, a good- natured and well bred gentleman"[2]
1712   Died in Dublin

*Picture of General Thomas Fairfax's portrait*
*Courtesy of the Earl of Rosse (Hawke descent)*

Whilst she was living in Dublin, Catherine's name headed up a Bill of Complaint, Bladen v Ashe, which has already been mentioned in Nathaniel's section where she and her siblings challenged the estate of the Duchess of Buckingham (prospective purchaser Ashe) to reinstate an annuity due to them and their father. If Catherine had depended on the outcome of the case to support her she would have been disappointed as the Duchess of Buckingham's estate was in receivership and all financial transactions had to go through, and be approved, by the courts.

---

[1] Life of Robert Fairfax of Steeton: Vice-Admiral, Alderman and Member for York 1666-1725 by Sir Clements Robert Markham, 1885
[2] A Life of the Great Lord Fairfax: Commander-in-Chief of the Army of the Parliament of England by Sir Clements Robert Markham, 1870

It is likely, therefore, that she lived very modestly in Dublin as her Fairfax uncle had barely the means to support himself. Further visits to London took place in 1707 and 1709 by Catherine and her uncle when, on the last return visit from Hollyhead to Dublin on a man-of-war, their journey was interrupted by the necessity to chase off privateers.

There were frequent references to Catherine being unwell in correspondence between Thomas Fairfax and his nephew, such as on 22nd April 1710 where Thomas wrote *"Poor Kate has been very ill but I hope now better"*. Then later in the same year, on 6th August her uncle described her as having her *"old distemper of headache but is pretty well over and rides on horseback very often"*. Catherine's headache's continued into the following year on 5th January 1711 followed by another episode of illness in March of 10 days' duration. She appears to have been of a sickly constitution and also, at this time, had an episode of pleurisy. By March of that year, however, she had rallied and writing to Robert on 30th March said:[1] *"Dear Cousin, I am glad of an opportunity to thank you and your lady for kindly remembering me, as also for the care of my poor sister Hamond. Pray God deliver her out of her troubles. I am in continual fear for her. I am glad she had the pleasure to see your sisters. I beg my humble service to my cousin and both your young folks and desire you will believe me sincerely dear cousin your ever affte coz and most humble servant. Kate"*

This letter is interesting for reasons which will become clear when her younger sister Frances is discussed later. It is dated 30th March 1711 and, within a matter of days, Frances' husband was dead at just 37 years of age. Frances was separated from her husband and would not let him know where she was, or have access to their children. She was literally in fear of her life and, the implication from the above sister Kate's letter, is that she had sought refuge and assistance from cousin Fairfax's family in London. Catherine stayed with her uncle until his death and, if she had been expecting a healthy inheritance from him (which perhaps she deserved) she was to be disappointed. Her father Nathaniel, writing to her younger sister Frances on 28th March 1712 described the circumstances at the end of his life and how he had eaten well, lit his pipe and.... *"thus died honest Thom Fairfax after a long life of great honours and influence, and as he did his relations little good in his lifetime, so he has given 'em no cause to rejoice at his death"*. He further wrote that Fairfax left *"no effects to bury him"* and, said Nathaniel, *"I am ashamed to write his circumstances"*.

*Marriage*

A couple of early sources[2] state that Catherine did not marry, however it is believed she did. Joseph Hunter in 'Familiae Minorum Gentium' Volume 3 indicated that Catherine may have married a Captain Fowke as he found a hand-written note in the margin of a copy of Thoresby's, which had been in the possession of the Fairfax family in America indicating she married a Captain Fowke. Knowing how close the Fairfax and Bladens families were, this therefore seems worthy of being valid information.

---

[1] A Life of the Great Lord Fairfax: Commander-in-Chief of the Army of the Parliament of England by Sir Clements Robert Markham, 1870, p225

[2] The Life of Robert Fairfax of Steeton by Clements R Markham - 1885. Harry Speight in 'Lower Wharfedale: Being a Complete Account of the History, Antiquities and Scenery of the Picturesque Valley of the Wharfe, from Cawood to Arthington - 1902

An exploration of connections between the Fowke and Bladen families does lead to a likely family with many possibilities yet to be explored. The descendants of the Fowke family of Brewood in Staffordshire headed up by Roger Fowke of Gunston, who had nineteen children, seems a likely branch.[1] At least three of this line were out in Spain and Portugal when Catherine's brother Martin Bladen was there and one line went to Dublin where Catherine was living until Fairfax's death. Sydenham Fowke has been suggested as a possible candidate (though with no real evidence) which, if so, means she probably married and died quite quickly afterwards as he remarried in 1721 and Catherine is not mentioned in her brother Martin's Will of 1726.

---

[1] Of those Fowkes in Portugal and Spain, both called Thomas, one was with Captain Theodore Vezey's Regiment, which Bladen took over and had come from the Inniskilling Regiment of Foot. Father and son, both called Thomas Fowke, were in service together and when the father became unwell, he stood aside to let his son take over as Captain, while he became his Vice. The father later was killed in service. These particular Fowkes are accounted for, but belong to a much wider family, with connections to Ireland. Fowkes, Hamond and Bladen all served in Spain/Portugal in Marlborough's Wars. Anthony Hamond was Deputy Paymaster to the British Forces in Spain. His boss was James Brydges (Duke of Chandos), Martin Bladen's very close friend. Martha Fowke (wife of Arnold Sansom) had her poems published in the 1720s by Anthony Hamond 1668-1738, politician, editor of *A New Miscellany* and writer/poet. Hamond also printed a poem of Martha's brother Thomas, later Governor of Gibraltar. Also Richard Swift (business partner to Jonathan Swift) published them too. Anthony Hamond had a duel with Lord William Pawlett where he sustained an injury to his leg. Pawlett was Nathaniel Bladen's boss at the Treasury. So this family have plenty of connections to the Bladens and, if Catherine did marry a Fowke, then this family seem the ideal candidates for further research. MSS Rawl D1207; Clio: The Autobiography of Martha Fowke Sansom 1689-1736

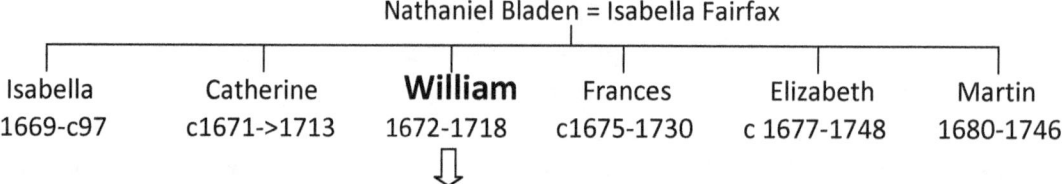

## William

William was the first son and third child born to Nathaniel and Isabella and was baptised in 1672/3 at Steeton, Yorkshire. He was admitted to the Inner Temple on 10th February 1688 where he spent four years and qualified as a lawyer.[1] His father's position as an official at the Treasury Department and as Steward to Lord Danby meant the family had good connections which helped to facilitate William's advancement. At just 19 years of age, he travelled to Colonial Maryland along with the new Governor Lionel Copley[2] who, as Danby's protégé would have been very well known to the Bladen family. Considering the political situation at that time it was a brave move for young William to have made. In England the Catholic King James II had been deposed in favour of the Protestant William and Mary and anti-Catholic sentiments spilled over to the colonies where the proprietorship of the Catholic Calverts (Lord Baltimore) had been thrown over and the colony came to the Crown. So, at a time when many fled the colonies due to unrest, William set sail for Maryland though he must have done so with some trepidation. Although initially based at St Mary's, a while later and against his wishes, the capital was relocated to Annapolis where his initial role was to assist the new Governor. Copley died within 18 months of arrival during which time, due to a shortage of good legal clerks in Maryland, William was quickly employed and settled into his first appointment as a Clerk to replace the Catholic Charles Carroll (the Settler) whose religion barred him from certain offices. Despite William taking his job, the two men became good friends and life-long business associates.

William got on well with the next governor, Francis Nicholson, who gave him additional appointments as Clerk to the various County Courts. William also served as Clerk to the Lower House, Clerk of St Mary's County, Clerk of Indictments in Prince George County and Deputy Collector of Annapolis. Some of these appointments were secured through the network of contacts he made in Maryland, or his father fostered in London, i.e. influential men such as William Blathwayt and Edward Randolph. His appointment, for instance, as Collector and Surveyor and Searcher of Annapolis would have made him Blathwayt's deputy. Some appointments were held for many years and others just for short periods, but there were plenty of opportunities for him to keep busy as he also became Clerk of the Lower House, Clerk of the Upper House and Clerk of the High Court of Appeal. To the accumulation of job titles was added Clerk of the Council, Clerk of Free Schools of Annapolis, Naval Officer of Annapolis[3] and Clerk of the Prerogative Office.

---

[1] Inner Temple Admissions Database
[2] The Royal Period of Colonial Maryland 1689-1715, David William Jordan, pp73-74, 1962. Copley arrived in Maryland prior to 6th April 1692
[3] Appointed by Nathaniel Blakiston. Commission stated 'Haveing Speciall Trust and Confidence in your fidelity Integrity knowledge and Circumspection, I do hereby Nominate Constitute and Appoint you the said W Bladen to be Navall Officer of the Porte of Annapolis'. Proceedings of the Council of Maryland 1698-1731

William also had responsibility for the Register of the Vice-Admiralty Courts in both the Eastern and Western Shores. He was a busy man.

In 1695 William married a Roman Catholic, Anne van Sweringen.[1] They married at St Inigoes Church in St Mary's County, Maryland[2] and their first child, Anne, was born within the year, son Thomas was born two years later. The van Sweringens had arrived in America in 1657 settling initially in a Dutch Colony in Delaware (New Amstel/New Castle) where Anne's father Gerrett[3] had various appointments as a councillor, deputy commander of the colony and sheriff. After the English captured the colony in 1664 the family relocated to Maryland where Gerrett became a member of the Council in 1694 and prospered in a variety of ventures. He was an inn-keeper, owned a coffee shop and a plantation as well as operating as a merchant trading between England and the colonies. He became one of the most prosperous men in the province and it is thought Gerrett gave his new Bladen son-in-law property after the marriage.

A few months later William[4] recommended to the Assembly of Annapolis that consideration be given to the provision of a printing press in order to enable *"printing the laws made every session"*.[5] In return for Bladen sourcing and importing the printing press[6] at his own expense, the delegates agreed that he would have a monopoly on official printing for the province. By May 1700 the printing process was set up and *"All the Laws of Maryland Now in Force"* was produced.[7] Unfortunately, errors were found in the print though it was never established who was at fault, whether William or his printer Thomas Reading, still it was the first of a few awkward incidents William was involved in. Complaints about the printing errors quickly reached the Board of Trade in London.[8]

Later in that year another unfortunate incident occurred when William was reported to have taken someone's horse without their permission. He was taken to court by a man called Thomas Pringle and the court directed him to pay 200 lbs of tobacco to Pringle.[9] This must have been embarrassing to William as he had just been appointed Clerk of Indictments in Prince George County where the incident had taken place.

---

[1] Anne van Sweringen c1679-1729

[2] William was not previously married to Letitia Loftus as has sometimes been suggested. The Loftus-Bladen marriage was between Charles Bladen and Letitia Loftus, Charles being the son of Dr Thomas Bladen of Dublin. Further details in Bunbury v Bolton 1721 TNA: HL/PO/JO/10/3/213/17, also TNA: HL/PO/JO/10/6/309 and TNA: HL/PO/JO/10/4/12

[3] Gerrett van Sweringen b1636, Reemsterdam, Holland, first wife Barbara de Barrette. Second wife (and Anne's mother) was Mary Smith married 5th Oct 1676, daughter of Hugh Smith. Will proved 4th Feb 1699

[4] MD.Arch. 19:466-67; 24:22,60,83,198; History of Printing in Colonial Maryland 1686-1776, Lawrence Counselman Wroth, 1922

[5] Ibid. There was another printer in Maryland before William, Dinah Nuthead, who appears not to have remained in business at the start of the public printing process in 1700

[6] Another branch of Bladens (who may be connected to William) was at this time based in Dublin where they had enjoyed the monopoly of printing for the King and also during the Commonwealth era

[7] History of Printing in Colonial Maryland 1686-1776, Lawrence Counselman Wroth, 1922

[8] June 1701, 11-14 CSP Colonial, America and West Indies, Vol. 19: 1701 (1910), pp296-301

[9] Court Records of Prince George's County, Maryland 1696-99, p7. Editors Smith and Crowl

The last of this spate of blunders was politically inspired. William (as Governor Nicholson's supporter) was overheard making a derogatory comment which led his van Sweringen in-laws to fear for his future. William had remained rigidly loyal to Nicholson who, at times, behaved vindictively towards colleagues. Allegations had been made that, on Nicholson's instructions, Bladen left detail out of records for the Journals of the Lower House, allegations that Bladen denied. Still, those who opposed Nicholson sought to undermine him at any opportunity and so, when Nicholson's staunch supporter William made a slip of the tongue, it was seized on. He was overheard to say that *"half the People of the Country .... [could be] ... Bought and Sold"*. Sentiments which, whether true or not, did not go down well when Assembly members heard.[1] Mother-in-law Mary van Sweringen feared William would lose his job but a severe shortage of legal clerks meant there was no-one to replace him and, of course, of paramount importance was the fact that he had the Governor's full support.

He survived the transgressions and settled into his busy life, enjoyed the full support of his peers and prospered and advanced his career at every opportunity. This was helped when Governor Nicholson, who was preparing to take up governorship of Virginia in 1698, assembled the Maryland Privy Council and recommended both Major William Dent and William Bladen to the new Governor Nathaniel Blakiston as loyal individuals willing to do their duty. In August of that year Nicholson, writing to the Board of Trade in London, lamented the lack of good clerks and advised them that he had moved William Bladen, who he found *"the most capable in all respects"*[2] from Clerk of the House of Delegates to Clerk of the Council, that being the reason for him signing both Journals (copies of which were sent to London).

As well as his administrative role in the Assembly, records do indicate that William held the title of Colonel in the militia by 1703[3] though it is suspected that this was more of an honorary title which was given to him by virtue of being on the Council for the Province. Another venture, by which William sought to enhance his personal income, was construction including organising municipal building projects.[4] He collaborated with Charles Carroll (the Settler) who was from one of the most influential families in the colony. The Carrolls were immigrants from Ireland and there were half a dozen relations all with prominent roles in Maryland's government. There may have also been a family connection between the two families through his sister-in-law Eleanor van Sweringen b1682 who had married a member of the Carroll family[5].

---

[1] MSA, XXIII, pp419-420

[2] CSP, America and West Indies, Vol.16, 1697-1698, ed. J.W. Fortescue (London, 1905), pp377-99

[3] His Lordship's Patronage; Offices of Profit in Colonial Maryland by Donnell MacClure Owings, MHS, 1953

[4] The Ancient City': A History of Annapolis in Maryland by Elihu Samuel Riley. 1887. William purchased land formerly owned by Thomas Gott on the south side of Severn River. It had been escheated to the State and that is when William bought it.

[5] Will of Mary van Sweringen 17 February 1712/13 (proved 5th September 1713) referred to her daughter Elinor Carroll. This branch of the Carroll family were probably ancestors of Thomas King Carroll, Governor of Maryland in 1830-1

Bladen and Carroll were the main contractors of the new State House[1] and prison and were also among the earliest owners of property at Bloomsbury Square in Annapolis, which had been named after the London Square inhabited by the Calverts, Lord Proprietors of Maryland. The Annapolis square is bounded by St John Street/College Avenue/Church Circle/Northwest Street and Calvert Street. Close by there is a blue memorial plaque on the corner of the William S James Senate building (corner of College Avenue).[2] Contained within scenic Bloomsbury Square are Bladen Street and Carroll Street, permanent reminders of the two early developers whose legacy is an area of beautiful Georgian buildings. Bladen and Carroll collaborated over several public building projects in the Province and, within a few years, were reputed to own half of the real estate in Annapolis between them.[3] Some of the buildings they constructed were rented to the use of the government.

*Secretary of Maryland - briefly*
On 15th April 1701 Governor Nathaniel Blakiston reported to the Board of Trade that Thomas Lawrence Jnr, Secretary of the Province, had died and Blakiston immediately recommended William Bladen for the post as Secretary, though with the proviso that if he thought Sir Thomas Lawrence (father of the Secretary, and previous Governor) was interested in the post that he would desist from making an appointment. *"Mr Thomas Laurence, HM Secretary of this Province, is this day dead of a feavour. On which occasion upon ye application of Mr William Bladen, a gentleman who for these ten years past has faithfully served HM in several imployments within this Province as Clark of Assembly and Clark of the council, as also in HM Customes here, wherein he has been serviceable beyond others in his station etc., I humbly presume to recommend him to your Lordships".*[4] The next day William was appointed Secretary of Maryland on an interim basis but, as it turned out, this was to be a short-lived appointment from April to November, as Sir Thomas Lawrence Snr had decided he did want the job (and fees that came with it). There is a record in the Board of Trade Journals of William being in England about May/June that year and attending the Board at its meeting on 17th May where he had been invited in to explain the many errors in the printing of the Province's laws (on his press).[5] This was unfortunate timing as his presence there was no doubt to bolster his chances of securing the post of Secretary on a permanent basis. William had support of his father who had done his best to lobby support in his favour, presenting a petition to the Board of Trade on 11th June 1701. In addition, William petitioned the King for the appointment, but Sir Lawrence won the day and, perhaps inevitably, this put the two men at odds from then on.[6]

---

[1] Price not to exceed £1,000. The Ancient City': A History of Annapolis in Maryland by Elihu Samuel Riley. 1887

[2] http://www.waymarking.com/gallery/default.aspx?f=1&guid=b13e6508-3f6a-4732-a931-a8b082b6cf50&gid=2

[3] Annapolis Pasts: Historical Archaeology in Annapolis, Maryland, edited by Paul A. Schakel, Paul R Mullins and Mark S Warner. 1998

[4] April 1701, 11-15 CSP Colonial, America and West Indies, Vol 19: 1701 (1910), pp157-163

[5] May 1701, 16-20 CSP Colonial, America and West Indies, Vol. 19: 1701 (1910), pp246-256

[6] JBoT, Vol. 1: April 1704 - January 1709 (1920), pp397-407. William made a further deposition regarding Sir Thomas Lawrence's complaints against Gov. Colonel Seymour in 1707

William never did regain the coveted job of Secretary but on 2nd May 1702 it was reported to the Board of Trade that William Dent, Maryland's Attorney-General was unwell and a replacement was needed for him. Bladen was appointed to this post in 1704 as well as becoming Registrar of H.M. Courts of Vice Admiralty.

Bladen enjoyed good relations with the new Governor who tried to reward William with a salary for his post (which had not previously enjoyed one)[1] and in 1705 representation was made to the Board concerning William's salary with an appeal for him to receive 100 *l*. for his appointment as Attorney General and the Board agreed. Neither the new Governor John Seymour nor William as Attorney General got on with Secretary Lawrence and so relations between high-ranking colonial officials were strained. Then, to add to the mixture, a hot-headed Irishman arrived in Maryland of whom it was said, *"Almost from day one of his arrival in the colony, Thomas Macnemara had been a disruptive force in Maryland. If ever a man merited the term "a wild Irishman", it was he."*[2] William and Macnemara came to know each other very well as Macnemara had been apprenticed as a lawyer to Charles Carroll, William's business partner. Macnemara had travelled to the province in the 1690s and converted to Protestantism so he could practice law. He had married Margaret Carroll,[3] a niece of Charles Carroll in 1702 but within five years Margaret brought her husband to court charging him with cruelty. Mary accused him of thrashing her 'merciless stripes'.[4]

The court had no hesitation in declaring: *"the said Thomas Macnemara towards his wife, manifested not only to the Chancellor, but to all Her Majesty's council in assembly, before whom he appeared not long since, the said Margaret, so battered, bruised and inhumanly beaten in most parts of her body, that had she not been of a constitution more than ordinarily strong, she could hardly have recovered it: and finding by daily expressions the said Thomas to be of a mad, turbulent, furious and ungovernable temper: therefore, for the preservation of the poor petitioners life ..."*[5] the court awarded her a legal separation. Thomas refused to pay his wife £4 quarterly as ordered by the court.

One of the many cases where Bladen and Macnemara opposed each other in court took place in 1705 where William was lawyer for a defendant called Thomas Hicks and Macnemara was the lawyer for the plaintiff William Seward (and his daughters, co-heirs Mary and Ann Seward). The dispute was over a land patent and went in Bladen's favour which, no doubt, irked Macnemara.[6]

---

[1] William was appointed a Vestryman at St Anne's Parish Church, Annapolis, in 1704, along with Col John Hammond, Mr William Taylard, Mr Amos Garrett, Mr John Freeman and Mr Samuel Norwood. 'The Ancient City: A History of Annapolis in Maryland' by Elihu Samuel Riley. 1887

[2] Princes of Ireland, Planters of Maryland: A Carroll Saga 1500-1782 by Ronald Hoffman, 2002

[3] Margaret's Will was proved 23rd February 1738

[4] 'Scarce any ways or means: The Separated Woman in Colonial Maryland 1634-1776' by Karen Ann Lubieniecki. 2007

[5] Ibid

[6] The background to the Seward v Hicks case was that William Seward's father George had obtained a warrant for 1,000 acres of land in 1674 and surveyed a tract called 'Sectar' comprising some 769 acres in Dorchester County. George, however, failed to complete the registration of his claim properly with the land office as his finances failed and he left the province with the paperwork not completed. Whilst he was absent for many years others petitioned for the same land on the basis that the rent was unpaid and the owner was overseas. In 1683 George's son William applied to resume the process but his patent was not allowed. The two lawyers

The reason for mentioning this case is that some five years later, William Bladen would again be facing Macnemara in court, though with Bladen being the plaintiff and Macnemara being the defendant accused of murder. Meanwhile enmity between Secretary Lawrence and Attorney General Bladen and Governor Seymour rumbled on through the years and Board of Trade records for July 1707 show William giving a deposition in a dispute between Sir Thomas Lawrence and Governor Seymour but Lawrence's complaint did not appear to have any evidence. The substance of Lawrence's complaint was that he wanted satisfaction for the losses he had sustained in office by removal of ordinary licences, such losses he alleged were caused by Seymour and William Bladen.[1] When Governor Seymour came to write his Will on 12th December 1708 he made mention of his friends Major General Edward Lloyd and William Bladen and, in a codicil, directed them to collect monies due to him in the Province. Lloyd became Governor after Seymour's death.

*Father's Assistance in England*
William had the benefit of unwavering support from his lawyer father in London and father and son worked jointly on issues that concerned individuals with ties to both London and Annapolis.[2] Such as on 4th February 1708, Nathaniel was about his legal business at the Inner Temple in London where he was witnessing a notarising document concerning the estate of an individual with connections to Maryland and his son William. The document was drawn up by Nathaniel Blakiston who was the grandson of John Blakiston[3] one of King Charles I's Regicides. Nathaniel Blakiston had himself been Governor of Maryland 1698-1701 and, when he returned to England, acted as Agent for Maryland from London.[4] William Bladen's father Nathaniel fostered relations with the many influential people in Maryland who visited, resided or had their children sent to England for an education. For example, Edward Randolph - Surveyor-General of H.M. Customs, an Englishman who was an important colonial administrator who appointed William to the post of Surveyor and Searcher of Annapolis.

Whilst in England in June 1702 and about to embark on his 17th sea voyage to America, Randolph wrote his Will and appointed Nathaniel Bladen and a Mrs Mary Fogg responsible for approving his daughter's choice of husbands when the time came for her to marry.[5]
Along with Nathaniel, daughter Catherine (who was visiting London from Dublin) signed the document as a witness.

---

based their arguments on whether there was sufficient evidence of due process to allow the patent and the final verdict was 'Judgment upon the demurrer for the defendant'. Macnemara, no doubt, felt aggrieved at losing the case and that is as far as matters went, until some years later (after William's death) when the matter was appealed. The Seward daughters took up the case again and it was later found in their favour. Oct 1725 court of Appeals confirmed the decree of the Court of Chancery. D. Dulany and I. George for the appellant (Sewards) and T Bordley for the appellee in the Court of Appeal

[1] JBoT, Vol. 1, pp 397-407 (1920)

[2] William brought a law suit against Joseph Owen, a Derby merchant who had settled in Anne Arundel County regarding a property transation whereby William was trying to recover funds TNA: C9/472/86

[3] 1603-49 John Blakiston

[4] Manuscripts of the HoL, Vol. 17, p646, date 3rd February 1705. Signed legal papers, along with William Banastre, concerning a case which he felt there was grounds for appeal. The appeal was lost

[5] TNA: PROB 11/473/238 Will of Edward Randolph, 7th December 1703 probate

Randolph was basically the King's tax collector in the colonies, a role which made him naturally unpopular. His first hand dealing with colonists, particularly the obstructive and independently minded ones of Massachusetts, gave him cause to report back to, and influence, the Committee for Trade and Plantations. He recommended the proprietary charters be revoked and challenged the legality of the Massachusetts one. He died in America in 1703.[1]

William Bladen's status was augmented in the colony when he was made Alderman of Annapolis in 1708. He was one of six of the original aldermen on the city's first charter and later that same year he was appointed Commissary General or Judge of Probate. A few months later William inherited land from his friend Philip Lynes[2] who had been a former Mayor of St Mary's City.[3] The land was near the Elk and Susquehanna Rivers and had been formerly formed by George Talbot proprietor and was part of a tract of 1,400 acres - Bladen had already bought half the adjoining section of land from Charles Carroll.[4] To this section he added another one quarter of Kent Fort Manor (one of the earliest English settlements in America) he had purchased from Foster Turbutt on 4th April 1710.[5] As well as leaving a bequest to Bladen, Lynes also asked that William Bladen have charge of his funeral, if Lynes died in Annapolis.[6] Also in the area of Elkridge, William was involved in buying some land from Col. Edward Dorsey called 'Major's Choice' (west of Waterloo and north of the Old Brick Church in Anne Arundel County). Edward was the heir-at-law of Edward Dorsey 'the Immigrant'.[7] From his father, Edward inherited a tract of land called 'Dorsey' which, after Edward's death, his widow sold to William Bladen in 1706 (Bladen's name appears as purchaser but it was probably a joint venture with Charles Carroll). Edward Dorsey (the father) it was claimed in a later chancery case, had intended his property to be left for his children's benefit and had petitioned the Assembly to be permitted to sell those properties for his children in 1704, though he did so without his son Samuel Dorsey's knowledge. All was well and property was conveyed to Charles Carroll/William Bladen in 1706 and the sum was £150 payable in three instalments at certain dates. Soon after, however, Edward Dorsey died and it was claimed Bladen/Carroll kept the land but made no payments. Samuel Dorsey brought the case to equity in 1711 against William Bladen and John Israel.[8]

---

[1] The New England Historical and Genealogical Register, Vol. 48, 1894

[2] Abstract of the Testamentary Proceedings of the Prerogative Court of Maryland by Vernon L Skinner, 2007. Item 19B: 36 dated 28th April 1705 *"John Contee Esq who married widow of John Coates was granted administration on his estate for the benefit of the orphans. Securities: Philip Lynes Esq., William Bladen"*

[3] Court session 11th July 1709, William was dealing with probate for Richard Colville (Inner Temple) age 43 and his wife Frances, age 28 and Madam Mary Carter, age 22, to Philomenon Lloyd and William Bladen to recover from Elizabeth Carter, widow, and administratrix of Richard Carter. Abstract of Testamentary Proceedings of the Prerogative Court of Maryland p1-206 by Jr Skinner (21:166)

[4] Maryland Historical Magazine, Vol 52, p.229. 1957. Also, from Provincial Court Deeds, Liber PL No. 6, f67, 107: Son Thomas sold Fort Kent Manor on Kent Isle with Court Baron and Court Leet on 8th July 1724 to Thomas Colmore (a London merchant) for £370-6-3d. Six months later Thomas also sold 2,000 acres in Fort Kent Manor, Queen Anne's County to William Staveley and James Bennett of London for £600.

[5] Ibid

[6] Maryland Calendar of Wills, Vols I - VIII

[7] House of Delegates met in Edward Dorsey's house when the State House burned down in 1704

[8] The Dorsey Family by Dorsey, Wright, Maxwell J Dorsey, Jean Muir Dorsey, Nannie Ball Nimmo

Although the outcome is not known, with Bladen being the Attorney General it is unlikely he was required to divest himself of the land. Some kind of resolution was achieved, however, because on 23rd March 1718 the above Samuel Dorsey sold a portion of land called 'Gatenby' lying on the Several River consisting of 100 acres to Mrs Anne Bladen (William's wife).

On 11th July 1710 William, as Attorney General for the Crown, brought an indictment for murder against fellow lawyer Thomas Macnemara[1] and his accomplice John Mitchell. The victim was a man called Thomas Graham who was murdered aboard *"a certain Sloop called the 'Sarah' of Maryland in Chesapeake bay (that is to say) in the County of Ann Arundell aforesaid with force and Arms (to witt Swords Daggers Gunns and Pistolls) upon a certain Thomas Graham, merchant, in the peace of God and the Queen"*.[2] The charges against him were only partially successful and Macnemara's defence was to plead "homicide by chance medley" (or accidental death). He subsequently travelled to England to appeal against the conviction against him and managed to get it reversed but further charges were brought: *"After several acquittals by petit jurors, the provincial justices raised the charges to manslaughter and ordered his right hand branded"*.[3] He was branded with an "M" for murderer.

Back in Maryland, Macnemara continued his errant behaviour and further incidents of assault led Bladen to bring new charges against the lawyer. A charge of assault on a young man led to Macnemara pleading guilty and attempts were made to prevent him practising law. Whilst Pennsylvania succeeded in preventing him operating in their province, he managed to keep practising in Maryland, despite repeated efforts to stop him. He even managed to continue acquiring new appointments when, in 1715, he became Naval Officer of Patuxent and then Clerk to the House of Delegates. Indictments continued against him right up to his death in 1719[4] when he died heavily in debt. Maryland State Archives has preserved many early records from when William became Attorney General, from 1704 through to his death in 1718 in the form of so-called 'Black Books'. Extracts from the collection of 1,600 papers concerning Bladen's activities have been included in the Appendices at page 202-205 and make interesting further reading.

As an aside, a snippet to mention from 1712 concerning William was that he was involved in what was perhaps one of the last witchcraft trials in Maryland. A woman called Virtue Violl from Talbot County was brought to court on charges of *"being seduced by the devil most Wickedly and diabolically did Use Practice and Exercise Witchcraft"* when she was accused of causing a woman to become lame and speechless. Virtue was found innocent of the charge and allowed to go free.

---

[1] Thomas Macnemara died deeply in debt in 1720
[2] American Legal Records, Vol. 1, p158-159, 162
[3] Princes of Ireland, Planters of Maryland: A Carroll Saga, 1500-1782, 2002, by Ronald Hoffman. Also Her Majesty (Queen Anne) v Mackenamara 1712
[4] Archives of Maryland, Vol.33 by William H Brown, Clayton Colman Hall, Bernard Christian Steiner. MHS 1913

The sheer number of projects William was involved in and the multiplicity of jobs he held started to take their toll. Still only in his early forties, the first sign that William's health was suffering came in 1713 when he asked delegates of the Maryland Assembly to agree to allow him an Assistant because he was *"now indisposed in his health"*.[1] After much persuasion they eventually agreed and William's son-in-law Benjamin Tasker was appointed. William said that the long sessions of the assembly had caused him *"great toil and fatigue in dispatching the publick business"* and from this point on he began to scale back on his commitments, resigning[2] some of his appointments from October 1716, though others he held on to until his death in 1718. During the last years of William's life his name cropped up occasionally in the Journals of the Board of Trade on routine matters and in only a couple of the volumes do the names of the two brothers, William and Martin Bladen, overlap in the years 1714-17.

Bladen had become wealthy during his years in Maryland because as well as purchasing land for himself, William acquired land by inheritance from friends, such as Lynes, and also on the death of his van Sweringen in-laws. Just five years before William's death, his mother-in-law Mary van Sweringen died and left property to William (To son William and heirs: "Painter's Rest" with "The Addition") including 1,900 acres of Cecil County 'at the head of Sasafrax River, house and lot in Annapolis (wherein Jno Jordain lives)'.[3] William's estate at the time of his death comprised a large library,[4] a printing press, 48 law titles, 26 slaves and 9 servants and, after his debts were paid, he had personal property worth £1,645 and at least 15,745 acres of land.[5]

Of the 9 servants William had, five were convicts. A group of 80, mainly Scotsmen, had been captured in the Jacobite Uprisings and had been taken at Preston in Lancashire and sentenced to transportation. They were: Thomas Potts, George Thompson, John Ramsey, Alexander Reind and Thomas Forbus.[6] All were transported from Belfast/Liverpool on 24th May 1716 on the ship 'Friendship' arriving on 20th August 1716. The terms of their transportation punishment was that they were required to become servants to whichever planter in Maryland had bought them but, when their prison term ended, they would have their freedom, the minimum term being 7 years. Since they arrived into Bladen's care in 1716 this means they would still have been with him at his death in 1718. Benjamin Tasker took three as did Philemon Lloyd and Thomas Macnemara took two of these convicts/servants.

*Photograph of William's grave in Annapolis, Maryland*
*Courtesy of William Cooke*[7]

---

[1] MSA XXVI, 87, Records of the Lower House
[2] His Lordship's Patronage; Offices of Profit in Colonial Maryland by Don
[3] Maryland Calendar of Wills Vol 1-VIII, Jane Baldwin 1904-1928. Abstract of Wills for both Gerret and Mary van Sweringen are in the Appendices, p227
[4] Cross-Howell Glover-Stoddert & Related Familys. Records Compiled by Kate Annelia Cross Vandervelde, 1959

[5] Edward Papenfuse et al, Maryland State Archivist & Commissioner of Land Patents 1973-2013. A Biographical Dictionary of the Maryland Legislature 1635-1789, 2010
[6] Immigrant Ships Transcribers Guild c2008. Immigrantships.net/v2/1700v2/friendship17160820.html
[7] http://tobaccoland.blogspot.co.uk/2011/12/William-bladens-grave-annapolis.html

William left no Will and wife Anne renounced her right to administer his estate in favour of her daughter Anne Tasker. On her behalf, husband Mr Benjamin Tasker took on the role of Administrator after his wife gave her consent.[1] William was buried at St Anne's Episcopal Church, Church Circle, Annapolis in the small graveyard at the Church. Close by William's grave, there is also buried his son-in-law Benjamin Tasker Senior 1690-1768 and his grandson Benjamin Tasker Junior 1720-60. His descendants went on to dominate politics at the highest level in Maryland for many generations.

*Legacy*

William left an impressive legacy in terms of his family's total domination of high office in Maryland politics. Charles Carroll of Carrollton (grandson of Charles Carroll the Settler who William had worked so closely with) in later years complained to Daniel Dulany Jnr that the government of Maryland had been in just one family's hands for too many years. He cited Tasker, Ogle, Bladen and Dulany, but in fact he could have cited many more names. Rosamund Randall Beirne, writing of Sir Robert Eden's Governorship,[2] which had resulted directly from his marriage to Caroline Calvert sister to the dissolute Frederick 6th Lord Calvert, described these Bladen families as a 'Court Circle'.

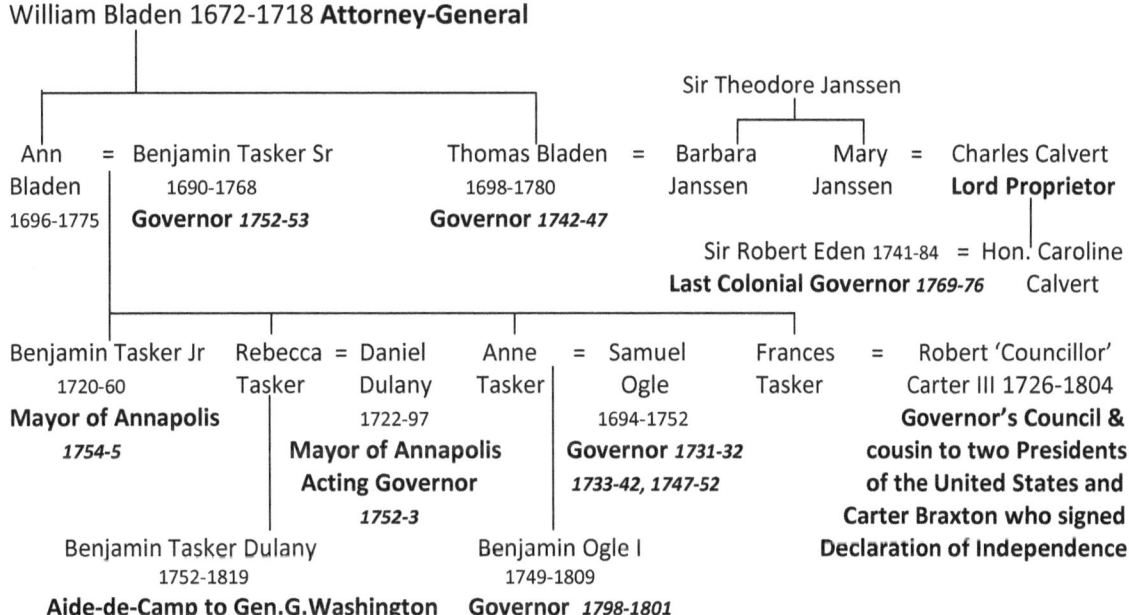

The following chart shows the main descendants who achieved high office:

---

[1] Test Proc. Lib. 23, fol 251, Maryland Historical Magazine, Vol. 5, 1910, p299 (314)
[2] Joshua Johnson, partner in an American merchant company told colleagues in Maryland *"Governor Eden owes very large sums here"*. Joshua Johnson's Letterbook 1771-74: letters from a merchant in London to his partners in Maryland. Joshua Johnson, Jacob M Price. LRS 1979. pp163-81

*Court Circle*

The Bladen family's influence over Maryland politics continued for decades after William's demise, through his descendants:

| Governors of Maryland | |
|---|---|
| 1731-2 | Samuel Ogle - husband of grand-daughter |
| 1732-3 | Charles Calvert - son's in-law relations |
| 1733-42 | Samuel Ogle - husband of grand-daughter |
| 1742-47 | Thomas Bladen - son |
| 1747-52 | Samuel Ogle - husband of grand-daughter |
| 1752-3 | Benjamin Tasker - son-in-law |
| 1769-76 | Sir Robert Eden - son's in-law relations |

*William's Descendants*

William's children and their spouses produced a coterie of relations who divided the most lucrative posts in government amongst themselves over succeeding generations. As well as those political 'giants' shown on the above chart, William's grand-daughter Elizabeth Tasker married Christopher Lowndes (English merchant and ship builder) and their descendants also held high office: their daughter Rebecca Lowndes married Benjamin Stoddert,[1] first Secretary of the US Navy. Other relations include Lloyd Lowndes who was Governor in 1896-1900, Edward Lloyd another Governor and Walter, the brother of Daniel Dulany II (the younger), who was Mayor of Annapolis.

William had more descendants than any other Yorkshire Bladen but, as most spent their lives in America it is beyond the scope of this book to include them. Indeed stories of the Taskers, Lowndes, Ogles and Dulaneys could fill several books on their own account, so for the purposes of this examination of Early Yorkshire Bladens, only those immediately connected with William or who returned to Yorkshire will be considered.

William and Anne had several children[2] but, since there is a great deal of information about two of their children (Anne and Thomas), the chronological order will be abandoned so those for whom there is less detail can be dealt with first.

---

[1] Memoirs of Benjamin Stoddert, First Secretary of the United States Navy by Harriot Stoddert Turner, Records of the Columbia Historical Soicety, Washington DC, Vol. 20 (1917), pp141-166
[2] St Mary's City Men's Career Files MSA SC 5094 - Maryland State Archives

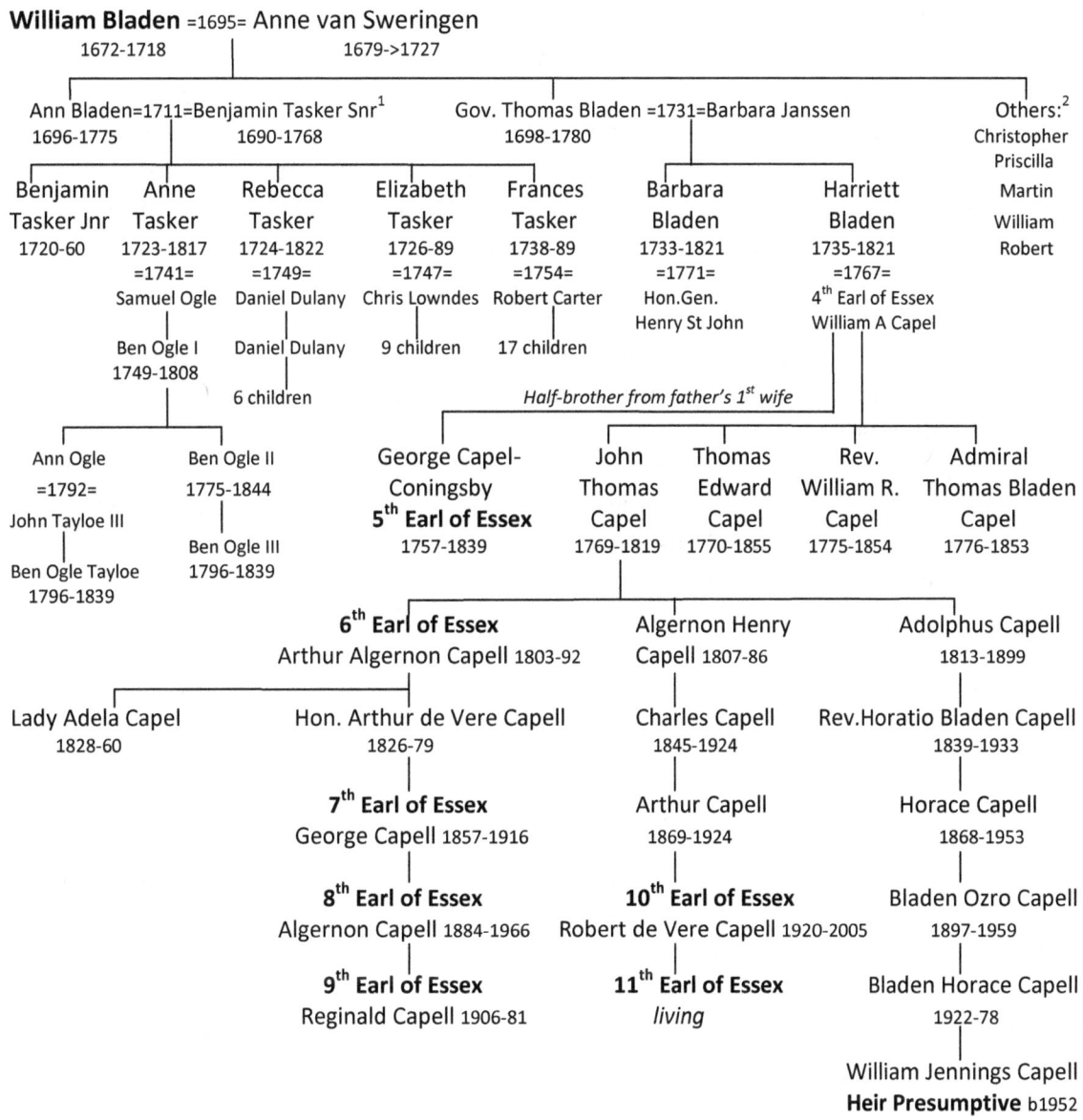

Surname spelling changed from Capel to Capell by Royal Licence on 23rd July 1880.

---

[1] Will of Benjamin Tasker, written 1766
[2] Records are incomplete for William's other children: Christopher b1700, Robert b1708

## Christopher Bladen

Christopher was born in Maryland about 1702 and only one record has surfaced on him so far which indicates he went to England and joined the army. 1731: *"Christopher Bladen, nephew to Col. Bladen, was appointed Ensign in Colonel Fielding's[1] regiment of Foot."*[2] Older brother Thomas would have been well acquainted with Hon. Lt-Colonel Charles Fielding who had been Captain of Pembroke's Horse. Fielding resided in Burlington Street, Mayfair, not far from Thomas Bladen's town house as Grosvenor Square.[3]

## Martin Bladen c1704-1749

Martin seems, like his brothers, to have left Maryland and resided in England after his father's death. Unfortunately it cannot be determined with certainty but it does seem likely, due to the size of his estate, that the following 1741 marriage relates to him: *"Mr Bladen, a Cheshire gentleman of a fine estate was married at Ormskirk in Lancashire to Mrs Wheatley of that place, an agreeable Lady with a fortune of 10,000 l."*. He died some eight years later but it is not known if the couple had children. Obituary: Martin Bladen of Wigan, Lancashire d. 5th April 1749.[4]

## Priscilla Bladen

Presumed to have died young because sister Anne was referred to as the *"only daughter of the Hon. William Bladen of Annapolis"*.[5]

## Anne Bladen

William's eldest child Anne married at just 15 years of age and travelled soon after to England on honeymoon taking her younger brother Thomas with her. This was probably the last time she would see her grandfather as Nathaniel Bladen died a few years later. In a letter to daughter Frances, Nathaniel described Anne Bladen's visit to England with new husband Benjamin Tasker (they had married in 1711): *"...Indeed on Wednesday last, Mr Harman underwent the trouble to bring me a great many proceedings to Earls Court where we were in much confusion in removing all the goods, and the next morning I came to town for my grandchild Nanny Tasker and her husband were to dine with us......."* Then in a postscript to the letter Nathaniel said:- *"I am now in Berk[e]ley Street[6] but you may direct as usual. I have some letters for you from Maryland which Nanny brought. When I see Mr Harman I shall give him them that he may send you 'em frank. She's the same face and person, only grown taller than her brother Thom, half the head, she is very grave and discreet. Her husband is eight years older than she is, viz 22, he is a sober modest young man, looks very young, in short they are but a boy and a girl.*

---

[1] Sometimes spelt Feilding
[2] Gentleman's Magazine 1732, Vol. 2, p587 and Ipswich Journal 15th April 1749 (G.M. 188)
[3] Survey of London, Vol. 31-32, part 2 (1963) pp566-72 (Burlington estate, Mayfair, north of Piccadilly)
[4] London Magazine and Monthly Chronologer, Vol. 10, 1741, p309, Gentleman's Magazine, No. 188
[5] Something about Dulaney (Dulany) Family and a Sketch of the Southern Cobb family by Benjamin Dulany 1815-59, Washington. A few sources state Priscilla Bladen married Robert Carter II (1704-34) but Carter married Priscilla Churchill
[6] Son Martin's residence in Westminster

*Cousen Brathwait was so obliging to equip her before she appeared here: she asked me when she first saw 'em – cousin do these two ly together? I answered, do you doubt it. Her clothes are exceedingly pretty and she becomes them well. And Thom was as fine as anybody, and they found him so when they came, but how long is the question. Mr Carroll and wife go this week, they have had my letters above half a year......"*[1] It is not known how often the Bladens in Maryland visited England as, from the change in Anne and Tom's appearance noted by Nathaniel, probably not that often.[2] After his daughter's marriage William gave the new couple plot 27 on a development of Annapolis land where he himself had purchased plots and after William's death, Benjamin Tasker purchased lots 36 and 37 from his father-in-law's estate. The young couple's home on plot 27 had burned down and so they enlarged the new plot and it became one of the finest homes in Annapolis, the property was on Market Street in Annapolis overlooking Spa Creek. He was appointed assistant to his father-in-law William Bladen in his later years as William's health declined. On 4th November 1718 Benjamin petitioned the Treasury Department at Whitehall to be Surveyor of the Customs at Annapolis, to be "appointed in case William Bladen is dead". In fact, by the time the Treasury had received Benjamin's petition and presented it to their meeting, Bladen had already died in August of that year.[3]

Benjamin cut a swath through politics, serving numerous terms as Mayor of Annapolis as well as being a Member of the Council of Maryland, Judge of the Prerogative Court, Acting Governor, Agent and Receiver-General[4] and, for a period of 32 years, he served as President of the Council. According to 'In Memoriam: Benjamin Ogle Tayloe' 1872, Benjamin attended the Albany Congress in 1754 and travelled on horse-back from Maryland to Philadelphia where he met up with Dr Franklin and the pair continued their journey to Albany together. Benjamin acquired large tracts of land as well as founding the Baltimore Ironworks Company. Benjamin and Ann had ten children, 5 boys and 5 girls though only half appear to have survived to adulthood. Since their descendants have no connection with Yorkshire, they are not covered in this volume.[5]

---

[1] Copy letter in the possession of Lord Rosse. Nathaniel Bladen to Frances Hamond, 30th September 1712

[2] The widowed Anne Tasker, née Bladen, is mentioned in her father-in-law's Will of 1766

[3] CTB, Vol. 32, pp107-114

[4] 'The Ancient City': A History of Annapolis in Maryland by Elihu Samuel Riley. 1887

[5] Another family connection which should not be overlooked is the Lloyd family, in fact two connections viz: Rebecca Tasker married Daniel Dulany (maternal descendant of Philemon Lloyd) and Anne Tasker's daughter Meliora Ogle married James Anderson, grandson of Edward Lloyd (brother of Philemon). Edward Lloyd brought 60 settlers in 1645 (including Dorseys). These related Maryland families frequently corresponded with Osgood Hanbury (brother in law to Sampson Lloyd III), for example: Daniel Dulany (senior) who was married thirdly to Elizabeth Lloyd, and Robert (Councillor) Carter, Benjamin Tasker (mentioned him in his Will), Anne Ogle (née Tasker) had Osgood Hanbury as her attorney, along with her son in law James Anderson and others had dealings with the Lloyds Hanbury partners. These Lloyds appear to descend from a Welsh puritan family (the Wye House Lloyds). Curiously, Sampson Lloyd II (b1698) who was the father-in-law of Osgood Hanbury (Quaker) began in partnership with John Taylor 1711-75 of 7 Dale End in Birmingham in 1765, originally called Taylor Lloyds Bank. John Taylor died just a few years after setting up the Birmingham banking partnership, but his descendents continued their association with the bank until the 1850s and may connect to the John Taylor who baptised his son John Bladen Taylor (baptised 1764). Although there appears to be no blood connection to the Bladen family, John Taylor 1738-1814 of Townhead Lancs and Abbot Hall in Kendall was serving in India as a Naval Surgeon for the EIC. He married Dorothy Northall (née Rumbold) - daughter of William Rumbold of

*Thomas Bladen 1698-1780*

William's son Thomas was born in Annapolis but, as just described above, was sent back to England for his education at age 11. This was common practice among those who could afford it as it was believed far better facilities were in England for a gentleman's education. Thomas was admitted to the Inner Temple[1] on 8th July 1712 and sister Anne and her husband remained in England until at least the end of September of that year. Thomas, during this time away from home, would have come under the care and guardianship of his family members, including grandfather Nathaniel, his Bladen aunts but, in particular, his Uncle Martin. Martin became very close to the young boy in exactly the same way that he became guardian and carer to his sister Elizabeth's son, Edward Hawke (both having lost their fathers in 1718) and his sister Frances's grand-daughter Catherine Brooke.

Thomas was 20 years old when his father died in Maryland and, to manage some of his father's real estate and other American holdings he made use of his brother-in-law Benjamin Tasker, who had been his father's assistant at the Maryland Assembly in later years. Thomas conveyed some of his assets over to Benjamin who, being situated in America, was better placed to manage affairs for him.[2] It is possible that Thomas was in Maryland when his father William died on 7th August 1718 because just days before, on 25th July, he had a lot surveyed in Annapolis, though this could easily have been arranged for him by his brother-in-law Benjamin Tasker who also had land surveyed. Land Office records show that Bladen, Tasker and his father's business partner Charles Carroll and violent lawyer Thomas Macnemara were the first to take plots of land in the centre of Annapolis in the area around the Public Circle (State House): Carroll had the first tract surveyed on the north-west of Duke of Gloucester Street (running to Market Street), Macnemara had the second tract surveyed (south-west of Duke of Gloucester Street) plus five others in the same vicinity, then Bladen and Tasker all had tracts in the centre of Annapolis.[3]

In England, Thomas's town residence in 1722-34 was in the Vintry parish next to the River Thames at the city end of Southwark Bridge in London[4] but thereafter he was in the parish of St George, Hanover Square. He disposed of some of his father's property and land in Maryland, but not all.[5]

---

the EIC in 1762 (her brother, Sir Thomas Rumbold, was the Governor of Madras and was there 1757-63) at the same time as Captain John Bladen Tinker so that may be where the families met. Dorothy's father William Rumbold was also of Low Leyton in Essex, again, there are Bladen connections there too as that is where Governor Thomas Bladen lived and was a short distance from Barking, Martin Bladen's residence. The year when John Bladen Taylor was baptised, in 1764 in Calcuta, was just before John Bladen Tinker made his return to England and, since it is known for certain that Tinker was in Calcuta, it seems likely that John Bladen Taylor may have been named for Capt. John Bladen Tinker

[1] Recorded as Thomas Fairfax Bladen on the Inner Temple Admissions Database. 1698-1780

[2] 11 Oct 1720, Thomas Bladen of the parish of St Anne's Westminster, son and heir of William Bladen, late of the City of Annapolis, MD, deceased conveys to Benjamin Tasker of the said city and province, gent, a tract called 'Woodchurch Rest' in Anne Arundel County (Anne Arundel County Records, Lib. CW. No. 1 fol 403). Maryland Historical Magazine, Vol. 5, 1910. P298 (313)

[3] 'The Ancient City': A History of Annapolis in Maryland by Elihu Samuel Riley. 1887

[4] London Land Tax Records 1692-1932, London Metropolitan Archives

[5] In September 1723, William Woodford (London agent for George Mason) was trying to meet Thomas to buy some of the land Thomas inherited from his father in Maryland. 'The Five George Masons: Patriots and

Thomas sold land his father owned at Fort Kent Manor[1] on Kent Isle with Court Baron and Court Leet on 8th July 1724 to Thomas Colmore (a London merchant) for £370-6-3d. Six months later Thomas also sold 2,000 acres in Fort Kent Manor, Queen Anne's County to William Staveley and James Bennett of London for £600. If not before, then by 9th September 1724 he had appointed an attorney in Annapolis to handle his affairs.[2] He was a very wealthy young man and kept interests on both sides of the Atlantic, and returned to live in America for a few years in the 1740s as Governor. His father William's interest in printing had led to the acquisition of a Print Shop in Maryland and in 1724 Thomas sold it to his brother-in-law Daniel Dulany. At some later point Dulany sold the property on to another family member, Sam Ogle for £160.[3]

Thomas was a gentleman with a good inheritance and so rumours that he "lived by gambling"[4] might well have been true which may have been why uncle Martin Bladen interceded at this point to use his friends to get Thomas a parliamentary seat and have him focused on a career. Thomas became MP for Steyning, a seat previously held by the son of the Duke of Chandos (Martin Bladen's good friend), a position he held from 1727 to 1734. He does not appear to have spoken in Parliament and voted with the government and his uncle: i.e. 1729 Civil List, 1730 Hessian Bill, 1733 Excise Bill and 1734 Septennial Act. During this time, again with money from his father's estate, he purchased Glastonbury Abbey from the Duke of Somerset for £12,000 (about £1m in today's money) or, a more romantic version of his acquisition is that he won it at dice from the 3rd Duke of Devonshire, William Cavendish,[5] which is also entirely possible.[6]

Thomas married on 14th July 1731 to Barbara Janssen[7] who was the second daughter of Sir Theodore Janssen.[8] Sir Theodore had been one of the very first residents of a newly-built Hanover Square[9] where Martin Bladen lived when in town and Theodore's younger brother William had been Principal Secretary for Maryland, though based in England. Barbara's sister Mary was Lady Baltimore (married to Charles Calvert the Proprietary Governor of Maryland, 5th Baron Baltimore) and this marriage paved the way for these Anglo-American families associated with the Bladens to achieve Governorship, i.e. Ogles and Taskers.

---

Planters of Virginia and Maryland' by Pamela C Copeland and Richard K MacMaster, Board of Regents of Gunston Hall, p58. 1989

[1] Provincial Court Deeds, Liber PL No. 6, f67, 107

[2] 9th Sept 1724. "Richard Hiller of London, gent, deposed that Thomas Bladen, son and heir of William Bladen Esq of Annapolis, Maryland, had appointed an attorney in Maryland (Lord Mayor's Court of London Depositions, Coldham, 1985)" Complete Book of Emigrants 1700-50, Peter Wilson Coldham, Baltimore 1988

[3] Personal Discipline and Material Culture – An Archaeology of Annapolis, Maryland 1695-1870. Jonas Green Print Shop by Paul A. Shackel. 1993

[4] The Dunciad in Four Books by Alexander Pope, edited by Valerie Rumbold, 1999

[5] A History of the County of Somerset: Vol. 9, Glastonbury and Street by M C Siraut, A T Thacker and Elizabeth Williamson, edited by R W Dunning. 2006

[6] After Thomas's death his two sons-in-law (General St John and the Earl of Essex) sold it on for £40,500. Later, in 1806 a James Rocke would buy the same estate for £75,000 and then began the process of breaking it down into portions

[7] Gentleman's Magazine, i, 310. Marriage on 14 July 1731 of Thomas Bladen Esq to Barbara and second daughter of Sir Theodore Janssen and parish register of St Stephen Walbrook 1716-97

[8] Sir Theodore Janssen 1658-1748, a French immigrant and wife Williamsa

[9] Resident at 1 Cork Street on the Burlington Estate, St James, Westminster from 1725-34

Barbara's father was a founder member and Governor of the Bank of England, having invested some £10,000. He was also a former Director of the South Sea Company and was financially penalised by Parliament when the 'bubble' burst.[1] Almost one month after their marriage, perhaps whilst still enjoying their honeymoon, the couple was reported to be on a ship that docked at Gravesend. The vessel 'Sea Nymph' was owned by Lord Baltimore[2] and the party on board included Lord and Lady Baltimore, Thomas Bladen [3]and his new wife Barbara (née Janssen) and John Highmore. The next day the party continued their journey to Spithead where they visited the squadron commanded by Sir George Walton before departing to continue their "Expedition of Pleasure".[4] Thomas was closely connected with the Russell family, Dukes of Bedford who owned Southampton House, later called Bedford House in Bloomsbury, and their main seat at Woburn Abbey. Thomas, the Janssens and Martin Bladen were known to play cards with the Dukes of Bedford,[5] the Bedfords were right at the heart of the administration of the day.

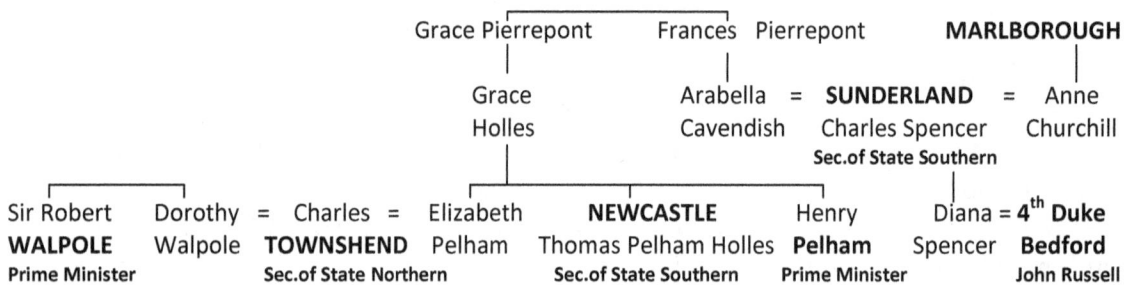

Later Thomas's youngest daughter would go on to marry a relation of the Duke of Bedford (Earl of Essex).

*Amersham Election*

After losing his seat at Steyning in 1734, Thomas stood twice for election as an MP for Amersham in Buckinghamshire; firstly in 1734 when he was defeated and then again in February 1735. He stood as a non-partisan candidate in opposition to the powerful Drake family who had control of the area. It was a tiny borough of less than 200 people and Thomas secured only 50 votes in the first election. It was only after incumbent Sir William Young vacated the seat in order to stand for a seat at Honiton in Devon that Thomas came to acquire it and he retained it until 1741, after which he went to America.

---

[1] Memoirs of Extraordinary Popular Delusions, Vol. 1 by Charles Mackay. 1841
[2] Sea Nymph was the same vessel that gave chase after pirate Stede Bonnet - the gentleman pirate in Carolina. Bonnet was eventually caught and hanged
[3] A newspaper report on Thursday 27 July 1732 (Derby Mercury) reported a tennis match taking place between Lord James Cavendish and Mr Bladen near the Haymarket, for 500 guineas, this match was a draw and had to be replayed five days later. Martin was known to be a great friend of Lord Cavendish's but it seems more likely that the Mr Bladen mentioned might have been Thomas Bladen, Martin's nephew who was nearer Lord James Cavendish's age and known as a great gambler and a fellow parliamentarian
[4] Stamford Mercury, Thursday 12th August 1731
[5] Woburn and the Russells, p98 by Georgiana Blakiston, 1980

His running partner in Amersham in 1735 was Thomas Gore (closely connected with Martin Bladen and his Tinker cousins). Gore was MP for Amersham from 1735-46 and then took over after Martin Bladen's death in 1746 as MP for Portsmouth 1746-47.

During the 1730s Thomas and Barbara began having children, first born Barbara arrived in 1733, then in 1735 youngest daughter Harriet was born. The family probably resided on the Glastonbury estate in summer but in the winter months they occupied a town house in London at number 9 (now actually number 10) Grosvenor Square which, at that time, would be a fairly new build. Thomas became MP for Ashburton[1] in Devon but, after a few years of the family being settled comfortably, he was offered and accepted an appointment as Lieutenant-General and Governor of Maryland and the whole family set sail in 1742 for America. Journals of the Board of Trade record on 10th March 1741 that the King had approved the recommendation by Charles Calvert Lord Baltimore for Thomas Bladen to be Deputy Governor of Maryland in the place of Sam Ogle, who had married Thomas's niece Anne Tasker that same year.[2] The decision to appoint Thomas as Governor came about through his connection with the Lord Proprietor of Maryland, his brother-in-law 5th Lord Baltimore  The two got on very well, in fact Thomas was Executor of Lord Baltimore's Will. Having his uncle Martin Bladen on the Board of Trade, the body responsible for recommending governors, would no doubt have been helpful too.[3] The relationship between Martin and his nephew Thomas was not confined to politics or a shared passion for gambling but from the late 1720s Martin had entrusted his nephew Thomas and made him privy to all his personal business. Thomas and Martin were very close and Martin made him a major beneficiary in his Will should his daughter not produce male heirs.

Thomas and his family travelled to America on a merchant ship within a convoy of vessels commanded by Captain Gordon of 'The Hound'. In a reference to Thomas's voyage to America, Martin wrote from Aldborough Hatch (his country home) on 29th May 1742 to his other protégé Admiral Hawke (who he affectionately called Ned): *"Dear Ned, I send this letter at a venture by my friend Bing, who goes in Sir Thomas Robinson's service to Barbardoes .... by a letter I lately received from your mother, she was then in good health, and that my nephew Tom Bladen, is made Governor of Maryland and sails at the same time with Sir Thomas Robinson."*[4] On 13th April 1742, a minute in the Journals of the Board of Trade records that Lord Baltimore, proprietary owner of Maryland, had proposed Abraham and William Janssen (Bladen's wealthy uncles) to act as sureties for Thomas Bladen *"for his observing the Acts of Trade and Navigation"*.

---

[1] Thomas 'won' the election to Ashburton on 20th February 1735, but it was uncontested. Sir William Yonge had decided to stand for Honiton in Devon instead

[2] Although Thomas's appointment is referred to in the official records as 'Deputy Governor', he was in fact 'Governor'; the title 'Deputy' was probably a deferment to the authority of the absentee Baltimore who had only once in 1732 been present in the colony. Sam Ogle would return to the post when Thomas Bladen vacated it some six years later

[3] Treasury Warrant issued 29th April 1742 Thomas Bladen, approved by His Majesty as Lt. Gov of Maryland, he having been nominated and appointed thereunto by the Right Honourable Charles Lord Baltimore Proprietor - CTB and Papers, Vol. 6, 1742-5

[4] The Life of Edward, Lord Hawke, Admiral of the Fleet: with some account of the origin of the English Wars in the reign of George II by Montagu Burrows, 1888

Like all other Governors, he duly took his oath to uphold those Acts which were unpopular with colonists as they forced them to use English vessels and more expensive English imports rather than those of rival colonial powers, in particular the Dutch.

On arrival in Maryland Thomas was honoured by news that a district in Prince George County, originally called Garrison's Landing, was to be renamed Bladensburg in his honour. Like others working in Maryland had found before him such as his father William, Thomas would be expected to hold multiple appointments simultaneously, beginning with Surveyor-General of the Western Shore and then Chancellor.

### 1744: Treaty of Lancaster

One familiar face Thomas found in the Maryland House of Delegates was his father's old partner Charles Carroll but, after an initial warm welcome, Bladen found the Lower House just as difficult to deal with as his predecessor Sam Ogle had.[1] Those elements which would eventually lead to the American Revolution were becoming palpable at this time as Assemblies increasingly challenged Governors' authority. There was, however, broad agreement that a solution to the problem with Indians had to be found quickly and one way to achieve this was to buy out any claims they had in Maryland. To that end, it was decided to appoint commissioners to look into the matter but the Assembly insisted on making their own selections. Governor Bladen considered this a challenge to his authority and declined to ratify proceedings and so the issue could not be progressed.

Later in 1744 and with no sign of a break in the impasse, Bladen decided to appoint his own commissioners, without reference to the Assembly, and those commissioners undertook Treaty negotiations with the Six Nations Indians and commissioners from Virginia and Pennsylvania, at Lancaster in Pennsylvania. Bladen said it was *"absolutely necessary, for the preservation of the lives and security of the property of His Majesty's subjects .... to enter into a Treaty with the Six Nations ..... in case of a rupture with France"* and the 1744 Treaty settled the western boundary of the province of Maryland.[2] For the sum of £300, the Indians renounced all claim to territory in Maryland.[3] This issue was one of Thomas's most significant achievements whilst in post.

### Description

There is a good description of Governor Thomas Bladen and his wife Barbara from the Treaty of Lancaster by one who attended on 19th May 1744.[4] William Black described being entertained by the Bladens with glasses of punch and fine wines. He described Thomas as *"in his Person inclining to be the larger Size of Men, Straight and well-proportioned, a Manly Face and Sanguine Complexion, seem'd Complaisant and free, of a Good Deal of Humour in Conversation, he had not a little Wit, and is allow'd to have a considerable Claim to Good*

---

[1] Thomas was given the military title of Colonel whilst in post, but this may have been an honorary title due to his rank in the government

[2] The Founders of Anne Arundel and Howard Counties, Maryland: A Genealogical and Biographical Review from Wills, Deeds and Church Records by J D Warfield. Copyright 1905, published 2008

[3] McSherry's History of Maryland, p110

[4] Journal of William Black, 1744 cited in The Pennsylvania Magazine of History and Biography, Vol 1., No. 2 (1877), pp117-132

*Sense, and every other Qualification Requir'd to Compleat a Gentleman; his Stature and Deportment is much becoming and adds not a little to the Dignity of his Office".*

Wife Barbara was also described as being "of middle Size, straight made, Black hair, and of a black Complexion much pitted with the smallpox, but very agreeable, and seems to have a great Stock of Good Nature, as well as Wit; she is a passionate Admirer of the Game Whist, which she is reckon'd to play admirably well; she is, by Birth, a French Woman, tho' not addicted to the Foppery of that Nation in appearance."

**Barbara Bladen née Janssen**[1]

*Governor's Mansion*

The most visible negative symbol of Bladen's tenure as Governor was the unfinished Governor's mansion which became known as "Bladen's Folly" or "Governor's folly". The Maryland Assembly had agreed in 1733 to allocate £3,000 to purchase land to rebuild the governor's residence but this was not enacted at the time. Then, with Thomas Bladen's arrival in post in 1742, it was decided to add a further £1,000 to the fund and four plots of land were purchased for the proposed building.[2] However, it quickly became apparent that Thomas's ambitious plans for the mansion outstripped the funds the Assembly had already approved and construction was halted when only the first floor of the building was completed. It was another stalemate and the building was left to decay for 40 years until 1784 when it was remodelled into the present day McDowell Hall, St John's College.

Another example of the difficulties Thomas faced with his Assembly occurred in 1745. Britain's war with France had, as part of the continuing War of the Austrian Succession, spread to the colonies and in June 1745 had resulted in a huge victory when British and New England troops captured the important French port of Louisbourg in Cape Breton, Canada - a fort which had concerned Martin Bladen at the Board of Trade for many years as he felt it was the area where the British Colonies were weak and vulnerable to attack. On 5th August 1745 Thomas called together a fully-attended session of the Maryland Assembly to inform them: *"This session was occasioned by a letter I have received from the Governor of New England, which shall be laid before you. You will find by it, that we are called upon to give our assistance towards securing to the obedience of our Sovereign the late acquisition of Cape Breton ...This service requiring the first place in consultations, and the speediest dispatch, I shall postpone the mention of any other matters to you, 'til we have discharged our duties upon this point".*

---

[1] Journal of William Black, 1744 cited in The Pennsylvania Magazine of History and Biography, Vol 1., No. 2 (1877), pp117-132. Picture of Barbara Bladen (Janssen) out of copyright

[2] The Ancient City': A History of Annapolis in Maryland by Elihu Samuel Riley. 1887

The Assembly responded by saying they were ready and willing to render assistance and that *"although exempted from the call for troops, they would proceed to raise a support"*.

Bladen's next step was to seek the Lower House's sanction of funds to support the garrison, however, members sat for a full week but no agreement was reached.

Instead, they responded by challenging Bladen to explain by what authority he had levied a tax on the freemen of Maryland. It was a power struggle. Bladen's response, after a few days of exchanges, was to angrily tell them *"you were resolved to treat me with the utmost indecency and ill manners ..."*. Instead he tried, and succeeded, to insist that such matters were secondary to the principal objective of supporting the Cape Breton garrison. Three days later the legislature relented and voted £1,000. That was not, however, the end of the difficulties Bladen faced. The Lower House continued to challenge his authority, particularly his grounds for enforcing a tax, *"We, therefore, hope you will agree with us, that it is a high infringement on the liberties of the people of Maryland to levy any taxes on them under color of law, as not only we, but our constituents generally conceived has been done in this case."*[1] Bladen encountered the same difficulties other governors faced in the colonies when Britain's right to impose taxes was beginning to be challenged and these difficulties continued until he left his post the following year.

*1746: Leaving America*

By 1746 his time in post was coming to an end as the difficulties of the job were becoming more pronounced. Previous incumbent and relation Samuel Ogle had found the post difficult to hold down because of the conflicting interests between the Proprietor Owners of Maryland and the Lower House. That may have been the reason he left the post, although another version is that he was dismissed because "he was tactless and quarrelsome".[2] So, on 16th May 1747[3] Thomas left Maryland with his family and returned to England, this time not to return. He was succeeded by Sam Ogle, his niece's husband, who had held the Governorship before Bladen. When Thomas left Maryland, he left his vast land acquisitions in the hands of his American relations. Many years later on 20th April 1773, Thomas and wife Barbara entered into an Indenture Deed with Daniel Dulany (husband of niece Rebecca) which would allow Daniel to act on their behalf. Some 3,742 acres of land, with all buildings thereon, which were held by Thomas were conveyed to Daniel Dulany for £100. The deed stated that, since Thomas was now resident in England, that it would be easier for Dulany to dispose of the land as he was present.[4]

Back in England he resumed his former lifestyle as a gentleman. He was a friend of John Jeffreys the notorious gamester who frequented White's Gentleman's Club.[5]

---

[1] The Ancient City': A History of Annapolis in Maryland by Elihu Samuel Riley. 1887
[2] A Biographical Dictionary of the Maryland Legislature 1635-1789 by Edward C. Papenfuse, et. al. 2010
[3] Other reports say he left on 2nd June on the 'Spencer' Frigate. Captain Adam Spencer but that they did not arrive in England until 11th November of that year
[4] Provincial Court Land Records, 1770-74, Vol. 726, p610. MSA
[5] In 1748 Thomas was involved in a mortgage (lease/release) involving the Jeffreys family. Thomas was himself a gambler and the mortgage was between him and John Jeffreys, fellow gamester and member of White's Gentleman's Club in St James. Jeffreys dissipated his vast inherited wealth and this mortgage appears to have been his selling off one of his estates at Pen-coed Castle, St Brides, Magor, Llandegang, Wilcrick and Undy in the counties of Monmouth and Wiltshire for £2,000, other parties signed the deed

Jeffreys dissipated his great inheritance and indeed, in 1748 Bladen entered into a mortgage deed with Jeffreys over his properties, no doubt to clear gambling debts. Bladen also had a passion for the horses. Many people of Thomas's acquaintance were involved with horses, racing or breeding and he was listed in 'Owners and Breeders of the 17th and 18th Centuries – of thoroughbred racehorses'.[1]

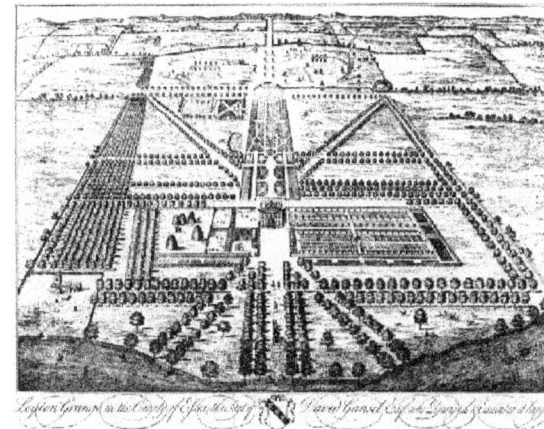

In 1754 Thomas purchased the Manor House at Leyton and renamed it The Grange. The house was built in 1720 and Thomas resided there until his death in 1780. The house was demolished in 1861 to make way for a housing development.

Picture, right, courtesy of David Chapman, Leyton and Leytonstone Historical Society.

**Thomas Bladen's home, The Grange, Leyton**

The Grange (left and above) was built in 1720 in the Palladian style by owner David Gansel with four classical female figures standing on the pediment. By the time Thomas Bladen owned the house, two additional wings augmented the size considerably. Garden layout may have been based on the union flag as the union of GB had only occurred a few years earlier.

In 1752 Thomas was the executor of the Will of Charles 5th Lord Baltimore (his brother-in-law) and 1765 saws his wife and two daughters receive a very large legacy following the death of Sir Abraham Janssen. Sir Abraham was uncle to Thomas's wife Barbara and left each of the ladies about 10,000*l*. This must have been very apt timing for daughter Harriet in particular who shortly afterwards became married to William Holles Capel (Earl of Essex) and the other daughter Barbara married in 1771 to General Henry St John.

On 11th March 1775 Thomas sold some paintings at Christie's Auction House, one painting was called 'Man and Girl Playing Cards' which was considered to be identical with a picture called 'A Man and Woman at Cards' attributed to Rembrandt.[2] Lot number 61, went for 65 guineas, being bought by the Bishop of Bristol (Dr Thomas Newton).

---

[1] He was owner of 'Bladen's Grey Horses'; other relations on the list include William Capel 3rd Earl of Essex owner of 'Smiling Ball', William Bentinck, 2nd Duke of Portland owner of 'Portland Arabian', John Hollis 1st Duke of Newcastle owner of 'Newcastle Turk and Paget Arabian', Benjamin Tasker Jnr importer of 'Selima' into Maryland, and Robert Walpole owner of 'Walpole's or Orford Grey Turk'. Owned 'Artistotle' whose pedigree in Bladen's own words was *"my brown horse Aristotle now sold to Mr Hodgin, bred by me, was got by the Cullen Arabian, his dam by Crab, his grandma by Hobgoblin, his grandma by the Godolphin Arabian out of a famous mare called White Cheek"*. American Turf Register and Sporting Magazine, Vol. 1. The London Chronicle reported in 1761 (Vol. 9, p590) that 'Mr Bladen's bay mare Essex Lady had won the purse of fifty pounds

[2] Claude Lorrain: The Enchanted Landscape by Martin Sonnabend & J Whiteley with Christian Rumelin, 2011

It was later acquired by 5th Baron Monson of Gatton Park in Surrey and was exhibited at the Royal Academy in 1886.

*End of Life*

The Last Will and Testament for Thomas[1] (see Appendices, p228) detailed the enormous wealth he amassed during his life. He owned the Glastonbury Estate, which would have been most of the town itself plus the abbey and lands and bequeathed them, plus property in Albemarle Street in London and all other property in America and England, to his cousin Martin Bladen Hawke, son of the great Admiral Hawke, in Trust. Hawke was to dispose of the same and the sums of money raised was to be paid for the marriage settlements for daughter Barbara who was married to Henry St John and his younger daughter Harriet who had married the Earl of Essex. A sum of £10,000 was to be paid to each. A similar sum was allocated to the children of his daughters, though only Harriet had children.

Thomas had paid handsomely to attract husbands for his daughters and they benefited enormously after his demise, which occurred in 1780 when he died aged 82 years. Thomas was buried at Leyton Churchyard,[2] St Mary the Virgin, Church Road, Walthamstow. Leyton and Leytonstone Historical Society have recently carried out a survey of the churchyard and plotted all the tombs. A visit to the church on a Thursday lunchtime, when the church is open for an hour or more, will enable the plot of graves to be viewed as it is displayed on the right in the chancel.[3] Wife Barbara's Will of 1780[4] directed that she be buried in the same vault next to her husband and stated *"I desire not to be nail'd up in my coffin until a week after I am dead"*. She left substantial sums of money to her daughters Barbara and Harriet and her sons-in-law, but with the proviso for her daughter *"that she shall not be liable to the continual debts or encumbrances of her husband Lord Essex"* and a similar statement for Barbara's husband. Barbara (the mother) died in 1784.

*Land Purchased in Maryland*

At the time of his appointment as Governor of Maryland it was reported that Thomas held 6,955 acres in Charles, Baltimore and Cecil Counties plus the land he inherited from his father in the counties of Anne Arundel and Queen Anne which amounted to some 15,000 acres.[5] Most of the land he inherited from his father was sold on and some of it was confiscated by the state in 1782. Thirty-five years after Thomas's death, in May 1815, there was a chancery case involving these grants and the assigning of them - Steuart et al., Lesse v Mason. By way of explaining the land holdings in Maryland that Thomas died possessed of, it is necessary to give a little background. Thomas had inherited a great deal of land in Maryland after his father's death in 1718 and some of his father's estate had been handed over to Benjamin Tasker to manage in situ. Whilst Thomas was in London, however, a man called William Woodford was trying to contact him with an offer to purchase some acres.

---

[1] TNA: PROB 11/1061/333 Will of Thomas Bladen, date 26th February 1780
[2] Lysons: The Environs of London: being an historical account of the towns, villages, p679
[3] Information courtesy of David Chapman, Leyton and Leytonstone Historical Society
[4] TNA: PROB 11/1113/112 Will of Barbara Bladen, written 18th February 1780, probate 5th February 1784
[5] A Biographical Dictionary of the Maryland Legislature 1635-1789 by Edward C. Papenfuse, et. al. 2010

Woodford was acting as Agent to George Mason (Treasurer of the Ohio Company) who was based in America and Mason was intent on buying up land in both Maryland and Virginia. Woodford wrote to Mason in 1723 saying *"I have yrs of 18$^{th}$ and 23$^{rd}$ Sept with copies of Deeds of Land to Buy of Mr Blayden whose lodgings I have been twice at but could not meet with him. Intend in a few days to go againe, his living at the other End of Town makes it ye more difficult to light of him, however hope to see him to give you an Acct per this Opportunity what can be gone in ye affair".*[1] Woodford eventually caught up with Bladen who indicated he would accept £150 for the land. It can be presumed that the sale went through because, as can be seen in the small table below, when Thomas returned to America in the 1740s, some 20 years later, he acquired large areas of land and, again, found a willing buyer in George Mason. One of the land transfers between Bladen and Mason, however, appears not to have been patented correctly and a Scottish Physician and Importer called Dr David Ross from Bladensburg took advantage when he heard about it from a frontiersman. The land concerned was at Wills Creek next to Fort Cumberland and any land near to a Fort was highly desirable and valuable, so Dr Ross applied to the land office for warrants for tracts in 1761: Wills Town, Buck Lodge, Sugar Bottom, Turkey Flight, Prized, Lawrence and Big Bottom (2,254 acres) but the Certificates were not to be found in the land office records. It was claimed that warrants had been issued to Bladen for some 6,305 acres and Dr Ross was claiming 2,254 of those.

It appeared that several of Bladen's patents had not been duly processed totalling some 4,012 acres. In subsequent depositions,[2] a Thomas Prather stated *"that some few days after Governor Bladen was out of office, Col. Cresap gave him, the deponent, a bundle of certificates to take to Annapolis, and informed him they were the last of Governor Bladen's certificates, and desired him to put them into the land office, which he did, and took a receipt therefore, which he delivered to Col. Cresap; that he saw Mr. Bladen the morning after he had delivered them into the office, who was vexed with Col. Cresap for not having returned the certificates sooner, as it would have saved him several fees of office."*[3]

| Date | Area | Notes |
| --- | --- | --- |
| 21 October 1743 | 2,000 acres | 1,000 acres located at Licking Creek |
|  |  | 1,000 acres between Old Town/Savage River/Evitts Creek and Wills Creek |
| 20 February 1744 |  | 1,900 acres of this 2,000 acres order still not executed - order renewed |
|  |  | 1,329 acres of this 2,000 acres order still not executed - order renewed |
| 28 June 1745 |  | Executed 100 acres for George Adam Wild |
|  |  | Certificates of survey issued: |
| 27 December 1745 |  | 100 acres called 'Fright' patented to John Flemmin (1761) |
|  |  | 248 acres to Daniel Cresap for 'Three Spring Bottom' |
|  |  | 260 acres to George Mason for 'Welchman's Conquest' |
|  |  | 240 acres to Thomas Bladen for 'Content' |
|  |  | 625 acres to Thomas Bladen for 'Cumberland' |
|  |  | 240 acres to Thomas Bladen for 'Providence' |

---

[1] The Five George Masons: Patriots and Planters of Virginia and Maryland. By Pamela C Copeland and Richard K MacMaster. Board of Regents at Gunston Hall. 1989
[2] Cases in the Court of Appeals of Maryland - Steuart, et al. Lesse vs. Mason, May 1815
[3] Reports of Cases Argued and Determined in the Court of Appeals, Maryland 1810-15, Vol. 3, by Thomas Harris and Beverley Johnson. 1826

| 3 February 1746 | 4,012 acres | Warrant granted to George Stueart who in turn assigned to Bladen 4,012 acres (to include above 2,000 acres) |
| --- | --- | --- |
| 16 April 1745 | 3,000 acres | Patented by Bladen to Dr David Ross: 300 acres to Wlm, Jn Mason for 'Pleasant Valley' 500 acres to George Mason for 'Walnut Bottom' 240 acres to George Mason for 'Hunt the Hare' 285 acres to Daniel Cresap for 'Dispute' 12 acres to Daniel Cresap for 'Three Spring Bottom' 160 acres to David Ross for 'Will's Town' 915 acres to David Ross for 'Big Bottom' |

The matter was brought by Benedict Calvert and George Steuart (Chief Justices of the Land Office) to the attention of the Governor, Horatio Sharpe as it was normal practice to inform the Governor of any difficult or contentious issues and seek his advice. Governor Sharpe's opinion was that, since Bladen had been negligent in procedural matters and so many years had elapsed above the usual timeframe for completing such transactions, that Dr Ross be entitled to have patents issued to him for the 2,254 acres. Thomas Bladen's estate lost many thousands of acres due to incomplete paperwork.[1]

*Children of Thomas Bladen and Barbara Janssen*

*Barbara*
First born daughter Barbara was baptised on 29th June 1733 at St George's parish church, Hanover Square, London. The lateness of her marriage in 1771 when she was 38 years of age, the absence of children from that marriage and her Will which made reference to her gratitude to Mary Anne Douglas, her carer, and *"my affliction"* may all suggest that Barbara suffered health problems, perhaps even have been an invalid, at least in later years. She married at the chapel of Cassiobury in Hertfordshire which was her brother-in-law's family seat to the Honourable Henry St John of Rockley in Wiltshire 1738-1818, brother of 2nd Viscount Bolingbroke, Frederick St John. One newspaper report of Barbara's marriage said: *"A treaty of marriage on foot, and in a day or two will be consummated, between the Hon. Henry St John Esq (brother to Lord St John) and Miss Barbara Bladen of St George Street, Hanover Square"*.[2] Immediately prior to marriage, Henry St John had been residing at 22-23 Savile Row in Mayfair, though rate returns show him renting only a part-house. After marriage in 1771, he moved to 1 Savile Row which was larger and lived in a house that had been occupied till his death in 1749 by Bryan Fairfax and his brother Ferdinando, the great-

---

[1] Armory: From the General Armory: Bladen of Glastonbury, Somerset: Gules, three chevronels argent. Crest - A greyhound's head erased ppr Motto, Toujours fidele (always faithful), the same three chevrons his grandfather Nathaniel used in his arms. Miscellaneous: Bladon. On 14th August 1928, a John McKno Bladon, applied to the College of Arms in London for a grant of arms which seems remarkably similar to Martin's: Three chevronnels between in chief two Mascles flory and in base an Annulet all argent. Motto Spe et Labore (by hope and exertion). Armorial Families by Arthur Charles Fox-Davies 1929. The York Herald was consulted and advised that the individual in 1928 seeking a coat of arms may well have seen and been influenced by finding a previous Bladen Arms in, say, Burke's and used it as a base for his own and the Herald of the day permitted it, even with no proof of a family connection. He said, *"the official practice today would be to avoid granting a design such as this could be genealogically misleading, unless some kind of connection between the families had been proven"*. The conclusion therefore is that there is no known connection between the two branches despite the identical motto and great similarity of design of Arms

[2] Kentish Gazette, Saturday 24 August 1771

grandsons of Thomas 1st Lord Fairfax of Cameron. The house next door, no 25-26, had been used by Governor Sam Ogle on visits to England in the period 1744-46.

Barbara's town address, when she wrote her Will many years later, was Audley Square in Mayfair, just round the corner from her sister Harriet at Curzon Street. She made bequests to her sister's Capel offspring and requested to be buried near her husband who had predeceased her in the St John family vault at Lyddiard in Wiltshire. She lived to be 88 years of age.

*Husband - Gen. Hon. Henry St John, of Rockley, Wiltshire 1738-1818*
Barbara's husband was the brother of Viscount Bolingbroke. Henry was an MP and military professional and, just before their marriage, was garrisoned on the island of Minorca, which been returned to British hands after Admiral Byng's 'failure to do his utmost' to relieve the island from the French in 1756 and been publicly executed for his failure.[1] After seven years under French occupancy Henry was part of a force despatched there.[2]

*Madness of King George*
Henry was referred to by acquaintances as a *"the Baptist"* and *"a man of pleasure"*.[3]
Back in England and, whilst languishing on his army half pay, Henry obtained an appointment in 1763 as Groom of the Bedchamber to Edward, Duke of York who was the younger brother of King George III. That same year he accompanied the Duke on his tour of the Mediterranean and in a letter to his friend George Selwyn[4] on 24th July, he wrote *"I am very happy to attend him in his travels in Italy, a country I wanted much to see"*.[5]

---

[1] Close by the Bladen and Hawke memorials in All Saints Church Bolton Percy there is a memorial to Frances Penelope Byng 1773-1796 daughter of Hon John Byng 1743-1813 5th Viscount Torrington. John was the nephew of Admiral John Byng 1704-57 who had been executed on "The Monarque" at Spithead in front of his crew. It is not clear what Frances's connection with Bolton Percy was, though her great-uncle Robert was godfather to one of the Lascelles children (a Yorkshire family with large land holdings in Barbados). In Martin Bladen's letter to Admiral Hawke, dated 1742, he made reference to Sir Thomas Robinson's appointment as Governor of Barbados. Nephew Governor Thomas Bladen was travelling with him en route. When Bladen says to Hawke that he is enclosing his letter to him via his friend Lyng who is to travel to Barbados in the service of Sir Thomas Robinson, it may be one of the Byng's he is referring to. Robert Byng had been Governor of Barbados from 1739-40 and may have died out there and it seems more likely that one of his relations was making the journey. Admiral Hawke took the place of Admiral John Byng after his execution

[2] There is reference to the two St John brothers in a letter from Horace Walpole to the Earl of Strafford in 1757 when he described their behaviour as to *"have been most abominable to Lady Coventry and that the chits deserved to be whipped"*. Walpole did not name them directly, but alluded to them as 'Lord and Captain Corydon', names used in one of Byron's novels. Henry's brother "Bully", Lord Bollingbroke had numerous affairs, including with Lady Coventry. She was Maria Gunning, who died in 1760 from use of toxic lead face make-up

[3] George Selwyn and his Contemporaries, with Memories and Notes, Vol. 1 by John Heneage Jesse, George Augustus Selwyn. 1843

[4] George Selwyn 1719-91 was an MP who sat in the HoC for 44 years but never made a speech. He had a strange interest in viewing dead bodies, was reputed to be a member of the Hell Fire Club and racked up debts from gambling. He was a life-long friend of the Duke of Queensberry - see Harriet Bladen

[5] George Selwyn and his Contemporaries, with Memories and Notes, Vol. 1 by John Heneage Jesse, George Augustus Selwyn. 1843, p259

They did not return to England until the end of 1764 but the tour had taken its toll on Henry St John and there were reports that his fatigue was such that often he was left behind to recover his tiredness whilst the rest of the party moved on.[1]

In early December 1766 he wrote again to his friend Selwyn complaining that he had lost £800 gambling and that he hoped to spend a few days at Woburn (Duke of Bedford) with his friends over Christmas. The reference to Woburn concerns political allegiances, St John was a Whig MP for Wootton Bassett who voted in Parliament for his family's interests, but when the Tories came into power, this put him on opposite sides of the political spectrum to the Bedfords (Russells), hence the remark he hoped he would still be welcome there by his former friends. He also lamented *"I was two years in opposition with the Bedfords, but I see no return of favour from them to me, which I think my brother and I have some right to claim"*.[2]

On 25th August 1767 he again accompanied Edward Duke of York on a tour of the Continent and their journey took them from Paris to Genoa at which point the Duke became ill but insisted on continuing the journey. They proceeded to Toulon and finally to Montpellier and by September 17th the party was at Monaco where the Duke's illness again returned but all efforts to get him back into health failed and he died. Henry St John accompanied the Duke's body back to England on HMS Montreal, a ship that had been despatched specifically to return the body home. In gratitude for his service, the King offered Henry St John the Lieutenant Colonelcy of Minorca (where he had previously been stationed) which he accepted, though later wished he had not. He later said *"I thank my stars (though I met with great indulgence from my late master, and was honoured with his friendship), that it is no longer my fate to follow the caprices of a young Prince"*.

Henry St John and his friend Selwyn were part of the gambling set at Brooke's, 60 James Street, London which was a Whig Gentlemen's Club favoured by the Prince of Wales and was a place where the gambling stakes were high. Not long after his marriage, Henry was appointed Groom of the Bedchamber (of which there were 12) to King George III which meant he was in very close contact with the monarch for the entire time of his 'madness' or, rather, illness. He only ended his role in 1812 when the King's deterioration led to the formation of the Regency in favour of his son, the future George IV. Despite his impressive military rank when he was finally appointed General, it was said of Henry St John ... *"In 1797 the King was informed that he was not fit for a military government, which was his ambition. Lord Glenbervie described him as 'General Henry St John of stupid memory and repute'."*[3] He also served on the staff in Portugal as Adjutant-General to Lord Loudon.[4]

*Harriet*
Thomas and Barbara Bladen's second daughter Harriet Isabella Bladen was born in 1735. She travelled with her family to Maryland in 1742, returning to England in 1747.

---

[1] HoC, 1754-90, Edited by Sir Lewis B Namier and John Brooke. 1985
[2] Ibid
[3] The History of Parliament, Vol.1, 1790-1820 Author R.G. Thorne. 1986
[4] The Royal Military Calendar containing the services of every General Officer in the British Army from the date of their first commission by John Phillippart, Vol. 1, 1815

The following is believed to be a reference to her; in a letter from Elizabeth Montagu to her cousin Gilbert West dated 2nd September 1752 from Royal Tunbridge Wells Spa Town. Montagu wrote ... *"I wasn't at the ball last night but the misses say it was a very agreeable one; perhaps they liked it the better as Miss Bladen was not there to outshine them, for so strong in woman is the laudable desire of pleasing, each would have that happy power confined entirely to her own person"*. Harriet was a celebrated beauty who turned quite a few heads, including one young man whilst at Tunbridge Wells that same year. It was the practice at the time for young men attending the Spa to compose verse for the ladies they admired and to leave the poems at the bookseller's shop. The verse was then displayed for general amusement.

One such verse was written about Miss Bladen who, it was said *"attracted all eyes, at least, if she captivated no hearts"*.[1]

**Harriet Bladen 1735-1821**
**by John Hoppner**

**On seeing Miss Bladen at Tunbridge:**

Ye sallow Sons of thought and care
Whose hearts ne'er panted for the fair,
Whose breasts no passion warms;
Leave your dull labours, and explore
With curious eye all Nature's store
To match my Caelia's charms.

Compare the blooming tints, that streak
With ruby glow her lip, her cheek
With those that paint the rose;
Her breath sends forth more rich perfume
Than Balm or Aromatic Gum,
Or sweetest flow'r, that blows.

Tell me what Iv'ry can be found
To suit each finger's polish'd round
That graceful decks her hand?
Her spotless rows of teeth excell
The pearly lining of the Shell
That glistneth on the Sand ...

German artist John Hoppner was not born until 1758, therefore the above painting must have been done in the period 1785-1805 when Harriet was known as the Countess of Essex and would have been at least 50 years of age. The painting was last sold at the New Orleans Auction Galleries in Louisiana. Lot 1701 in the December 2008, sale made $1440 (£925).[2]

The poems were meant to be complementary, though the reference to Caelia's charms perhaps does not chime too well, since Caelia was a fairy queen ruler of an island populated by women who had slain their warmongering husbands.

---

[1] General Account of Tunbridge Wells, cited in The Early Letters of Bishop Richard Hurd 1739-62, Edited by Sarah Brewer, 1995
[2] Reproduced with the portrait owner's permission (who wished to remain anonymous)

In 1754 her father purchased The Grange at Low Leyton in Essex, depicted on the rear cover of this book, and the family settled into a genteel lifestyle with attendance at Bath in the summer season and Tunbridge Wells in the winter, both being overseen by Beau Nash, Master of Ceremonies. Some ten years later, Harriet was still enjoying the good life and attended a concert at a Mrs Forster's on 3rd March 1764 where she, along with Lady Denbigh and Miss Campbell sung for the company.[1] At another concert at Carlisle House a few days later Harriet again sang for the company with Mrs Hubbart. Carlisle House was a large mansion at Soho Square/Sutton Street rented by Madam Teresa Cornelys, an opera singer and entertainer who put on lavish balls in a concert hall and ballroom in her house.

*Marriage*
Inevitably, the time came for Harriet to marry, and marry well. Harriet's father Thomas Bladen, as previously mentioned, was very well known to the Dukes of Bedford (Russells) and played cards with them. Sister of the 3rd and 4th Duke was Elizabeth Russell who married William Capel, 3rd Earl of Essex and so the Essex family was already well known to the Bladens. This certainly seems to have paved the way for the marriage of Elizabeth Russell's son William Capel (4th Earl) who married Harriet as his second wife. The fact that Harriet had such a wealthy father and attractive marriage settlement would have made it a desirable match on both sides. A reference to her marriage occurred in a letter exchange between the Rt. Hon Philip Dormer to his son, Earl of Chesterfield. *3rd Mar 1767 "Lord Essex was married yesterday to Harriet Bladen and Lord Strathmore last week to Miss Bowen, both couples went directly from the church to consummation in the country, from an unnecessary fear that they should be tired of each other, if they stayed in town."* William Capel's first wife had been Frances Hanbury-Williams (wealthy traders involved in banking with the Lloyds family) from whom William had inherited the estate of Hampton Court (15th century castle came to Hanbury-Williams from their Coningsby descent and later sold to Richard Arkwright of Cromford in Derbyshire).[2]

*Social Life of Countess of Essex*
There's a fascinating snippet of what Harriet's Bladen's life was like (as Lady Essex) taken from Arthur Irwin Dasent's book[3] where a house-by-house account of life and residents of Piccadilly in the early 18th century was described. At 138 Piccadilly (still exists today), Dasent described a celebrated resident,[4] 4th Duke of Queensbury known as Old Q, who was hosting a party for 23 people and Lady Mary Coke (cousin to Georgiana, Duchess of Devonshire) gave an account of it (dated about 1770):[5]

---

[1] Correspondence of Elizabeth Harris at Whitehall to James Harris Jnr at Oxford. G1251/2 cited in Music and Theatre in Handel's World. The Family Papers of James Harris 1732-80 by Donald Burrows and Rosemary Dunhill. 2002, p415, p417

[2] The Art Journal, Vol. 33. 1871. Note: this not the Hampton Court Palace in Surrey, home to Henry VIII

[3] Piccadilly in Three Centuries: With Some Account of Berkeley Square and the Haymarket by Arthur Irwin Dascent, 1920

[4] William Douglas, 1725-1810, 4th Duke of Queensbury

[5] It is likely that the Queensbury's were family friends with the Bladens. The Queensbury's (probably father of above) visited Spa to take the waters in 1734 - same time as Colonel Martin Bladen was there. The British and the Grand tour by Jeremy Black, 1985, p87

*"The house is very fine and fitted up with a great deal of taste. There are three and twenty people; The Duchess of Grafton,[1] The Duchess of Hamilton, The Duchess of Buccleuch, Lady Coventry, Lady Essex, Mrs Fitzroy, Mrs Pitt and Lady Susan Stewart. Rest were all men. ....The liveries of the Duke's servants were of green and silver and everything that wealth and a sense of luxury could suggest was requisitioned to entertain his guests at the house-warming"*. The really interesting comments that are made about the above ensemble are that *"Lady Essex had been Miss Harriet Bladen and an old flame of her host"* but then so too was Lady Mary Coke who wrote this account and many, many others.

### *Janssen Inheritances*

As well as large marriage settlements from their father, the two Bladen daughters also received large inheritances from their maternal Janssen relations. Their mother Barbara Bladen Snr received 10,000 *l.* from her brother Sir Abraham Janssen, who also gave Barbara Jnr and Harriet the same amount. The residue of Abraham's estate went to his brother William of Cheshunt in Herts.[2] William Janssen's daughter, though married, was childless and so after the death of the Earl of Essex in 1798/9 Harriet petitioned the House of Lords to bring a Bill[3] concerning the division of her uncle Captain William Janssen's estate, this was in advance of the demise of the principle beneficiary as the legacy then fell to the next generation.[4]

---

[1] The Duchess of Grafton was Anne Liddell, the 28 year old wife of the Prime Minister, Lady Coventry (this was actually Barbara St John, née Bladen), the Duchess of Buccleuch was a Montagu, Mrs Anne Pitt (frequently referred to in Walpole's letters) and Lady Susan Stewart was Lord Galloway's daughter, Lord Galloway was buried at Kensall Green just behind Harriet's son's grave (Admiral Thomas Bladen Capel). Old Q (still called Lord March) had been made Lord of the Bedchamber to King George III

[2] Reported in the Derby Mercury on 22nd February 1765

[3] Journal of the House of Lords, Vol. 45. 1805. Countess of Essex et al Leave to Exhibit a Petition for a Bill

[4] There were four heirs to William's estate; Harriet (née Bladen), Barbara Saint John (née Bladen), Catherine Anne Janssen who had married John Blackwood (the younger) and Henrietta Janssen (a niece of William's) who had married Lorenzo Moore. The four became principal legatees because the principal intended legatee, Williamsa Janssen, daughter of William, was by 1805 in her fifties and with no children, although she was married to the Hon Lionel Damer (1748-1807 of Came House, Winterborne, Dorset, 3rd son of the Earl of Dorchester) but both would later die without issue in 1825. So, the four next beneficiaries decided between them that in order to make matters easier after Williamsa's demise, that they would make an application to divide the Janssen estate in Dorset up in advance of Williamsa's death and, presumably, with Williamsa's permission. As some of the heirs were minors (i.e. the infant children of Henrietta Moore and the Hon John Thomas Capel and Lady Caroline) then, legally, Harriet and the other petitioners needed to ask Parliament for consent to proceed. The chancery document was interesting for confirming some family relations, i.e. that Harriet's sister Barbara Saint John had no children in 1805 (and was past child-bearing age) and therefore no heirs, etc. The chart below shows the heirs to Captain William Janssen's estate, some 26+ people. One of the heirs, Ogle Capel Theodore Moore (who was engaged in naval duties serving on 'Sea Horse' at the time of this case) had expressed an interest in taking on the estate, which was pointed out in the legal Petition and so the Court was petitioned. *"Accordingly, upon reading the petition of the right honourable Harriett Countess Dowager of Essex, the Honourable John Thomas Capel and Lady Caroline Capel on behalf of themselves and Arthur Capel, Harriet Capel, Georgiana Capel, Louisa Capel, Maria Capel and Horatio Capel, their infant children; the honourable Henry Saint John and Barbara his wife; Henrietta Moor on behalf of herself and Charles William Soulegee Moore, Williamsa Caroline Mary Moore, Calvert FitzGerald Moore and John James Moore her infant children; and of Henrietta Catherine Moore and Georgiana Elizabeth Moore, praying leave to bring in a Bill for the purposes in the said petition mentioned. "IT IS ORDERED, that the consideration of the*

Harriet Bladen and the Earl of Essex had a still-born son within a year of marriage, so the Hon. John Thomas Capel born the following year was their eldest, but not the principal heir, as that honour belonged to the Earl's son from his first marriage. After the 4th Earl of Essex's death, his son from his first marriage, George Capel Coningsby 1757-1839 became the 5th Earl and, under the terms of his grandmother's Will, adopted the additional surname Coningsby. After the 5th Lord's death the title went to Harriet Bladen's grandson Arthur Algernon Capell (now spelt with two L's) 1803-92, the eldest son of Harriet's eldest Hon John Thomas Capel.

*Children of Harriet Bladen and the 4th Earl of Essex*
Harriett had four sons from her marriage to the 4th Earl of Essex;[1] one was an Admiral who was present at Trafalgar with Nelson, the second one was a priest, the third one was in command of a regiment at the Battle of Waterloo, and the fourth one and eldest.... well, let's start with him first:-

*Hon. John Thomas Capel*
Harriet's eldest son John's godfather was Lord Henry Cavendish 1732-1804, a relation. Cavendish dined with Lord and Lady Essex in 1769 (about the time that John was born) after which he noted *"Mr Bladen [Thomas] and my sister Harriet were the other gossips"*. John joined the Coldstream Guards in 1789-90, along with his younger brother Edward though he managed to maintain an impressive social life at the same time as, on 16th September 1790 the Bath Chronicle reported John attending a music evening in Gloucester with a distinguished guest list: R.H. Prince William his son, Dukes of Gloucester, Norfolk and Beauford, Marquis of Worcester, Lords Edward and Arthur Somerset, Earl of Rochford, Lords Henry Fitzgerald, Apsley and Ducie etc. He had secured (or purchased) an appointment as a Cornet in the Earl of Dalhousie's Independent Company (lowest grade of commissioned officers) though by 24th January 1791 he was on half-pay.

What happened next is not clear, as Dalhousie's Company was posted to Martinique in June 1792 but, by May of that year, John was still in England and about to marry. *"Caledonian Mercury - 17th May 1792: MARRIED: Friday evening by special licence Hon. John Thomas Capel 2nd son of the Earl of Essex and Lady Caroline Paget eldest daughter of the Earl of Uxbridge. The ceremony was performed by the Bishop of Worcester at the Earl of Uxbridge's house in Old Burlington Street in the presence of the Countess of Uxbridge, the Earl and Countess of Essex and a few other near relations of the young couple, who soon after set off unaccompanied in a chariot and four, attending by two servants, for Cassiobury Park, Essex, where they will honeymoon"*.

---

said petition be, and is hereby referred to Mr Baron Thomson and Mr Justice Le Blanc who are forthwith to summon all parties concerned in the bill and after hearing them are to report to the house the state of the case with their opinion thereupon, under their hands; and whether all parties, who may be concerned in the consequences of the bill have signed the petition and also that the Judges have perused the Bill, do sign the same". Williamsa left a raft of legacies to relations, including £1,000 each to Edward Capel, Hon Bladen Capel and Rev William Capel. Hertfordshire Archives and Local Studies DE/M/216

[1] Each son received £1,000 bequeathed to them by their aunt, Lady Anne Capell of Russel Farm in Watford

The couple went on to have 13 children. The Earl of Essex title went to his father's son from his first marriage but, since that son died without a legitimate heir, the title reverted in due course to John's line of descent. In 1803 John was a Captain in the Light Infantry Company of the Sussex Militia but he also at this time put himself forward as a candidate to be MP for Montgomeryshire to succeed the late Francis Lloyd, but he lost to Charles Williams-Wynn. Meanwhile, like many aristocratic men of his day, he was gambling and running up debts which, by 1804, had reached a staggering £20,000. An appeal for financial help was made to his half-brother, the 5th Earl of Essex, who did offer to assist the family, but the conditions were unacceptable. He would only render financial assistance if John surrendered his children to his half-brother, in particular his new-born son and heir Arthur (who would become the 6th Earl of Essex).

So the couple carried on without the Earl's help and somehow managed to avoid bankruptcy.[1] Help was, however, forthcoming from another direction in the form of Lord Uxbridge, his father-in-law who secured two posts for John: the first was Receiver-General for Taxes of the Land Assessed and Property Taxes for Staffordshire and the second was as Colonial Secretary for Berbice in British Guiana.[2] John's income brought in £4,000 per annum but, through various commitments and large debts, he was only left with one quarter of that to support his family. The Staffordshire appointment was from at least 1804 to 1811 because in 1806-7 John arranged to have a Deputy Receiver-General appointed to assist him who would be the person who did the actual work, John would put his signature to the accounts yearly, and in 1810-11 he was still in post.

Some years later, in 1821, a parliamentary select committee was convened and minutes were taken of a meeting between a Mr Cobb and Mr Spooner who had been Deputy-Receiver-Generals in Capel's tenure, Capel was deceased by this time. Questions were asked of them, including from the time when Capel was in office.

*Where did Mr Capel reside?* He resided the greatest part of the time near Atherstone.
*Is that in the County of Stafford?* No, I think his house was in Leicestershire, it was just on the border of Leicestershire and Warwickshire.
*Where did he reside at any other part of the time?* Part of the time in Colebrook in Buckinghamshire.
*Did not he afterwards go abroad?* He did.
*For several years?* 2 or 3 years.
*And died abroad?* Yes.
*During the time he was Receiver-General did he ever transact any business whatever?* Swearing to the accounts.
*Did he act in any way except swearing to the annual accounts?* No he certainly did not.
*By whom were those accounts made out?* Generally by myself or my clerk, I overlooked them myself and the clerk generally did the writing.
*Do you know where he had any connection with the County of Stafford, any property or anything to do with the County?* Not to my knowledge.

---
[1] The Capel Letters, 1814-17, Edited by the Marquess of Anglesey. 1955
[2] Debrett's Peerage by John Debrett, p75

*Was he connected in any way with the County of Stafford?* By marriage.
*Did you give any security to Mr Capel?* No, not to Mr Capel, to the Board we joined with Mr Capel.
*Do you happen to know who Mr Capel's securities were?* I think part of the time my father, Mr Wilberforce and Mr Matthias Attwood.
*Was it land security?* Bonds, as it always is.
*Then Mr Capel was in the receipt from 12 to 13 or 14 hundred a year, finding no other security whatever than his bond?* No, certainly not.
*The other part of the security was found by yourself?* Yes the sum Mr Capel received might not be so much as that, but it was thereabouts.[1]

The answers above from John's assistant shows that practical help was also given to the couple from his mother-in-law who had them live with her at various Paget family residences in Staffordshire and other counties. It has also to be said that it seems a strange appointment for a man who had managed his own finances so badly and had a problem with gambling, to have responsibilities as a Collector of Taxes for Staffordshire and responsible for collecting large quantities of money. The second appointment secured for John by his in-laws was as Colonial Secretary for British Guiana. His income from this post was 1,607 Marks and the Lt. Governor of Berbice Henry William Bentinck received 4,392 Marks though it is thought neither of them visited the colony.[2] How long he managed to retain that income, however, is debatable as Parliament was taking steps to prevent absentee colonial administrators and on 6th May 1814 the Colonial Offices Bill was debated, this was an attempt to force those individuals who held offices in the colonies to discharge their duties in person, rather than accepting the fees and appointing proxies. Whether John continued with his gambling is not known but his burgeoning family needed to find a way to live more cheaply and their solution to the problem was to look to the Continent where the cost of living was significantly lower than in England. It was also desirable for the Capels to live somewhere the creditors could not easily get to them.

Now that the Peninsula Wars had ended and Napoleon Bonaparte was contained on Elba, Europe gave a collective sigh of relief and John started in earnest to look for a suitable place to relocate his family. Preference for The Hague was swiftly dismissed as there was no suitable large property to be found, so the next destination of choice was Brussels where they found a property to rent and on 4th June 1814, they set off for Dover to cross the Channel, that is to say parents (Hon. John Capel and Caroline) and daughters (Harriet aged 21, Georgiana 19, Maria 17, Louisa 15, Horatia aged 13, Jane aged 9, Mary aged 6, Amelia aged 3 and baby Adolphus) made the journey but the couple's elder sons were left behind in England where they attended school, and even in the holidays still remained in England with their Uxbridge relation, at Lord Essex's insistence (as he was funding some of their schooling).

---

[1] Parliamentary Papers, HoC; minutes of evidence taken before Select Committees, Vol. 8, p135 (Reports from Committees: militia, receivers general, malt, royal burghs, Ireland & c, Vol. III, 23rd January to 11th July 1821
[2] Colonial Journal, 1816

Only one son Algernon aged 7 accompanied them, but soon after he returned to England for his schooling. Along with them, the Capels took a ladies-maid, two other maids, a housekeeper/nanny, a nursery maid and a governess.

From The Ship Inn at Dover, where they had many days wait, the party eventually crossed over to Calais and then sailed onwards to Dunkirk when they were to travel by inexpensive barge to Bruges but their carriages could not be accommodated on the barge, so they continued their journey by carriage to Ghent and onwards to Brussels. It was to be seven weeks before they were reunited with their luggage. Brussels was an exciting place to live at the time but getting more crowded by the day as thousands of soldiers were assembling there, as well as many English people known to the Capels travelling en route to Paris or Spa. There were visits by the Prince of Orange and the Duke of Wellington and the family hardly needed to interact with locals at all as there was such a large English community there. At the same time as the Capels had relocated to Brussels, the Duke of Richmond moved his family there, also for reasons of economy. The two men would already have been well acquainted as Richmond had been MP for Sussex where Capel had been based and Richmond was also placed in command of the reserve force in Brussels. Several months into their residence, as winter approached Capel and Richmond arranged to leave their families for a few days and go on a Grand Wolf Hunt about fifty miles away in the Ardennes. John returned from the visit feeling unwell and with painful rheumatism.

By the following spring of 1815 Lady Caroline was pregnant with her 13th child and, unknown to the family, Bonaparte had escaped Elba, arrived in Paris and was on his way to Brussels. When news did reach them there was panic and civilians left Brussels in their droves, including the Capels' servants and the woman who was to assist Caroline with birthing. The Capel family hurriedly formed a contingency plan to escape to Holland if Napoleon should attack Brussels. Order, to some extent, was restored however with the arrival in Brussels of Lord Wellington (who had decided to keep his own niece with him) and this instilled confidence in the community and the panic subsided to an uneasy calm. A few months later the family moved from their town house to Le Château de Walcheuse just two miles north of Brussels which, at that time, would have been set in secluded woodland in the grounds of the Palais de Laeken.

*Waterloo - Duchess of Richmond's Ball*
However things did not remain calm for too long as the family had jumped out of the frying pan straight into the fire. Bonaparte was now reported to be heading for Brussels with an army of 100,000 troops where he hoped to re-establish himself. It was even rumoured that he had stationery pre-printed with the Palais de Laeken as his address, the official residence of the Monarchs of Belgium and a place Bonaparte had stayed at in 1804 with Josephine. He knew the British/Prussian armies were coalescing in that area and meant to make his spectacular come-back in Brussels.[1]

---
[1] The Capel Letters 1814-17 edited by The Marquis of Anglesey. 1955

Things changed quickly for the Capels, from their arrival in Brussels when they had enjoyed endless parties, balls and soirees just months earlier they were now in an area where the entire British army was forming its base and Bonaparte and his army was heading directly for them. Laeken was just a few miles north of Waterloo.

The Capel ladies wrote letters to their mother/grandmother the Countess of Uxbridge where they described what was happening at the time. On 10th June (8 days before Waterloo), one of the Capel daughters wrote: *"At present we have 200 Brunswickers quartered here, but they are soon to be removed. There is regular little Parade of above 200 men in the Courtyard every day. Their Dismal Black Uniforms & Deaths head Caps look so pretty...the Duke of Wellington gives a Grand Fête Champêtre next week. Mama say she [is] determined not to stir from this place unless for something very brilliant. We have not made the same determination & therefore mean to make Papa Chaperone us to a ball at the Duchess of Richmond in a day or two."*[1]

John's brother Edward's army unit arrived in the area and, like many others, he was to take part in both the Battles of Quatra Bras and Waterloo. How popular Edward was with his brother John is hard to say, but it was said that there had been a conversation in the family regarding Caroline's latest baby's name and the name Edward was dismissed as it was said that one person such as he with that name was quite enough. Others arriving in Brussels included cousin, Martin Bladen Edward Hawke and his three months' pregnant wife who rode close to the Battle of Quatra Bras 'out of curiosity' as was the custom at the time, a dangerous practice vividly portrayed in the Vanity Fair novel.[2]

With so much good company in town Capel's friends, the Richmonds, held a ball which has been called *"the most famous ball in history"*. Amongst the list of invited guests of 200+ there was *"Mr and Lady Caroline Capel and Miss Capel"* - in fact it was daughters Georgiana and Marie who attended with their father whilst the heavily, nine months pregnant Lady Caroline stayed home. Also in attendance at the Duchess of Richmond's Ball on the eve of the battles was Hawke's wife. During the ball Wellington received news of Bonaparte's location, which was much nearer than expected, and immediately ordered his men to rally and prepare for action. Within twenty minutes of this news the rooms were cleared and the soldiers, who made up a good proportion of the male guests, were gone leaving the ladies to weep in fear. A couple of days later, whilst the Battle of Waterloo was in progress, Caroline wrote to her mother and told her how Bonaparte had caught everyone off guard crossing the border *"like a thief in the night"*.[3] Then a few days later after the victory of Waterloo, Caroline described the horror the family faced, of wounded soldiers filling their courtyard in the dismal wet, dark weather. She described the anxieties the family faced and how her husband went to Brussels to try to arrange transportation for them in case Wellington should lose the advantage. Rumours of what the French would do next were rife and Capel found that the banks were closed and that there was not a horse or barge to be found in the town for love nor money.

---

[1] The Gentry Stories of the English: 1790s-1840s: The Capels, Brussels and Lausanne
[2] Lord Hawke: A Cricketing Legend by James P. Coldham
[3] The Capel Letters 1814-17 edited by the Marquis of Anglesey. 1955

Caroline was particularly worried because of their isolated location, that any straggling group of French soldiers could render them harm, but as the news of Wellington's victory was reinforced their worries subsided. The news of Caroline's brother, the 1st Marquis of Anglesey who had led charges at Waterloo was not so good, his wounded leg had to be amputated without anaesthetic. Lady Hawke's brother, Nisbet, who was at both Quatre Bras and Waterloo was with the 13th Light Dragoons and had been left for dead on the battle field.

A few months later John Capel continued to have health problems and Caroline lost the child she had been carrying, which would have been her 13th. John was weak and thin. The heat, combined with "the pestilential air of Brussels" with dead soldiers buried in shallow graves combined to make it feel like an unhealthy place to live. The lease on the Capel's house on the Rue Ducale was nearly up and so thoughts turned to moving on and Neufchâtel in Switzerland on the banks of Lake Geneva was considered. They set off in 1816-17 for the Château Belair at Vevey, crossed the Alps and arrived at Lake Geneva. It was rumoured in England that they escaped from Brussels *"without paying anything"*, but Caroline denied this. She felt the new château was too small, but was adequate and the children loved the vineyards surrounding it. Writing in 1816, she referred to the cost of living being higher there than in Brussels and to the appalling weather and how, out of 152 days, they had 130 of constant rain. A better house, therefore, was sought and found in Lausanne at Montbenon to which they all relocated and everyone appeared happy with it. This is also the time that another prominent party of individuals were in Switzerland and also visited Lausanne and also were hemmed in by the bad weather: Lord Byron and the Shelleys, the result of Mary Shelley's cabin-fever was the Dracula stories. The family settled in Lausanne and in 1817 the first of their daughters married when Harriett married David Okeden Parry-Okeden (assumed the Okeden surname under the terms of his maternal grandfather's Will).

This was to be the first and last wedding of his children John would see as by 1818, after suffering from convulsions and being *"in a state of insensibility"* John was dead.[1] Lady Caroline and her family continued to live in Lausanne for some years after his demise and daughters Georgiana and Maria also married there. Further details of his children's marriages are included in the genealogy at the end of this book. Caroline died on 9th July 1847 at midnight (at the age of 74 years) and was buried at Kensal Green Cemetery in North-West London on 14th July.

### *Major-General Thomas Edward Capel*
The second of Harriet Bladen's sons was Edward who had a distinguished military career which began in 1794 with the 1st Regiment of Foot Guards, the Coldstream Guards, and service in Flanders under the Duke of York.[2] He was rapidly promoted and in command when the Napoleonic Wars commenced.

---

[1] The Capel Letters 1814-17 edited by the Marquis of Anglesey. 1955
[2] Royal Military Calendar, or Army Service and Commission Book, Vol. 3, edited by John Philippart, 1820

The 1st Regiment became combined with the 3rd and Capel was present at the Battle of Carunna in 1809 after which, on return to England, he was presented to the King (or, more likely, due to his illness to the soon-to-be Prince Regent) at a Royal Levee. Later, his regiment was sent to Quatra Bras in Belgium and Waterloo[1] where he met up with older brother John Thomas Capel and the Hawke families. Although there is a record of him marrying in December 1814 to the niece of a Brigadier Maretti of Cadiz, it is not thought she lived very long as there is no further mention of her. Edward continued in his military career and had no children. He became Gentleman Usher of the Privy Chamber with an income of 200 *l.* per annum. Edward wrote the following short letter to a relation following the funeral of his mother Harriet:

To William Cavendish-Scott Bentinck (4th Duke of Portland)-[eldest son of the Prime Minister] re: The Death of Harriet Bladen (Lady Essex) - on black edged, mourning paper ....
From: Cassiobury 21st March 1821 *"My Dear Duke, I regret most earnestly that you have not been informed from the Executor Lord Clarendon of the death of my poor mother, and of the burial which took place this day. Believe me, I would not intentionally have been guilty of any disrespect to yourself - I therefore hope you will allow me to plead the excuse of being had a great deal of painful duty to perform, besides having myself been very unwell. Believe me, my dear Duke, Your humble servant, Edward Capel"*.[2]

In the 1851 census, Edward (General Capel) was living at 14 Charles Street, Hanover Square in London with a butler, footman, a housekeeper and a housemaid. Soon after, he wrote his Will and left his property and possessions to his two surviving brothers Hon. and Rev. William Robert and Admiral Thomas Bladen Capel. As well as his brothers his original Will left the usual bequests to servants who should be living with him at the time of his demise, but then at the last moment he added a codicil revoking the servant bequests, except for just one servant James Fryer (who was also with him on the 1841 census) who was instead granted an annuity, but the others were removed as legatees.

### Hon. & Rev. William Robert Capel

The third son of Harriet Bladen and the Earl of Essex was William Robert Capel who was born in 1775. He pursued a career in the church where he was fortunate to receive the assistance of his half-brother the 5th Earl of Essex in securing ecclesiastical appointments. However, despite this, he found himself being sued by his brother over a fox-hunting incident. William was a priest with a passion for both fox-hunting and cricket. The hunt, with William in charge, had damaged fencing on the Earl's Cassiobury estate and legal action was brought for trespass in 1809 which the Earl won. William was also involved in an accusation that he was negligent in his ministerial duties by the Bishop of London. Steps were taken to appoint a curate (with a stipend) but William did his utmost to resist the newcomer, it was reported at the time they were seen 'racing for a reading-desk in church'. William was married to Sarah Salter and they had seven children, some dying as infants.[3]

---

[1] Gentleman's Magazine and Historical Review, Vol. 197
[2] Copy letter from the Manuscripts and Special Collections at the University of Nottingham, Lenton Lane, Nottingham - PwH/475
[3] TNA: PROB 11/2206/296, Will of the Hon. and Rev. William Robert Capel, Clerk, Vicar of Watford

*Admiral Sir Thomas Bladen Capel*

The fourth son of Harriet Bladen and the Earl of Essex was born on 25th August 1776 and became an Admiral of distinction who was at the Battle of Trafalgar with Nelson.

Following in the footsteps of his famous cousin Admiral Hawke, the youngest son of the 4th Earl of Essex, Thomas Bladen Capel was put on the navy's books by his parents as a child in order to begin his naval career at the first possible moment in 1792. He served time initially as a mid-shipman before becoming an Acting Lieutenant in 1796. He became one of Nelson's protégés in 1797 and was made Signal Lieutenant on HMS Vanguard, which was Nelson's flagship at the Battle of the Nile. Immediately after the Battle in 1798, the fleet made for Naples as Nelson was suffering severe headaches and in need of rest. Bladen Capel was on hand[1] to liaise with William Hamilton, the British Ambassador to Naples, whose wife Lady Hamilton would become Nelson's mistress. Bladen Capel was commissioned to take a copy of despatches to London, advising the Admiralty of Nelson's success, which guaranteed the Admiralty's approval of Nelson's request that Capel be made up to Commander, the other copy of despatches had been captured by the French so he was the first to bring them the good news. He also took the sword of the French Admiral Blanquet who had surrendered at the battle. Nelson wrote to them that Bladen Capel was *'a most excellent officer'*.[2] The Sword was presented to the Lord-Mayor of London on 15th October 1798 with a message from Nelson:

To: Rt.Hon. Lord-Mayor of London  From: Vanguard, Mouth of the Nile, August 8, 1798

*"My Lord, I have the honour of being a Freeman of the City of London and I take the Liberty of sending to your Lordship the sword of the Commanding French Admiral (Monsieur Blanquet) who survived the Battle of the Nile and request that the City of London will honour me by accepting it as a remembrance that 'Britannia Still Rules the Waves' which that she may ever do, is the fervent prayer of your Lordship's*

*Most obedient servant, Horatio Nelson'*[3]

Collingwood, Nelson's number two, said of Bladen Capel *"The extraordinary exertion of Capt Capel saved the French Swiftsure and his ship the Phoebe together with the Donegal, afterwards brought out the Bahama"*.[4] Nelson's commendation worked and Capel was appointed Captain of the sloop Alecto and was commissioned to patrol the coast of Spain and then in 1803 he was given command of HMS Phoebe, a 36-gun frigate. As Nelson's Mediterranean campaign commenced and Villeneuve was pursued to the West Indies, Bladen Capel was instructed to remain in the Mediterranean to watch the Egyptian approaches, Sicily and Sardinia. At the Battle of Trafalgar Capel was in command of HMS Phoebe and was situated to the left rear of Nelson's flank, with the other frigates. Although the ship was not directly involved in the fighting, her orders were to relay signals and stand ready to assist.

---

[1] MS 37076m British Library Board, ff 30-36 Letters of Nelson and Sir William Hamilton, Envoy at Naples

[2] The Naval Gazetteer, Biographer and Chronologist; containing a history of the late wars from 1793 to 1801; and from 1803-1815 and continued, as to the biographical part to the present time. Compiled by John William Norie, p69. 1827

[3] Letters and Dispatches of Admiral Horatio Nelson 3-9 August 1798. The War Times Journal

[4] Nelson Despatches. Nicholas vii, p219

Phoebe did intervene to save the French prize Swiftsure from destruction as mentioned above by Collingwood.

After Trafalgar, Bladen Capel served in America where it is possible he met up with Admiral Robert Fairfax, his relation, who was also there at the time. At the end of that war he was back in England in command of one of the Royal Yachts. He was appointed Rear-Admiral in 1825, made KCB (Knight Commander) in 1834 and then, two years later, became Commander-in-Chief of the East Indies Station until 1837.

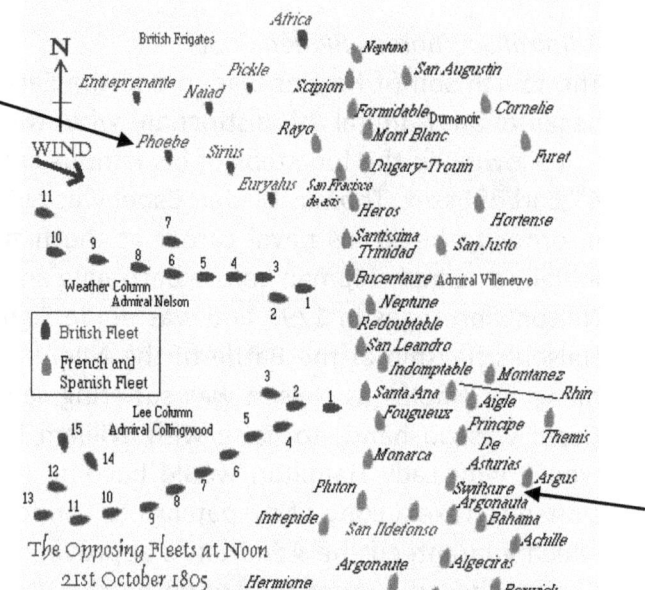

The Admiral's social life was recorded in the Court Journals: in February 1835 he attended a dinner at Clifford House by the Baroness Dowager de Clifford along with Sir Charles and Lady Coote, Lord John Fitzroy (son of a former Prime Minister) and Lady Champagne.[1] In 1849 he corresponded with William Baillie-Hamilton, Secretary of the Admiralty regarding the missing Sir John Frankland who, some years earlier, had led to voyage to map the North West Passage but never returned. His widow pleaded with the government to send a search party to find him and his crew but it was subsequently learned that all had died of cold and starvation in the Canadian Arctic. Bladen Capel returned to England and in 1852 was made GCB (Knight Grand Cross, Order of the Bath) and was later appointed to sit on the Committee that arranged the issue of the Naval General Service Medal for those who had been at Trafalgar. He died in 1853 and was buried at Kensal Green Cemetery in North West London: plots 10680. His wife died three years later and was buried in plot 7112. The 1805 Club has pencilled in the Admiral's grave for restoration, as they have done an excellent job of renovating many of the graves of those Captains who were at Trafalgar.

Admiral Capel[2] married Harriet Catherine Smythe in 1816 (daughter of Francis George Smythe of Upper Brooke Street) and the couple had no children.

---

[1] The Court Journal, Court Circular land Fashionable Gazette, Vol. 7

[2] His half-brother was George Capel Coningsby, 5th Earl of Essex and in 1821 the Admiral was consulted over a delicate matter concerning his half-brother. The Earl had married twice but had no legitimate heir and his illegitimate daughter Harriet 1808-37 had a Governess called Ann Tiler. Ann was probably a relation of Reynier Tiler who was the House Steward at Windsor Castle. The Earl, who had been separated from his wife for some time, corresponded from various locations (Woburn Abbey, Cassiobury, Holland House or the Brooks's Club) daily with the Governess during 1821 as she had taken his daughter to France where they resided at the Place Vendôme de Neuilly and the Champs-Élysées and, within the correspondence, there would always be a separate letter, written in French, to his daughter. The Earl and the Governess exchanged interesting letters commenting on events of the day, the hot topics at the time being the death of Napoleon, the Coronation of George IV and the farce surrounding the estranged Queen Caroline's attempts to attend the coronation and her forcible exclusion. Although it is not known what the delicate matter was, the Admiral was asked by the Governess to 'intervene' between the Earl and his daughter

Dame Harriet's Will, probate 1866,[1] showed her estate to be under £18,000 in value and her husband's possessions were disposed of as follows:[2] the Trafalgar Cup and a snuffbox with a picture of Lord Nelson painted on and a bloodstone snuffbox presented to Admiral Bladen Capel by Lord Mark Kerr were to be given to the Earl of Essex. Lord Kerr had been Captain of a frigate 'Fisgard' patrolling the straits of Gibraltar in the lead up to the Battle of Trafalgar when Villeneuve's fleet had slipped out of Toulon heading for the Atlantic and Kerr[3] had immediately sent the news to Nelson. Harriet was the beneficiary of Joseph Ryall's Will when she acquired three Jamaican slaves.[4]

## OBITUARY - New York Times, 1853

Recent deaths: "ADMIRAL SIR THOMAS BLADEN CAPEL G.C.B. who died lately at the advanced age of 76 years was in active service for 31 years. He was the youngest son of William, 4th Earl of Essex. He entered the Navy March 22nd, 1782. After participating July 23rd 1795 in Lord Bridport's action, he was appointed May 16th 1796 as acting Lieutenant. In April 1798 Mr Capel was appointed to the Vanguard. He served as signal-lieutenant at the Battle of the Nile, he was advanced, August 4. He was in command of a frigate at the battle of Trafalgar where he was on Nelson's left flank, and at its close saved from destruction the prize ship of the line Swiftsure. He commanded afterwards La Hague [Hogue], and shared in the warfare with the United States".

Admiral Bladen Capel has a deserved place in history as one of Nelson's 'Band of Brothers'.

All Souls' Cemetery, Kensal Green, North London
IN MEMORY of Admiral the Honourable Sir Thomas Bladen Capel who departed this life on 4th March 1853 thus closing a long and distinguished career of service to this country during which time he served actively for thirty-one years from his entry into the Royal Navy until his death.

Brick grave in mortar - 6 coffins contained.

**Kensal Green Visited 5th July 2008[5]**

---

[1] England and Wales, National Probate Calendar (Index of Wills and Administrations) 1858-1966. Death date 30th July 1866, probate 22nd September 1866, Middlesex Principal Registry

[2] Most of Dame Capel's possessions were bequeathed to Capel relations. Her estate in Jamaica was left to a cousin Henry Leach. Reported in The Morning Post, Saturday 13th October 1866

[3] Vice-Admiral Lord Mark Kerr 1776-1840, third son of 5th Marquess of Lothian. Scottish family with their English residence at Charlton (Jacobean House) near Greenwich

[4] www.ucl.ac.uk/lbs/oerson/view/22858 Legacies of British Slave-ownership

[5] Grant of assignment dated 8th March 1853 for £15.15 to The Honourable Dame Harriet Capel of 22 Rutland Gate Hyde Park, Westminster. Names of persons interred: Admiral the Honourable Sir Thomas Bladen Capel 1853 and Hon the Dame Harriet Capel 1866. Top right of the picture, shows a series of steps and this is the very large monument to George Stewart, 8th Earl of Galloway who was married to Lady Jane Paget (d.1842) and who was mentioned in the letters of Lady Adela Capel at Cassiobury. Lady Paget was daughter to Henry Paget 1st Earl of Uxbridge, who led a charge at Waterloo and she was sister to Cassandra who married John Thomas Capel. The daughter of the Earl of Galloway and Lady Jane Paget was Lady Jane Stewart 1798-1844

*Lady Adela Caroline Harriet Capel*

On a lighter note, actually much lighter, the grand-daughter of above John Thomas Capel (via son Arthur Algenon) left a wonderful diary in 1841-42. The young 13-14 year old girl, Adela, kept a diary for one year and, from this, we get some interesting insights into the contact she had with her great-uncle Admiral Bladen Capel and his wife. Lady Adela was the daughter of the 6th Earl of Essex and lived at Cassiobury House (the Capel seat in Hertfordshire) and the Admiral seemed to live on the estate at "Little Cassiobury" - this was obviously his country residence as 22 Rutland Gate was his home in town.

Marian Strachan, in her introduction to 'The Diary of Lady Adela Capel of Cassiobury'[1] described how Admiral Thomas Bladen Capel and his wife Harriet *"were both involved in various ways in helping to develop the interests and skills of their young great-niece Adela, and she visited them often"*. It is not proposed to reproduce all the diary entries here as they are of a routine nature. But one or two extracts only:

Sunday May 2, 1841 ...... *Rose at 7. After breakfast went to church. In the afternoon lessons until half past three; heard two claps of thunder, took a walk about the garden and picked some radishes for tea, they were very good. In the evening Uncle Bladen showed me how to arrange my microscope.*

Wednesday November 10, 1841.... *Rose at half past 7. After breakfast walked to Little Cassiobury and received from Aunt Bladen some piano exercises and a letter from grandmama.*

Wednesday December 29, 1841 .... *Rose at half past 8. After breakfast I could not go out because it rained. In the evening went to a party at Aunt Bladen's. We had famous fun, leaping, dancing and playing at various games. We arrived home a little after 12 o'clock.*

**Adela married in Dublin at the age of 28 to Archibald William, 13th Earl of Eglinton and Winton. Adela's father provided a marriage settlement of £5,000. Adela died in childbirth.**

---

who married George Spencer-Churchill, 6th Duke of Marlborough. Admiral Bladen Capel's sister-in-law Lady Caroline Capel (née Paget) is also there. Other relations are buried nearby: Hon B E Henry Blackwood, son of Hon 2nd Lord Dufferin, Isabel Maud Stewart, youngest daughter of Randolph 9th Earl of Galloway and of Harriet Blanch, daughter of the 6th Duke of Beaufort - some of the latter being in the large Galloway tomb which contained upto 16 persons. Also nearby are Paget/Turners.

[1] A Victorian Teenager's Diary. The Diary of Lady Adela Capel of Cassiobury, edited by Marian Strachan, Hertfordshire Record Publications, 2006

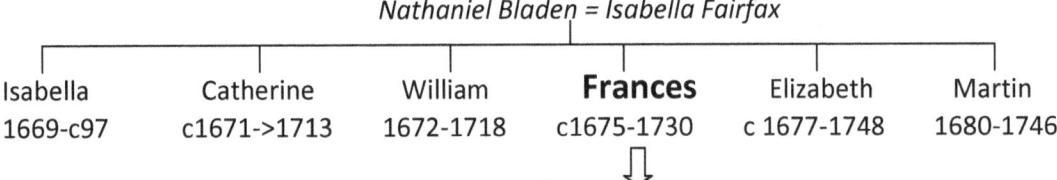

## Frances

Turning now to Frances, the fourth child and third daughter.

### 1697: Marriage

Considering the Bladen family were Yorkshire Protestants and so closely connected to the Fairfax family who were parliamentarian leaders in the English Civil War and equally strong Protestants, it is amazing how many of their children married into Catholic families. First eldest daughter Isabella married a Vavasour, then eldest son William married into the van Sweringen family, albeit in Maryland, where perhaps there was more tolerance of Catholics than there was in England. Then when Frances married, she did so into one of Yorkshire's most stalwart Catholic families, the Hamonds/Hamonds of Scarthingwell. Frances and her new husband William Hamond knew full well they were marrying without the approbation of his family, indeed entirely without his father's knowledge, and so kept their union secret. The decision to marry was probably prompted by the arrival of the couple's eldest daughter Catherine Maria who was born a few months later. Initially they were not residing together but, at some point within the first two years of marriage, news of their status got out and the reaction of father-in-law Gervase Hamond Snr could not have been worse.[1]

It cannot be known whether it was his son and heir's decision to marry without permission that angered him the most, or the fact that he married outside of the Catholic faith, or even Frances's lack of fortune. Just after the couple married, Frances and her sisters had been involved in a chancery suit over a failed annuity from the Duchess of Buckingham. The Bladen sisters had claimed[2] that whether they ate or starved depended on the Buckingham annuity and marriage settlements had depended on it. In any event, the minute her father-in-law heard of the marriage, he made life as difficult as he could for both his own son and Frances. The other possibility is that there was a pre-existing poor relationship between William and his father which was brought out into the open with the son's unexpected marriage. There is evidence of William being a weak character who led a dissolute lifestyle.

Over 170 letters concerning Frances are in the possession of the Yorkshire Archaeological Society and most have been transcribed by Archivist Kirsty McHugh, to whom I am indebted. They allow the harrowing story of Frances to be pieced together in the early, turbulent years and are referred to frequently throughout this section.

---

[1] Catholic Record Society: Lancashire Registers IV, Volume 23, p14 of 56: shows Gervase Hamond Snr's father William Hamond marrying Joan Middleton who was the widow of Francis Hungate. The Hungates married into the Gascoigne family, hence Gervase Hamond Jnr being, later in life, called "of Parlington" (Gascoigne home)
[2] TNA: C5/310/9 Bladen v Ash, 1700

By 1701 news of the marriage was common knowledge though, from a letter between Frances and Mrs Leeds (who signed herself 'your affectionate kin and servant') the couple were still living apart.

Mrs Leeds was a go-between they used to communicate with each other and, after passing Frances' letter to William Hamond, Mrs Leeds stated that William had *"parted with his woman who took [the] coach yesterday for London."* It is difficult to read too much into this comment but William's lifestyle was a major factor in the difficulties this couple were to experience and probably his own early death.[1] Seven months later Frances found refuge at Hazlewood Castle which was the home of her Vavasour in-laws. Sister Isabella Bladen, who had just recently died, had lived there as wife of Peter Vavasour and at that time the house was under the patronage of Sir Walter Vavasour, who was also a Catholic.

Outline of the Hamond family and Descendants of Frances:-[2]

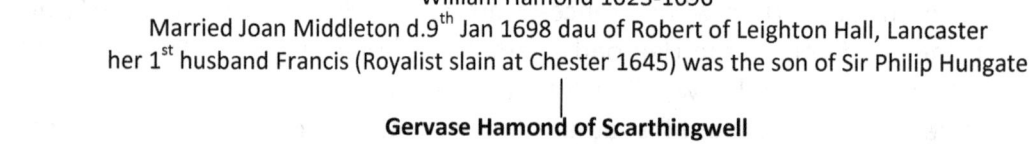

William Hamond 1623-1696
Married Joan Middleton d.9th Jan 1698 dau of Robert of Leighton Hall, Lancaster
her 1st husband Francis (Royalist slain at Chester 1645) was the son of Sir Philip Hungate

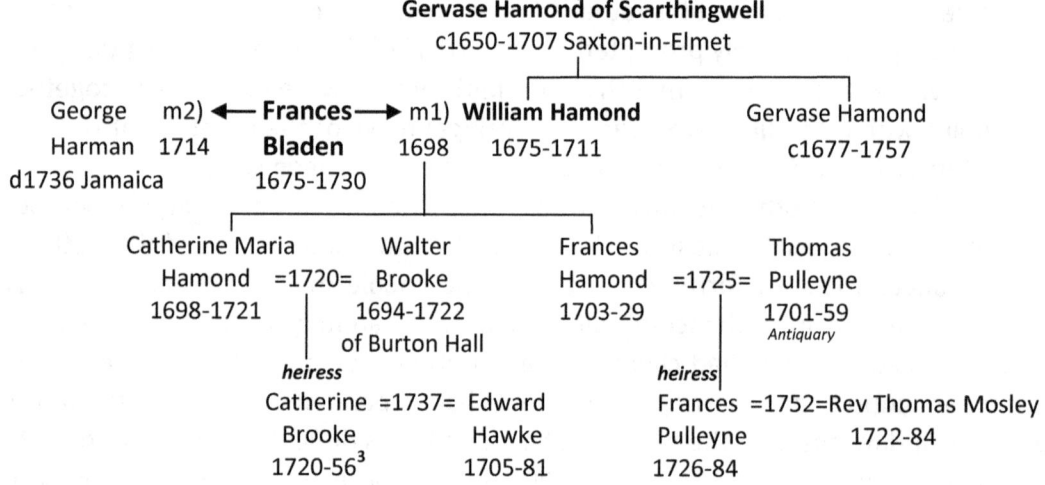

Her father-in-law's response to the news was to state he did not believe a marriage had actually taken place and he refused to acknowledge it.

---

[1] YAS: MS 614 a/1 Letter Mrs Leeds to Frances Hamond 13th May 1701
[2] Recusant History, Vol. 6 – The Catholic Society, 1962
[3] Dugdale's Visitation of Yorkshire, Vol. II, 1665-6 and Vol. 3 pp443-4. The above chart is taken from records in Saxton-in-Elmet parish register. Walter Brooke (husband of Catherine Hamond) was the eldest son of Gabriel Brooke (according to Familae Minorum Gentium, p879) and, of interest therefore, East Riding of Yorkshire Archives Services has a Will for Mary Bowlin of Pontefract DDCL/1593 dated 13th November 1778 which makes a Bladen and Catherine Hawke (née Brooke d1756) as beneficiaries, along with nephew Humphrey Osbaldeston, Calisthenes Marshall and Mary Firman. All of which suggests Walter Brooke belonged to the main Osbaldeston-Brooke line of Gateforth which descends from William Osbaldeston of Hunmanby and Anne Wentworth. Interestingly, William's son Sir Richard b1650 married Elizabeth Fountaine d.1697 whose parents were John Fountaine of Melton and Elizabeth Monckton (see chart on p27). John and Elizabeth Fountaine were the beneficiaries of Dr Richard Berry referred to in Robert and Nathaniel's chapters

Just how William reacted to the situation is not apparent as it seems to have been Frances who took on the burden of trying to find a solution. She appealed to her father for advice and wrote to him saying *"We are both in such concern that we hear not from you that we are almost mad and knows not what to do. Pray write to us and tell us what we shall do. I find they will do all they can to hinder us from giving the writings but will prolong the time to make us run more in debt. So dear father pray do what you can and as speedily as possible with full directions to us how to proceed. In haste I beg your blessing for your dutyfull daughter"*.[1] The 'writings' Frances referred to was documentation to prove their marriage had taken place. The couple had obtained copies of the parish register entry to prove to William's father that it had occurred. In the New Year and, conscious that her lawyer father was about to depart for London for the start of the new court term, Frances wrote again on 17th January informing him of a meeting that had taken place in York between attorneys for each side where one swore that William's grandfather had left him an annuity of £100 a year.[2] This would at least have provided Frances and her girls with something to subsist on because it does not appear that William had any kind of occupation or any other way of supporting them. He was entirely dependent financially on his father and his expected inheritance.

The Bladens called on their Fairfax relations for assistance and Frances wrote *"my cousin Fairfax knows more of this so can tell you, having carried the priest's letter to my father Hamond."* The priest who married Frances to William Hamond was a Mr Pue and he sent Frances a certificate to prove the validity of their marriage with a note saying *"Be it known to all people whome it may concern that Mr William Hamond (son of Gervase Hamond Esquire of Scarthingwell) and Mrs Frances Bladen were joined in Lawful matremoney by me Maurice Pue"*.[3] Frances indicated elsewhere that she believed their marriage to have taken place in *"I in King William's reign"*, or 1689 which, if so, would mean the couple married after their first child was born. Mr Pue had also written to Gervase Hamond Snr on 7th June 1700 to confirm in writing that the marriage had taken place. *"Honoured Sir, having had your son Mr William Hamond his permission, I thought it my duty to acquaint you that I married him to madam Frances Bladen and I hope there marriage will daly receive the blessing of almighty God together with those of an indulgent Father. I am sencable I may in some measure deserve your censure that this notice cometh to you to late, but I hope you will consider not only the apprehension Mr Hamond was in of your displeasure but all so the particular obligation of secrese which they lay upon your obliged humble servant...."*

So for almost two years, from at least June 1700, Gervase Hamond Snr had been aware of the marriage but continued to refuse to acknowledge it, even after the priest produced the marriage certificate. He commenced legal action against the couple in 1702 by which time their two further children, both boys, had died. Just before the marriage the Hamond family received a substantial inheritance when William's grandmother and heiress Joan Hungate died.[4]

---

[1] YAS: MS 614 a/2 Letter from Frances Hamond to Nathaniel Bladen 15th December 1701
[2] YAS: MS614 a/3 Frances Hamond to Nathaniel Bladen 17th January 1701/2
[3] YAS: MS 614 a/4 Frances Hamond to Nathaniel Bladen 5th April 1702
[4] Dugdale's Visitation of Yorkshire, Vol. II p49, 443

In 1701 William took legal action against his father, Hamond v Hamond, citing the 'Act for Further Preventing the Growth of Poperie' suing him for his maintenance and he successfully secured an income of £100 a year for his family's support. His father's estate, which brought in £800 a year was ordered to pay the sum but considering William had debts of £700, it was but a drop in the ocean. The couple now had two daughters and William had been pawning jewellery and other possessions in order to provide money for them to live on. The means by which the aggrieved father raised £100 to pay the couple was to borrow money against his estate which, after his death, son William would be bonded to repay. He then set about exerting his influence to persuade anyone giving his son's family shelter to turn them out. Fellow Catholic, Sir Walter Vavasour of Hazlewood, duly obliged Hamond and Frances wrote to tell her father the distressing news, saying he *"has ordered all the servants in his house that either dos or has ever done anything for one shall go away at Mayday, so it is time to look about for myself."* A further comment Frances made shows her to be still living apart from her husband .... *"Sir Walter* [Vavasour] *has writ a letter to my husband tho' he was at that time in the house, to bid him take me away from his house in the holly days".* So by Easter Frances was looking for somewhere else to live and, it seems, it was only Frances and her daughters, not William Hamond. Two days later, writing on 7th April 1702, Frances told her father that William *"is going to see if he can perswade the tenant that is in the Toulson House to take me because I must go from here, if not there if he can git me at any other place"*.[1]

After leaving Hazlewood, Frances next went to reside with Gascoigne relations at Parlington from April 1702.[2] Sadly the stay there was to be short-lived too because almost immediately they were visited by the father-in-law's steward, Dick Wright, who served subpoenas on Frances, her husband and *"from whence he went to Parlington to service my brother Gascoigne and sister with one"*.[3] In need of legal representation, William Hamond told his wife he was considering approaching Anthony Hamond as being *"one of the same name"* to ask if he would *"defend him against there juggling and cheating"*. Anthony had just been appointed a Commissioner for Stating the Public Accounts and would, in later times, become Deputy to "Princely Chandos", Martin Bladen's good friend.

Anthony's wife Jane was the daughter of Sir Walter Clarges whose second wife Jane Herbert was a descendant of Philip, Earl of Pembroke, referred to earlier in Nathaniel Bladen's section as the murderer who evoked Parliamentary Privilege to escape punishment. So despite there being plenty of family connections, the notion to approach Anthony Hamond came to nothing, or it was rejected, as the couple obtained legal advice from elsewhere.

---

[1] YAS: MS 614 a/5 From Frances Hamond at Hazlewood to Nathaniel Bladen 7th April 1702
[2] Related to Hamonds through Hungate marriage of William Hamond
[3] Reference to 'brother Gascoigne' would be Sir John Gascoigne 1662-1722 (actually the husband of Gervase Hamond's half-sister Mary Widdrington 1669-1722). Gervase Hamond Jnr's mother Catherine Widdrington 1649-97 married first Roger Widdrington of Harbottle (a distant relation) and secondly she married in 1673 Gervase Hamond 1650-1707. The Gascoignes were at Parlington and the name crops up again in the Hawke section when son and heir Thomas Gascoigne was accidentally killed whilst out riding with Martin Bladen Edward Hawke

Five weeks later and writing from a different address at Oglethorpe (about 10 miles north of Scarthingwell) Frances clarified the sequence of events to her father: *"The reasons why we did not declare our marriage at ye first were these: ..... Father Hamond .... would disinherit my husband if he did not marry as he pleased ...... Nor did we refuse to give my Father Hamond proof of our wedding, for as soon as that was called in question that we heard of it, we sent to ye priest who married us to give my Father Hamond an account of it himself, since he did not believe our word (and ye witnesses being dead), which account my cousin T. Fairfax[1] carried to Scarthingwell, where my sister and he believed his son married, but yet he would not pardon him and to excuse himself afterwards when, pressed by several worthy persons to give us a maintenance, he said he would if we were married, but those 'ifs' were not put in till my cousin Fairfax was gone out of ye country"*.[2] The priest who married the couple even visited Scarthingwell to see Hamond, who pretended not to be home at the time as he did not want to see him. Only one side of the correspondence between Frances and her father has been seen but, from the response given it is clear that Nathaniel Bladen asked his daughter whether she had compromised her religious belief, to which she replied *"as to religion, my dear Father, I did not change mine for any human respects"*.

At some point during the dispute as to whether their marriage had actually taken place, the couple decided to put the question beyond doubt *"... my husband and I did there renew our consent before ye above said witnesses"*.[3] How Frances managed to have a child and keep that child and her marriage secret for so long is revealed in the same letter previously referred to. William and Frances had been frantically trying to find those who had witnessed their wedding to make statements to the unbelieving father-in-law but they were deceased. One of those individuals mentioned and who was still alive was Mr Charles Jackson who, in 1697 and seven months before the birth of daughter Catherine Marie, Frances said *"He was ye man who was to have taken care of me when I was with child for I was to have laid in at Newcastle"*. In the event Mr Jackson was not called as a witness because William Hamond knew Jackson to be a close friend of Mr Ord who was great friends with Gervase Hamond and he feared would come under his influence and give unreliable testimony. Clearly then, if Frances had gone away to Newcastle to give birth, it was to conceal the event which also seems to confirm that the marriage took place after the pregnancy was discovered.

One extraordinary detail that emerged in a letter between Rev Pue and Frances on 7th June 1700[4] was the priest's own fuzzy memory on the marriage date: *"I send you accordingly to your order two certificates but whether you should inclose one of them in your father's letter I leave to your discretion tho' I think it is not necessary being I cannot upon account of my ill-memory be positive in the date of them, tho' you may easily put the date to them for that will be expected and looked upon as very materiall."*

---

[1] Henry, Thomas and Brian Fairfax were involved in trying to assist the couple. That is to say brothers Thomas 5th Lord Fairfax and Henry Fairfax of Toulston son of 4th Lord Henry Fairfax and their cousin Brian Fairfax
[2] YAS, MS 614, 19th May 1702, Frances Hamond to Nathaniel Bladen
[3] YAS, MS 614 dated 19th May 1702, Frances Hamond to Nathaniel Bladen
[4] YAS, MS 614 - letter dated 7th June 1700 cited in a/4 of 5th April 1702 Frances to Nath Bladen

This seems to suggest that Gervase Hamond's anger may be related to the fact that the marriage took place after the pregnancy began or, indeed, maybe after the birth itself and the priest's bad memory and record-keeping did not help matters.

What started as a private dispute between father and son over his marriage, escalated into a religious battleground, where the Protestant cause was incensed to prevent Catholic supremacy. This all took place just a few years after the Popish Plot and fears and disdain for Catholicism were palpable. The son consulted with the Lord Archbishop of York and leading Protestant families in Yorkshire whilst the father had the full backing of the Catholic Benedictine Order and had the highest ranking Catholic families to support him. A few months later in August, Frances was exhausted from a visit to consult the Lord Abp on their troubles and, on her behalf, William wrote to Nathaniel Bladen, this being the sole letter seen from him. He described Frances having been encouraged by His Grace and how there was a determination to assist Frances *"rather than lose to a papist family"*. In turn, Gervase Hamond was busy consulting his Catholic contacts and had several meetings alluded to by William who said, the *"Holy Order of the Benedictins here are now and have bine several times with my Father at York and will leave noe stone unturned to there own interest."*

William ended the letter with an appeal for money: *"Prey remember our debts, a hundred a year for the three last past, with the debt at Barston [Bramham?] will set alright, and to assist upon something to begin the world with would not be amiss, for we are as bare as well can be. Alsoe prey remember the little charg my father hath and as likely to live as myself, and that we are young and may have a great charge of children. Soe dear sir in hast. Prey excuse the paper its all we have in the house. I am your obedient son Wm Hamond."*[1]

Since leaving Parlington the couple, now seemingly living as a family, resided at Toulston (area of Oglethorpe/Bramham) just a few miles away from Scarthingwell where they were heavily involved in defending themselves against Gervase Hamond's legal proceedings. A lawyer, Mr West,[2] had been appointed to represent them and Frances's cousin Henry Fairfax was assisting. Fairfax, wrote to Nathaniel Bladen, advising him on progress. He described how William had gone to York *"having got his Father's proposal, which in many respects are far short of what His Grace would have done"*.[3] So it seems that the intervention of the Lord Abp was successful in getting the father-in-law to come up with a proposal for the couple's maintenance with a figure of £120 per annum now being mentioned but the indication was that he would not pay off their debts. However such a sum barely covered their large debts and William subsequently applied to the court to increase it because his family was growing and such a small sum could not maintain them. William claimed that his father was deliberately impoverishing his estate by chopping down trees for a quick profit and having no care for their future re-growth.[4]

A few weeks later the correspondence refers to the couple being advised they were to be given some money by Gervase Hamond (possibly via a third party) but, Frances told her father, I *"desired him to pay it to my own hand, not my husband's."*

---

[1] YAS: MS 614 a/6 William Hamond to Nathaniel Bladen, 7 New Square, Lincoln's Inn, 5th August 1702
[2] YAS: MS 614 a/7 Frances Hamond at Toulston to Nathaniel Bladen at Lincoln's Inn, 22nd August 1702
[3] YAS: MS 614 Henry Fairfax to Nathaniel Bladen, 5th October 1702
[4] TNA: C9/168/52 Hamond v Hamond, 1701 and TNA: C 6/428/57 Hamond v Hamond, 1709

This suggests that either Frances did not feel her husband was trustworthy with money or that perhaps she wanted to avoid confrontation between father and son and a meeting place of the White Horse in Tadcaster was agreed. Mention was made of the Fairfax family suggesting that the Hamond family difficulties would best resolved in Parliament as *"my Lord Fairfax [5th Lord] would gladly have our business in parliament, which everyone says would be the better for us (no bribes can be entered there)"* and that Sir William Lowther, former Sheriff of Yorkshire and MP, *"had been at London to suffer unto us all the mischief he can"*.[1]

So many people had become involved in the case, too many to mention here but it demonstrates why contacts were so powerful when Sheriffs, Archbishops, Lords and even religious orders could be called on to put pressure on the opposing side. The Bladens, of course, made full use of their hugely influential Fairfax relations and, in a reference to her cousin Brian Fairfax, Frances described how the couple were about to travel to London (9th October 1702) and how, on their return, they were hoping to go and live in their house [Fairfax's] and that they hoped Nathaniel Bladen would join them so they could repay him for the trouble he has gone to in assisting them. Frances said *"I hope you will live with us, as long as you live, and if I outlive you I promise I will bury you by my mother"*. Well, Frances did outlive her father but although the burial place of her mother is well known as being at Bolton Percy, it is not known if Nathaniel was ever buried next to her as details of his final burial place have yet to emerge.

A few weeks later it was Christmas and both William Hamond with Frances's cousin Brian Fairfax were to attend Scarthingwell to wait on Gervase Snr with an order for which William was to receive the agreed allowance to him. It was stipulated that William was to attend in person but when William and Brian arrived they found Gervase Hamond 'supposedly' out. They were told by the steward to return the next day when he would be at home, which they did, only to be told the same thing again. On the third day, the order was sent by a servant but the father refused to pay it until the son appeared in person. William attended the next day, but only to find that his father could not see him as he had a heavy cold. On the fifth attempt to see his father, William arrived to find a group of men there who, Frances later told her father, *"did all they could to make my husband fall out with them, but God be thanked he behaved himself with all the meakness, tho' his younger brother did challenge him to a fight"*.[2]

Payment was eventually made but then Frances and her husband had to duck and dive to avoid detection as word got out in Tadcaster that they had funds and all their creditors chased after them for settlement. They hired a coach, in a false name and Frances wrote *"Nobody here knows of our going but the bearer and Mrs Mary, my cousin Fairfax's servant, who takes care of the house goods"*.[3] The intended destination of the couple was probably London to the safety of cousin Admiral Robert Fairfax's town house in Searle Street or accommodation he arranged nearby for them.

---

[1] YAS: MS 614 Frances Hamond to Nathaniel Bladen, 9th October 1702
[2] YAS: MS 614 a/8 Frances Hamond at Toulston to Nathaniel Bladen at Lincoln's Inn, 30th December 1702
[3] Ibid

The next step the unforgiving father-in-law took was to make out his Will[1] to disinherit William in favour of his second younger son Gervase (Jnr) who was blind but who was also a Catholic. The Will directed that he was to have the use and income from the Scarthingwell estate and there were other bequests to brother (in-law) William Hungate £10, Mary Anderton of Scarthingwell £300, Katherine Treadway £10, his steward 20 guineas, Christopher Bailey servant £10, and then at the end of the Will he bequested to his eldest son William Hamond a derisory 20 shillings *"in full of what he may claim or demand out of any part of my real or personal estate (except the entail estate)"*.[2] No doubt the reason he left his son a mere 20 shillings was a legal technicality, if the son was included in the Will even for a single penny then he could not later challenge it claiming that he had not been considered, but it was clearly an attempt to divert everything within his power away from son William.

**Scarthingwell Hall**

What the father could not alter though, and which his Will grudgingly alluded to, was the entail. This is a reference to the grandfather's Will who devised part of his Scarthingwell estate to William the grandson and his heirs and Gervase Hamond Snr could not interfere with that arrangement, though he did everything else in his power to ruin the couple's lives. The Will was drawn up on 19th/20th July in 1706 along with Indentures of lease and release which put the Hamond estate into the hands of Sir Reginald Graham (Widdrington relation) of Norton Conyers and Thomas Gill of Ripon in Trust until the father-in-law's death at which time he directed the younger son, Gervase Junior to inherit.

---

[1] TNA: PROB 11/496/5 Will of Gervase Hamond of Scarthingwell (see Appencies p230). 1707
[2] Catholic Record Society (Great Britain) Lancashire Registers IV (Vol. 23) and TNA: C5/242/39 Hamond v Graham (Sir Reginald), 1711
[3] 'Lost Heritage - England's Lost Country Houses; www.lostheritage.org.uk' (Thanks to Matthew for permission to use photograph). Noted in a book entitled 'The Beauties of England and Wales, or, Original Delineations, Topographical, Historical and Descriptive of each County, Vol XIV, dated 1819 by a collection of authors, p629

Within a few months Gervase Hamond Senior died and his passing must have been an enormous relief to the young couple who immediately moved into the Hamond family home of Scarthingwell Hall with their two daughters. A letter from Brig. General Thomas Fairfax (in Dublin) dated 19 September 1707 to his nephew Admiral Robert Fairfax (at his country house at Newton Kyme near Tadcaster a short distance from Scarthingwell) said ... *"I am mighty glad my niece Hamond is peaceably settled at Scarthingwell. You will have a good neighbour of her. I hope to see you all in old Yorkshire before I die"*.

Unfortunately the couple was not left in peace at Scarthingwell for long because their occupation of the estate was challenged by the younger son and those who held it in Trust via the Indentures of Lease and Release.[1] At the same time, on 25th October 1707, William brought a Testamentary Appeal in the Exchequer Court against the Will.[2] Perhaps it was due to the stress of the legal problems that, no sooner had William and Frances settled into the splendour of Scarthingwell, then serious cracks in their relationship became apparent. The only letter between the couple, dated 18th March 1710, revealed major problems with William's behaviour and lifestyle which had driven Frances and her two daughters to leave the house for their safety. Frances wrote, *"I doe assure my dear I would doe all that's in my power to oblige you, but you can't blame me after what has happened to take a little care of myself. I don't love to enter into perticulars tho I can't be without some apprehensions of danger. So if you'l deliver up all your armes to whome you please and admit me with cousin Mary Fairfax and your cousin Middleton, who if you wou'd leave him but for halfe an hour what he hath to say I'm sure you wou'd 'ave as an opinion of him as ever you had. His chief business is to serve you and wou'd be glad to git an end of these differences that he may goe back to London again which will be much more to his advantage than staying here. But he hath given his word for my brother[Martin] to stay till there's a good end made or at least till my brother comes down or he can assure my relations that you treat me very kindly and then he will send down your children to Scarthingwell till such time I shall have small encouragement to think of it. I have so much tenderness for them not to let them run any hazards but heartily wish we could understand one another for I do declare I would doe all that's in my power to serve you and am, my dear, your affectionate wife and humble servant. F Hamond."*[3]

Frances was residing in London in Denmark Street near St Giles Church and relied on her relations to help. It is known that her brother Martin Bladen was in England for three months in early 1710 attending the Treasury Department in London answering questions about his regiment's spending. Martin had instructed his Fairfax relations to ensure the safety of Frances and her daughters and it is thought cousin Admiral Robert Fairfax helped with accommodation for Frances in London. The behaviour of William Hamond is worrying from this letter and Frances feared for her own safety and that of her children, perhaps with good cause because, among the inventory of his possessions at her husband's death was a pair of pistols, the arms referred to in her letter.

---

[1] TNA: C5/242/39 Graham v Hamond. Reginald Graham Plaintiff v Frances Hamond, widow, Katherine Hamond and Frances Hamond. Property in Scarthingwell, Saxton, Biggin, Little Fenton etc in Yorkshire. 1711
[2] 1699 Act to Prevent the Further Growth of Popery. Also Borthwick Institute: Test.CP.1701/1 Appeal
[3] YAS: MS 614 a/9 Frances Hamond to William Hamond at Scarthingwell, 18th March 1710

Frances had moved to London and had possibly one of her sisters staying with her but she concealed her address from her husband. She used Mrs Leeds who resided in the vicinity of Scarthingwell, who we have previously encountered, as a go-between to pass letters to her husband and also get news of him. Mrs Leeds was concerned about him *"pray God madam let me hear if you can, what they intend to doe with Mr William and how matters are likely to goe"*.[1] Although not expressed explicitly in the letters, it is supposed that William was living a licentious lifestyle and probably drinking and gambling heavily. The last two letters from Mrs Leeds will be the last we hear of William Hamond who died shortly afterwards. In the first, dated 22nd April 1710 she told Frances she had managed to find William's location, that he was at *"Miss Thompsons at the Two Blue Flower Potts in the Broad Way in St Giles Field"* possibly in the company of another woman as Mrs Leeds asks her to *"make what inquiries you can and what this woman is"*.

The final letter from Mrs Leeds to Frances referred to William having visited her but he had not being in good humour. Some of the housemaids at Scarthingwell were leaving and William suspected that Frances and Mrs Leeds were behind it. William may also have brought the above woman to Scarthingwell as Mrs Leeds mentioned *"For my part I never saw her, but Betty did but did not shew her the respect she expected which she complained sadly of your spouse"*. Mrs Leeds also hinted that the letters between Frances and herself may have been getting intercepted *"... but I perceive by Mr Mann ther is straing doings with some, for both your letters and mine are seen and stopt ..... I have not received any from you this three weekes"*.[2]

As previously mentioned, there was a letter from Catherine Bladen, Frances's sister in Dublin, to their close relation Admiral Robert Fairfax[3] dated 30th March 1711,[4] only a matter of days before William Hamond died, where she thanked him *"for the care of my poor sister Hamond, Pray God deliver her out of her troubles. I am in continual fear for her"*. The implication being that their Fairfax relation had helped Frances, either living with his family in London or arranging safe accommodation for her where her husband could not find her and the children. Catherine Bladen's prayers were answered remarkably quickly and her sister Frances was, indeed, delivered out of her troubles as within days William Hamond was dead.

*William Ham[m]ond was buried 15 April 1711 at age 37 years.*[5]

"Here lyeth William Hamond of Scarthingwell Esq who married Frances, daughter of Nathaniel Bladen, of Hemsworth in the County of York Esq and had by her issue Catherine Maria, Frances and William. Obit 14th die Aprilis, anno 1711, aetatis suae 37."[1]

---

[1] YAS: MS 614 a/10 Mrs Leeds to Frances Hamond at Denmark Street, 10th April 1710
[2] YAS: MS 614 a/12 Mrs Leeds to Frances Hamond at Denmark Street, 20th May 1710
[3] Admiral Robert Fairfax 1666-1725 was in command of the Bonaventure, Conception, Ruby and Entreprenant and was present at the Battles of Bantry Bay 1689 and Beachy Head 1690. He was presented with a silver cup by Queen Anne for his part, during 1704, of the capture of Gibraltar
[4] YAS: MS 614, Catherine Bladen to Admiral Robert Fairfax, 1711
[5] Saxton-in-Elmet parish register

He was buried at Saxton in Yorkshire. William had written his Will just seven days before he died and described himself as being *'very weak'* and named Frances as his executor and entrusted the care of their two daughters to her. Crucially, he directed that his daughters were not to marry before the age of 21 years without their mother's consent and, if they did, Frances would be entitled to remain at Scarthingwell and derive the income from the estate for as long as she wished. Within weeks of burying her husband, new legal proceedings were brought against Frances and her two daughters.[2]

| | |
|---|---|
| 1701 | Hamond v Hamond. William sued his father Gervase Senior for maintenance |
| 1706 | Jul 22nd: Gervase Hamond Snr made his Will, to the benefit of his second son |
| 1707 | Apr 25th: Gervase Hamond Snr died |
| 1707 | Apr: William and Frances Hamond took possession of the estate |
| 1708 | Oct: William Hamond filed a Bill against his brother Gervase Jnr |
| 1710 | Nov 3rd: Lord Chancellor Cowper declared Gervase Snr's estate should pay his debts and all parties to submit their accounts |
| 1710 | William Hamond was unhappy with the outcome and asked for a re-hearing |
| 1710 | Nov 18th: New hearing was gone through but the Order was unaltered |
| 1711 | Apr 15th: William Hamond died |
| 1711 | Jul 5th: Executors of Gervase Hamond Snr brought action against Frances and her daughters |

The widowed Frances continued to reside at Scarthingwell and claimed the estate as the property of herself and her children. She refused to pay those debts of her father-in-law that were outstanding but was obligated to provide Gervase Jnr with an annuity from the entail on the estate (300 marks) and, significantly, that annuity to the younger brother also gave him power to prevent Frances from disposing of the Scarthingwell estate. Frances relied heavily on her lawyer father Nathaniel at this time and there were numerous exchanges of correspondence between the two dating from 1712-13 as he sought to advise her on how to manage proceedings.

In a letter, written after William's death, attorney Francis Taylor wrote to Frances saying *"some of your neighbourhood have been insisting strange notions in his head for they now talk of Mr Hamond's being 'non compos mentis' at the time of making the Will"*. The allegation that Frances's husband was not sane when he wrote his Will, however, was disputed by those who witnessed it, one of whom was the elderly Fairfax[3] chaplain William Topham. It was likely no more than a rouse for some of the Hamond creditors to challenge William's Will and the Hamond title to the estate. The probate process, however, had gone through satisfactorily.[4]

Cousin Robert Fairfax wrote to Frances on 11 January 1712 and from the letter's contents he had clearly not attended William's funeral as he asked for details of how it went.

---

[1] The History of the Parishes of Sherburn and Cawood, with notices of Wistow, Saxton, Towton. William Wheater
[2] TNA: PROB 11/532/279 Will of William Hammond, written 1711, probate 1st April 1713
[3] Chaplain to Lady Fairfax (Chaloner) at Newton Kyme. He died 1720
[4] YAS: MS 614 Francis Taylor to Frances Hamond, 16th October 1715

He also made reference to another event that happened at this time, the death of Thomas Fairfax in Dublin who her sister Catherine Bladen was taking care of. Robert Fairfax asked Frances *"Did you fortell his death in a dreme as they tolde me you did that of poor cousin Henry Fairfax?"*[1] This was a reference to Henry Fairfax 1659-1708, son of the 4th Lord Fairfax, who had been trying to help Frances, along with his brother the 5th Lord Thomas Fairfax and their cousin Brian. Frances was left to continue the legal battles as her husband's death brought death duties and she was also chased by her husband's creditors. Despite the annuity due to Gervase Junior, Frances tried to improve her financial position by selling part of the estate. Scarthingwell did not just comprise the Hall, it included several messuages and farm lands, hereditaments, tenements and rents from land and property in Saxton, Biggin, Little Fenton, Kirk Fenton, Barkston and Townton. Such vast and valuable estates involved numerous parties, not just immediate Hamond descendants. A 1717 court deposition stated that William's Will *"did empower the said defendant his wife to sell and dispose of such part only of his land tenements and hereditaments in Kirk Fenton, Little Fenton, and Biggin in the County of York as would fully pay and discharge all his debts, funeral expenses and legacies therein mentioned"*. This was in response to calls from creditors who had been trying to force the sale of more of the estate.

Francis Taylor, the attorney who had been helping Frances, decided to buy a portion of the estate for himself. With the sum of 5,300 *l.* which this sale raised, Frances could repay some debts and mortgages, she could also repay Gervase Jnr his portion of £412-9-7d and the residue would go to Frances's daughters, as they retained one-third ownership of the estate. The family had also retained a portion of the estate which included a common meadow, as was their right under the grandfather's Will. The creditors, however, claimed that the sale price of 5,300 *l.* was insufficient to cover the debts.

These were the parties involved in chancery: -v- William Wright of Tadcaster, yeoman
| | |
|---|---|
| William Hamond (died) | Gervase Hamond |
| Wife: Frances Hamond | Thomas Gill - Trustee (died) |
| Daughter: Maria Catherine Hamond | Mary Anderton, spinster (bequest £300) |
| Daughter: Frances Hamond | Reginald Graham - trustee and executor of Will |
| William Wickham | Robert Lofthouse of Tadcaster, yeoman |
| Wilfrid Tolson | Richard Standish of Barkstone, yeoman |

The death of William Hamond brought Frances a new financial crisis. During the probate process, money was held by the courts for the children's portion[2] and a bankruptcy notice was issued against the estate.[3] Solely because the grandfather had devised a portion to the children of Frances, the family managed to remain at Scarthingwell but Frances relinquished a London townhouse in Great Russell Street where she had been living at the time of her husband William's funeral.

---

[1] YAS: MS 614 b/58 Robert Fairfax to Frances Hamond, dated 11th January 1711 (n.s.)
[2] TNA: C5/242/39 Hamond v Graham (Sir Reginald), 1711
[3] London Gazette – 4th August 1713 published a notice that the Scarthingwell estate was to be sold

In William Hamond's Will he acknowledged his 'dire' financial situation: *"I being very[1] sensible that my debts amount to a very great sum over and above what my personal estate will pay and satisfy I therefore do hereby will and fully empower my executrix hereafter named to sell and dispose of such part only of my land, tenements and hereditaments as will pay and fully discharge my debts"*. Other debts were recorded as *"... 175 ounces of plate which was pawned in his life time to Peter Dove of St James Market for securing £40 with interest (at 10%) .... and a parcel of linen and some plate also pawned in his lifetime to Rowland Isles for £20 ..... also a gold watch [of Frances] which her husband formerly gave her, which she used to wear but was pawned in his lifetime to Mr Wright, a goldsmith for £12 ..... and two rings which she used to wear and were also pawned in his lifetime for securing 5 guineas (at 15% interest)."*

Many years later, when the younger brother Gervase Jnr wrote his own Will in 1737,[2] he summarised his interpretation of these events and the situation regarding his father's estate. Gervase seems not to have been married (or no wife surviving) as there was no reference to a wife, a wife's family or any children in his Will proved in 1757. Instead he made bequests to his nephews and nieces in the Gascoigne family, that is, descendants of his half-sister Mary Widdrington and Sir John Gascoigne, children mentioned mainly being Elizabeth Gascoigne married to John Plumpton and Sir Edward Gascoigne 1697-1750 who married Dame Mary Hungate, daughter of Sir Francis Hungate.[3] He described himself as being 'of Parlington', formerly of Scarthingwell, so perhaps he went to live with his Gascoigne close relations after the Scarthingwell estate went to the Hawke family (descendants of Frances). He also described how his father had devised the estate to him in 1706 and that Sir Reginald Graham (a Widdrington relation) and Thomas Gill were his father's joint executors. He referred to the numerous law suits arising from that Will involving Frances Bladen and her daughters and that around 1715 the courts had decreed that the Scarthingwell estate should be sold but, on appeal, this was overturned and delayed during the minority of the daughters of Frances as they were one-third owners of the estate (from the grandfather's Will).[4] This is how Frances came to still be residing at Scarthingwell after her husband William's death in 1711 and in receipt of rents for Little Fenton with Biggin, Saxton, Scarthingwell and Barkston. Gervase Jnr made various bequests in his Will, including small sums for mourning to his nieces Catherine Maria Brooke and ____Pulleyn) which is curious since both of his nieces were dead when he wrote his Will in 1737, Catherine Maria Brooke(née Hamond) died in 1721 and Frances Pulleyne (née Hamond) died in 1729 (see chart p156). It is presumed, therefore, that he was referring to his grand-nieces Catherine Brooke and Frances Pulleyn who were aged 17 and 11 years respectively at that time and he left them a derisory one guinea to buy mourning rings.

---

[1] TNA: PROB 11/532/279, Will of William Ham[m]ond dated 1711 (Appendix p230)
[2] TNA: PROB 11/830/313 - Will of Gervase Hamond, written 1737, died 1756, probate 1757 (Appendix p231)
[3] Sources for chart: Dugdale's Visitation of Yorkshire, Vol. 2, pp443-444; Reports of the Cases in the High Court of Chancery and Publications of the Surtees Society, Vol. 62, by Mrs Alice (Wandesford) Thornton; Ducatus Leoientis, or, the Topography of the Ancient and Populous Town and Parish of Leeds and parts adjacent by Ralph Thoresby, 1715, (Hungate pedigree)
[4] TNA: C11/1120/18 Hawke v Graham. The deposition of Gervase Hamond Jnr in this Cause was taken 12th June 1756 which must have been just a few weeks before he died, as his Will was proved 27th April 1757

Sir Edward Hawke immediately challenged the Will: 'Petitioning for administrative rights over the goods and chattels of Gervase Hammond, deceased, late of Parlington; Knight' along with his co-petitioner Thomas Pullan [Pulleyn].[1] Gervase also stated that, about this time, the courts confirmed that he was entitled to two-thirds of his father's estate by an order of 1715, meaning his nieces were entitled to one-third (that is, one-sixth portion each). The main beneficiary was his friend Sir Walter Wagstaff Bagot of Blythfield, Staffs. Gervase did not amend his Will in the years after 1737 and the situation changed due to numerous chancery cases.[2] Occupancy of Scarthingwell passed from Frances Bladen and her two children during their minority, probably initially to Reverend Thomas Mosley who, Gervase stated, was granted administration of the estate of Frances after her death.[3] Mosley, through his wife Frances (née Hamond), acquired her one-sixth portion of the estate, then at some later point it passed to the Hawke family. In May 1740 Gervase Hamond had made a payment to Sir Edward Hawke and his wife Dame Catherine Maria regarding Catherine's portion. In 1756 Hawke, his wife and Thomas Pulleyne (now widowed and remarried) took Gervase Hamond Jnr and Rev Thomas Mosley to court over the estate, Thomas Pulleyne and Mosley being father and son-in-law.

Scarthingwell was structurally altered and added to by succeeding generations, though the original 17th century part of the house remained and was incorporated as servants quarters (less the gables). Home at various times, to the Hamonds, Harman (when Frances Bladen moved in after remarriage), then later Admiral Hawke, then to his eldest son. Hawke descendants sold it in 1948 to the Maxwell family who added a new wing and a chapel (modelled on the Chapel Royal at Munich). The church survives but the house was demolished in the 1960s.[4]

Nathaniel Bladen continued to assist daughter Frances with her legal difficulties after her husband's death. In a letter from September 1712, he wrote to urge Frances to be careful how she replied to legal documents he had glanced at because they seemed to "*bear so hard among your husband's weak side*".[5] At times, this correspondence between father and daughter was carried by the man who would become Frances's second husband, Captain George Harman. Harman was an army officer and[6] Frances married him in 1714 but, exactly as at her first marriage, kept it secret, though this time for a different reason; as a widowed woman she was able to conduct business and sell property but as a married woman her affairs would have to be handled by her husband, that was the law. Captain Harman, however, was perhaps not in the best position to conduct business as by 1715 he was away from home with the army fighting in the Jacobite Rebellion.

---

[1] Borthwick Institute: TEST. CP. 1757/1, Borthwick Institute GB 193, Exchequer Court, 1 piece
[2] TNA: PROB 11/830/313 Will of Gervas Ham[m]ond of Parlington, 25th May 1757
[3] TNA: C11/1120/18 Hawke v Graham. 1757
[4] Burial of Madam Hamond, wife of Gervase Hamond of Scarthingwell 1 Jan 1697 and burial of Gervase Hamond of Scarthingwell 28 April 1707, page 111; then William's own burial on 17th April 1711, he had died on the 14th: birth and burial also of Frances, daughter of Walter Brooke of Towton Hall, gentleman; death of Catherine, wife of Walter Brooke buried 22 Nov 1720, Saxton-in-Elmet parish register
[5] Copy letter in the possession of Lord Rosse, Nathaniel Bladen to Frances Hamond, 30th September 1712
[6] George Harman was named in Colonel Martin Bladen's Will drawn up in 1726

Perhaps, more likely, the experience Frances had from her first marriage made her cautious about trusting her future and her children's to a husband. In letters between Frances and her attorney Taylor, there were references to the rebels' movements in the north, Frances feared their arrival near Scarthingwell travelling south from Scotland where the Old Pretender had briefly occupied Perth. At one point, she sent her two daughters away to Admiral Robert Fairfax's family in London, for safety. Taylor wrote to Frances on 16th October 1715 to say he had received a letter from her husband from Barwick (in Elmet) where his regiment had been stationed. The troops were at nearby Barnham Moor ready to challenge Jacobites travelling south. Barnham was a good strategic point being located next to the Great North Road and close to crucial river crossings.[1]

Although Gervase Junior succeeded in 1715 in getting the courts to award him two-thirds of the Scarthingwell estate and ordering that the estate be sold, there was an immediate appeal which prevented the sale and judgment was reversed in deference to the daughters of Frances still being minors, and any action to sell the estate was held in abeyance until the daughters were of full age. This news had not yet filtered out to the creditors of William Hammond who had been waiting four years for their bills to be paid. Attorney Taylor told Frances *"I have been attack'd since my coming to town by several of Mr Hammond's creditors to know why wee are so dilatory in disposing of the estate for payment of debts, and withal they threaten to set up a purchase in town and sell it to the best bidder"*.[2]

Meanwhile, by 7th February 1716 the Jacobite threat was diminishing and Taylor wrote again to Frances keeping her informed: *"Wee have nothing from Scotland of the rebels being defeated, but yesternight wee made illuminations and rejoicing for their abandoning Perth upon the approach of our army without leaving the courage to strike a stroak"*.[3] The good relations between Frances and her attorney, however, soon became strained when he finally discovered that Frances was, in fact, married. He was mortified as, in the meantime, he had purchased a portion of her estate for himself and was worried about the legality of the transaction. Writing on 17th October 1716 (though now addressing himself to the husband George Harman) he said .... *"Sir, I have very well considered and have been likewise advised that my estate at Fenton is very precarious, for that your Lady at the time of expecting the conveyance was married, which if true, nothing could pass to me by these deeds because a married woman can do no act in Law without the consent of her husband and such consent must appear upon record, which must be either by a fine or recovery.*
*I am told your marrying has been of two years standing or upwards and the reason why it was not made publick enough, but really I think (with submission) something of this matter should have been [told] to me that I might have prepared securities accordingly. Most of my fortune that I have been labouring for all my life depends upon this stake and it would be pretty hard (after my time), that my wife and children should suffer through my inadversity, therefore must hope you'll make me easy in this ...."*.[4]

---

[1] YAS, MS614 (a/63), Letter to Frances Harman (Hamond/Bladen) from Francis Taylor
[2] YAS: MS 614 a/46 Francis Taylor to Frances Hammond, 9th July 1715
[3] YAS: MS 614 a/63 Francis Taylor to George Harman, 7th February 1716 n.s.
[4] YAS: MS 614 b/13 Francis Taylor to George Harman, 17th October 1716

The purchase and the court settlement of the Hamond estate gave much needed funds to Frances and on 24th September 1716 Taylor wrote to George Harman to advise that the family's creditors were invited to the George Inn at 2pm to receive money owed.[1] The George Inn at 19 Coney Street was one of the most important Inns in the North of England.

The Inn was demolished in 1867 and, writing in 1901, Harper wrote of it *"when it went to make way for new buildings, York lost its most picturesque Inn"*.

It was a medieval timber-framed building, with the York Courant next door and Fairfax House just round the corner.

**The George Inn, York:[2]**

George Harman and Frances muddled through the legal complexities but that was not the only difficulty they had to contend with. In further correspondence, George alluded to the family's difficulties with one daughter in particular:[3] *"the treatment I have met with from one of them may convince you what reason I have to fear it. I can expect but little favour from her who shews neither duty nor affection to the best of mothers."* Eldest daughter Catherine Marie had married Walter Brooke without her mother's consent and Gervase Hamond Jnr, writing to George Harman in November 1718, expressed his regret at the news, *"I am extremely .... surprised at what you tell me and very sorry for it. I always was of opinion she never would have married but by advice and consent of her mother"*.[4] Immediately the marriage had taken place Catherine's in-laws got involved in her portion of the Scarthingwell estate and threatened to take legal action against William and Frances. The worry and tension between the Harman household and Taylor was palpable in their letters to each other over the Brooke family's involvement. Taylor contemplated bringing a Bill in Equity as he feared the Brookes' actions could threaten possession of his own property. Harman wrote back quickly, overnight, to Taylor urging restraint and for him to join forces with them against Brooke as he felt, should Brooke carry out his threats, both Taylor and Harman family homes would be under threat and the estate could *"devolve on Mr Hamond,"*[5] that is, Gervase Hamond Jnr the blind/Catholic. Brooke's actions, he continued *"should he succeed in it, as I'm sure he can't, he would cut himself (as well as others) out of the estate"*.

---

[1] List of creditors: Richard Fawkingham of Towton, Mr & Mrs Hartley, William Briggs of Tadcaster, John Hutton of Barkston, Richard Standish of Barkston, Mr Leeds, Matthew Harrison of Saxton, Widow Lease of Ryther, William Thompson of Newton and Thomas Slothard of Uskelfe
[2] Reproduced with permission from Mick Armitage
[3] YAS: MS 614 b/36, Francis Taylor to George Harman at Scarthingwell, 15th July 1719
[4] YAS: MS 614 b/31 Gervase Hamond Jnr to George Harman at Scarthingwell, 23rd November 1718
[5] YAS: MS 614 George Harman to unknown recipient, 12th March 1718

Taylor's frustration at George Harman's inability to locate a crucial deed boiled over a few months later: *"I know it is amongst your writings, but you have overlooked it. Therefore, pray once more cast your eye over them and send it to be copyed, that it may be lodged with the rest of the deeds"*.[1]  It is probable that George Harman was playing for time by claiming to be unable to locate the deed because when it was finally found he rejected Taylor's request to see it.  So Taylor suggested it be deposited with a third party, but Harman was still hanging on to it saying on 9th September *"as it is a matter in which my wife and the children (as well as myself) are concerned you cannot blame me for being a little cautious"*.[2]

One month later Taylor replied, *"Dear Captain, I am amazed that a man of your penetration should not be convinced thoroughly by this time that yours and your ladies interests are upon the same footing with mine"*.[3]  Taylor feared that if the deed was to be "accidentally" destroyed, the children when they became of full age, could claim the whole estate as well as Taylor's own purchase.  Harman replied a week later *"Tho' I confess my penetration is very shallow, yet I was not mistaken in my opinion of the children being as deeply concerned in the contested deed as any of us. In my opinion tis by that they hold their estate, as well as ours. If that deed had not been made, their uncle* [Gervase, blind catholic - as male heir] *might put in for the whole, and who could oppose him ...."*[4]

Time passed but in July 1719 Harman was still clinging on to the precious deed. Taylor wrote *"If you cannot be perswaded to deposite them in a third persons hands, I must be forced to find out some method for the security of myselfe and family, for as the case now stands it is very precarious ..."*.[5]  Still Harman would not let go of the deed as he considered it central to ownership of Scarthingwell and, of course, Taylor considered it essential that it be lodged in safe third-party hands, to protect his own interests.[6] Taylor's words fell on deaf ears, as Harman replied pleading poverty *"... what can I do, the children are in my debt. I had very little above £40 per annum to maintain them both with. One of them* [Catherine] *has thrown herself wholly out of my management and threatens to sue me, for no other reason that I can think of but because I have been too easie, kind and indulgent to her"*.[7] In the following months Taylor re-ignited his threat of action to force Harman to hand over the deed and, when he got no response, threatened legal action and also made reference to payment of a fine, which had been due when the marriage of Frances to Harman had become known.  His last letter prompted Harman finally to hand over the remaining deed into the custody of a third party (Alderman Fairfax , a relation) and Taylor wrote again on 26th December to thank him.[8]  Despite the threat of chancery proceedings Taylor and George Harman remained on good terms and their correspondence continued throughout the 1720s though was of a more routine nature.

---

[1] YAS: MS 614 b/32 Francis Taylor to George Harman at Scarthingwell, 11th March 1719
[2] YAS: MS 614 b/29 George Harman to unknown recipient, 9th September 1718
[3] YAS: MS 614 b/30 Francis Taylor to George Harman at Scarthingwell, 9th October 1718
[4] YAS: MS 614 b/30 George Harman to unknown recipient, 15th October 1718
[5] YAS: MS 614 b/36 Francis Taylor to George Harman at Scarthingwell, 15th July 1719
[6] George Harman had a brother in Maryland 1718
[7] YAS: MS 614 b/36 Reply. George Harman to Francis Taylor, date after 15th July 1719
[8] YAS: MS 614 b/39 Francis Taylor to George Harman at Scarthingwell, 26th December 1719

*Death of Frances*
Frances died in 1730 and in a letter dated January 1730/1 from Walter Brooke [close relation to Walter who married Catherine Hamond] to George Harman, Brooke wrote to say he had heard, with some surprise, of the death of Frances some weeks previously. She was buried 29th November 1730 at St Marylebone's, Westminster and, since both her daughters had predeceased her, Scarthingwell went to their heirs.

*Daughter Catherine*
Catherine Hamond, the 'difficult' daughter of Frances, had married Walter Brooke of Burton Hall[1] in 1718. He was a descendant of Humphrey Brooke (Brookes had been settled in the counties of York since the time of Queen Elizabeth I) and expanded their estate by purchasing the Gateforth Manor from Lord Darcy in 1564. Catherine and Walter had a single surviving daughter also called Catherine born in 1721. Both Catherine Snr and her husband Water Brooke died young, Catherine being only 23 years of age, and Walter was just 28. With the death of this young couple, their sole daughter Catherine Brooke became the new joint heir to Scarthingwell and relations clamoured to give her a new home (no doubt mindful of her great inheritance). On 9th February 1722 Richard Braithwaite (for the Harmans, a Fairfax/Bladen cousin), who was an attorney, wrote to George Harman advising him that he had "*entered a caveat against anyone's taking tuition of Mr Brooke's child*".[2] Young Catherine was looked after, until 1730, by her grandmother Frances. Her Brooke relations, however, had sought administration of Walter Brooke's possessions and also by extension the orphaned child, to be theirs but Catherine Brooke seems to have been brought up by her Bladen relations after her grandmother's death.

Over a year later, in April 1723, and Braithwaite was still handling the legal wrangling over the infant heiress's future having just returned from the assizes and was engaged in preparing a schedule of effects. In the final letter she received from her attorney in 1724 reference was made to papers Frances was searching for where Taylor insisted the paper was with her "*it should have been lodged with you for the sake of the young lady*". George Harman, after his wife's death, was probably obliged to vacate Scarthingwell and final letters from him show that he was staying with Colonel Bladen in Hanover Square in London where the grand-daughter was brought up and Martin no doubt had a hand in engineering her match with her cousin, Admiral Hawke who he was also guardian to.

*Daughter Frances*
The other younger daughter of Frances Bladen (Hamond/Harman), Frances Hamond, like her sister died young at only 26 years of age after marriage in 1725 to Thomas Pulleyne[3] of Burley-in-Otley.

---

[1] Burton Hall was located 10 miles south of Tadcaster
[2] YAS: MS 614 b/47 Richard Braithwait of York to George Harman, 9th February 1722
[3] The Pulleyns of Yorkshire, Catherine Pullein, 1915. Thomas was the son of Thomas Pulleyne d.1709 of Bilton and Anne Fairfax, daughter of Captain John Fairfax of Menston Thomas remarried when his daughter was about 13 years old to Mary Sterne

Their sole surviving daughter, Frances Pulleyne, thereby lost her mother at the age of three but she did, at least, have her father and his family to raise her. Frances Pulleyne married in 1752 to Rev. Thomas Mosley.

With the death of the three women at the centre of the Scarthingwell inheritance (Frances and her two daughters), their interests now passed to their respective infant daughters and the families they subsequently married into.

Litigation between the parties stretched forward in time.

|      |                | Plaintiffs                         | Defendants                  |
|------|----------------|------------------------------------|-----------------------------|
| 1755 | Hawke v Graham | Admiral Hawke & wife               | Gervase Hamond              |
|      |                | Thomas Pulleyne [*father v dau.*]  | Rev Thomas & Frances Mosley |
|      |                |                                    | Sir Bellingham Graham       |
| 1805 | Mosley v Taylor| Thomas Pulleyne Mosley & wife      | Thomas Taylor               |
|      |                |                                    | Lord Edward Harvey-Hawke    |
| 1806 | Mosley v Hawke | Mosley                             | Hawke                       |
| 1810 | Mosley v Hawke | Mosley                             | Hawke                       |
| 1820 | Hawke v Brooks | Lord Edward Harvey-Hawke           | Brookes                     |

123 years after Frances Bladen married William Hamond, issues surrounding Scarthingwell were still being worked out as individuals died and their descendants continued the litigation. As further marriages took place, the shared interests of these families were not restricted to the Scarthingwell estate, they included the Manors of Burley and lands at Otley, Kirk Fenton, Halifax and the advowson of Burley Church which would have come to the families via the Pulleynes. George Harman died in 1737. He had been sent to Jamaica as a Captain in one of the independent companies. Of the five captains sent there four, including Harman, had died and only one (Captain Les Bane) survived.[1]

The Scarthingwell estate remained in the Hawke family. Ultimately, the Pulleynes, with an interest in half of Scarthingwell, sold their portion to Admiral Hawke, some time prior to 1774. By then Martin Bladen Hawke (son of the Admiral) was living at Scarthingwell as a country residence as the Admiral made his home down south. Since Martin Hawke had married in 1771 it is perhaps likely that the father made the house over to the newly-wed couple at that time. He was also known to have advanced his son a huge sum of £11,000 to make improvements to Scarthingwell.

---

[1] Stamford Mercury, Thursday 21st July 1737

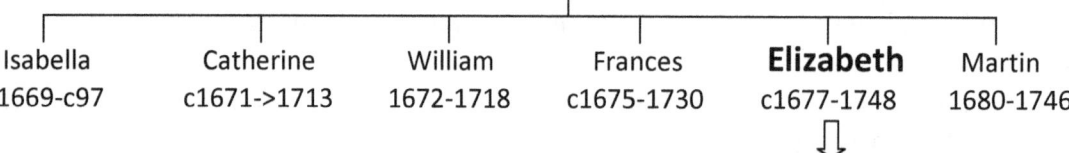

Nathaniel Bladen = Isabella Fairfax

| Isabella | Catherine | William | Frances | **Elizabeth** | Martin |
| 1669-c97 | c1671->1713 | 1672-1718 | c1675-1730 | c1677-1748 | 1680-1746 |

*Elizabeth*

Elizabeth was born about 1677, the fifth child of Nathaniel and Isabella Bladen.

Pictured right:
Elizabeth Bladen holding her son Edward Hawke
(*Picture courtesy of the Hawke family*)

She married at age 21 to James Ruthven but was widowed within a year and there were no children from the marriage.

**Elizabeth Bladen**

First husband Colonel James Ruthven was a soldier under the command of Colonel Francis Collingwood and his regiment was sent to the Leeward Islands in 1698/99: Petition of the L.-G., Council and Assembly of St. Christopher's to the King: *We, your Majesty's most dutiful, loyal and obedient subjects, return our sincere and hearty thanks to Almighty God for the blessings of a glorious peace established by your Majesty's most sublime wisdom and courage, the happy influence whereof we now enjoy, etc. And whereas your Majesty hath been graciously pleased to send a regiment of soldiers under the command of Col. Francis Collingwood to these your Majesty's islands, thereby giving a full and clear demonstration of your Majesty's tender regard for our safety.* Copy Endorsed, Rec'd. June 26, Read Sept. 21, 1699.[1]

James wrote his Will,[2] which is in the Appendices p232, immediately before setting off on the journey.[3] Luttrell stated that on 1st August 1699: "*Collonel Collingwood, who went with his regiment to the Leeward Islands, is dead there; as also his lady and daughter, with many of his officers and soldiers*". Collingwood's vessel probably came under attack from the French as England was at war with France and her far-flung colonies at the time, hence soldiers being despatched to St Kitts to strengthen its defences. Ruthven was also dead and Elizabeth was left widowed at just 22 years of age.

Five years later Elizabeth married a lawyer called Edward Hawke, a colleague of her father's in the legal profession.

*Inner Temple Records*
According to the Admissions Database for the Inner Temple, Edward Hawke, gentleman, was admitted to the Temple on 5th May 1685 and was called to the bar on 29th May 1693.

---

[1] CSP Colonial, America and West Indies, Vol. 17: 1699 and Addenda 1621-1698 (1908), pp181-196
[2] Will of James Ruthven, see Appendices, p232
[3] TNA: PROB 11/453/310, Will of James Ruthven, Written 1698, Probate 1699

His admission to Lincoln's Inn was dated 7th February 1717/18 where it was stated he was the son and heir of Thomas Hawke, a merchant, and his address was City of London. The Assistant Librarian at Lincoln's Inn elaborated a little further on this and stated the names of two of Edward's manucaptors: they were Thomas Trengrouse of Constantine in Cornwall and John Squibb of Truro. These sponsors were either kinsmen or men of good standing, say in the legal community, who would vouch for him. There is an early record of a John Squibb of Truro being a lawyer and also Thomas Trengrouse (b.19th Aug 1673) was a lawyer, having been admitted to the Inner Temple on 17th May 1705. Some sources claim that Edward Hawke was descended from the Cornish Treraven branch of Hawke:

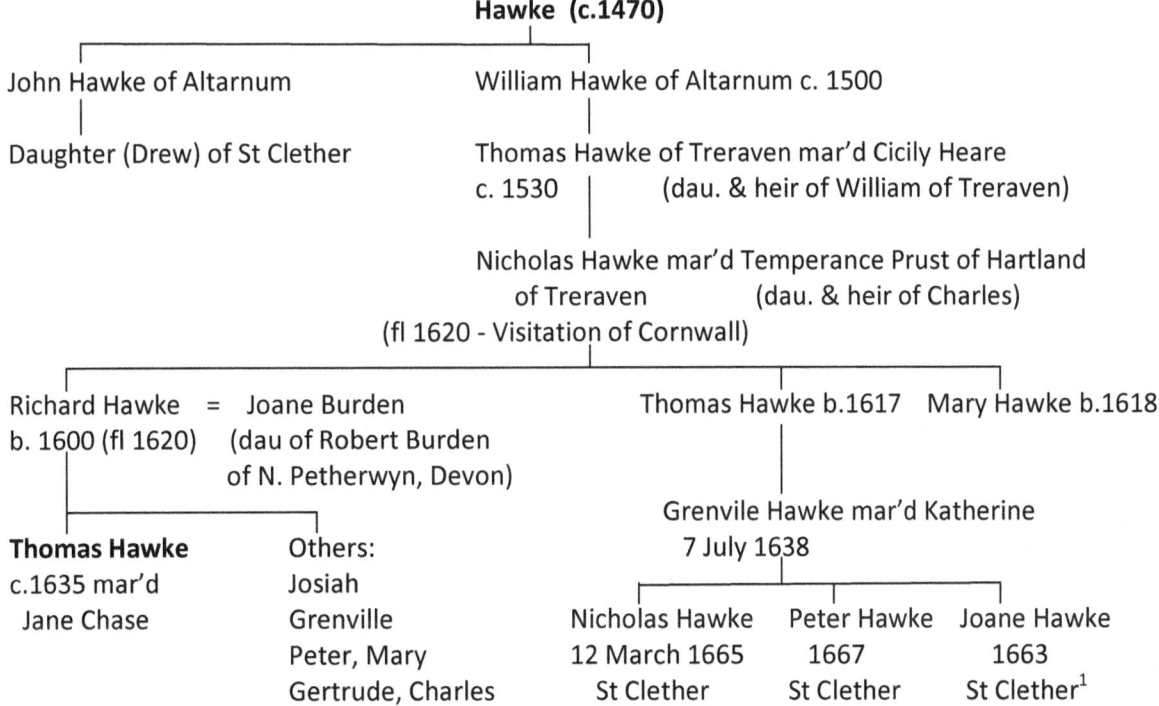

In which case he was probably the son of Thomas Hawke married to Jane Chase. The above chart was compiled from information in the 1620 Visitation of Cornwall and an Indenture kindly provided by Jenny Bussey, a Hawke researcher, but it is important to stress that it is an outline for illustrative purposes only and so far no conclusive evidence has been found to confirm this.

A marriage date of around 1704 seems likely for Edward Hawke and Elizabeth Ruthven (née Bladen) with three known children being born to them: Edward in 1705 (later Admiral), Thomas in 1707 (died young) and Frances.

---

[1] The Visitation of the County of Cornwall in the year 1620 by Lt. Col. J.L. Vivian and Henry H. Drake 1874

Just before he married Elizabeth, Westminster Rate Books show Edward residing at Charing Cross (East Side) St Martin-in-the-Fields in 1692 and paying a rent charge of 5/- in a property with a yearly rate value of £25.1.

He also occupied what looks like business premises at New Exchange, also in St Martin's with a yearly rate value of £8 for 1693.

Photograph of portrait reproduced with permission of the Hawke family

In 1707 Edward wrote a poem with an unappealing title:

**Edward Hawke 1667-1718**

*'A Poem upon the Law. Occasioned by a late Act of Parliament Entituled: An Act for the Amendment of the Law, and The better Advancement of Justice Together with A character of, and a panegyrick upon my Lord Keeper And the twelve judges by a Gentleman of the Inner Temple London By Edward Hawke (Barrister at Law)'.* Edward was dismissive about the chances of the poem being well received when he said *"As for the poem itself, mankind may censure it as they please: 'tis the first and, in all probability will be the last, I shall ever trouble them with."*[1] He was right, it does seem to have been his only poem.

"To the right honourable William Cowper Baron of Wingham, Lord Keeper of the Great Seal of England. PREFACE, Considering England ingag'd in a most just and necessary War, in defence of our Religion and the Liberties of all Europe, my Thoughts naturally led me to look into the first Rise of Government in general, and of those Laws, Customs and Constitutions in particular, which we Receiv'd from our Ancestors, and have so often and so Honourably contended for.

**A Poem upon the Amendments Made to the Law**
From Sala's Banks our Constitutions came,
Ancient as Fear, Necessity or Fame.
To Albion first Hengst and Horsa brought
Teutonick Rights, and Cimbrian Customs taught;
And Time, that best instructs us how to chuse,
Did British Laws and Saxon Gods refuse.
Say Heaven-born Muse, for only you can paint,
The King, the Soldier, Confessor and Saint;
Who various Laws in wild Confusion plac'd,
With Beauty, Order, and Connexion grac'd:
Did happy Kings in Legal Fetters bind,
Let loose to Good, from Ill confin'd."

---

[1] Ruddock F. Mackay. Admiral Hawke, p3. 1965

In 1714-16, probably benefiting from his brother-in-law Martin Bladen's position as a Chief Officer at the Royal Mint, Edward secured a small post there:-

**Salaries:-**

| | | |
|---|---|---|
| Sir Isaac Newton ) | Chief Officers | 450 Marks |
| Sir Richard Sandford ) | | |
| Martin Bladen ) | | |
| Dr John Francis Farquier | Assistant | 100 Marks |
| Edward Hawke[1] | Keeping the Ledger Book | 40 Marks[2] |

Montagu Burrows, who wrote a biography of Edward and Elizabeth's son Admiral Edward Hawke, wrote in 1888 that Edward *"retired to Bocking [Docking] in Norfolk and died in 1718 aged 50 years"*. Since this was a comparatively young age to be retiring, it is perhaps more likely that Edward's health was failing at this time.

*Elizabeth's Third Marriage to Isaac Sharpe*

Seven years after Edward's death, Elizabeth married again, for the third and final time to Rev. Isaac Sharpe on 18th July 1723, London. Little more is known about her life afterwards except for a brief mention in a letter of 1742 when her brother Martin wrote to her son Admiral Edward Hawke and said *"by a letter I lately received from your mother, she was then in good health"*. Elizabeth seems to have spent her final years living in Yorkshire and had died by 1748. Her son, who was at sea at the time, made arrangements that a friend should organise a large memorial wall tablet to be erected at Bolton Percy church in Yorkshire to commemorate his mother (see the next page).

*Elizabeth's Descendants*

Elizabeth and Edward Hawke had two surviving children, one daughter Frances about whom very little is known and a son Edward whose illustrious career has been well chronicled.

**Frances:** All that is known about Frances is that she married a son of Dr Henry Maule of Dromore, Ireland.[3] However, the two known sons of Henry Maule were Thomas (died unmarried) and James (married twice and had three children).[4] Montagu Burrows in his biography of Admiral Edward Hawke suggested that Frances was alive in 1742 but she was mentioned in very vague terms, more a supposition that she was probably still alive, no more.[5] Maule is an old Scottish name dating back to Norman times and it was Henry Maule's grandfather who settled in Ireland (possibly Surveyor-General of Irish Ports). Henry himself was a Protestant Bishop who married three times but it is said he only had children from his first marriage.

---

[1] TNA: AO 1/1669/491: The Royal Mint principal officers
[2] CTB, 1660-67 Preserved in the Public Record Office, Vol. 30, Part 1
[3] Debrett's Peerage of English, Scotland and Ireland; and also stated in Stockdale's Peerage of England, Scotland and Ireland, Vol. 1, by Barak Longmate
[4] Clerical and Parochial Records of Cork, Cloyne and Ross, William Maziere Brady, 1864
[5] The Life of Edward, Lord Hawke, Admiral of the Fleet: With Some Account of the Origin of the English Wars in the reign of George II. Montagu Burrows, page 122

Despite the lack of evidence, it does seem at least possible that Frances Hawke did marry a Maule. Amongst letters held by Trinity College in Dublin there is correspondence from Abp William King regarding Henry Maule dated 1717 where he was recommending him for a preferment.[1] As Martin Bladen took on a guardianship role for his nephew Edward, then he would surely have done the same for niece Frances and he could very well have put forward Maule who would have been known to him. Frances may have been residing with Martin's sister Catherine in Dublin at the time and Martin himself was resident in Dublin from 1715 to 1717.

The following is Elizabeth's memorial:

*Sir Edward Hawke*

The Most Honourable Order of the Bath and Vice-Admiral of the Blue Squadron of His Majesty's Fleet. MDCCXLVIII (1748).
In Memory of the best mothers (Sharpe), the monument was created by her only son.

Other names on the memorial are Edward Hawke, Harriet Bladen* and William Fairfax.
Right at the top of the monument amongst a broken triangle of marble a vase/crown shaped ornament, displays the Bladen Family Crest of three inverted chevrons.

*Harriet Bladen was the daughter of Gov. Thomas (Elizabeth's nephew). That family had returned from Maryland the previous year. Elizabeth would have therefore been Harriet's great-aunt.

**Memorial to Elizabeth Bladen, Bolton Percy Church**

---

[1] TCD MS 2833/140, dated 3rd April 1717 from Abp King (in Bath)

Outline of Elizabeth's descendants showing the lines of descent for Lords Hawke and the Earls of Rosse:-

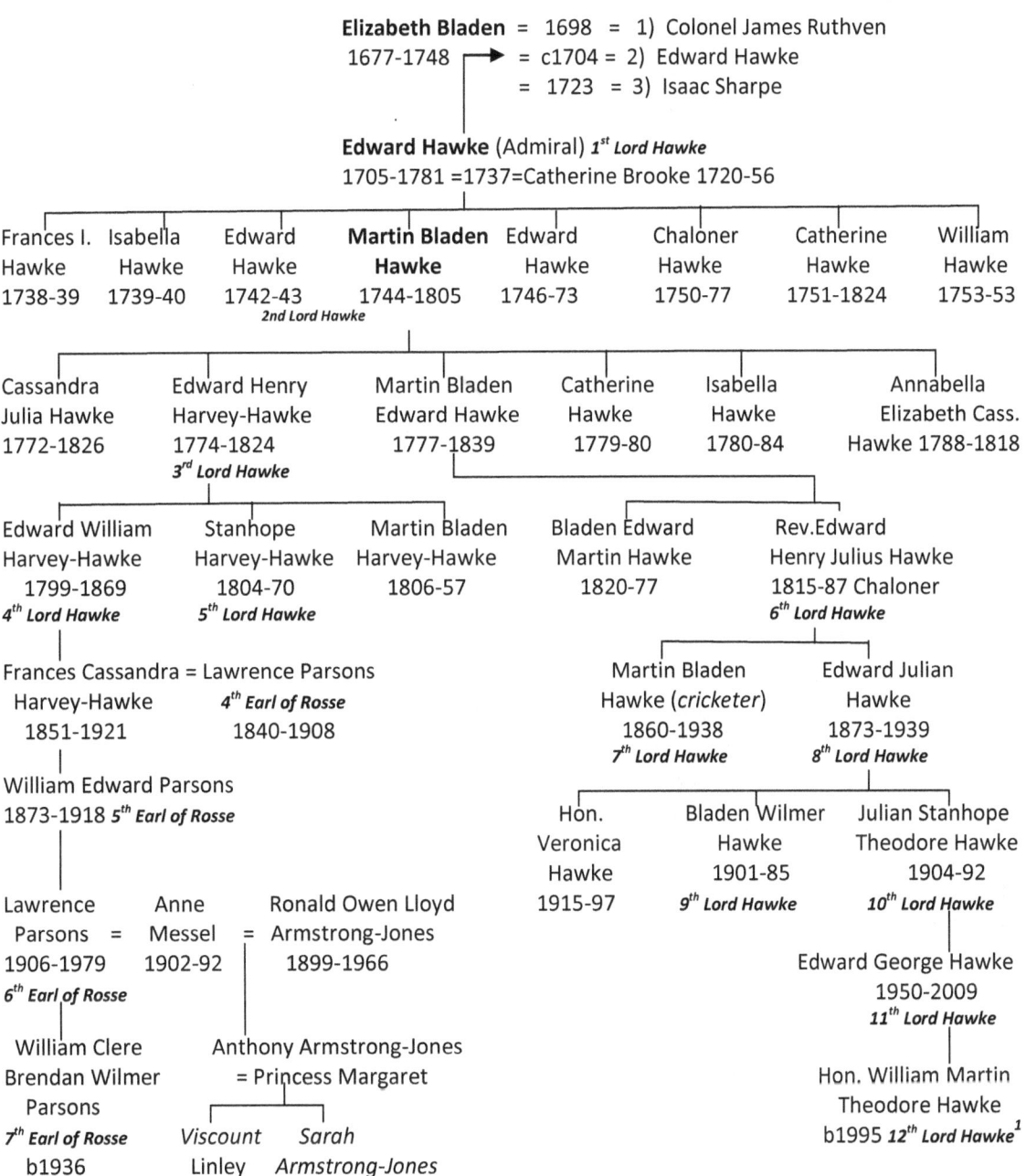

[1] Sources for chart: Familiae Minorum Gentium by Joseph Hunter. Burke's Peerage, Baronetage and Knightage, 107th edition, 3 Vols

**Edward:** All of Elizabeth's known descendants come from her son Admiral Edward Hawke. Elizabeth lived long enough to see her son rise to become a Captain and achieve success in the navy though it is not known if she was still alive when he became Knight of The Bath and was feted by both King and Parliament. She would have been immensely proud of him if she had happened to read the Newcastle Courant of 31st October 1747 when the following story about her son appeared: *"His mother was sister to the late Hon. Col. Martin Bladen, sometime one of the Lords Commissioners of Trade and Plantations and was born in Yorkshire. It is confidently asserted by those who have heard it from his mother that, when he parted with his father at his first going to sea, who exhorted him to behave well and said he hoped to see him a captain, the youth replied "A Captain! Sir, if I did not think I should become an Admiral I'd never go". He was some years a Lieutenant in the Navy but on March 20, 1733 was made a Captain of the Flamborough man-of-war at Jamaica by Sir Chaloner Ogle. In the famous action in the Mediterranean he commanded the Berwick and he behaved in so gallant a manner under two ill-matched Admirals that at the next promotion of flag officers 15th July 1747 he was appointed Rear-Admiral of the White.*

*On 14th October 1747 being sent out with a fleet to intercept a French Squadron bound to the West Indies he fell in with them at latitude 47 deg 50N and longitude 1 deg 2W of Cape Finestre and after giving them a hearty drubbing on this occasion he was created a Knight of the Bath and was raised to the rank of Vice-Admiral....."* Of course there may be some artistic licence in the article but it is nonetheless true that Admiral Hawke went on to become one of Britain's greatest naval commanders, after defeating and blockading the French fleet at Quiberon Bay, thereby preventing a planned invasion of Britain. Sadly there is insufficient space in this volume to do his career justice but biographies of Hawke have been produced by those better qualified to comment on his career.

As mentioned previously in the section for Frances Harman/Hamond/Bladen, her granddaughter Catherine Brooke came into the care of Martin Bladen after 1730 where Catherine would have had plenty of opportunities to get to know Martin's nephews, who he also acted as guardian to, Thomas Bladen and Edward Hawke. By 1737 Edward and Catherine (some 15 years age difference) were married. They had a civil ceremony at Somerset House, which was then registered just across the road at St Mary le Strand Church and were living with, or nearby, the Bladens as there were two infant burials for Hawke babies at Barking near Aldborough Hatch, his uncle's residence following the marriage.

Bladen, through his position on the Board of Trade and his contacts at the highest levels, was instrumental in forwarding and assisting Hawke's career[1] and early advancement. So, by the time war commenced with Spain in 1739, Hawke had worked his way up through the ranks and was well placed to command. In 1742 and 1743 Hawke occupied a town residence at Queen Street, St Margaret's parish in Westminster for £30-2/- 6d. Following the death of his uncle Martin Bladen in February 1746 (n.s.) Edward, who was present at Martin's death, took charge of aspects of Martin's estate in so much that he undertook to accompany Thomas Tarrant, Martin's Steward and Secretary (and creditor) to do an inventory of Martin's possessions. He also signed a Memorandum of Agreement with the creditors to commit to bring in the debts.

---

[1] Oxford DNB

Hawke's career advanced even after the downfall of Walpole where it could have been expected that his 'guardian' Martin Bladen (Walpole's steady supporter) would have lost the power to influence those around him for preferment, but Hawke prevailed and went on to gain respect being distinguished for his service at the Battles of Toulon and Finisterre capturing nearly all of the French ships. Hawke's approach in battle was not to engage with the enemy until they were within pistol range and his tactics were successful. At the Battle of Toulon some 200 of the Spanish enemy were killed compared to just 6 of his own men. The Battle of Cape Finisterre (2$^{nd}$) was even more spectacular with some 4,000 Frenchmen being killed and six captured ships being brought into Portsmouth Harbour. Hawke's successes won him the applause of the King and he was granted the Order of the Bath in addition to being made MP for Portsmouth.

Through his wife, Hawke acquired substantial property from the Brooke/Hamond families, not least of which was Scarthingwell Hall in Yorkshire where it is known he spent some time, but his naval duties would have demanded his location near the ports in the south and so Sunbury in Richmond and later Swaythling in Southampton became home. It is not known how many more voyages wife Catherine took with him, but the Navy demanded his continuous service. He was appointed to command the Neptune and Mars and soon found himself promoted to Rear-Admiral of the White and second in command of the Channel Fleet. 1748 saw him promoted to Vice-Admiral of the Blue and Admiral in Command of the Western Squadron. He was required to take over command after Byng was 'ill' and the loss of Minorca to the French. In 1755 Hawke promoted a young Lieutenant William Locker 1731-1800 to Captain and, in gratitude, William named his next child Edward Hawke Locker 1777-1849. Captain William was at Quiberon Bay with Hawke and it is believed he taught Hawke's naval tactics to Nelson.

Whilst serving in the Mediterranean, his wife Catherine died in 1756 and he immediately asked for leave to be with his family at this time but the demands of naval command did not allow him to grieve for long, within months he was appointed a full Admiral and sailed with Boscawen. All did not go perfectly well though as Hawke, perceived his authority was being undermined and briefly resigned but he was persuaded to remain in post as imminent fears of a French invasion turned everyone's attention to preparations to blockade the port of Brest. Using the distraction of gale-force winds, some of the French fleet had slipped out of the port and Hawke gave chase, following them into Quiberon Bay. Conflans, commanding for the French, did not believe that Hawke would dare follow him into the treacherous bay at Quiberon across dangerous reefs, but he did. Six French ships were either sunk or captured and the rest were scattered and the threat of a French invasion receded, safeguarding not only England but also the future of India and Canada too. Hawke, for his part, was a national hero! He returned to England to a Reception by the King and in gratitude for his service to his country he was granted a generous pension of £2,000 per year for two lives. Hawke was also known to have been given some 20,000 acres of land in Florida by Governor Sir Richard Russell,[1] though other reports state that he requested the land in order to establish a plantation but that the Governor selected it for him.

---

[1] The 20,000 acres of land Hawke acquired are situated in the southern part of Fleming Island. A river running due south of Hawke's plantation, called Black Creek, was renamed in his honour as Hawke's River. Hawke's

His final years of employment saw him serving as an MP and First Lord of the Admiralty where his abilities and effectiveness was not equal to his dashing exploits at sea. His resignation in 1771 was ostensibly claimed to be on health grounds but was more likely due to the difficulties many encountered at that time from the interference of the Princess Dowager of Wales and her 'Carlton House Junto'. Hawke was also an Elder Brother of the Trinity House from 1761-81, an organisation founded by King Henry VIII in 1514 to oversee lighthouse operations, deep sea pilotage and also acted as a naval charity. Another prominent Elder in later years would be Winston Churchill. He continued to enjoy the support of his King at this time but did not enjoy good relations with Pitt.

Hawke's daughter Catherine, who had some mental health difficulties, continued to live with him at Hawke House in Sunbury (near Richmond) whilst Hawke's son Martin lived with his family at Scarthingwell Hall in Yorkshire when in the country. Hawke died in 1782 and was buried next to his wife at Swaythling Church in Southampton where there is a large memorial: *"This monument is sacred to the memory of Edward Hawke, Lord Hawke, Baron of Towton in the County of York, Knight of the Bath, Admiral and Commander-in-Chief of the Fleet, Vice-Admiral of Great Britain &c., who died October 17$^{th}$, 1781, aged 76. The bravery of his soul was equal to the dangers he encountered; the cautious intrepidity of his deliberations superior even to the conquests he obtained. The annals of his life compose a period of naval glory unparalleled in later times: for wherever he sailed victory attended him. A prince unsolicited conferred on him dignities which he distained to ask. This monument is also sacred to the memory of Catherine, Lady Hawke, his wife the beauty of whose person was excelled only by the accomplished elegance of her mind. She died October 27$^{th}$ 1756, aged 36. In the conjugal, parental and social duties of private life, they were equalled by few, excelled by none"*.

PROPERTIES:
7 George Street, Hanover Square - from 1729-1762 and Swaythling House, Southampton
Hawke House, Sunbury - from 1762+ purchased from Trustees of Hamond Estate (built 1703)
Hart Street, Bloomsbury Square - from 1762 (an Admiralty house) occupied by his son Martin
Scarthingwell Hall, Yorkshire - occupied by his son's family from 1774
Towton Hall, Yorkshire - some time occupied by Martin Bladen Edward Hawke

*Admiral Hawke's children*
Of the eight children that Edward and Catherine had, four were infant deaths, two further sons (Chaloner and Edward) died young and unmarried, and only son Martin and daughter Catherine were alive at the Admiral's death. The only descendants from Hawke came from son Martin, as Catherine did not marry. She died at Sunbury aged 73 years.[1]

---

agent Alexander Gray was in situ to run the plantation which was manned entirely by Negroes and it quickly produced a healthy return. After Hawke's death his son, Martin Bladen Hawke continued to run it until Florida was returned to Spain. The slaves were shipped to Dominica. Hawke's neighbours were Sir Richard Russell and James Crisp (replaced later by Francis Levett). Source: The Early History of Clay County: A Wilderness that Could be Tamed by Kevin S. Hooper. 2006

[1] St Marylebone, Westminster, parish register

```
                    Admiral Edward Hawke = Catherine Brooke
                                        |
    ┌───────────────────┬───────────────┴───────┬───────────────┐
 Martin Bladen       Edward              Chaloner          Catherine
   Hawke             Hawke                Hawke              Hawke
     ⇩
```

*Martin Bladen Hawke (2nd Baron) 1744-1805*

After attending Eton School, Oxford University and Lincoln's Inn Martin, in 1769, was reported to be renting a house near Lisle in France where he was busy learning the French language before returning to England to commence his parliamentary career. Martin stood as a Whig politician for Saltash, a seat he held for six years, and, when he did speak in Parliament it was mainly on naval matters. As well as inheriting great wealth from both his Bladen and Hawke relations, he was named as one of the two lives in receipt of an annuity from 7th March 1760 in recognition of his father's service to the country which was worth £2,000 per annum.[1]

*Presented at Court*

In 1771, aged 27 years, he married Cassandra Turner 1746-1813 (daughter of Sir Edward Turner of Ambrosden in Oxford). The couple were married by Dr Theophilus Leigh, Master of Balliol College Oxford who was Cassandra's grandfather's brother (and he was also the grandfather of author Jane Austen). Two weeks after their marriage Martin and Cassandra were presented at Court to Their Majesties at St James's Palace. The Hawkes had six children with two dying as infants. After marriage, the couple briefly lived in Hawke's admiralty house in Bloomsbury Square before moving, about 1774, to Scarthingwell Hall in Yorkshire.[2] Cassandra, now Lady Hawke, had a novel published in 1788 called 'Julia de Gramont' and this appears to have been her only literary publication although her sister, Lady Saye and Sele, alluded to the existence of a second, unpublished, manuscript. Here's an extract from her lacklustre novel:- *"Good Heavens! What an interesting picture struck my view! In a verdant alcove of intermingling jasmine and roses, sat the loveliest of women! Each snowy arm encircled a blooming cherubim! These sweet innocents were adorning with flowers her shining ringlets! How shall I describe her countenance? It spoke all the mother: her cheek was animated with the glow of pleasure, smiles of maternal fondness dimpled around her mouth and in the mild effulgence of her eyes beamed more than usual lustre".* Extracted from Julia de Gramont, 1788, by Cassandra Hawke.

The quality of the writing, or lack of, meant the novel was destined for obscurity though perhaps the novelist Fanny Burney read it. Burney wrote about meeting Lady Hawke in February 1782 when Cassandra and her sister, Lady Saye and Sele, along with their wealthy brother Sir Gregory Page-Turner, were at a dinner for a Mrs Paradise. Burney described an uninspiring meeting she had with the Turner siblings which she terminated as soon as she could ....

---

[1] Parliamentary Reg History of the Proceedings and Debates of the HoC 6th session, 4th Parl.
[2] Le Faye - Chronology of Jane Austen, p169

*"I took, however, the first opportunity of Lady Hawke's casting down her eyes and reclining her delicate head, to make away from this terrible set"*.[1] Cassandra Hawke was cousin to novelist Jane Austen, their common ancestor being their great-grandfather Theophilus Leigh. This branch of the Leigh family descends from the Sir Thomas Leigh who walked in front of Queen Elizabeth I on her ascension to the throne. Of three sons of Theophilus, Cassandra's grandfather was William Leigh and Jane Austen's grandfather was Rev Thomas Leigh. A third son of Theophilus was another Rev Thomas Leigh who had a son of the same name. In 1794 author Jane Austen's brother Francis was in the Royal Navy and his patron, Sir Henry Martin, Commissioner and Governor of the Royal Navy Academy had died on 1st August. Jane's mother Cassandra Austen (née Leigh) wrote a letter and handed it to her cousin Rev. Thomas Leigh (mentioned above) and requested that it be presented to their cousin Cassandra Lady Hawke (née Turner, grand-daughter of William Leigh).[2] The idea was that her husband, Martin Bladen 2nd Lord Hawke, was to be asked to help, to see if anything could be done to assist Francis Austen's naval career, if Martin could use his influence at the Admiralty to this end.[3]

Jane Austen certainly knew and met her Turner and Hawke relations but perhaps not too often. Lady Cassandra Hawke's sister, Elizabeth Turner married Lord Saye & Sele. When Jane Austen was only 12 years old in 1788 and visiting her relations she learned that her cousin's husband Lord Saye & Sele had locked himself in a room in his home at Harley Street and then committed suicide in a rather bizarre fashion: he cut his throat with a razor, then stabbed himself with his sword,[4] then tried to drown himself. Some years later, when Jane again encountered these relations, she heard that Lady Saye & Sele was offered some boiled chicken to eat, but declined, saying that after her husband "had destroyed himself" she had eaten nothing but boiled chicken for a fortnight but had not been able to touch it since!"[5]

Returning to Martin Bladen Hawke; in 1774 he won selection to stand as an MP for York beating his opponents viz …. 110 Hawke, 63 Charles Turner and 57 Lord John Cavendish. The candidates paraded through the streets of York on horseback before going into the Guildhall for the results. However he did not succeed in the election.

*American Judas*
One of Martin Bladen Hawke's friends was Benedict Arnold who had become a General in the American War of Independence winning many battles against the British, but by the 1780s became an infamous turncoat and switched to the British side. After the initial fanfare of his arrival in London which included meetings with the King to advise him on colonial policy, interest in him waned but Lord Hawke became a good friend. In 1792 a member of the House of Lords, the Earl Lauderdale, slandered Arnold and, in response, Arnold challenged him to a duel.

---

[1] The Diary and Letters of Madame D'Arblay, Vol. 3, 1788-96. Some of Fanny's brothers were in the Navy and accompanied Captain Cook on two voyages
[2] Stoneleigh Archive DR.18/10/18 Southampton, dated 1794
[3] The Diary and Letters of Madame D'Arblay, Vol. 3, 1788-96
[4] Hampshire Chronicle 1788, 18th July
[5] 'Jane Austen: The Woman, Some Biographical Insights by George Holbert Tucker, 1994

Lord Hawke volunteered to be Arnold's second and the second for Earl Lauderdale was Charles James Fox, the parliamentarian. After Arnold had fired off his shot he waited for Lauderdale to return fire but it never came. He refused to return fire and the seconds had to intervene to conclude matters. Arnold had attended the duel for satisfaction, but if Lauderdale did not return the shot then satisfaction had not been obtained. Hawke and Fox negotiated a solution which saw Lauderdale apologise to Arnold (rather than take a shot).[1]

*Board of Agriculture*
In 1793 Hawke had a letter from Sir John Sinclair who had a plan to set up a Board of Agriculture. Hawke was enthusiastic about agricultural reform though he was uncertain about a venture in the current climate, i.e. French Revolution, but despite his initial misgivings agreed to join the Board as one of its earliest members. From his Scarthingwell estate in Yorkshire, Hawke became quite an authority on agricultural matters. Of his estate he had 150 acres for crops (turnips, barley, clover and wheat) plus 50 acres for moss/peat. He ploughed with a pair of oxen and kept 350 sheep plus Scottish and Irish cattle. He was the author of the Agricultural Survey of the West Riding, written in 1799, where he gave advice on such matters as warping (irrigation) etc. Martin's descendants will be looked at, following a few words on his siblings.

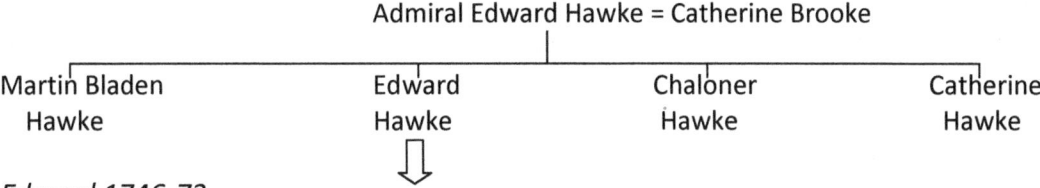

*Edward 1746-73*
Edward was the second child bearing that name born to Admiral Hawke, the first was born in Barbados 1742-43 and died young. He was a Major based at Gibraltar in 1767 when there is a record that he and Ensign William Bosvile of the Guards decided to pay a short visit to the Barbary Coast in North Africa. They had invited a newly arrived Ensign Alexander Lindsay to join them but his commanding officer refused him leave.[2] Hawke and Bosvile went to Morocco and it was said Hawke asked a 'renegado' - *"if you would tell him the arguments which had induced him to turn Mahomedan, he would follow his example, provided they were good and convincing"*. The response was *"I cannot assign my reasons but the truth is, I am not Christian"*.[3]

In published pedigrees, it is said that Edward died on 2nd October 1773 unmarried (Stockdale and Kearsey's). However, there is other evidence to contradict this. There is a record of a Lt. Colonel Hawke of the 6th Regiment, son of Admiral Hawke marrying in Dublin on 5th October 1773.

---

[1] The Life of Benedict Arnold, his patriotism and his treason by Isaac N Arnold, 2006
[2] Lives of the Lindsays, or a Memoir of the Houses of Crawford and Balcarres, Vol. 2, by Alexander Will Crawford, Lord Lindsay. 1849
[3] Universal Magazine of Knowledge and Pleasure containing original communications. Vol. XX, July-December 1813

Also, there is a personal account of Edward's fate[1] which supports the connection with Ireland. John Baker, a barrister at the Middle Temple and one time Solicitor-General of the Leeward Islands was at his home in London on 15th October 1773 when he received a visit from his son-in-law Henry Swinburne (the travel writer).[2] John Baker wrote in his diary that day that Swinburne[3] told him that Sir Edward Hawke's 2nd son of 3, the Colonel, was *"lately killed in a duel in Ireland"*. Clearly the marriage and duel were no more than a few days apart at most, so a reasonable assumption may be that there was a direct connection between them.[4]

```
              Admiral Edward Hawke = Catherine Brooke
    ┌──────────────────┬──────────────────┬──────────────────┐
Martin Bladen       Edward            Chaloner           Catherine
   Hawke            Hawke              Hawke              Hawke
                                         ⇓
```

*Chaloner 1749-77*

A third son Chaloner Hawke was named for Admiral Hawke's close friend Admiral Sir Chaloner Ogle.[5] According to the parish register of Saxton-in-Elmet, Chaloner was a "cornet of the Royal Regiment on North British Dragoons, 3rd son of Edward Lord Hawke of Sunbury by Catherine, his wife, daughter of Walter Brooke of Gateforth, died 16 September and buried in the chancel in Saxton Church, 3 Oct (age 28)". Killed on the road by a post chaise, he was making a return journey from Twickenham where he may have been lodging to

---

[1] The Diary of John Baker, Barrister of the Middle Temple by Philip Chesney Yorke, 1931
[2] Henry Swinburne 1743-1803 was a well known travel-writer. Author of 'Travels through Spain 1775 and 1776' and 'Travels in the Two Sicilies 1777-80'. Henry married Martha Baker (aka Louisa/Patty) who was John Baker's daughter by his second marriage to Mary Ryan. Martha/Louisa was courted by Charles Carroll of Maryland (Charles Carroll of Carrollton 1737-1832, only Roman Catholic to sign the Declaration of Independence in 1776) who had desired to marry her around 1763 but she was not yet of an age to marry and there was some anxiety regarding the marriage settlement (because she had four brothers and Charley Carroll's father was concerned the financial arrangements might not work to the Carroll family's favour) and whether she would want to relocate to Maryland. They had been introduced in Paris where Carroll had been on a grand tour of the Continent and met Martha who was a student at Ursuline Convent, Rue St Jacques on the left bank of the Seine, Paris, both families were Catholics. He went on to marry Mary Darnall 1749-1782. A few years after Henry Swinburne married Martha they set off for a six year tour of the Continent, particularly France, Spain, Italy and Germany where they were frequent visitors to European courts. Their son Joseph had Emperor Joseph II of Austria as his godfather and another son was a page to Marie Antoinette. 'Princes of Ireland, Planters of Maryland: A Carroll Saga, 1500-1782', 2002, by Ronald Hoffman
[3] Swinburne was a good friend of Sir Thomas Gascoigne and the pair travelled to Italy, attending the Neapolitan Court and they also went to Sicily. Gascoigne's son died in October 1809 in a riding accident whilst hunting with his good friend Martin Bladen Edward Hawke in Retford, Nottinghamshire
[4] The Diary of John Baker, Barrister of the Middle Temple by Philip Chesney Yorke, 1931, p268
[5] Sir Chaloner Ogle 1681-1750 was held in high esteem by Hawke. As a young teenage midshipman he would have heard the story of Ogle's capturing of the famous pirate Roberts who, with two ships and 300 fellow pirates under his control, encountered Ogle off the Coast of Africa. Ogle passed his vessel off as being merchant class initially and after a battle the first ship of pirates surrendered. Hawke wrote to Sir Chaloner Ogle's widow in 1760 advising her that he had named his son after Chaloner Ogle

London[1] possibly having visited Sir Chaloner Ogle who was known to have lived at Twickenham.

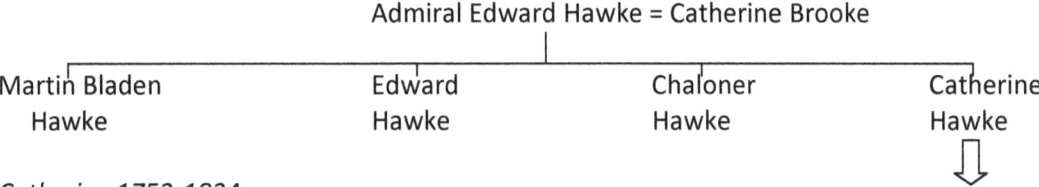

### Catherine 1752-1824

Catherine never married and her father's Will in 1781 was very revealing as to Catherine's life upto that point as her father referred to her as "melancholy" and he hoped she would regain her "sanity". One contemporary simply stated she was "*mad*".[2] A great portion of the Will was given over to Catherine's future care with the appointment of two servants to take care of her for the rest of her life (sisters Sarah and Mary Birt). Hawke bequested them property and money and Catherine was to be given everything she could need, but he also made provision for Catherine in case she should regain her sanity and became capable of making her own will. She was to have £500 per year income plus a carriage, coach man, foot boy and two maid servants. He also left her plate, including "table china given to me by the late Captain John Tinker, china from Goa in the East Indies",[3] jewels, furniture etc, but if she did not regain her sanity, then the executors were instructed to pass on her bequests to Cassandra Hawke, the Admiral's granddaughter. Catherine lived to be 76 years of age, dying in 1824 at Hawke House in Sunbury, near Richmond in London. The two servants Sally and Mary Birt were thought to be the sisters of a Lieutenant John Birt who had served under Hawke. Lieutenant Birt had been assigned to the 10 gun cutter Lapwing, but died 1764 when the ship was sunk. Jeremiah Tinker was, along with Sarah Birt, one of the Trustees.

### Admiral Hawke's Grandchildren

As previously stated, of the Admiral's children only son Martin Bladen Hawke 1744-1805 had children to continue the name. Two of Martin's sons (Edward and Martin) would begin two distinct lines of descent. But first, a run through of Martin Bladen Hawke's children:-

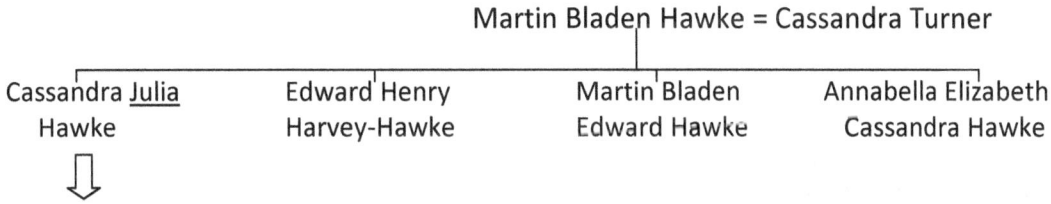

### Cassandra *Julia* Hawke 1772-1826

Cassandra, who called herself Julia, was married three times, having been widowed by her first two husbands.

---

[1] The Diary of John Baker, Barrister of the Middle Temple, by Philip Chesney Yorke, 1931, p268
[2] The Diary of John Baker, Barrister of the Middle Temple, by Philip Chesney Yorke, 1931, p268
[3] TNA: PROB 11/1086/21, Will of Rt Hon. Edward Lord Hawke of South Stoneham, Hampshire

After the death of her first husband, Samuel Estwick in 1793, Julia's cousin Jane Austen, who was apparently intrigued by the notion of women marrying more than once and knew Julia well, wrote to her sister Cassandra Austen in 1800 and said: *"Mrs Estwick is married again to a Mr Sloane, a young man under age, without the knowledge of either family, he bears a good character however"*.[1] Rev Stephen Sloane, son of Hans Sloane,[2] was just 19 years of age when he married Julia in 1800. He completed his MA in 1809 and had the sinecure Rectory of Gedney in Lincs from 1806-12. He died at his father's home in Upper Harley Street in London on 16th April 1812.[3]

Julia's third and final marriage was to Thomas Frederick Green, a comic actor. He appeared in Bath on 5th October 1816 as Sir Benjamin Backbite in Sheridan's 'The School for Scandal', then in Romeo and Juliet on 8th June and The Citizen on 14th June the following year.[4] The couple married at Park Street, Grosvenor Square but, after marriage, Green appears not to have kept up his stage work. Julia had no children and her Will was a sad testament to how her life ended.[5] She bequeathed part of her estate to her husband but the other part was to servants Julia Maria Spencer and Emily Rosina Spencer (their mother was Jane Cork, who Julia had already settled £1,000 on plus an annuity for the two daughters). The two Spencer girls, however, disappointed Julia in her final days when, in her bed and dying, she added a codicil to her Will revoking the inheritances to them...... *"I revoke anything relative to my ornaments of every kind, as dated in my Will of December 1825, as those girls I have brought up for about 14 years and preserved in every way, neglected me and treated me unkindly whilst I have been dying and wanted their care and while I have been quite alone only came to me only now and then and have quite broken my heart, yet I wish they may marry to their satisfaction. No doubt I shall soon be obliterated from their memory as I appear to them to be dead already"*. She also said *"I am deeply grieved that I could not live to pay my creditors"* and there was also reference to her recent losses, presumably financial losses.

Her husband, at her death, was in Boulogne and was referred to as being late of Manchester Square. Julia mentioned in her Will that her husband was in possession of a copy of her Will (with him in Boulogne) though he would not have been aware of the codicils that she added. About the time Julia died, there was litigation, Green v Hawke,[6] that is to say Julia's husband Thomas Frederick Green v Martin Bladen Lord Hawke (Julia's brother). Julia would have received an inheritance when the last of her parents died in 1813 so the litigation may have been regarding Julia's marriage settlement - or, perhaps, lack of one.

---

[1] The Letters of Jane Austen by Jane Austen, 2010
[2] Stephen's great-grandfather William was the elder brother of Sir Hans Sloane 1660-1753 whose huge private collection of plants etc formed the basis of the British Museum's collection. Sir Hans Sloane was a doctor to Queen Anne, George I and George II and travelled to Jamaica with the 2nd Duke of Albemarle mentioned in the companion book on Martin Bladen. Stephen's father Col. Hans Sloan was MP for Southampton and Colonel of the North Hants Regiment
[3] West Yorkshire Archive Service has copies of legal documents for Sloane v Hawke WYL115/DZ/510, box 2W, which date from 1812. Records from Foster, Index Eccles; Clerical Guide
[4] The Piozzi Letters, 1817-21, Vol. 6; p288, Volumes 1817-21 by Hester Lynch Pioizzi, 2010
[5] TNA: PROB 11/1714/57, Will of Hon. Cassandra Julia Green, 1st July 1826
[6] TNA: C13/1475/68 Green v Hawke, 1826 and TNA: C13/1788/22 Green v Hawke, 1827

Her father had appointed trustees to invest £20,000 @ 3% for the benefit of his younger children[1] but Julia's inability to pay her creditors when she died suggests her fortunes seriously declined somewhere along the way.

```
                    Martin Bladen Hawke = Cassandra Turner
    ┌───────────────────┬───────────────────┬───────────────────┐
Cassandra Julia    Edward Henry       Martin Bladen      Annabella Elizabeth
    Hawke          Harvey-Hawke       Edward Hawke       Cassandra Hawke
                        ⇩
```

*Edward Henry Hawke 1774-1824 3rd Lord (Harvey-Hawke from 1798)*
Born Edward Henry Hawke, he adopted the Harvey-Hawke surname at the time of his marriage on 29th August 1798 to Frances Anne Harvey 1772-1810 who was the 2nd daughter and heiress of Stanhope Harvey of Womersley Park.[2] There were three children from Edward's marriage to Frances Harvey: Hon. Edward William Harvey-Hawke; Capt. Hon. Stanhope Harvey-Hawke and Martin Bladen Harvey-Hawke. Some years after his wife died, Edward was involved with Augusta Elizabeth Corri who claimed a marriage had taken place between them. Hawke initially introduced her to his acquaintances as Lady Hawke but later brought chancery proceedings against the lady, claiming that no such marriage had taken place and that she should desist from using the name. The lady concerned (who was already married) believed a marriage had occurred and the Judge, who was less than impressed with either of them, threw the case out.[3] Edward died at his Regent's Park home in London.

### Earl of Rosse Line of Descent
Edward's son, called Edward William Harvey-Hawke 1799-1869, became the 4th Baron Hawke of Towton. There were no children from his first marriage to Elizabeth Frances Ramsden and one daughter Frances Cassandra Harvey-Hawke 1851-1921 from his second marriage to Frances Featherstonhaugh in 1848. Edward was the Master of the Badsworth Hunt in Yorkshire (one of the oldest hunts in England). His favourite horse was 'Tipton Slasher' and his favourite hounds were Dowager, Dairymaid, Randle, Freeman and Social. Properties: Towton Hall, Scarthingwell Hall, Womersley Park, Yorkshire.[4] He died from a fall from his horse when he broke his collar bone. Daughter Frances married Lawrence Parsons, 4th Earl of Rosse. Continuation of the Rosse line of descent is shown in the genealogy at the end of this book.

---

[1] DR18/8/22/6 28th August 1823 Shakespeare Centre Library and Archive
[2] It was said that Benjamin Bailey 1791-1853 (friend to the poet John Keats) was the Hawke family's private chaplain
[3] http://www.slaw.ca/2009/01/14/jactitation-of-marriage-%E2%80%93-the-unnecessary-legal-phrase-of-the-day/. The court dismissed the suit brought by Hawke
[4] 1858 at a dinner in Pontefract, presented with a painting of him sitting on Tipton Slasher, the horse he had ridden for 16 years

```
                    Martin Bladen Hawke = Cassandra Turner
                                      |
  ┌─────────────────┬──────────────────┼──────────────────┬─────────────────┐
Cassandra Julia   Edward Henry    Martin Bladen      Annabella Elizabeth
    Hawke         Harvey-Hawke    Edward Hawke          Cassandra Hawke
                                       ⇩
```

## Lord Hawke Line of Descent

### *Martin Bladen Edward Hawke 1777-1839*

Martin Bladen Edward Hawke was a bit of a character. He was a typical gentleman of his day being passionate about all sporting matters but, after an excellent education, seemed not to choose to distinguish himself in a career. He acquired some honorary military ranks and appointments but otherwise seems to have given his life over entirely to recreation. If some of his friends were any measure, he was probably a gambler, being ranked with gamblers Lord Yarmouth and Ball Hughes in this regard, who were exiled in France.[1] He did, however, seem to excel in hunting, fishing, shooting and sport, all sports.

From as early as 1812, Hawke seems to have been well acquainted with Lord Byron as they moved in the same circle, with common friends such as Hay, who accompanied Byron to Pisa, Italy and all partook of boar-hunting.[2] One incident that was recalled by a Captain R. N. Gronow in 1820 relates that Hawke was invited to join a shooting party into the Forest of St Germain in France with the Duc de Berri (Charles Ferdinand, younger son of the King of France). On arrival Hawke was informed that it was not good etiquette for him to take a shot before His Royal Highness. However, the instant Hawke spotted a cock-pheasant in flight he instinctively shot it and the bird fell down at the Duke's feet. The Duke cried out in English: *"Who the devil are you sir, who have disobeyed my orders?"* Hawke duly told his name and the Duke replied, *"A droll name yours is Mr Hock"*. To which Martin replied *"Oh, sir, your Royal Highness must be acquainted with it already, for my grandfather Admiral Hawke's name was well known in the French navy"*. There is no record of the Duke's response and the following day, at the opera, the Duke was assassinated by a man called Louvel.[3]

As master of a hunt Martin made a career out of his passion for sports and may have had some interest in politics too. There is no record of him standing for parliament but he may have been active on others' behalf in getting support at election time. The Gentlemen's Magazine of 1826 showed Martin and his family living at Towton Hall not far from Scarthingwell, the place where the Lords Hawke took their title and one of their seats. Martin himself never became Baron Hawke, as the title fell to his older brother Edward initially, then the title passed to his nephew Stanhope (who died unmarried) before finally the title came, after his death, to Martin's own son Edward who became the 6th Baron. Martin was a keen fox-hunter and owned a pack of hounds whilst living in France and would hunt in the area between Calais and Boulogne. He was a man with many friends, some of whom recalled tales of him.

---

[1] 50 Years Recollections, Literary and Personal with Observations on Men by Cyrus Redding
[2] Autograph letter signed 'Byron' to Capt. John Hay - on sale in 2014 for US$12,310
[3] Reminiscences of Captain Gronow, Vol. 3, 1865. Celebrities of London &Paris

One wrote about the experience of dining at Martin's French chateau:- *"He filled me full of champagne, and started me on the road home with my face towards the horse's tail, and on a horse without a bridle"*.[1] Another recounted that he had a profound dislike of flies. How, a group of people were to go on a journey with him, but Martin kept everyone waiting because he would not eat his breakfast until every fly in the room had been killed and so began swiping them one by one, until one solitary fly was left, perched on the sugar bowl. He swiped with his napkin and got the fly but in the process sent scalding hot water into his guest's lap.

*Fighting Duels*

Martin was an excellent shot and engaged in two duels; first with his fourth cousin Colonel Mellish (The Meteor of the Turf) whom he wounded in the arm. Mellish was aide-de-Camp to the Duke of Wellington and Sir Ronald Cranford Ferguson in the Peninsula Wars. His father, Charles Mellish, was Executor of Stanhope Harvey's Will. It was subsequently reported that Mellish was, in fact, in danger of losing the arm from the shooting injury. Mellish and Hawke had been returning in a coach from an election rally in York when they got into a dispute. Mellish was also a gambler, owned a thoroughbred horse Sancho that won the St Leger at Doncaster and was good friends with the Prince (future Prince Regent and then George IV). The second duel took place in Brussels against Baron Smeiton[2] where Hawke took a shot but did not return it.

*Later Life*

A composer of poems, in 1806 he wrote: 'Trafalgar: or Nelson's Last Triumph' and the following is an extract of a Herald speaking to Napoleon:-

>A Herald came and thus the King address'd:
>Thy fleet, great monarch, in Trafalgar's Bays
>With Spain combin'd alas! have lost the day;
>Villeneuve is captur'd and Gravina* fled
>But England mourns her mighty Nelson dead!
>Still France shall mourn, on many a distant day
>The dread destruction of Trafalgar's Bay.

* Gravina was a Spanish Admiral at Trafalgar.

Martin was inconsolable at the death of his daughter with many saying the event took the life out of him and his health declined after 1837. He died of angina pectoris. He stood 5 feet 8 inches tall and weighed about 13 stones, died on 14th September 1839, aged 62 years. He wrote his Will earlier in that same day and gave his address as "late of Towton Hall" being at the end of his life in Tours, France.[3]

---

[1] The Sporting Review, ed Craven, The Late Honourable Martin Hawke: A Sketch of his Sporting Career by Nimrod. Duel took place in June 1807 (reported in the Hull Packet, Yorkshire). Hawke's second in the duel was Tom Gascoigne who would be killed two years later whilst out riding at Lord Scarborough's hunt with Hawke

[2] Light Come, Light Go; Gambling, Gamesters, Wagers, the Turf by Ralph Neville, p11. 1909

[3] TNA: PROB 11/1921/276 Will of Hon. Martin Bladen Edward Hawke of Tours Indre et Loire, France

```
                    Martin Bladen Hawke = Cassandra Turner
    ┌──────────────────┬──────────────────┬──────────────────┐
Cassandra Julia    Edward Henry      Martin Bladen     Annabella Elizabeth
   Hawke           Harvey-Hawke      Edward Hawke      Cassandra Hawke
                                                              ⇩
```

*Annabella Elizabeth Cassandra Hawke 1788-1818*
Last of the children of Martin, 2nd Lord Hawke was Annabella. There were two other children; Catherine who died as a baby and Isabella who died within one year. Annabella Hawke was born in 1788 and did not marry. She wrote 'Babylon and other poems' published in 1811. One reviewer of the poem said *"Babylon is a very unequal poem. It contains some exceedingly animated passages and some passages which are altogether as tame. On the whole, however, it merits greatly counterbalance its defect. The smaller poems are, in general, elegant.*[1] She died at age 30 after suffering for a long time from a "fatal complaint", so said her obituary in Gentleman's Magazine. She died at Chapel Street, Grosvenor Place, London, in the arms of her childhood friend, Miss Stacpoole and the obituary described her as well educated and devoted to religion.

That completes the examination of Elizabeth's early descendants, for further Hawke descendants please see the Genealogy in the Appendix.

---

[1] The Poetical Register and Repository of Fugitive Poetry for 1801, 1815, F.C. and J. Rivington

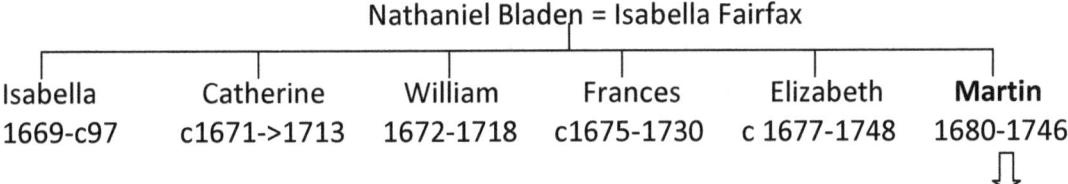

## Martin

Second son and youngest child of Nathaniel and Isabella Bladen, Martin is the subject of a separate book to accompany this volume, called 'Martin Bladen: A Biography' and so only a brief summary of him is provided here.

Born in 1680, Martin spent his early years in Yorkshire. After attendance at Westminster School and St John's College Cambridge, he undertook training in the legal profession, though did not practice as a lawyer. Immediately after this, he joined the army and also married about the same time. His first few years in the army were based in Dublin where, for two years, he languished on half-pay whilst it was decided what to do with his regiment. Regimental commander, Thomas Fairfax was Martin's uncle and Fairfax had Martin's sister Catherine residing with him and so Martin would have been among friends and relations in Ireland.

Following marriage to Mary Gibbs two children were born shortly afterwards though only one daughter Isabella survived. The Gibbs family had just returned from a few years residing in the North Carolina/Virginia area where father-in-law John Gibbs had assumed the governorship of North Carolina when the previous incumbent left. Mother-in-law Elizabeth Gibbs (née Pride) was the great-niece of 1$^{st}$ Duke of Albemarle, General George Monck, who was instrumental in bringing about the Restoration of King Charles II and, in gratitude for his contribution, Charles bestowed vast estates on Monck. When George died his Pride relations expected a healthy inheritance from him but were unfortunately disappointed. George left his estate to his son and other relations, such as the Earls of Bath. Then, when his son and heir Christopher died without heirs, yet again the Gibbs/Pride families expected a share of the estate and, yet again, they were to be disappointed. The Moncks had not looked favourably on their niece marrying the son of a regicide (Thomas Pride) whose family had connections to Oliver Cromwell and so took steps to disinherit the couple. Monck's other relations, such as the Earl of Bath, were the principal beneficiaries although Martin Bladen's mother-in-law Elizabeth Pride and her brother did receive some inheritance from Christopher Monck, so the grudge was only applied to the niece, and better relations were restored with their children, the next generation. Eventually the much-disappointed Prides instigated legal proceedings against those who had inherited from the Moncks and Martin Bladen became one of the named parties. Over the period of 15 years, most of the legal challenges failed but there were two successes for the Pride/Gibbs/Bladen parties.

In 1702, when war was declared on France and Spain, Martin's regiment (under a new commander) travelled to Flanders to fight in 'Marlborough's Wars'. Bladen was made Aide-de-Camp to the Earl of Galway and promoted to Captain, then Major and finally made a Colonel during the years which saw him move constantly between Spain, Portugal and Gibraltar. He was, however, recalled from his command to answer questions in London about irregularities in his regimental spending.

The large allowance he received for clothing and sustenance for his regiment had accounting discrepancies and he spent three months at the Treasury explaining them. At last Bladen returned to Spain but immediately sold his colonelcy and retired from the army. A few months later he was required to attend an inquiry by Parliament where his explanations were deemed unsatisfactory and it is believed, like most other high ranking officers, he used some of his regimental money for his own benefit.

With his army career over, Bladen turned to politics for his future and became an MP in both the English and Irish Parliaments. He managed to secure an appointment as Comptroller at the Royal Mint and, in the General Election which followed, secured a second seat in the English Parliament. Close friend Robert Walpole offered him a post as Envoy to Switzerland which Bladen declined, before offering him the post of joint Chief Secretary to the Lord Justices of Ireland, a post which saw him working for the Duke of Grafton and the Earl Galway, his former army commander. Bladen accepted the post and held it jointly with Charles Delafaye and immediately he arrived in Dublin became embroiled in a factional dispute with Alan Brodrick, the Lord Chancellor. He made powerful friends through this posting, including Joseph Addison, Secretary of State for the Southern Department, and the Duke of Sunderland and it is thought these two men were responsible for his next appointment as Lord Commissioner for the Board of Trade and Plantations.

Wife Mary died in 1724 after a long illness, during which time their daughter Isabella was sent away to live with the family of James Brydges, the Duke of Chandos who was close friends with Bladen. Isabella went through a clandestine marriage with John Tinker and gave birth to their first son shortly afterwards. The daughter's marriage, which produced another son, seems to have lasted barely two years before son-in-law John Tinker left the country to serve with the South Seas Company at Portobello, Panama. He returned some years later and, with Martin Bladen's assistance, secured the post of Governor of the Bahamas where he remained for the rest of his life and had a second family. Neither Tinker nor Isabella was free to remarry though and Isabella waited for many years after Tinker's death before she remarried to George Blount.

All of Martin Bladen's descendants come from the two sons between John Tinker and Isabella. Martin most likely had an illegitimate family himself, though all but one member of the family died in his lifetime. The surviving male son died a few years after Martin but had not married, nor had any relations, so the line died out.

Throughout the twenty years of Walpole's long domination of Parliament, Bladen remained working alongside him and supporting him, even though the Walpole/ Newcastle doctrine of 'wise and salutary neglect' of the colonies scotched any proposals for reform that Bladen may have had. When asked to report to ministers on the state of the colonies and proposals for their future, his recommendations, though largely based on previous workings of the Board, were for a 'colonial utopia' where, for instance, American colonists were obedient to the Crown, paid their quit-rents and governors' salaries, engaged only in manufacturing which was not in competition with Britain's manufacturers and, in times of war, could unite together to fight rival colonial powers and heed Britain's call to arms. Above all, he believed the colonies' purpose was to enrich the mother country.

As the years progressed Bladen's vast knowledge and experience of colonial matters made him indispensable to the Secretary of State and he was often asked to join Privy Council meetings when subjects concerning his expertise were on the agenda. When war came, in 1739, he was heavily involved in preparations. Indeed, he had been attending the conferences with Spain (Treaty of Pardo) and talking 'peace' at the same time as planning Cathcart's Expedition when war eventually broke out. Bladen spent almost thirty years at the Board of Trade and kept working there until a few days before his death.

Much changed for Bladen's private life from the 1720s following the South Sea 'bubble', the death of his first wife and the unexpected marriage of his daughter and heiress. From this point on Martin's financial position was weakened. It is thought he made losses on South Sea, Royal African Company and East India Company stock as, from the mid-1720s onwards he began raising money against all that freehold property he had purchased in earlier days. He married the heiress Frances Foche who had a plantation in the West Indies and property in England and used the money he raised against his own freehold property to build her a house, Aldborough Hatch, near Barking in Essex. He thereby impoverished his own estate (and his daughter's inheritance) in favour of not only his new wife, but her 10 year old daughter Mary, who was also to have £10,000 as a marriage portion. How all of this made his own daughter Isabella feel can only be guessed at, as her own marriage portion was significantly less than this amount and her father's 'refinancing' had seriously reduced the inheritance she had been expecting. Martin seems to have spent the seventeen years he was married to Frances having little contact with daughter Isabella.

When he died in 1746, Martin had 91 creditors and owed substantial sums of money which far exceeded the value of his personal estate to settle. His second wife Frances would claim that he left her in a destitute situation with all her furniture and possessions seized by bailiffs and creditors (though not her real estate). The administrators of both Martin's and Frances's estates were locked in battle for some years and eventually the probate court ordered Martin's estate at Barmoor in Northumberland to be sold to satisfy his creditors. Those assets that were passed down to Martin's descendants were those obtained by John Tinker, rather than Bladen, who purchased several of Bladens' properties for their benefit.

Bladen put a great deal of effort into his political career at a time when some of his colleagues preferred to take their salary and make little contribution. He was, however, hampered in creating a significant legacy by a doctrine of laissez faire and the experience of a generation who had lived through the South Sea Bubble and now wanted caution in government spending. His attempts to shore up Britain's mercantile supremacy over the American colonies saw him introduce what may be termed 'Bladenite' policies which Benjamin Franklin responded to with anger. Franklin saw such policies as Anti-American and he voiced his resentment in the Pennsylvania Gazette. Such rumblings of discontent would, in later years, lead to resistance to paying taxes to the Crown and protestations of 'no taxation without representation'.

Bladen's response to the challenging American colonies which were developing faster than Britain's ability to contain them was for a bicameral 'Plantation Parliament'. It was a compromise solution because what he actually wanted was all American Colonies, charter and proprietary, returned to the Crown.

In later years he resigned himself to the knowledge that could never happen and his suggested Plantation Parliament was the next best outcome. It was never intended to be a stepping stone to independence, however, it was to be headed by a Royal nomination and the upper chamber was to be comprised of Crown appointed individuals with only the lower burgesses elected locally. Others feared it was only one step away from a tool which could be used against the Crown in troubled circumstances and so the proposal never came to fruition.

Bladen was a professional diplomat and politician who was fiercely loyal to the Crown and saw the role of colonists as merely supporting the status quo of Britain's mercantile supremacy. All those elements which eventually led to the American Revolution began under Bladen's watch and, if Walpole and Newcastle had adopted a more hard-line stance in handling colonies, Bladen would not have hesitated to go along with it.

# Legacy

England was thinly populated in the 17th century compared to today, with less than 6 million people (reduced in part by the plague epidemics), yet the early Yorkshire Bladens managed to find themselves right at the heart of national events.  At least, they were servants to those eminent noble families in Yorkshire whose lives shaped history.  The actions of the King and Parliament and the changing dynamics between those vying for power in the State all directly affected those around them, those dependent on them for patronage and advancement and those subject to their will.

The first of the Bladens, Robert, managed to live out his life without interference from the State and national events. He made extensive use of his wife's Lacy family connections and the set-backs he encountered in his life emanated from his own business activities and the loss of support he suffered from Wortley.

Son John, however, lost control of his own destiny when the Civil War erupted.  From then on his life-story was a mere sub-plot to the main event which engulfed the country. Despite working for the Fairfax family and being a Captain in the Parliamentary Army, he lost the support of Lord Fairfax and was labelled a turncoat and his future then was not his own to command.

John's only child Nathaniel was left to deal with the consequences of both his parents' early deaths but also his grandfather's messy finances and diminished estate.  He also had his own difficulties dealing with the Danby family.  Danby himself was not well liked by his peers, one of whom described him as *"the most hated minister that had ever been about the King"[1]* and Danby's son Latimer and daughter Plymouth certainly did not treat Nathaniel well.  What Robert and Nathaniel shared in common was that they both put their faith in the wrong people.  For Robert it was Dr Berry the 'universal money lender' and for Nathaniel it was the friendless, ungrateful Danby, supposed guardian Wrightson and Lady Theodosia Ivy, the forger.

It took until the fourth generation for Yorkshire Bladens to escape the yoke of servitude to the nobility. Nathaniel's children flourished. Eldest son William's career in public service in Maryland as eventual Attorney General broke the mould and then younger brother Martin Bladen's political career as Lord Commissioner for Trade and Plantations saw him also excel.  The advancement of each son was, however, heavily predicated on having good connections and patronage.  How well each performed in their jobs did, to a great extent, also depend on what was happening both nationally and internationally, but then ..... that is perhaps always the case. From this fourth generation, the Bladen descendants have widely dispersed being more numerous in America for William's descendants and, from Martin's, the distribution is global but smaller.

---

[1] Statement by Gilbert Burnet 1643-1715, Bishop of Salisbury

The Early Yorkshire Bladens were ordinary people living through extraordinary times. They thrived through making highly advantageous marriages in days when family connections were essential to secure patronage and preferment. Once in positions of power they immediately took the opportunity to promote their own interests and those of their relations. They also thrived by making themselves indispensible to 'the great and the good' they served: they were servants of the Parliamentarian Fairfaxes, but also servants to the Royalist Wortley and Savile families. In the case of Nathaniel's son William, as Attorney General in America he curried favour with successive Maryland Governors and became immensely rich in the process. Although his life was cut short by his early death, his legacy was secure and his descendants dominated Maryland politics for several generations.

Younger brother Martin served first Marlborough in the army and then later Sir Robert Walpole in government and also benefited from patronage, being caught in the wake of those great figures around him. By their support and his own marriage to an heiress, he too enriched himself (though his fortunes later waned). Likewise their sisters all married, though with varying degrees of success, but they all married very well and, though the paths were not always smooth, their descendants were well provided for.

Whilst the very earliest Bladens in Yorkshire may not have achieved greatness in their own right and their abilities may be deemed quite ordinary, they prospered by being of service to the leading figures of the day. Despite multiple different set-backs and errors of judgement, the family prevailed and, numerically, from Nathaniel's generation onwards they were established, prosperous and deserve to be remembered.

Bladen

# Appendices

## ADVICE TO A SON
### Author: Nathaniel Bladen, 1694
### Recipient: Martin Bladen

*This section 'Advice to a Son' is duplicated in the companion book 'Martin Bladen: A Biography' as it concerns both Nathaniel and Martin Bladen.*

Martin was presented with a 100 page, 20,000 word manuscript from his father in 1694 when he was 14 years of age which, as the title suggests, was instruction to the young man on how to conduct himself. Nathaniel methodically worked through the different aspects of life and then passed on his thoughts and recommendations to his son. His extensive work is quoted in short sections but, due to the length of the manuscript, it is mostly paraphrased for brevity. He began by saying, "You are now entering upon the theatre of the world where everyone must act his part, which part yet I know not, but if it be your fortune to act that of a beggar, do it with as much grace and complacence as ye can".[1] Nathaniel was paraphrasing either 'As you Like It' and "*All the world's a stage and all the men and women merely players*" or, more likely, 'The Merchant of Venice' where Shakespeare said "*A Stage where every man must play a part*". Nathaniel had, of course, no idea which direction his son's future would take and where the boy's inclination for a career would take him and, with his eldest son now settled and living in America, his attention turned to Martin and his future. In advising Martin how he should prepare for his future, he urged him to embrace practical experiences as well as theoretical: as an example he compared the knowledge gained by travelling versus that gleaned merely by observing a map. The 'Advice' is full of inspirational sayings, mixed with shades of Shakespeare and wise pronouncements as well as some Ancient Roman oratory which makes it difficult to know if Nathaniel was passing on original words of wisdom or presenting his son with the collective thoughts of forebears. There were frequent references to the leaders, mathematicians and scientists of Ancient Greece and Rome which, no doubt both Nathaniel and Martin could relate to. However, Nathaniel warned his son that, although studies of Archimedes, Aristotle, Galen, Plato, Socrates and Pythagoras were of great interest in their own right, advanced mathematics, abstract and philosophical studies may be of no use to him in paying one single debt and providing for his family or succeeding in the world. Of metaphysics he said it was the "needless work of curious brains, are accordingly pleasant, but pleasure without profit is a flower without a root".

PERSONAL: "If ye design to make yourself happy look to your thoughts before they come to be desires and entertain no thoughts which may blush in words". He advised Martin to practice observation, humility and charity to others and not be heard to speak badly of either friend or enemy nor trust everything heard of others. He warned his son to compliment someone to others (rather than directly) as they would be receptive and join in that good opinion. On the other hand, he should tell someone off directly, not to others. Use civil language and good behaviour. Keep your promises, pay your debts and retain your honour and honesty. Soberly consider actions before you take them but then remain decisive when a decision is taken and do not turn back from it. Take good reasoned counsel, not rash advice. "Demosthenes says the greatest good that can happen to us in our life is to be happy but there is another thing not inferior to that and without which the first cannot subsist, to carry ourselves with prudence for grant that nature hath everything requisite for great use; yet if you do not conduct her, then is apt to founder". If you achieve great fortune, you must have it sitting on a solid base and you must act small and discrete, not boastful which will cause offence. On popularity, he said "He that builds upon the people, builds upon the sand. Witness .... the Earl of Essex in the reign of Queen Elizabeth of England."

CAREER: "My advice to you is that you seriously apply yourself in the study of the law of this nation, being the most excellent for their justice and wisdom. If not to practice the law, yet to gain so much knowledge therein as to defend yourself and estate from ye Robin Hood felons in it. If ye be not disposed, ye must lay up one-third of your revenue to preserve your other two, or else it will be assuredly undone." Be quietly industrious and proactive but do not waver if success is not instant. If something happens to your disadvantage, seek a delay, to buy you thinking time. But a delay in a matter which is to your advantage may be a costly error to be avoided. Never rely on the honesty of other men. Be cautious of matters that require great haste as fraud and deceit may be involved. If misfortune comes your way, do something, inaction will produce no result. Beware of unharnessed ambition which can lead to a mighty fall. Aim to make your life comfortable only. Private life is more happy than that of a Prince.

RELIGION: Pray to God in the morning about what you are to do and ask for his blessing, then at night pray for his pardon for what you have done; repent every day so that on the final day you have only one day to repent of. Serve God and keep his commandments. "That religion to me seems best which is most rationale, especially if we consider how much of interest the strong impressions of education, there is in that which many call religion. I do not speak thus that ye should try the Articles of ye Creed by touchstone of Aristotle. Be content with a single faith in God, the comforts of a good life, the hopes of a better upon true repentance and take ye rest upon ye authority of the church".

KING: "Next to ye duty to God I require that ye preserve your loyalty to your King, never sell honour to purchase the brand of a traitor." Do not allow his name to be sullied. "Kings have quick ears and long hands, they catch afar off and their blows are dangerous." He said "It is better for a Prince to be parsimonious than liberal."

---

[1] V.a.346 Folger Shakespeare Library, Washington

GOVERNMENT: "Government is the greatest security of freedom, for as obedience in subjects is the Prince's strength, so is the same their own safety, therefore they who weaken ye Sovereign's power, infringe their own security." In old times it was said that Honesty was the Best Policy, but in modern days Politics is the best Honesty.

MARRIAGE: "There is one more step to make your life comfortable and to advance your fortune and that is well to dispose of yourself in marriage is certainly a business which requires grave consideration". Do not go to meet your match travelling Post, pick a virtuous woman, marry for love but have a mind to her finances too. Passion will develop but, in time, will die out. "Never marry so much for a great living as a good life, yet a fare wife without a portion is like a brave house without furniture; ye may please yourself with your prospect, but there is nothing to keep you warm. Be sure you love her person better than her estate, for he who marrieth where he doth not love will be sure to love where he doth not marry".

BE CONTENT: with a single faith in God, a good comfortable life and hope of repentance. Gain respect by being humble and of good humour. Wisdom comes from slow beliefs. Be modest in discourse and not too vehement. Reputation, wisdom and wealth usually go together: reputation produces good opinion, "Opinion riches, riches honour". Do not put all your kindness and charity in one place alone, scatter it. If something is without your power to control then it should be beyond your care, let God handle the rest.

The above summary of Nathaniel's manuscript represent about half of his 'Advice', the bulk of the remaining text is by way of warnings about the pitfalls of life but also it is evident that Nathaniel was trying to direct Martin away from a certain kind of lifestyle that appeared superficially appealing but was not. He used a translation of a Greek/Roman called Lucian to give a detailed description of the reality of being a courtier or working for a noble family, but first the warnings ....

WARNING: "Man is naturally wicked, never does well but upon constraints and they will show their natural malignity so often as they have opportunity to do it nearly. Reputation and poverty make man industrious but it is ye Lord that makes them good". Take care in your letters and correspondence and with whom you entrust information in case it is produced against you one day. Take special care around servants in this regard. Do not over-talk, this is a weakness and vanity in men. Take care with intemperate or unruly men, act as Solon would have as a mediator; say something well or keep silent when you may use observational skills. Do not give away knowledge that can be used as a power against you later. Be careful how you treat the vulgar people as there are many of them whereas there are few learned men. Of revenge and interest, blood does not appease. Being disobliging to just one man can do you more harm than being obliging to ninety-nine, one resentful individual can be the source of your ruin more so than the other happily obliged individuals. Control your passions always: when passion enters the front door, wisdom goes out the back. If you have authority over others you must have even more over yourself. Have nothing to do with a passionate man and ignore trivial offences rather than quarrel otherwise you may yourself be perpetually inconvenienced and ultimately at a loss to them. "He that makes himself a sheep shall be devoured by ye wolf". Injure no-one so they will not seek a way to injure you. "It was a principle in Julius Caesar not to be eminent amongst his magnificos, but to be chief amongst inferio". Never make friends with a coward or a drunkard and never bribe friends. Be cautious as today's friend may end up being tomorrow's enemy. Never engage in suits of law as you risk your estate and, whatever your eventual career, study the law so that he may protect your estate. Do not flatter, but always use civil language and prudence. Filter information out to people slowly so you can assess their reactions before making a large announcement. If you should happen to fail in a venture, retreat to your own privacy to retrench. Your hopes may fade but your quiet peace return.

MONEY: "Study not only to preserve your estate but justly to increase it, money is the hire of fortune and Lord Paramount of this world". If you have little money, do not go into society very often but when you do then you should spend your money. Lost fortunes rarely generate love and respect and adversity does not often meet with friendship. Every man's perception of what is sufficient wealth to be happy varies. Whatever the size of a man's estate if he has no wants, then he is happy. Those in control of their estates are more likely to be happy, as they are not dependent on others. A poor husbandman with no unfulfilled needs may be happier than a Prince who is beset with endless needs. "Riches are power, the keys to greatness and makes the access to home more easy and open". Of himself, Nathaniel said "I am not by my constellation destined to be rich, neither do I much care for the more a man hath the more he wanteth and riches were to be sought after above all things, if they brought content".

FAVOURITE TO A GREAT PERSON: "You must study to enworthy yourself into the face of some great person, upon whom you must lean rather than upon your own virtues, if not, you will be like a hop without a pole upon the ground to be trampled upon". Converse with those more accomplished than yourself and higher than your station, not below. Honour and preferment rarely automatically follow from virtue without some assistance. Nathaniel's message to his youngest son was - beware, if it becomes your destiny to seek your career and fortune by being a favourite to a great person. Of all the doors of opportunity that may open here, the Prince holds all the keys. And you must learn a courtier's arts to handle your Prince. If you are a favourite, others will eye you with jealousy and lobby against you, waiting for you to slip and give them an opportunity to denounce you. If such libels are ignored they will evaporate mostly, but occasionally can cause your ruin depending on the circumstances, you must beware. For your security always be truthful but confide in none and prepare stratagem to counter your enemies at the right moment. A favourite can be in a perilous state, at the complete mercy of their master's whim. Nathaniel goes to great lengths to warn his son off from choosing this path, mainly by including in his 'Advice to a son' a transcript of Lucian's De Mercede Conditis. Lucian (A.D. 125-180+) was a native Syrian who wrote in Greek but was a Roman Citizen and was a public rhetorician on such topics as philosophy, rhetorical exercises and fictional narratives. But the purpose of Bladen extensively translating this particular piece of work, was the subject matter. Lucian wrote about well educated Greeks who went to work for wealthy Romans. He described how they were treated as little better than slaves and, to secure their posts, had to endure degradations. Although it is never explicitly stated by Nathaniel, it is known that he also spent his entire working life - after receiving a first-class education - in the employ of eminent statesmen (Danby) and nobility and perhaps in some way felt this subject related to his similar lifestyle: serving nobility but not being of noble blood though being far superior to the servants in the household -occupying a kind of no-man's land where he was neither one thing nor the other. Knowing some of the legal tangles Bladen got into with his employers it would be surprising if he did not feel some bitterness towards those he served. The translation describes in fascinating detail the humilities that the well educated Greeks put themselves through to obtain posts with the wealthy Romans, how they were required to have the skills of a courtier but dare not offend anyone for fear of losing their livelihood or popularity. The servants, who were incredibly conscious of status levels, would serve the best wines and foods to the noble family but lesser cuts and poorer wines to the lower status individuals. One incident relayed by Lucian describes how he was forced to endure a never-ending banquet where wave after wave of courses were served as the host was determined to impress his guests with the finest of foods, but that the courses were endless and he feared to refuse any food in case it caused the host offence. How the hours rolled on and on so slowly but still the food kept coming and sleep beckoned. Then, how the very next morning, he was called to meet his noble host and discuss terms of his employment - in front of the very men he had the previous night dined with. A reluctance to answer the question, in front of the company, of how much money he expected in return was greeted with an insistence for reply. Lucian found himself telling his host that he would accept whatever his host felt his skills were worth - to which the retort was that there were many who would envy Lucian's position and would gladly do it without thought of pecuniary reward! So, this is how, in time, he found himself ensnared into a role he described as little better than that of a slave; entirely at his 'Emperor's' beck and call, day or night.

If Nathaniel saw fit to include Lucian's tale in his Advice to a Son, then it would seem he was trying to warn him against ever contemplating servitude to a noble family by opening his eyes to the reality of that life. Perhaps the inclusion of the lengthy translation was well worth it because Martin did not follow his father's footsteps and become Steward to a noble family, but chose a political career instead after his military service. At the time Nathaniel was writing, he himself was 52 years of age and his youngest son Martin was just 14 and had not yet fixed on what his future would be.

Contained with Nathaniel's 'Advice' is a poem which can be attributed to Martin. Not only is the handwriting different, but a short index - in Martin's own hand - states it to be his but is unfortunately not dated. The title is "Woman" and seems out of place with the restrained writings and poetry of the mature Martin of later years, so perhaps was written when he was adolescent:

**On Woman**
Ye heavenly powers why did ye bring to light
That thing called Woman, nature's oversight
That she bred tyrant full of mysery
That gilded weather cock of vanity
A wayward forward and a constant evil
A seeming saint, sole factor for ye devil
Were she proud, poxt, painted or more
Patch't, perjured, plagued, all ye were be no more
I could forgive her and connive at that
But she is worse and may in time forestall
The Devil's proxy, damning of us all

The final two lines are in unreadable Latin - so the poem may lack its 'punch line'. In any event, clearly Martin got over his idea of women as the "devil's proxy" and went on to marry twice.

*William Bladen*
## Additional Information on William Bladen when Attorney General
**Extracts from the Calendar of Maryland State Papers No. 1: Black Books. Early preserved records of the proprietary and royal period, comprises 1,600 papers in the Black Books. (State of Maryland)[1]:-**

9th September 1704 Walter Campbell (Dorchester) to William Bladen Annapolis. Sent a mortgage and record of transfer for the land of Philip Clark; desires a Writ of Ejectment if Mr Bladen approves. Clark's Negroes have been undervalued. Names: William Edmonson, [Nicholas] Low, [Hugh] Eccleston. [11]

8th September 1705. Robert Gettey, Chaptico, St Mary's County. To William Bladen Annapolis.
Mr [John] Cood refused to serve the writ on [George?] Foster, probably because he was security for Foster; wants to take action against Cood; asks assistance for Mr Carvall when he comes to Annapolis. Names: Col [Henry] Darnall, Mr Randall. [15]

1706 [Provincial Court Proceedings]. John Collins vs Robert Howard. Howard was called to answer a charge by Collins that he entered with force and arms a tract of land called St Martein's, or the Happy Entrance, which tract Wrixam White devised to Collins for a term not yet expired; Collins being ejected says he is denmified to the value of £200 and brings this suit; his attorney is William Bladen. On verso: unless the tenant in possession of the premises, [Robert Howard] appear to this declaration at the next Provincial Court, he will confess judgment and possession will be delivered to the plaintiff [John Collins]. [19]

[1706] [Provincial Court Proceedings]. Her Majesty vs James Butler. The jurors present that James Butler, on 6th June 1706, contracted a marriage with Johan Carroll; Hannah Butler his former wife was then alive, she had not been beyond the seas seven years nor absent from him seven years together. Signature: W[illiam] Bladen, Att[orney] Gen[eral].Witnesses: Geo. Valentine and T.Tench [20]

[1706] [Provincial Court Proceedings]. Her Majesty vs James Butler. Copy of 20 in another hand.
Signature: W[illiam] Bladen, Att[orney] Gen[eral].Witnesses: George Valentine and Thomas Tench [21]

18th Feb [1705/6] W[illiam] B[laden] [Clerk to the Council]. [To the Lords of Trade and Plantations]
Letter from England delayed; laws to be enacted concerning priests and Quakers; crimes committed by Benjamin Celile, Humphrey Hernaman, Richard Clarke and Rachell Freeborn; sale of Cole and Hernaman to the Barbadoes; misrepresentation of Bladen's conduct by Sir Thomas Lawrence, Secretary of the Province; orders concerning the convoys. Note at bottom of p4, "Write to Colonel Smallwood to send his evidence", Joseph Walters Overseer of Highways, Thomas Stonestreet, constable of Piscataway. [22]

[May 1706] [Provincial Court?] List of cases to be tried. George P[arker] vs William Chew, debt; William Heywood vs Daniel Pearce, trespass on the case; case against Thomas Howell, administrator of Jacob Regnier, debt; Samuel Chew has come into the Court of Chancery and given sufficient security for the return of his Negro slaves, which Benjamin Ball has taken and unjustly detained; Tabitha Norest, Charles Wright and Katherine his wife, executors of Robert Norest, who was executor of Francis [She]ppard vs ___ and William Coursey, administrators of Richard Sweatnam, debt; save ms the same, debt; Benjamin vs Francis Dallahide, debt; William Roach vs Joshua Guybert, trespass on the case; Hez[ekiah] Linthicum vs William Gambell, debt; George Parker vs Henry Roberts, debt; same vs. The same debt; William Smith vs. Gabriel Burnham; Walter Taylor vs. Edward John, and William Stevens, a plea wherefore they entered a tract of land and took timber thereon; Jacob Regnier vs. Isaac Frippier, debt. Attorney in the cases: William Bladen [23]

May [1706] Provincial Court Proceedings. William Finch vs John Atkey. Finch, by William Bladen his attorney, says that Atkey was his Factor for 1682 to 1703; he was to dispose of one chest of apothecary's medicines and make a profit rendering an account when required to do so. This he has not done. [24]

After 14th May [1706] Provincial Court Proceedings. Her Majesty vs Thomas Whichaley. The jurors present that Whichaley swore that a certain account was true, once before Philip Briscoe and William Herbert, Justices of Charles County and again on 16th May 1704 before Thomas Smithson and his associate justices of the Provincial Court; the account charged that there was due Whichaley a balance of 16,297 lbs of tobacco from the estate of Captain John Raynes whereas no sum was due. Signature: William Bladen, Attorney General. [25]

11th July 1706 Governor John Seymour to W[illiam] B[laden] Attorney General. Seymour desires that [James] Butler be prosecuted for his second match with Joyce Carrole, the former wife is alive, as Mr Carrole and Mr Wilson can testify. [27]

2nd September 1706 Samuel Handy Senior (Somerset County) to William Bladen, Annapolis.
Handy has already written Bladen and [Thomas] Bordeley by Benjamin Idelot but for fear of miscarriage sends the present letter by James Strawbridge - he thanks Bladen for his care of the letter he (Handy) received from Captain Hyede. Handy is glad [John] Smith is taken and trusts that Bladen will take care to summon the evidences; they are George Gentels who lives at Mistress Whit's on the Patuxent a little above Walter Smith's and Hezzacaiah Bussey. On verso "Kingsbury & Chew Act". [28]

20th September 1706 J[ohn] West (Somerset County) to William Bladen.
Many persons in the county are dissatisfied with the laying out of the port and the town. As to the port in Wicomico there is not a more commodious place in the Province, it is approved of by all the masters and mates that have lately left. The incommodiousness of Round Hill where it is planned to move the port will be apparent. It will be a pity should the growing hundreds of the north side of the river be deprived of the privileges with which they are now invested by law. The loss of tithe of Port Pocomoke is the cause of all the trouble. As the town on Coulbourne Creek in Annemesroc River, the original layout has been changed. This has been done to right the damage caused to Nathaniel Horsy by the first commissioners for towns, certain lots included in the town as first laid out have been returned to him; those who had built on those plots have had others allowed them; some selfish persons are dissatisfied with this; if Horsy's petition is rejected again, as it was when the town was first laid out a year ago, he will be utterly ruined. As to the charge that the new town is mostly swamp it can be said that there is scarcely any better or more level land in the country. There are several good landing places for sloops; West is just recovering from a six week [illness] so cannot undertake the voyage to Annapolis. [30]

20th September 1706 Arthur Smith (Dorchester County) to William Bladen, Attorney General, Annapolis. Theodore Bonner falsely prosecuted a suit against Smith in the name of Alexander Wall and recovered judgment and costs without the knowledge of Wall; to recover these damages Smith brought an action in the Dorchester County Court which Bonner removed to the Provincial Court by a Certiorari. Bladen is asked to manage this cause. [31]

---

[1] Maryland State Archives

## Appendices

22$^{nd}$ September 1706 Council Proceedings. The following members were present: Thomas Tench, Robert Smith, John Hamond, Edward Lloyd, James Sanders, William Corsey, Kenelm Cheseldyn and William Holland. Sir Thomas Lawrence's misrepresentations in England are refuted, the interposition of the Governor John Seymour in the matter of security to William Bladen was wholly in Lawrence's favour. At the death of Colonel William Dent, the attorney of Lawrence, the Council made enquiry and learned that Lawrence had made over the fees of his secretary's office to Bladen for the payment of a certain sum of money, so it was ordered that Bladen should pay the Clerk and the Deputy Secretary out of Sir Thomas' fees; by the deposition of Thomas Bordley, there never was any transaction to take away the record of the Land Office out of the secretary's custody. [32]

10$^{th}$ November 1706 Flower Walker of Chester, to William Bladen of Annapolis. John Israel promised to see Bladen and pay £15 on Walker's account, the remainder of the account will be sent by some careful hand. If Israel has not paid then Walker will pay when the first London fleet arrives. He hopes Bladen will not be so unkind as to sue him. [33]

23$^{rd}$ Nov 1706 Wrixham White (Somerset County) to William Bladen, Annapolis. It is thought that Robert Howard intends to remove himself and his estate by stealth, Bladen is asked to send the execution with the bill of costs against Howard in such a manner that it will be executed on either his goods or body. White wants the Writ of Ejectment against Howard to be served; he also asks Bladen to send his [White's] patent belonging to the land called Fishing Harbor, for which an ejectment was brought against John Blizzard. [34]

[1707?] William Roach of St Mary's County to Michael Macnemara Annapolis. Desires summonses for Charles Garnert, Benjamin Reader and Richard Reader; assured of prompt payment. Signed with his mark. Name: William Bladen [35]

[1707] Provincial Court Proceedings. Her Majesty vs Elizabeth Wallis. The jurors present that Elizabeth Wallis, being great with child of J Hunt, privately gave birth to a child on 10$^{th}$ October 1706 and murdered it. Signature: William Bladen, Attorney General. Witnesses: John Anderson, Mary Anderson, Sarah Joslin On verso: Ignoramus, Henry Wriothesley, Foreman [36] - see 49-51

[1707] Provincial Court Proceedings. Her Majesty vs Thomas Wintersell. The jurors present that Wintersell on 25$^{th}$ December 1706 having two counterfeit pieces of money, like the coins of the Low Countries called Dog Dollars, used them deceitfully as payment. Signature: William Bladen, Attorney General. Witness: Richard Snowden. On verso: billa vera Henry Wriothesley, Foreman [37]

[1707] Provincial Court Proceedings. Her Majesty vs Elizabeth Clarke. The jurors present that Elizabeth Clarke, wife of Richard Clarke, deceitfully uttered 15 pieces of counterfeit money, like unto the coins of Spain and the Low Countries.
Signed: William Bladen, Attorney General. Witness: Richard Snowden. On verso: billa vera Henry Wriothesley, Foreman [38]

[1707?] Provincial Court Proceedings. Her Majesty vs Thomas Wintersell. The jurors present that Wintersell, knowing Richard Clarke to stand outlawed for having conspired to overthrow the government, did receive and aid him on 4$^{th}$ May 1707. He assisted Clarke to escape into Virginia; on the day he was received Clarke saw Johana Harrison, wife of Charles Harrison, and threatened to run her through with a sword if she ever revealed his presence. Wintersill threatened to burn her house if she told on him or Clarke. On 7$^{th}$ May Wintersell again received Clarke and abetted him in his conspiracies. Signature: William Bladen, Attorney General. Witnesses: Samuel Young, William Bladen. On verso: billa vera Henry Wriothesley, Foreman [39]

[1707] Provincial Court Proceedings. Her Majesty vs Margaret Cane. The jurors present that Margaret Cane privately brought forth two children and on the same day beat and burned them to death. Signature: William Bladen, Attorney General
On verso: testimony of the witnesses. Joseph Brown: [Thomas] Odel called him to a child put into the ground - one was fair, the other was dirty parched and had its skull broken; Charles Walker; he and his wife came to see child buried; Thomas Odel; she (Margaret Cane) always denied being with child, he went "to a gum", they put ashes in and fetched the male child, the female was found burned. Sarah Odel; (Margaret) was asked if she was not in travail but she would not own it. [40]

7$^{th}$ March 1706/7 James Stoddert of Mount Calvert to William Bladen Annapolis.
Margaret Cane, servant of Thomas Odel, was suspected of having murdered two bastard children. She stands charged by her own confession of having lately been begotten with child, she was privately delivered of two children and put them into a tub of ashes, covering them with hot embers. Whether they were dead or alive is unknown. Stoddert has committed her to jail without bail, he has not bound over the evidence to the Provincial Court but sends their names that they may be summoned. They are: Thomas Odel, Sarah Odel, Joseph Brown and Charles Walker. On verso: Joshua Cecell by Mr Bate. [41]

8$^{th}$ March 1706/7 George Wiseman to William Bladen of Annapolis. Wiseman has lately arrived at Whit's Landing in the ship 'Ardin', Captain Thomas Markin, commander, he hopes Bladen has ended with Vincent Hemsley and gotten his [Wisemans] due from him; when Wiseman departed Captain Pullman was so unkind as to not let him come ashore and see Bladen. He requests Bladen to let Robert Bradley or William Wilkinson know how 'this Hemsley' has served him. [54]

May 1070? Provincial Court Proceedings. Her Majesty vs Edward Hamond and Donough Dennys Jr.
The jurors present that Hamond and Dennys contriving to scandalise the true Christian religion performed an obscene ceremony of baptism on 10$^{th}$ December 1705. Signature William Bladen, Attorney General. Witnesses: Walter Collins, George Day. Clerk: John Beal. On verso: Ignoramus, Henry Wriothesley, Foreman. [61]

May 1707 Provincial Court Proceedings. Her Majesty vs Anthony Drew. The jurors present that Drew, on 1$^{st}$ October 1706, made an assault upon John Law and knocked him down with a small fowling piece. Signature: William Bladen, Attorney General. Witnesses James Law, David Price, John Parker, John Williams. Clerk: John Beal. On verso: ignoramus, Henry Wriothesley, Foreman. [62]

10$^{th}$ May 1707 John Waters, Somerset County to William Bladen of Annapolis. Waters desired William Bladen to appear as attorney for him against Vincent Hemsle administrator of James Bosle; he hopes to see Bladen before the trial and receive his directions, the cause of his (Hesle's) arresting Waters is presumably that he (Waters) is said to have carried Dr Stenalling out of the province; but he can prove that he carried neither him nor anything that belonged to him. Waters has already written to Bladen by Mr Worthington. He wants two summonses: one for Thomas Maddox, the other for Mr David Shehea. [64]

28$^{th}$ Sep 1707? Joshua Gulbert, Clements Bay, to William Bladen of Annapolis. Charges fraud in the High Court costs against his son Luke, blames William Roche who is a menace to the lives and properties of his neighbors. Names: James Welsh, Oswald Dasch, Thomas Chamberling and Richard Frisby. [68]

17$^{th}$ Feb 1707/8 Council Proceedings. The following Members were present: The Governor (John Seymour), Thomas Tench, Francis Jenkins, Colonel William Holland and Colonel William Coursey, Captain John Daracot complains that by the Act of Assembly for the Encouragement of Towns, he is barred from trading in his accustomed place since no towns are there. It is the opinion of the Governor and Council, together with Colonel Thomas Smith, late Speaker of the Lower House and Justice Edward Lloyd that Daracot would not be liable to the penalties of the Act if he should sell his goods elsewhere and that no advantage should be taken against him until next September. Signature William Bladen, Clerk of the Council. Archives of Maryland XXV, 234. [69]

16th April 1708 Kenelm Cheseldyn (Sheriff, St Mary's County). To William Bladen, Annapolis. [Thomas Trueman] Greenfield has shown Cheseldyn a bill of costs demanded of him by Mrs Keech; it is a very erroneous [enormous?] one; Greenfield is willing to pay his due, but Cheseldyn has advised him first to hear from Bladen, for till the suit in Chancery is over, nothing, in Cheseldyn's opinion, is due; it seems that the bill should have been revived upon the death of [Mr] Keech; but Cheseldyn leaves it to Bladen to say whether Greenfield should pay. Note to Greenfield [from Bladen]; Mr Keech cannot take out any execution against Greenfield for the cost of the non-suit his father had against him unless he has revived the judgment by a scire facias; since the Land Law is repealed, it will be possible to maintain __ Neck for Greenfield. [71]

30th November 1708. Mary Contee, Charles County. To the Governor [John Seymour] and the Upper and lower Houses of Assembly. The petitioner's late husband, Col John Contee, made his will and intended to sign and seal it as soon as Hickford Leman should come to him; but he died suddenly before this was done; the widow prays that a bill may be brought in to make the will valid. At bottom of pages, on 6th December the Governor [John Hart] and Council in Assembly recommends to the House of Delegates that the petitioner's counsel may bring in a bill to confirm Col. Contee's will. Signed William Bladen, Clerk. On verso: the Lower House grant leave, on 6th December, to bring in a bill as prayed. Signed Richard Dallam, clerk, petition and message sent by John Salter, Philemon Hemsley, Thomas Robbins, Daniel Marreartte. [74]

1st Dec 1708. The Governor [John Seymour] and the Council in Assembly. To the Lower House of Assembly. In answer to the message by [Samuel] Worthington and others the Governor declares that he has ample authority from the Queen to erect cities and boroughs; what he has done in favour of making this place [Annapolis] the seat of government was with a true regard to the interest of the province. Signed: William Bladen, Clerk of Council. Sent by Edward Lloyd and Col. William Holland. [77]

2nd December 1708. The Governor John Seymour and Council in Assembly to the Lower House of Assembly. The Board assents to the reports of the conferees (appointed for enquiring into the Charter of Annapolis). Signature: William Bladen, Clerk. Archives of Maryland: III, 148-2 [ 80]

6th December 1708. The Governor [John Seymour] and the Council in Assembly. To the Lower House of Assembly. The Governor and Board are well satisfied with the reason for referring the question of itinerant justices until the next session. Signature: William Bladen, Clerk of Council. Archives of Maryland: XXVII, 239 II, 90-2 [84]

8th December 1708. The Upper House of Assembly. To the Lower House of Assembly. In answer to the message by [William] Wilkinson, Capt [Richard] Jones, [Philip] Lee and [Thomas] Covington, the Upper House thinks it reasonable to address Her Majesty and are willing that the county justices should regulate the ordinary licenses till otherwise provided.
Signature William Bladen, Clerk of the Council. [87]

13th December 1708. The Council [To the Upper and Lower Houses of Assembly]. Message concerning "the admission of attorneys to plead in this Province; attorneys admitted in Great Britain by the Sovereign with the approval of the Courts; such a regulation in this Province will benefit the people; Courts can suspend any attorney for misbehaviour; the Governor has not given leave to keep store outside of towns. Signature William Bladen to the Council. Names: Capt John Daracot, Capt John Jefferson, Thomas Covington, Philemon Hemsley, Thomas Greenfield, Philip Lynes. Archives of Maryland XXVII, 248-249. 91, III, 49 [91]

1710 The Council in Assembly. Extract of the minutes: negotiations concerning the relief of "aggrievances"; a list of bills passed by the current session of the legislature. Signature: William Bladen, Clerk of the Council. Names: William Dixon, Christian Swornstedt, William Edmondson, Richard Bridges, Mr Hall, Col. Whittington, Mr Hemsley, Mr Bradford. [102]

[1710?] Message regarding the State's debt to Mr Bladen, the furnishings for the Governor's house ....
D. Incomplete and unsigned. 2pp. Archives of Maryland: Ref: 103, I, 23 [103]

20th May 1710. The Lower House of Assembly. To the Upper House of Assembly. James Calder, Dr Charles Carroll, Col. Robert King, Vachel Denton, Col Thomas Colvill and William Stoughton have been appointed to confer with Benjamin Tasker, George Plater and Edmund Jenings of the Upper House. Signature: Michael Macnemara, Clerk Lower House, [104]

24th October - 4th November 1710. The Council (in Assembly). Journal of Proceedings: a short session agreed upon, business of the council concerning taxes, the Indians, the Palatines, the Provincial Court, the carrying of letters, the importation of bread and other agricultural produce and the appointment of an American Agent to England; petitions and other business
Names: Col William Holland, Col Thomas Greenfield, Col Charles Greenberry, Samuel Young, John Hall, Lt Col Walter Smith, Philemon Hemsley, Thomas Bordley, Robert Tyler, Samuel Worthington, Nathaniel Dare, Capt John Franklin, Thomas Hicks, John Hodson, Maj Charles Hamond, James Bowles, Col William Coursey, Richard Dallam, Philip Jones, Walter Campbell, Joseph Hill, William Bladen, Christian Swornsteadt, William Hickman, Gerrard Slye, Col James Smallwood, Col Philip Hopkins, Gerard Foukes, John Bradford, James Wallace, Rev Edward Butler, Daniel Mariarte, Col James Maxwell, John Hurst, Magdalena Edmonson, John Edmondson Jr, John Edmondson Sr, James Edmondson, Thomas Edmondson, Col William Whittington, Robert Skinner, Capt Crabb, Maj Thomas Ringold, James Harris, Capt Edward Scott, Capt Hans Tilman, Col Thomas Addison, John Dansey, George Asque, George Muschamp, Lt Col Nicholas Low, William Dixon, Gov John Seymour, Ann Lynes, Philip Lynes, James Frisby, John Nicholas, Wittin Edmondson, James Presbury, John Gresham, Major Joseph Wilson, Maj John Hamond, James Young, Earl of Sunderland, William Taylard, Col Walter Smith, Richard Bridges, Col Robert Finley, Major Levin Gale, Samuel Phillips, Mr Hudson, Henry Jowles, Mr Pearce, Mary Seward, Ann Seward, William Seward, George Seward, Col Robert Quarry, Mr Page, John Clements, Thomas Rennolds, John Salter, Col Thomas Ennalls, Col Nathaniel Blakiston, Philemon Lloyd, Maj Storey, Robert Ungle, Mr Robins, Mr Macall, Aquila Paca, Edward Wright. Tract names: Richardson's Choice, lector endorsed. [107]

25th October 1710. The Council in Assembly to the House of Delegates. Message summarising the action of the Governor and Council on the laws passed by the Assembly during the current session. Signature William Bladen, Clerk to the Council.
Names: Colonel Blakiston, James Crooke. Archives of Maryland: 109, I, 20-3 [109]

1st November 1710 The Council in Assembly to the House of Delegates. Message concerning "The aggrievance offered by ye Grand Jury" Signature William Bladen, Clerk of the Council. Note: Sent by Mr Young, Col Greenberry, Mr Hall and Col Whittington". [113]

4th November 1710 House of Delegates, to the Council. Message concerning the appointment of an Agent. Signature: R Darram, Clerk of the House of Delegates. Note "by Mr Worthington". [119]

## Appendices

3rd November 1711. An Act empowering Robert Roberts to sell a tract of land recently belonging to John Toas. Roberts was obliged to pay £231 Sterling in which sum he was bound for Toas who ran away - the wife of Toas, a sister of Roberts' and two children have been maintained by Roberts since the departure of Toas. It is therefore enacted that Roberts shall have authority to sell 4,500 acres of land belonging to Toas as compensation. Signatures: Richard Gallan, Clerk of the House of Delegates, William Bladen, Clerk of Council, Edward Lloyd President. Archives of Maryland XXIX, 75, XXXVIII, 138-139. Ref: 124, III, 186. [124]

1715 Philip Fedderman, Sheriff of Dorchester County, to Governor John Hart and the Council.
The petitioner's term as Sheriff began with a commission from Edward Lloyd which will expire in June. Since there never has, during his term of office, been near as much tobacco as there used to be, he has been unable to pay the public dues. He therefore prays that the three year limit on the sheriff's term may be extended to enable him to meet the public claims and save his character. Verso: 4th May 1715 read an order to lie on the table till the law related to the sheriff's office is revised. Signed William Bladen, Clerk. Archives of Maryland. Ref: 127, VIII, 64. [127]

1715. John Dorsey, Sheriff of Baltimore County to Governor John Hart at the Council. This petitioner first commissioned as Sheriff by Edward Lloyd prays that his term may be extended beyond the three year limit in order to enable him to pay the public dues which till now have been impossible because of the small quantity of tobacco raised. Verso: On 9th May 1715 read an order to lie on the table until the bill relating to the sheriff's office is revised. Signed William Bladen, Clerk. Archives of Maryland. Ref: 128, VIII, 67. [128]

1715. Christ Church, Calvert County. Petition of the Parishioners to the Governor John Hart and the Council in General Assembly.
The Petitioners are put to an extraordinary charge to support a church and chapel and yet do not have opportunity to perform their duty and service suitable to every Sabbath. They pray that the delegates of the County may lay before the Governor a true account of the profits of the two parishes found in it. If these profits are thought sufficient for the support of three ministers the Governor may support suitable action. Verso: read and rejected by the Governor and Council 28th May 1715. Signed William Bladen.[129]

3rd May 1715 The Governor John Hart and Council. An Act pledging the support of the Province to the new King George I. Verso: by the Governor and Council in Assembly read the first time 3rd May 1715 and will pass and signed by order of William Bladen, Clerk to the Council. Read in Council the second time and passed with no objections. Archives of Maryland. Ref: 132, VII, 73. [132]

3rd May 1715. Thomas Hicks, Dorchester County, to Governor John Hart and the Council in Assembly. Benjamin Woodward and his wife, co-heirs of William Seward, the heir of George Seward, having obtained through a petition the passage in the Lower House of an Act giving them title to a tract called Sector, Hicks claiming a right in the said land - prays that he may be heard by his Counsel before the Board. Ordered by the Governor and Council in Assembly, 3rd May 1715 that the petitioner be given notice to attend, with his counsel, at 5 o'clock in the evening. Signed William Bladen. Archives of Maryland. Ref: 133, VIII, 62. [133]

3rd May 1715. Benjamin and Mary Woodward to Governor John Hart and the Council.
Mary Woodward, late wife of William Seward, son of George Seward petitions together with her husband on behalf of Mary and Ann Seward, daughters and heirs of William - since the bill passed in favour of Mary and Ann, by the Lower House concerning the tract of land called Sector is delayed through the endeavours of Thomas Hicks, the petitioners pray that by their counsel they may present their case before the Governor and Council. On verso: ordered by the Governor and Council in Assembly 3rd May 1715 that the petitioners with their counsel be given notice to attend at 5 o'clock in the evening. Signed William Bladen, Clerk. Archives of Maryland. Ref: 134, VIII, 63 [134]

6th May 1715. Conference of Members of the Upper and Lower House at Assembly. Colonel William Coursey was elected Chairman and William Bladen, Clerk. It was resolved that tobacco should be shipped earlier than usual, it would be advantageous if coopers would set up their casks earlier than usual. It was decided that coopers be paid upon execution at the rate of 80lbs of tobacco or 6 shillings 6d for every ton of cask. Members of the Council present: Colonel William Coursey, Colonel Samuel Young, Colonel Thomas Addison, Colonel Richard Tilgman. Archives of Maryland. Ref: 135, II, 84 [135]

6th May 1715. Conference of Members of the Upper and Lower Houses of Assembly: Colonel William Coursey is elected Chairman and William Bladen, Clerk. Two royal instructions are considered apropro of the order to revise the laws and send a complete body for His Majesty's approbation or disallowance. It is agreed that all such laws that need amendment be reinacted at the present session. All of the laws are to be transcribed onto parchment and sent under separate seals.
Archives of Maryland. Ref: 136, II, 85 [136]

13th, 16th, 18th May 1715. Conference of Members of the Upper and Lower Houses of Assembly.
Colonel Edward Lloyd is elected Chairman, William Bladen Clerk. The Conference considered the enlarging of tobacco hogsheads. The Royal Instruction of 26th June 1711 relating to the gauge of hogsheads was read, the conferees are of the opinion that it would be in vain to propose any law, even when it is necessary, when it is proposed to ask permission of His Majesty for making the law and enlarging the gauge, the Conferees from the House of Delegates say that they have no instruction to consider that, but will return for further directions. The Conference adjourns until 16th May and then again until 18th May. The majority are of the opinion that the present law of fixing the gauge of hogsheads be continued until 15th May 1716. [139]

17th May 1715. The Governor John Hart and Council to the Lower House of Assembly. The Council proceedings are defaced and torn for want of being well bound. A good well bound paper book should be provided at public expense. Signature: William Bladen, Clerk of the Council. Verso: message drawn up and intended to be sent to the delegates. Archives of Maryland: Ref: 141, III, 103. [141]

26th May 1715. The Governor John Hart to Evan Jones, Deputy Collector of the Port of Annapolis.
An order is given to go on board the Colchester Adventure whose master is Jeremiah Sampson and make search for all such hogsheads of tobacco as exceed the gauge fixed by an Act of Assembly. The Governor is to be given an account of the marks and numbers of each hogsheads as exceed the gauge. Signature: William Bladen, Clerk of the Council. Archives of Maryland, ref: 144, II, 95. [144]

6th June 1717. Robert Ungle, Treasurer of the Eastern Shore, Public Account.
The public stock of the Eastern Shore in currency shows credit amounting to £306 - 15 shillings 6d, the sum of the balance left on 1st October and various duties collected; £236-14 shillings -1d have been drawn, leaving a balance of £70 - 1shilling - 5d; the same public stock in Sterling cash shows credits amounting to £62-15shillings-1½d; £31-9 shillings have been drawn, leaving a balance of £30-6 shillings-1½d; the duty of 3d per hogshead on tobacco for arms etc has amounted to £13-3 shillings-9d; expenditure for salary amounted to 6 shillings-7d leaving a balance of £12-7 shillings-2d; the naval officers mentioned in the account are Steven Knight, Arnold Vel.

## Chronologies

**Nathaniel Birkhead**

| | |
|---|---|
| c1582 | Born (had a sister Mary) |
| 1590 | Father Martin died. Mother was Alice Lacy (daughter of John Lacy of Cromwellbothom) |
| 1590 | Father appointed 4th Earl of Huntingdon, Sir George Hastings 1540-1604, as Guardian to his sons TNA: C142/225/104 |
| 1593 | Emmanual College, Cambridge (Alumni Cantabrigiensis) |
| 1599 | Co-signed lease on Kirby Hall with Ambrose Vaux/Involved with Baddesley Clinton Manor House, Warwick |
| 1601 | Co-signed lease ref Manor of Isham |
| 1602 | May 3rd: admitted to Grays Inn |
| 1605 | Married Elizabeth Dale at Colleyweston[1] (received £1,000 marriage settlement) |
| 1620 | Purchased Hague Hall jointly with Robert Bladen, Inherited property at Aislaby from his brother Daniel's Will Donated 10/- a year, with his mother Mary [step-mother]) to Wakefield Grammar School |
| 1622-3 | Witnessed father-in-law's Will (Roger Dale) |
| 1630 | May 2nd: permission to alienate 30 acres of Harden, Yorkshire to Stephen Farrand[2] |
| 1630s | Leased land to Colonel Morrice of Pomfret Castle |
| 1642 | Royalist sympathiser in the Civil War (compounded for a fee later) |
| 1649 | Feb 12th: wrote his Will |
| 1649/50 | Jan 23rd: buried;[3] Apr 24th: Will proved |

**John Lacy**

| | |
|---|---|
| 1561 | Born |
| 1565 | Baptised |
| 1579 | Married Alice Birkhead 1561-85 (daughter of Martin Birkhead) |
| 1580 | Daughter Elizabeth born - she later married Robert Bladen abt 1603 |
| 1581 | Daughter Sarah born - she later married Richard Waterhouse (of Shibden Hall) |
| 1587 | Married Ellen Lister 1566-1603 |
| 1590 | Sold Old Syddall Hall to John Scolfield of Coley |
| 1605 | Sold the Chapel of St Annes to Robert Lawe of Halifax for 5 Marks |
| 1612 | Sold the Manor House of Cromwellbotham to Thomas Gledhill |
| 1638 | Died |

**Robert Bladen**

| | |
|---|---|
| c1582 | Approximate birth date |
| c1603 | Married Elizabeth Lacy, dau. of John Lacy 1561-1638 and Alice Birkhead 1560-85 |
| 1604 | Baptism of son John, at Southowram, Halifax (St John the Baptist, Halifax parish register) |
| c1605 | Baptism of daughter Elizabeth |
| c1608 | Steward to the Wortley family of Wortley Hall in Yorkshire |
| c1614 | Wortley leased Carlton farm to Bladen - 4m from Wortley Hall |
| 1615 | Bladen's family were living at Denton/Askwith[4] on Fairfax manorial land[5] |
| 1616 | Owned/purchased land in Hemsworth (mentioned in Coney v Bladen) |
| 1616 | May 23rd: met with Sir George Radcliffe about wall memorial for uncle Phillip Waterhouse |
| 1616 | Agreement with Richard Sunderland and Coney re land in Barlby |
| 1616 | May 31st: met with Sir George Radcliffe re leasing of land |
| 1617 | Bladen v Illingworth - chased up bad debt from Richard Illingworth/Edward Holdsworth |
| 1617 | Purchased 3 farms, including Bullinghire Hall |
| 1617 | Family moved to Hemsworth (sub-let or lived at Bullingshire Hall) |
| 1618 | Indenture to receive profits of goods of outlaws and felons - along with Richard Berry |
| 1619 | Indenture between Robert Bladen and Mary Wainwright to take her son Thomas as his Ward |
| 1620 | Robert Bixxon of Skircoat having difficulty getting money from Robert writes to Sunderland |
| 1621 | Bladen v Boyne - litigation re money matters TNA: C5/592/74 (Thomas Boyne), Yorkshire |
| 1622 | Bladen v Parkin - Chased up bad debts from Thomas and John Parkin of Hemsworth TNA: C3/337/48, C3/336/94 and C21/B27/13 |

---

[1] The Genealogist New Series, p84 dated 1915. Roger Dale had a son also called Roger Dale, born 1595, a daughter Anne and a daughter Elizabeth who married Nathaniel Birkhead. He also had a nephew William Dale

[2] Wife Elizabeth was also mentioned on these papers. 'A Calendar of the docquets of Lord Keeper Coventry 1625-40', Vol. 36-37

[3] South Kirkby Parish Registers

[4] Barnsley Archives: SpSt 60240 (55/22) Bargain and Sale between Sir Francis Wortley of Wortley and Robert Bladen of Askwith and Richard Kaye of Hoylandswaine re Tithes of corn and grain

[5] Barnsley Archives: SpSt 60327/22 (145/20, 21 and 22) Bond for Wainwright Wardship

## Appendices

**Robert Bladen (cont/...)**

| | |
|---|---|
| 1622 | Bladen & Hey v Thomas & John Parkin - as above TNA: C4/30/16 |
| 1623 | 20th August. Wrote to Sunderland re-arranging a meeting |
| 1624 | Bowe v Bladen - money matters Middlesex TNA: C3/333/58 |
| 1625 | Indenture between Robert Bladen and Richard Berry |
| 1625 | Lease on Carlton farm was renewed for 21 years (to 1646) |
| 1626 | Advice to Wortley to purchase a worthless Manor |
| 1626 | Nov 14th: Indenture between Robert Bladen and Richard Berry |
| 1627 | Nov 16th: Indenture between Robert Bladen and Richard Berry |
| 1628 | Con[e]y v Bladen. TNA: C2/ChasI/C58/58 |
| 1629 | Dec 17th: Indenture between Robert Bladen and Richard Berry |
| 1630 | Berry & Robert Bladen et al v Elizabeth Redhead - Robert's cattle on disputed land TNA: DL4/79/5 |
| 1630s | Earl of Danby v Berry (& Bladen) - dispute over sale of fee farms TNA: C2/ChasI/D1/19 & D44/33 |
| 1630s | Danby v Bladen TNA: C2/ChasI/D28/5, C22/624/18 |
| 1630s | Bladen v Munday - money matters TNA: C2/ChasI/B15/43 |
| 1630s | Cary v Bladen - money matters TNA: C2/ChasI/C29/8 |
| 1630s | Bladen v Flathers - money matters TNA: C2/ChasI/B21/25 |
| 1630s | Bladen v Gill - money matters TNA: C2/ChasI/B69/46 |
| 1630s | Bladen v Phillips - money matters TNA: C2/ChasI/B137/59 |
| 1630s | Bladen v Cundy - money matters TNA: C2/ChasI/B5/53, C21/B7/23 |
| 1630s | Bladen v Wood - money matters TNA: C2/ChasI/B86/9 |
| 1630s | Bladen v Walker - money matters TNA: C2/ChasI/B104/12 |
| 1630 | Left Wortley's employ |
| 1630+ | Began working for Sir William Savile as a steward |
| 1631 | Son John corresponded/employed by 1st Lord Fairfax of Cameron |
| 1631 | Mortgaged a property to Dr Robert Berry for 550 Marks |
| 1632 | Dec 11th: Indenture between Robert Bladen and Richard Berry |
| 1634 | Dec: Indenture between Robert Bladen and Richard Berry |
| 1635 | Dec 4th: Indenture between Robert Bladen and Richard Berry |
| 1636 | Bladen v Wortley - concerning Bladen's leased Carlton farm from Wortley (21 yr lease from 1625) TNA: C21/B19/16, C21/B19/23 |
| 1637 | Dec 14th: Indenture between Robert Bladen and Richard Berry |
| 1637 | Involved in land dispute with Hemsworth Hospital, along with Berry, TNA C205/14/29 |
| 1638 | Property was sold for 500 l. to a Mr Baker. Dispute with Berry as to whether sum was repaid |
| 1638 | Father-in-law John Lacy sold the Manor House of Cromwellbotham to a Thomas Gledhill |
| 1639 | Jul 14th: Indenture between Robert Bladen and Richard Berry |
| 1642 | Wortley & Bladen v Sir Nicholas Tempest C4/27-2/76 |
| 1647 | Died, administration of his estate granted to wife Elizabeth[1] |
| | Jan 4th: 1653 Burial of wife Elizabeth, Hemsworth[2] |
| | <u>Litigation after his death concerning his estate</u> |
| | 1651 Baker v Fountain (& Elizabeth - Robert's wife) TNA: C10/12/16 |
| | 1690 Bladen v Fountain - grandson Nathaniel sued over his grandfather's estate |

**John Bladen**

| | |
|---|---|
| 1604 | Mar 24th: baptised Southowram, Halifax parish |
| 1615 | Living at Askwith/Denton |
| 1622 | Attended St John's College, Cambridge |
| 1624 | Mar 6th: admitted to Gray's Inn, London[3] |
| 1631 | London based. Corresponded with Lord Fairfax.[4] 1st Lord Thomas Fairfax of Cameron |
| 1634 | Jun-Jul: Dublin wrote to Lord Fairfax from Ireland, reporting on political events |
| 1636 | Donated two books to Grays Inn[5] |
| 1636 | Aug: wrote: "Miscellaneous Observations of the Principal Matters in this Court and State" |
| 1637 | Called to the bar[6] |
| 1641 | Oct 2nd: married Margaret Birkhead at South Kirkby, Yorkshire |
| 1642 | Joined the parliamentary army as Lieutenant in Col. Thomas Grantham's Regiment |

---

[1] YAS. University of York, Borthwick Institute: Admon Bladen Robert, Hemsworth, Doncaster Archives, Oct 1647. Fol 501, MF 1180. Wills of York Registry 1627-36 administrations and 1627-52 YAS Vol. 35

[2] Hemsworth Parish Register

[3] Foster's Admissions to Grays Inn, p175. (John, son and heir of Robert of Hemsworth), gent

[4] ©The British Library Board, Manuscript Collection, MS 28051, f109

[5] Parergon, Vol. 14

[6] Ibid

**John Bladen (cont/...)**

| | |
|---|---|
| 1642 | Son Nathaniel was born (named for his Birkhead grandfather) |
| 1642 | Wife died. She was nowhere mentioned in documents relating to Nathaniel's upbringing |
| 1643 | Jan: Captain in Fairfax's parliamentary army[1] |
| 1643 | Aug 27th: appointed to the Defence Committee for Hull |
| 1645 | Mar: named in Royalist Composition Papers regarding Sequestration of Property |
| 1645+ | Date of death - Nathaniel Birkhead's Will of February 1649 referred to him as deceased |

**Nathaniel Bladen**

| | |
|---|---|
| 1642 | Oct: baptism. Probably named after his grandfather Nathaniel Birkhead (who was a lawyer) |
| 1645 | Aft Mar: father died |
| 1652 | Chancery Bill: Lindsey v Watson TNA: C6/46/146 - between his two Birkhead Aunts |
| 1655 | Chancery Bill: Bladen v Watson TNA: C22/768/14 - between Birkhead descendants |
| 1656 | School: Sheffield – Mr Potts is mentioned in his admission to Cambridge |
| 1661 | Matriculated |
| 1661 | At the Cockpit area of the Inns of Court |
| 1661 | May 6th: attended St John College, Cambridge[2] |
| 1662+ | Corresponded with Robert Wrightson |
| 1663 | Aug 28th: Exercised his power of Advowson of Hemsworth Church[3] |
| 1664 | Resided with Uncle Linsey, c/o Mrs How's House, St James, Petty France, London |
| 1666 | Oct 19th: admitted to the Inner Temple[4] |
| 1666 | Receiver of Arrears of Prize Ships, along with Charles Osborne (brother of Danby) |
| 1667 | Working for the Earl of Danby and his family |
| 1668 | Mar: marriage to Isabella Fairfax at Steeton |
| 1669 | Sep 2nd: baptism of daughter, Isabella at Wandsworth, Surrey |
| 1671 | Birth of daughter, Catherine |
| 1671 | Sold the Manor of Haworth and Harden for £80 to a William Midgley, gent |
| 1672 | Mar 21st: birth of son, William at Steeton |
| 1673 | Nov 3rd: called to the bar |
| 1675 | Birth of daughter, Frances |
| 1677 | Mar: wrote a letter to 4th Lord Henry Fairfax 1631-88 urging him to stand for Parliament[5] |
| 1677 | Birth of daughter, Elizabeth |
| 1680 | Birth of son, Martin |
| 1680 | Arranged the funeral of the Earl of Plymouth (paid for by the King) |
| 1680 | Steward to Danby's daughter, the widowed Countess of Plymouth[6] |
| 1681 | Still engaged with the Treasury ref Receiver of Arrears etc of Prize Ships |
| 1681 | Fairfax & Topham v Wrightson & Bladen TNA: C10/142/2 |
| 1682 | Jul 10th: named on a British Patent – mill for making paper and plasterboard |
| 1683 | Living at Gardines/Gardiners Lane, St James Piccadilly (near Duke Street), Westminster |
| 1683 | Living at Duke Street, St Margaret's Westminster, also had premises around the corner at Gardiner's Lane (business). Still there at 1686 |
| 1685 | Birth of son Charles – died infant[7] |
| 1685 | Sold land and the advowson in Hemsworth (prior to 1685) to Wrightson |
| 1685 | Nathaniel travelled to Portsmouth with Edward Osborne, Viscount Latimer |
| 1686 | Jun: referred to in a letter from Admiral Robert Fairfax (nephew) to his mother[8] |
| 1686 | Aug: residing in Duke Street, Westminster,[9] |
| 1686 | Sep: kept prisoner by the Countess of Plymouth |
| 1686 | Sep: early, escaped from Countess's house and went straight to Wallingford House |
| 1686 | Reward to anyone who could find Bladen, so the Countess could prosecute him |
| 1686 | In custody in Southwark Debtors Gaol |
| 1686 | Nov 6th: Admiral Robert Fairfax writes of Nathaniel having "fled from hence and absconding himself at Appleton House" |

---

[1] Hull History Centre, C BRS/7/19, 53 Bodl., MS Fairfax 30, folio 129

[2] Alumni Cantabrigiensis

[3] Hunter's South Yorkshire, Vol. II, 1828/31

[4] The Inner Temple Admissions Database

[5] Royal Commission on Historical Documents Reports Part 9

[6] Plymouth v Bladen 1686 2 Vern 31, 32

[7] Harleian Society Books, Register of St Margaret's Westminster

[8] Life of Robert Fairfax of Steeton by Clements R. Markham 7 June 1687

[9] Westminster Rate Books, 20th March 1686 show Nathaniel renting property: Mr Blayden of Duke Street, St James Piccadilly, St Margaret's Westminster. Rent £2- 6/-

# Appendices

### Nathaniel Bladen (cont/...)

| | |
|---|---|
| 1686 | Nov 13th: Countess of Plymouth took legal action against him for disposing of £2,000 of her money, without her knowledge[1] |
| 1686 | Nov: cases stopped by the Countess herself and Nathaniel freed. (Non-suit) |
| 1686 | Dec: spent Christmas at Yorkshire |
| 1687 | Feb: Countess tried unsuccessfully to bring another legal action against Nathaniel |
| 1688 | Obtained an annuity from the Duchess of Buckingham for £100 per year |
| 1688 | Jan 26th: rode out with Admiral Robert Fairfax and others to meet Lord Charles Fairfax of Gilling[2] |
| 1690 | Wife Isabella wrote to Admiral Robert Fairfax |
| 1690 | Bladen v Pembroke |
| 1691 | Oct 25th: death of wife Isabella Fairfax from spotted fever – probably typhus |
| 1692 | Death of Lady Frances Fairfax. Nathaniel joint executor with Thomas Fairfax |
| 1696 | Brought legal action against Francis Williamson and others - re: money matters, Middlesex |
| 1698 | Death of eldest child, Isabella Vavasour |
| 1699 | His annuity from Duchess of Buckingham (daughter of 3rd Lord Fairfax) was terminated |
| 1700 | Bill of Complaint brought by his daughters against Duchess of Buckingham for loss of an annuity |
| 1701 | Address (in letter to daughter Frances) as New Square No. 7, Lincoln's Inn, London |
| 1701 | Wrote a Treatise 'On the Antiquity and Constitution of the Six Clerks Office' |
| 1702 | Witnessed, with dau. Catherine, the Will of Edward Randolph – Surveyor General of HM Customs |
| 1706 | Legal representative in a case in Wigan, Lancs at the sign of the Three Legs of Man (Attorney General v Thurston Heakin) |
| 1712 | Sep 30th: Dined with grandchild Nanny (Anne Tasker) and her new husband Benjamin Tasker |
| 1712 | Corresponded with Lady Altham - see section on Tom Fairfax 1633-1712[3] |
| 1712 | In a letter dated 1712 he referred to 'cousin Braithwaite' (this is Richard Braithwaite[4] - Nath's cousin via Fairfax/Ogle line) |
| 1712 | Sep 30th: Living at Berkeley Street/Square with son Martin |
| 1712 | Dec 16th: letter to daughter Frances[5], says he is very ill. The seal on this letter[6] appears to be a lion rampant and three inverted Vs (Fairfax/Bladen heraldry) |
| 1713 | Mar 28th: letter from Nathaniel at Berkeley Street, to daughter Frances[7] where he says "I cannot read what I have writ" |
| 1713 | Mar 28th: last letter to daughter Frances |
| 1713 | Probably unwell after this point - son Martin appears in Plaxton v Bladen in 1713 in his stead |
| 1716 | Daughter Frances seeks advice on what to do about the Hemsworth estate |
| 1717 | Referred to in a letter by William Fairfax |
| 1717+ | Probable date of death |

### Isabella Bladen

| | |
|---|---|
| 1669 | Sep 2nd: baptised[8] |
| c1688 | Marriage to Peter Vavasour |
| 1690 | Mentioned as "cousin Bell" in a letter from Robert Fairfax to his mother |
| 1691 | Named on her mother's Memorial Plaque |
| 1692 | Named in her grandmother's Will as 'Mrs' Isabella - therefore married by 29 October 1692 |
| 1698 | Was alive after her sister Frances' marriage in 1697 |
| 1698 | Probable date of death |
| 1700 | Chancery document stated her to be deceased |

### Catherine Bladen

| | |
|---|---|
| 1671 | Estimated birth date |
| 1696 | Catherine was in Dublin with Uncle Thomas Fairfax |
| 1700 | One of the parties in Bladen v Ash (annuity from the Duchess of Buckingham) |
| 1702 | Jun 15th: in London with her father where she witnessed Edward Randolph's Will |
| 1707 | Jun 2nd: wrote from Dublin to her cousin Captain Robert Fairfax in London |
| 1707 | Sep: In London visiting her Fairfax cousin at Searle Street, nr New Square, Lincoln's Inn (St Clement Danes parish) |
| 1709 | Returned to Dublin (via Hollyhead) on a man-of-war |
| 1710 | Apr 22nd: Uncle Tom described Kate as recovering after being very ill |

---

[1] Bridget, Countess of Plymouth alleged he disposed of £2,000 without her knowledge

[2] Admiral Robert Fairfax, Markham

[3] Cited in copy letter in the possession of Lord Rosse. Nathaniel Bladen to Frances Hamond, 30th September 1712

[4] Richard Braithwaite-Nath's cousin via Fairfax/Ogle line–See Ltr to George Harman. Apr 1723

[5] Letter from Nathaniel Bladen to daughter Frances at Scarthingwell

[6] Transcript of some Hawke family papers

[7] Letters from Nathaniel to daughter Frances supplied by Nicholas MacLean-Bristol

[8] Wandsworth Parish Register, baptisms

## Catherine Bladen (cont/...)

| | |
|---|---|
| 1710 | Aug 6th: Kate's uncle describes Kate as having her "old distemper of headache but is pretty well over and rides on horseback very often" |
| 1711 | Jan 5th: Dublin |
| 1711 | Mar 30th: letter described Kate has having been very ill for 10 days, but recovered. |
| 1711 | Letter to Admiral Fairfax - she described her fears for sister Frances |
| 1711 | An undated letter (though from about this time) referred to "Caty having a pleurisy" |
| 1712 | Mar 11th: in Dublin with her uncle when he died, aged 80 |
| c1715 | Marriage to a Captain Fowke |
| c1717 | Estimate date of death, not mentioned in her brother's Will of 1726 |

## William Bladen

| | |
|---|---|
| 1672/3 | Mar 21st: baptised at Steeton[1], Yorkshire (born 27th February 1672/3) |
| 1688 | Feb 10th: admitted to the Inner Temple[2] (not called to the Bar) |
| 1692 | Went to Maryland (19 yrs old) initially to St Mary's City – appointed Clerk (in place of the Catholic Charles Carroll)[3] |
| 1692 | Jun 7th: Assembly awarded him 1,600 lbs of tobacco as Clerk |
| 1692 | Oct 24th: Assembly awarded him 4,000 lbs of tobacco to transcribe copies of Laws |
| 1693 | Apr 8th: 1 of 3 Deputies to apprehend Col. Peter Sagar and Thomas Smith for conspiracy |
| 1693 | Admitted to Provincial, Cecil County and Prince George County Courts Appointed Attorney-General |
| 1693 | Royal Governor Copley died |
| 1693 | Jul 6th: new Governor Francis Nicholson in post, appointed William to a Committee to Inspect Provincial Records |
| 1694 | Bladen had signed a petition not to move the capital to Annapolis (13th November) |
| 1694 | Signed a Declaration of Loyalty to King William |
| 1695 | Married Anne van Sweringen 1680-aft 1727 at St Inigoes in St Mary's County, Maryland (daughter of Garret van Sweringen and Mary Smith - Catholic Immigrants 1690s) |
| 1695-7 | May 9th: appointed Clerk of the Lower House[4] |
| 1695-8 | Appointed Clerk of St Mary's County[5] |
| 1696 | Governor Nicholson accused of taking bribes |
| 1696-8 | Appointed Clerk of Indictments - Prince George County |
| 1696 | Took someone's horse without permission - Justices ordered him to pay 200 pounds of tobacco to the horse's owner[6] |
| 1696 | Assaulted |
| 1696 | Sep 30th: Set up a printing press for the Maryland Assembly's use[7] |
| 1696 | Birth of daughter Anne |
| 1697 | Appointed Deputy Collector of Annapolis (for 5 months only) from 20th October |
| 1697 | Appointed by Edward Randolph as Surveyor and Searcher of Annapolis |
| 1697 | Appointed Clerk of the Council; Clerk of the Upper House and Clerk of the High Court of Appeals |
| 1698 | Register of Vice-Admiralty - Court of Eastern Shore (5 yrs) |
| 1698 | Birth of son Thomas |
| 1698 | Register of Vice-Admiralty - Court of Western Shore (5 yrs) |
| 1698 | Appointed Clerk of Free Schools of Annapolis (15 yrs) |
| 1698 | Appointed Naval Officer of Annapolis (for over 19 years) |
| 1698 | Mother-in-law Mary van Sweringen swore (before Governor Nicholson) that Bladen could be thrown out of his job because he said "half the people of the Country [were] bought and sold"[8] |
| 1698 | Wrote to Abp Tenison thanking for his assistance in amending Maryland's laws[9] |
| 1699 | Aug 14th: Clerk of the Prerogative Court (for 10 months only)[10] |
| 1699 | Part owner of a ship, Tyrone (of London) |

---

[1] Life of Robert Fairfax of Steeton, by Clements R. Markham. Last of the Bladens to be baptised there

[2] The Inner Temple Admissions Database, 10th February 1688

[3] Charles Carroll 1660-1720, Attorney General of Maryland, 1688-9 (until the unrest by the council against the Catholic proprietors)

[4] Journals of the Upper and Lower Houses

[5] Edward C. Papenfuse, Maryland State Archivist and Commissioner of Land Patents

[6] In the 17th century, Maryland used tobacco as its primary medium of exchange because tobacco was a home-grown product

[7] After he obtained permission, it took a further 3-4 years to import the press and set it up, errors were found in Bills by delegates and, by 1701, he was no longer actively involved in the printing process - though maintained ownership of the equipment

[8] Maryland Archives, XXIII, 406, 447

[9] Lambeth Palace Library FP/1-40 1626-1822

[10] Test. Proc. Lib. 18 fol.3

# Appendices

**William Bladen (cont/...)**
| | |
|---|---|
| 1700 | Birth of son Christopher |
| | Nathaniel Blakiston was appointed Governor |
| 1700+ | Assumed responsibility as public printer |
| 1701 | Apr 16th: appointed Principal Secretary of Maryland[1] |
| 1701 | Nov 19th: suspended as Secretary as Sir Thomas Lawrence wanted the job (and fees for it) |
| 1701 | May-Jun: In England lobbying to secure his appointment as Secretary |
| 1701-3 | Responsible for building the new state prison (25'x15') with 2' thick walls |
| 1703 | Appointed Deputy Surveyor of Customs (for over 20 years) after Edward Randolph's death |
| 1703 | Appointed to the Court of Anne Arundel County |
| 1704 | John Seymour took over as Governor of the province |
| 1704 | Province's Statehouse burned down and Bladen requested funds to rebuild it |
| 1704 | Vestryman of St Anne's Parish in Annapolis (14 years) |
| 1704 | Appointed Attorney General of Maryland (for over 13 years)[2] |
| 1704 | Sir Walter Campbell 1659-1724, Sheriff of Dorchester County MD wrote re Philip Clark's land |
| 1704 | Birth of son William |
| 1705 | Wrote to the BoT regarding Sir Thomas Lawrence's misrepresentation of his conduct |
| 1705 | Allied himself with Charles Carroll (snr) in property purchases in Annapolis |
| 1705 | Visiting England (Bladen v Owen TNA: C9/472/86), money matters ref Joseph Owen of Derby |
| 1705 | Lawrence complained to the BoT about Bladen "charging for copies of the Upper House Journals" |
| 1707 | Made a deposition regarding Sir Thomas Lawrence's complaints against Gov. Col. Seymour |
| 1708 | Alderman of Annapolis (one of the six original aldermen on city's first charter)[3] |
| 1708 | Responsible for commencing building of the new State House[4] |
| 1708 | Birth of daughter Priscilla |
| 1708 | Commissary General or Judge of Probate (for 10 years)[5] |
| 1708 | Delegate to the Lower House (1 month) |
| 1709 | Inherited land from his friend Philip Lynes' Will, one time Mayor of St Mary's City |
| 1711 | Defendant, along with John Israel, in a suit brought by Samuel Dorsey |
| 1711 | Jul 31st: daughter Ann married Benjamin Tasker |
| 1712 | Significant inheritance from his van Swearingen mother-in-law (Mary) |
| 1713 | William gave 18,000 pounds of tobacco to Francis Dollahide (Francis put up 200 acres of his land as collateral, he basically mortgaged 200 acres to secure the tobacco from Bladen) |
| 1714 | New Governor John Hart took up post |
| 1716 | Purchased rebels transported from Belfast (Thomas Forbus, Thomas Potts, George Thomson, John Ramsey Alexander Reind)[6] |
| 1718 | Aug 7th: died, Maryland. Buried on 9th August in an elevated memorial at St Anne's Church in Annapolis[7]. Died intestate |

**Frances Bladen**
| | |
|---|---|
| 1675 | Date of birth calculated from mother's memorial which listed children in chronological order |
| 1697 | Marriage to William Hamond |
| 1698 | Birth of first daughter, Catherine |
| 1701 | No financial support from Hamonds, Frances/William running up debts |
| 1701+ | Possible birth (and death) of two sons William and Martin who died as infants[8] |
| 1702 | Hamond father-in-law challenged legality of Frances' marriage to William |
| 1702 | Frances/William living at Hazlewood Castle (home of Sir Walter Vavasour[9] her sister Isabelle's relations) |
| 1702 | Frances forced to leave her home by Hamond family. Servants dismissed |
| 1702 | May 19th: wrote to her father from Oglethorpe |
| 1703 | Birth of second daughter, Frances Hamond, baptised St Clement Dane's Church, London |
| 1706 | Father-in-law wrote Will cutting out Frances's husband[10] |
| 1707 | Death of father in law Gervase Hamond |

---

[1] Prov. Court Rec., Lib. TL. No. 2 fol. 343

[2] Council Journal 1699-1714, p. 528

[3] Riley's Ancient City, pp. 80, 86, 88

[4] Ibid

[5] Charles Co. Rec.

[6] History of Maryland from the Earliest Period to the present Day J. Thomas Scarf. Baltimore John Piet, 1879 (I: 386-387)

[7] Register of St Anne's, Annapolis

[8] Dugdale's Visitation of Yorkshire and Familiae Minorum Gentium

[9] Walter Vavasour raised a regiment for King Charles I in the English Civil War

[10] TNA: PROB 11/496/5, 1707, actually left him 20 shillings (less than he left his servants)

**Frances Bladen (cont/...)**

| | |
|---|---|
| 1707 | Sep 19th: moved into Scarthingwell[1] by the 19th[2] |
| 1708 | Claimed to have had a dream foretelling the death of Henry Fairfax (cousin)[3] |
| 1708 | Commencement of legal proceedings relating to the estate of Gervase Hamond |
| 1710 | Frances had taken her two daughters and was not living with husband |
| 1710 | Apr: William Hamond was living at Two Blue Flower Pots Inn, St Giles |
| 1710 | May. Frances believed her letters were being intercepted |
| 1711 | Sister Catherine was concerned for Frances.[4] "Pray God deliver her out of her troubles" |
| 1711 | Death of her husband, William Hamond (died in debt, aged 37 years) |
| 1712 | Sep 30th: first mention of George Harman in Nath Bladen's letters |
| 1712 | Hamond family bankruptcy notice published in the London Gazette[5] |
| 1713 | Frances is unwell (fever),[6] brother Martin settled some of her debts for her[7] |
| 1713+ | Used solicitor Francis Taylor for herself; Nicholls continued for children |
| 1714 | First of many letters between Frances/solicitor Francis Taylor concerning property problems Scarthingwell, Kirk Fenton[8] |
| 1714 | 2nd Feb. Frances prepared to sell[9] |
| 1714 | Jun: At Scarthingwell with George Harman[10] |
| 1714 | Married to Captain George Harman but did not tell her solicitor[11] |
| 1714 | Nov 2nd: Frances unwell[12] |
| 1715 | Feb 7th: Frances unwell[13] |
| 1715 | May 17th: Hamond v Hamond Case is heard |
| 1715 | Jun 4th: Alderman Miller interested in buying estate, did not know about annuity to Gervase at this point, deal fell through later |
| 1715 | Jul 9th: solicitor Taylor besieged my Frances's creditors wanting the estate to be sold to pay them off. He offered to buy[14] |
| 1715 | Sep 24th: Lady Preston showed interest in purchasing[15] |
| 1715 | Nov 11th: Frances fearful of the Jacobite Uprising. Sent daughters to London for their safety.[16] |
| 1715 | Nov 19th: Captain Harman away on military service.[17] |
| 1715 | Dec: Harman returned to Scarthingwell by December at the end of the Northern Expedition[18] |
| 1716 | Jun 2nd: Frances unwell[19] |
| 1716 | Chased by debtors. Goes to chancery to get money for her daughters |
| 1716 | Solicitor Francis Taylor buys a part of the estate from Frances |

---

[1] The Beauties of England and Wales, or, Original Delineations, Topographical, Historical, and Descriptive of each County. Vol XIV; dated 1819 by a collection of authors, on p629 details information about the seat of the Right Honorable Lord Hawke

[2] Letter from T Fairfax to Admiral Robert Fairfax dated 19 September 1707, Limerick

[3] Letter to Frances from Robert Fairfax 11 January 1710

[4] Letter Cath Bladen to Robert Fairfax, dated 1711 (Source: Admiral Robert Fairfax, by Markham; 1885)

[5] London Gazette 6th August 1713 says Hamond family have gone bust and the properties are to be sold

[6] Nathaniel Bladen's letter 28 March 1713

[7] YAS MS614 Nathaniel Bladen to Frances, dated 28 March 1713 (last letter from Nathaniel)

[8] YAS MS614 Letter Francis Taylor to George Harman, Scarthingwell, 9 May 1719 "the estate taile upon Scarthingwell and Fenton etc"

[9] YAS MS614 Letter from Francis Taylor 2 Feb 1714, preparations for sale of Fenton, preparing and distributing the particulars in, for example, coffee houses to find a buyer. 12 March 1714, he thinks the time is right to try and sell as it is Assizes time in London and that the estate is to be sold for 300 p.a.

[10] YAS MS614 Letters from Francis Taylor (15 June 1714) now addressed to Scarthingwell

[11] In her brother Martin's Will, drawn up in 1726, Frances and husband Harman are both left legacies

[12] YAS MS614 Letter from Francis Taylor to George Harman, Scarthingwell. 2 Nov. 1714

[13] YAS MS614 Letter Francis Taylor to George Harman, Scarthingwell, 7 February 1715

[14] YAS MS614 Letter from Francis Taylor to George Harman, Scarthingwell, 12 March 1715

[15] YAS MS614 Letter from Francis Taylor to Frances Hamond, Scarthingwell, 24 Sept.1715

[16] YAS MS614 Letter from Francis Taylor to Frances Hamond, Scarthingwell, 11 Nov 1715. Where he reassures her that her fears are groundless that Rebels have been repelled ... "Between Argyle and Marr and that the rebels are beaten which I hope will be confirmed". 19 November 1715

[17] YAS MS614 Letter from Francis Taylor to Frances Hamond, Scarthingwell, 19 Nov. 1715

[18] YAS MS614 Letter from Francis Taylor to George Harman, Scarthingwell, 3 Dec. 1715

[19] YAS MS614 Letter from Francis Taylor to George Harman, Scarthingwell, 2 June 1716

# Appendices

**Frances Bladen (cont/...)**

| | |
|---|---|
| 1716 | Oct 17th: Francis Taylor discovers Frances is married |
| 1718 | Quarrel over a marriage settlement concerning daughter to Walter Brooke of Gateforth[1] |
| 1718 | George Harman does not get on with Frances's daughter Catherine and the Brooke family[2] |
| 1719 | Daughter Catherine Brooke threatens to sue George Harman[3] over her interest in the estate |
| 1721 | Death of daughter Catherine |
| 1722 | Legal action by Brooke over guardianship Frances's grandchild. Richard Braithwaite (Bladen cousin) acting for and trying to support George Harman[4] |
| 1729 | Death of daughter Frances |
| 1731 | Death of Frances Harman (née Hamond/Bladen) |
| 1731 | Jan 4th: Capt George Harman resided at Martin Bladen's house in Hanover Square, London[5] |
| 1737 | Death of Captain George Harman in Jamaica[6] |

**Elizabeth Bladen**

| | |
|---|---|
| 1677 | Approximate birth of Elizabeth |
| 1698 | Nov 6th: married firstly to Colonel James Ruthven at Lincoln's Inn Chapel, Holborn[7] |
| 1699 | Widowed within one year |
| 1699 | Husband's army service sent him to West Indies where he died |
| 1704 | Married secondly to Edward Hawke |
| 1705 | Son Edward Hawke born |
| 1707 | Son Thomas born, died infant |
| 1716 | Daughter Frances born |
| 1718 | Husband Edward Hawke died |
| 1723 | Jul 18th: married thirdly to Isaac Sharpe |
| 1726 | Brother Martin wrote his Will referring to his sister Elizabeth Sharpe[8] |
| 1735 | Third husband, Isaac Sharpe died[9] |
| 1742 | May 29th: mentioned in her brother Martin's letter to Admiral Hawke as being in good health |
| 1747 | Mentioned in a Newcastle newspaper as living in York[10] |
| 1748 | Died in Yorkshire (memorial plaque at All Saints Church, Bolton Percy) |

**Colonel Martin Bladen**

| | |
|---|---|
| 1680 | Born at Bolton [Percy], Yorkshire and educated at a private school |
| 1691 | Oct 25th: mother died and grandmother a few months later (Jan 1692) |
| 1692 | Older brother went to America |
| 1694 | Father wrote 'Advice to a Son' |

---

1 Brookes bought their Manor from Lord Darcy in 1564 and Walter was a direct descendant of Humphrey Brooke

[2] Letter from George Harman to Francis Taylor 12 March 1718 MS614 YAS

[3] Letter from George Harman to Francis Taylor 15 July 1719 MS614 YAS

[4] Richard Braithwaite to George Harman, Pontefract, 9 February 1722. Richard Braithwaite (lawyer) was a cousin of Nathaniel Bladen. (Actually Isabella Fairfax's father, Sir William Fairfax 1609-44, it was his sister Ursula who married James Chaloner; their daughter Mariana Chaloner married Richard Braithwaite in 1659). So the term 'cousin' is used somewhat casually here. MS614 YAS

[5] Letter from Walter Brooke, Gateforth to George Harman, Hanover Square, Holly Street, London. Walter Brooke tells of his surprise at hearing of her death MS614 YAS

[6] The Harleian Society papers "Obituaries; Harman (Capt) bro. of Colonel Bladen July 1737 (H.R.C. 14)

[7] Vicar-General Marriage Licence Allegations 1694-1850

[8] Martin Bladen's Will, written in 1726, refers to a legacy to his sister Elizabeth Sharpe, Elizabeth had been widowed by the death of Edward Hawke in 1718. So, if she married for a third time, it had to be between 1718 and 1726 and, there is a marriage of Isaac Sharpe to Elizabeth Hawks (note S, not E after name). Also the Harleian Society records refer to Elizabeth being also known as Sharpe (also Sharp is on her memorial at Bolton Percy Church).

[9] The Will of Isaac Sharpe is dated 4 Feb 1735, proved on 14 Feb 1736. Left his estate portioned between children and wife Elizabeth. Family: wife Elizabeth, sister Dorothy Sharpe, children Isaac, b.1694, Thomas b.1697, James b.1699 and Daniel b.1701. Grandchildren Bransill, Isaac and Lancelot (b.1735). It is believed that Isaac Sharpe married, firstly, to Anne Reyner in 1692 at St Dunstans, Stepney

[10] Newcastle Courant, 7 November 1747

# Early Yorkshire Bladens

**Colonel Martin Bladen (cont/...)**

| | |
|---|---|
| 1695-97 | Westminster School, London, King/Queen's Scholar at St Peter's College[1] |
| 1697 | Apr 17th: matriculated St John's College, Cambridge; admitted pensioner[2] |
| 1697 | Dec 12th: Ensign in uncle Colonel Thomas Fairfax's Regiment of Foot |
| 1698 | Mar 23rd: Admitted Inner Temple |
| c1699 | Marriage to Mary Gibbs |
| 1700 | Nov 24th: called to the Bar[3] |
| 1700-1 | Army half-pay[4] |
| 1700 | Approx birth date for Isabella (heiress) daughter |
| 1702 | Went to Flanders/Spain with Pearce's Regiment |
| 1702 | Birth of son George Monk Bladen |
| 1702 | Wrote a pamphlet on the Albemarle chancery case (Sherwins) |
| 1703 | Named as a defendant in the Albemarle case |
| 1704/5 | Translated 'Caesar's Commentaries of his Wars in Gaul and Civil War in Pompey' |
| 1705 | Commissioned Captain |
| 1706 | Mar: Captain in Sir Charles Hotham's new Regiment of Foot, in Spain and Portugal |
| 1707 | Aide-de-camp to the Earl of Galway |
| 1707 | Battle of Almanza |
| 1707+ | Military operations in Spain, Portugal and Gibraltar |
| 1708 | Additional army post: Officiating Judge Advocate |
| 1708 | Additional army post: Provost Martial |
| 1708 | Commissioned Major |
| 1708 | Sep: guard/garrison at hospital in Portugal |
| 1709 | May: Present at the Battle of La Gudina/La Caya, Portuguese/Spanish border |
| 1709 | Defendant again in the Albemarle chancery case |
| 1709 | Colonel of a regiment in Spain,[5] received £15,497-4-9d for troop subsistence and uniforms |
| 1709 | Dec: based at Gibraltar |
| 1710 | Feb to Apr: Attended the Treasury in London to explain regimental spending |
| 1710 | Jun 25th: sold his Commission to Colonel Vesey[6] |
| 1710 | Jun: Wrote to Captain Hoffman/Hussein,[7] copied to Walpole |
| 1710 | Aug: returned to England with Galway |
| 1711/12 | Attended parliamentary enquiry into regimental spending |
| 1712 | Wrote 'An Impartial Enquiry Into the Management of the War in Spain, by the Ministry at Home' |
| 1712 | Visited Royal Tunbridge Wells Spa Town (seen in Ralph Thoresby's Diary) |
| 1713 | Plaxton v Bladen |
| 1713 | Paid the creditors of his sister Frances |
| 1713 | Mar: returned from a visit to Lord Galway (Ireland) and sister Catherine (? marriage) |
| 1713 | Aug: (General Election) defeated as MP Saltash, Cornwall |
| 1713 | Oct: MP for Kinsale, Ireland with Francis Barnard |
| 1713 | Nov: member of the Hanover Club |
| 1714 | Living at Dean Street, St Anne's Parish, Soho, London |
| 1714 | Oct: attended Coronation of King George I |
| 1714 | Dec: Comptroller of the Royal Mint (to 1728) |
| 1715 | Jan: Defeated as MP Saltash, Cornwall (for the second time) |
| 1715 | Jan: MP for Stockbridge jointly with Thomas Brodrick/John Chetwynd (to 1734) |
| 1715 | Sep: declined the post of Envoy to Switzerland |
| 1715 | Oct: Chief Secretary to the Lord Justices of Ireland, Duke of Grafton and the Earl of Galway |
| 1715 | Nov 1st: Privy Councillor of Ireland (to his death in 1746) |
| 1715 | Nov: MP for Bandonbridge, Irish Parliament (to 1727), jointly with Francis Barnard |
| 1715 | Nov: dispute with Irish Lord Chancellor Alan Brodrick |
| 1715 | Dec 8th: spoke in Irish Parliament ref the King's promise to continue supporting Protestants |
| 1716 | Apr 13th: Dublin Assembly awarded him the Freedom of the City, along with Charles Delafaye |
| 1716 | Apr 16th: wrote to R. Walpole from Dublin Castle |
| 1716 | Aug: attended the Board of Trade for the first time as a guest to present Portuguese Ambassador |

---

[1] DNB Vols. 1-20, 22

[2] Alumni Cantabrigiensis

[3] Inner Temple Parliament

[4] CTB, Vol. 16, 1700-01

[5] 26th Oct English Army Lists and Commission Registers 1661-1714, Vol. 5 1702-07. Charles Dalton

[6] Journal of the Society for Army Historical Research, 1989. Issues 269-276

[7] Cholmondeley Papers, CUL, Ch(H) Corr, 619. Amongst Robert Walpole's correspondence, may have been copied to him as Walpole was still Secretary of War in 1710

# Appendices

**Colonel Martin Bladen (cont/...)**

| | |
|---|---|
| 1716 | Presented a report to Stanhope from the Lord Justices (Ireland) |
| 1716 | Bladen informed the Dublin Assembly that the College of Dublin had chosen the Prince of Wales as their Chancellor. Bladen delivered the King's reply and acceptance |
| 1717 | Apr 2$^{nd}$: back in London |
| 1717 | Apr 13$^{th}$: Abp King visited Martin in London (who was out), spent time with Mary |
| 1717 | Apr 22$^{nd}$: Offered post of Envoy Extraordinary to Spain. Declined by May 31$^{st}$ |
| 1717 | Jul 19$^{th}$: appointed Commissioner of the Board of Trade and Plantations |
| 1717 | Joined the Freemasons |
| 1717 | Director of the RAC (to 1726) (along with Chandos, Thomas Crisp, Earl of Craven and Viscount Fauconberg)[1] |
| 1717 | Visited by William Byrd II 1674-1744, founder of Virginia |
| 1718 | Took on the wardship of his nephew Thomas Bladen when William Bladen (brother) died |
| 1718 | Took on the wardship of his nephew Edward Hawke when Edward Hawke Senior (brother-in-law) died |
| 1719 | Mar 1$^{st}$: purchased land and properties at Panton Street and Panton Square, London |
| 1719 | Director of the Royal Academy of Music, along with Duke of Chandos (to 1728) |
| 1719 | Sep 3$^{rd}$: Commissioner to the Court of France (to 1720) |
| 1720 | May: verbal attack by Jonathan Swift |
| 1720 | Attended Michael Dahl's house/studio with Duke of Chandos for portraits to be painted |
| 1720 | Purchased the Barmoor Estate in Northumberland |
| 1720 | Member of the Court of Assistants of the RAC of England along with Chandos |
| 1720 | Involved in buying/selling shares: South Sea/RAC and EIC |
| 1721 | Purchased property and land on the south side of Hanover Square in London |
| 1721 | Sep 8$^{th}$: produced a large report to the King on the state of the Colonies |
| 1722 | Rumoured to be in the running for the appointment as Speaker of the House of Commons |
| 1722 | Began relationship with Jane Porter (three illegitimate children) |
| 1722 | Renewed lease on Ketton Hall in Rutland prior to 1723[2] |
| 1722 | Apr: wife Mary was unwell and travelled to Spa to take the waters |
| 1722 | Apr: daughter Isabella was sent to live with Duke of Chandos (family friend and matchmaker) |
| 1723 | Aug 26$^{th}$: visited at Hanover Square by Ralph Thoresby the Antiquarian |
| 1724 | Jan 29$^{th}$: wife buried at St Mary's, Sunbury |
| 1725 | Chancery complaint regarding purchase of Panton Square properties |
| 1725 | Divested himself of RAC stock and directorship |
| 1726 | Jan 5$^{th}$: Wrote his Will |
| 1726 | Spoke in the Commons on the Treaties of Hanover and Vienna |
| 1727 | Feb 6$^{th}$: daughter married John Tinker |
| 1727 | Feb 28$^{th}$: marriage allegation between Martin Bladen and Frances Foche |
| 1727 | Mar 28$^{th}$: Indenture to transfer freehold estate at Barmoor to Hopton Haynes and Thomas Sykes |
| 1727 | Mar 29$^{th}$: marriage settlement to Frances |
| 1727 | Apr 3$^{rd}$: marriage to Frances Foche at St Martin-in-the-Fields, Westminster |
| 1727 | May 10$^{th}$: resigned from the Royal Mint within weeks of Sir Isaac Newton's demise |
| 1727 | Oct 19$^{th}$: Indenture/Marriage Settlement for John Tinker-Isabella Bladen £7,730 |
| 1727 | Oct 22$^{nd}$: Coronation of King George II |
| 1728 | Jun: Congress of Soissons (to June 1729) |
| 1728 | Report to Lord Townshend on Carolina, Nova Scotia and New England[3] |
| 1729 | Nov: Treaty of Seville |
| 1729 | Angrily denied that the Board of Trade had ignored a trader's petition for assistance[4] |
| 1730 | Rebuilt Aldborough Hatch at great expense, 14,000 l. |
| 1730 | Sister Frances died. Took a guardianship role to her grand-daughter Catherine Brooke |
| 1730s | Justice of the Peace in Barking/Ilford Essex |
| 1730 | Voted in favour of a subsidy towards the maintenance of the RAC's forts and settlements |
| 1730 | Feb 4$^{th}$: spoke in the debate on the Hessian Troops[5] |
| 1730 | Jun 19$^{th}$: complained that parliamentarians wanted Board of Trade papers |
| 1730 | Jul: John Tinker (son-in-law) departed for Panama |
| 1730 | Sep 7$^{th}$: met the seven chiefs of the Cherokee Nation for peace ratification |
| 1730 | Nov: met Arthur Dobbs regarding the North West Passage |
| 1731 | Trustee for the estates of the Earl of Buchan and Lord Cardross of Scotland |

---

[1] Freedom's Debt: the RAC and the Politics of the Atlantic Slave Trade 1672-1752 by William A. Pettigrew, 2013, Appendix 1X, 4,p. Thomas Crispe was also a Factor at Cape Coast Castle

[2] Gentleman's Magazine, Vol. 220, p610

[3] TNA: CO5/4 folio 159-62

[4] Knatchbull Diary

[5] HMC Egmont Diary, i, 29 Martin Bladen's Speech - TNA: SP 36/21/198, date 1730, on the Hessian Bill

**Colonel Martin Bladen (cont/...)**

| | |
|---|---|
| 1731 | Attended Hampton Court Palace for a Privy Council Meeting re trade and Jamaica |
| 1731 | Spoke in support of the Sugar Bills along with his friend Lascelles |
| 1732 | Attended Antwerp Conference as a Commissioner and Plenipotentiary to set tariffs |
| 1732 | Jun: drafted and supported the Hat Bill |
| 1732 | N. Carolina Assembly in Edenton ordered a county to be named after him, Bladen County |
| 1733 | Mar: supported the Molasses Act |
| 1733 | Apr: supported the unpopular Excise Bill, Walpole was forced to withdraw it |
| 1734 | Bladen Precinct established/later called Bladen County in 1739 |
| 1734 | Feb: voted against the motion to prevent Commissioned Officers being removed by the Crown |
| 1734 | Mar: voted against the motion to Repeal the 1715 Septennial Act |
| 1734 | Wrote, from Hanover Square, to Sir Robert Walpole regarding present state of Jamaica |
| 1734 | Apr: appointed MP for Maldon, Essex (to 1741)[1] |
| 1734 | Dec: took depositions for Earl Tylney regarding Dick Turpin's Gregory Gang robberies |
| 1734 | Long speech in the Commons defending the Govt over lack of repayment of National Debt |
| 1735 | Jun 13th: borrowed £400 from Isaac Drew, secured by a bond |
| 1735 | Jul-Aug: travelled to Spa to take the waters |
| 1735 | Report to Newcastle 'Reasons for the Immediate Peopling of Nova Scotia'[2] |
| 1736 | Apr: Porteous Riots |
| 1736 | Jul-Aug: long summer visit for mineral waters at Spa |
| 1736 | As a JP, gave an address in support of the King from JPs and freeholders of Essex |
| 1737 | Took part in a debate for the Reduction of Interest on the Redeemable National Debt |
| 1737 | July 18th: in Antwerp for six months |
| 1737 | Oct 8th: visited the Prince of Orange-Nassau and wife[3] Anne Hanover |
| 1737 | Wife Frances in Paris (perhaps both she and Martin travelling to Breda) |
| 1738 | Jan 1st: returned to England from Antwerp |
| 1738/9 | Plenipotentiary to adjust the peace with Spain along with Ld Monson, Sir Charles Wager and Mr Hurt (merchant) |
| 1738 | Sep: petitioned the Duke of Newcastle for son-in-law Tinker to be Governor of the Bahamas |
| 1739 | Jan: Treaty of Pardo |
| 1739 | May 2nd: Newcastle asked Bladen to look into the King's title to Carolina |
| 1739 | Oct: outbreak of war between Britain and Spain |
| 1739 | Oct: attended a cabinet meeting about stopping Spain accessing silver mined in Peru/Mexico[4] |
| 1739 | Nov 27th: spoke in the debate on the King's suggestion to raise marines from the standing army |
| 1739 | Dec 27th: produced 'Reasons for Appointing a Captain-General for the Continent of America' |
| 1739 | Negotiated on fixing boundaries of Carolina[5] |
| 1739 | Wrote to Newcastle concerning the export of sugar[6] |
| 1739 | Appointed Plenipotentiary, along with Arthur Stert, for Catholic liaisons |
| 1740 | Apr 1st: voted against the motion to repeal the bill to remove tax on Irish yarn: those against 120: those for 20 (Bladen had brought in the 1716 Bill in Ireland regarding tax on linen)[7] |
| 1740 | Involved in organising Lord Cathcart's expedition against Spanish interests in America |
| 1740 | Martin was reported to be "dangerously ill"[8] |
| 1741 | Feb 13th: voted against the motion for removal of Walpole |
| 1741 | Feb 17th: borrowed £400 from Thomas Tarrant (his Steward and Secretary) |
| 1741 | Dec 16th: step-daughter died (daughter of Frances née Foche/Jory) |
| 1741 | MP for Portsmouth, safe Admiralty seat (till death in 1746) |
| 1742 | Walpole resigned |
| 1742 | Feb 18th: rumoured that he was to be impeached for his share in the Spanish convention |
| 1742 | Dec 10th: spoke in support of Hanoverian troops |
| 1742-3 | Involved with Churchwardens Accounts, St George, Hanover, Westminster Archives |
| 1744 | Voted against Pelham's proposal to put extra duty on sugar |

---

[1] Alumni Cantabrigiensis

[2] Colonial State Papers Vol. 41, nos 592, 454-8

[3] Letter, dated 8 October 1737 from Martin Bladen to Sir Charles Wager. University of Edinburgh: RCHM lxxii 328-9 Title Laing Manuscripts ii 641, 20

[4] The Emergence of Britain's Global Naval Supremacy; the war of 1739-1748, by Richard Harding, p60, The Opening Moves, October 1739-Jan 1741; The main thrust: the west or east indies. (The Anglo Spanish War which became the War of Austrian Succession)

[5] TNA: SP 36/47/191, 20th April 1739 Colonel M Bladen, Aldborough Hatch, to Courand

[6] TNA: SP 36/47/245 folio 245, 30th May 1739 Colonel M Bladen to Duke of Newcastle

[7] HMC, Egmont Diary, 1739-47, Vol. 3, p126

[8] Caledonian Mercury 23rd Dec 1740 Tuesday

# Appendices

**Colonel Martin Bladen (cont/...)**
| | |
|---|---|
| 1745 | Apr 7/8th: Home at Aldborough Hatch burgled |
| 1745 | Apr 10th: Last speech in parliament ref Courts-martial for Admiral Mathews and Lestock[1] |
| 1745 | Attended Westminster for a meeting on land tax |
| 1746 | Feb: reported to be on the point of death[2] |
| 1746 | Feb 15th: died, buried St Dunstan and All Saints, Stepney[3] |

**William's Daughter - Anne Bladen**
| | |
|---|---|
| 1696 | Born in Maryland |
| 1711 | Jul 31st: married Benjamin Tasker Snr (1690-1768), Belair, Prince George Co, Maryland |
| 1712 | In England, in Nathaniel's letters (grandfather called her "Nanny") |
| 1720 | Birth of son Benjamin Tasker Junior |
| 1723 | Birth of daughter Anne |
| 1724 | Birth of daughter Rebecca |
| 1726 | Birth of daughter Elizabeth |
| 1738 | Birth of daughter Frances |
| 1770 | May 11th: Wrote her Will |
| 1775 | Died. Will proved 9 December |

**William's Son - Governor Thomas Bladen** (Inner Temple Records refer to him as Thomas Fairfax Bladen)[4]
| | |
|---|---|
| 1698 | Born in Annapolis, Maryland, America |
| 1712 | Sent to England for his education, admitted Inner Temple 8th July, not called to the Bar |
| 1718 | His father, William, died in Maryland |
| 1720 | Oct 11th: conveyed inherited land in Annapolis to his brother-in-law Benjamin Tasker |
| 1727 | MP for Steyning in Sussex to 1734 |
| 1729 | Appointed to a committee to improve the roads in Cambridge |
| 1731 | Jul 14th: marriage to Ms Barbara Janssen,[5] sister to Lady Baltimore |
| 1731 | Occupied number 9 (now 10) Grosvenor Square, London (house built 1726-7)[6] to 1738 |
| 1733 | Purchased Glastonbury Abbey for £12,000 (£1m in today's money)[7] |
| 1733 | Birth of daughter Barbara |
| 1734 | Defeated in the election as MP for Amersham in Buckinghamshire |
| 1735 | Feb: defeated again in the election as MP for Amersham in Buckinghamshire |
| 1735 | Birth of daughter Harriett |
| 1735 | MP for Ashburton, Devon (instead of Sir William Yonge)[8] to 1741 |
| 1742 | Jan 29th: returned to Maryland, appointed Lt-Gen and Governor[9] to 1747 |
| 1742 | Sep 21st: commenced working as Governor |
| 1742 | Bladensburg named in his honour |
| 1742 | Served as Surveyor-General of the Western Shore[10] to 1746 |
| 1742 | Appointed Chancellor to 1747 |
| 1744 | Concluded a Treaty with the Six Nations Indians at Lancaster PA[11] |
| 1744 | Signed, along with his brother-in-law Benjamin Tasker, an Address of support to the King |
| 1745 | Three Warrants for land purchased in Maryland: 2,000 and 3,000 acres |
| 1746 | Conflicting interests of Proprietors and lower house made his job difficult |
| 1747 | Mar 12th: ended his term as Governor of Maryland |

---

[1] Cholmondeley MSS, CUL

[2] The Caledonian Mercury on 20th Feb 1746 reported "This evening Martin Bladen, MP for Portsmouth lay at the point of death at his home in Hanover Square". Martin was buried on 14th February it is presumed the paper's 'news' lagged a little behind actual events

[3] Musgrave's Obituary, Whincop; Biog. Dram. G.M. 107; L.M. 101; Parl Register, Jacob 1, 282.

[4] The Inner Temple Admissions Database

[5] Gentleman's Magazine, i, 310, Marriage on 14 July 1731 of Thomas Bladen Esq to Barbara the second daughter of Sir Theodore Janssen at St Stephen Walbrook & St Benet Sherehog in London

[6] Survey of London: Vol. 39 pp172-195: The Grosvenor Estate in Mayfair, Part 1 (General History) edited by F H W Sheppard, 1977. Thomas Bladen was listed as first occupant, 10 shillings rent from 1726

[7] Glastonbury Abbey the legendary home of King Arthur and Queen Guinevere

[8] Gentleman's Magazine, February 1735

[9] Archives of Maryland, Biographical Series

[10] Maryland State Archives

[11] Herringshaw's Encyclopedia of American Biography of the Nineteenth Century, p118

## Early Yorkshire Bladens

**William's son Thomas Bladen (cont/...)**

| | |
|---|---|
| 1747 | May 16th: left Maryland province as Thomas 6th Lord Fairfax arrived in Virginia |
| 1747 | Nov 11th: returned to England |
| 1749 | Town residence Albemarle Street, Parish of St George Hanover Square (Poll books) |
| 1751 | Executor of the Will of Charles 5th Lord Baltimore |
| 1754 | Purchased The Grange, Leyton, Essex[1] |
| 1761 | Sheriff of Low Layton, Essex |
| 1762 | 'Aristotle' was entered for the King's Plate at Birford. The Races were to include stag hunting and would be attended by the Duke of Marlborough who brought along his hounds |
| 1763 | Ran a chestnut colt in the Chelmsford Races (50 l.) over 2 miles |
| 1763 | Jun 14th: via his attorney (Benjamin Tasker in America) sold some land to Col George Mason |
| 1765 | Wife and daughters received a large legacy when Sir Abraham Janssen died |
| 1763 | Churchwarden at Low Leyton, Essex |
| 1764 | Surveyor of Highways |
| 1767 | Mar 3rd: daughter Harriet married William Anne Holles Capel (Earl of Essex) |
| 1771 | Aug 31st: daughter Barbara married Henry St John in Watford, Herts |
| 1773 | Deed with Daniel Dulany to sell their American lands 3,742 acres |
| 1780 | Feb 2nd: Died (aged 82) |

**Daughter of Thomas - Barbara Bladen**

| | |
|---|---|
| 1733 | Baptised |
| 1771 | Aug 3rd: married Henry St John |
| 1798 | Named in the Janssen Inheritance Case |
| 1821 | Apr 5th: Wrote her Will[2] probate 1st August 1821 |

**Henry St John (husband of above)**

| | |
|---|---|
| 1738 | Baptised, parents John St John 2nd Viscount St John and Anne Furnese |
| 1747 | Eton to 1753 |
| 1754 | Dec 31st: Ensign 2nd Foot Guards of the Coldstream Regiment |
| 1758 | Jan 12th: promoted to Captain 18th Foot, Royal Irish Regiment, then stationed in Ireland |
| 1760 | Jan 12th: advanced to rank of Major 91st Regiment of Foot |
| 1762 | Feb 13th: promoted to Brevet Lt-Colonel and based at Minorca |
| 1763 | His Corps was disbanded at the peace of 1763, placed on half-pay |
| 1763 | Groom of the bedchamber to the Duke of York (until 1767) |
| 1763 | Accompanied the Duke of York on his tour of the Mediterranean (to 1764) |
| 1766 | Lost £800 gambling |
| 1767 | Went to Montpelier with the Duke of York |
| 1767 | Was with the Duke of York at Monaco when the Duke died. Brought his body back to England |
| 1767 | Nov 9th: appointed by the King Lt-Colonel 67th Regiment of Foot, Minorca |
| 1768 | May. Set out for Minorca, returning in October. Returned again briefly in 1770 |
| 1771 | Aug 3rd: married Barbara Bladen |
| 1772 | Groom of the bedchamber, to King George III (until 1812) |
| 1774 | MP for Wotton Bassett |
| 1776 | Jan 11th: received the Brevet Rank of Colonel |
| 1778 | Nov 27th: appointed by George III to be Colonel of the 36th Regiment of Foot[3] |
| 1779 | Feb 19th: advanced to the rank of Major-General |
| 1780 | MP for Wootton Bassett |
| 1787 | Sep 28th: advanced to the rank of Lieutenant General |
| 1797 | Jan 16th: advanced to the rank of General |
| 1816 | Jun 29th: wrote his Will |
| 1818 | Apr 4th: died (after retaining colonelcy of the 36th Regiment of Foot for 39 years) |
| 1818 | May 8th: Will proved[4] |

**Daughter of Thomas - Harriet Bladen**

| | |
|---|---|
| 1735 | Jul 25th: baptised at Westminster |
| 1765 | Large inheritance from uncle Sir Abraham Janssen, annuity of 200 and lump sum of 2,000 |

---

[1] The Manor House at Leyton was purchased from Sir John Strange, Master of the Rolls, by Thomas Bladen in 1754 when it became known as The Grange. Bladen's heirs sold it to a Nathaniel Brassey (church warden) in 1780. Leyton and Leytonstone Historical Society: The Great Houses of Leyton and Leytonstone, 'The Grange' by David Ian Chapman, 2007

[2] TNA: PROB 11/1647/43, Will of Hon. Barbara St John, widow of St George Hanover Square

[3] Debrett's Peerage of England, Scotland and Ireland, revised and corrected by John Debrett

[4] TNA: PROB 11/1604/134, Henry St John, date 8th May 1818

## Appendices

**Daughter of Thomas - Harriet Bladen (cont/...)**
| | |
|---|---|
| 1767 | Mar 3rd: marriage to the 4th Earl of Essex |
| 1768 | Jan 5th: birth of a still-born son |
| 1769 | Mar 2nd: birth of son John Thomas Capel |
| 1770 | Birth of son Thomas Edward Capel |
| 1775 | Completed a watercolour painting[1] |
| 1775 | Apr 28th: birth of son William Robert Capel |
| 1776 | Aug 25th: birth of son Thomas Bladen Capel[2] |
| 1799 | Husband died |
| 1805 | Commenced chancery case for Janssen inheritance |
| 1817 | Visited by relation Mr Ogle Tayloe from America |
| 1818 | Wrote her Will, then added 8 codicils through to 1821[3] |
| 1821 | Last address: Curzon Street, Mayfair near her sister's house at Audley Square |
| 1821 | Mar 29th: date of final codicil |
| 1821 | Apr 8th: Will proved |

**Elizabeth's Husband - Edward Hawke (Senior)**
| | |
|---|---|
| 1667 | Feb 17th: born St Paul's Covent Garden, London. Parents Thomas (a merchant) and Jane Chase who married 1662 |
| 1685 | Admitted to the Inner Temple, abt 18 yrs of age |
| 1692 | Residing Charing Cross |
| 1693 | May 29th: called to the Bar |
| 1704 | Marriage to Elizabeth Bladen |
| 1705 | Birth of son and heir Edward (later Admiral) |
| 1707 | Birth of son Thomas, St Giles, Cripplegate, London (died infant) |
| 1707 | Wrote 'A Poem Upon the Amendments Made to the Law' |
| 1714 | Working for or with Martin Bladen at the Royal Mint Keeping the Ledger Book[4] (to 1716) |
| 1716 | Approx. Birth of daughter Frances |
| 1718 | Admitted to the Inner Temple |
| 1718 | Died |

**Elizabeth's Son - Edward Hawke (Guardian Martin Bladen)**
| | |
|---|---|
| 1705 | Feb 21st: born in London (Lincoln's Inn)[5] |
| 1718 | His father died and he became a ward of his uncle Martin Bladen |
| 1717 | Joined the navy aged 12 (according to the 7th Lord Hawke's Reminiscences book) |
| 1720 | Feb 10th: entered the Navy, appointed by warrant a volunteer in the Frigate Seahorse (W.Indies) |
| 1723 | Mother's marriage to Isaac Sharpe |
| 1725 | Jun 2nd: passed his naval examinations, Lieutenant on the Galleons Reach |
| 1726 | First sea-cruise under Sir Charles Wager (relief of Gibraltar), spent 1 month in Portobello Panama |
| 1726 | Lieutenant on the Kinsale (West African coast and West Indies) |
| 1727 | Unemployed for almost 2 years |
| 1729 | Apr 11th: appointed 3rd Lieutenant on the 'Portland' |
| 1729 | Nov 25th: appointed Lieutenant on the 'Leopard' |
| 1730 | 5 months on half pay |
| 1731 | May: on the Edinburgh (severely damaged in the Bay of Biscay) 4th Lieutenant |
| 1732 | With his first Captain on the North American station on the Scarborough |
| 1732 | 1st Lieutenant the Kingston (Jamaica) (flagship of Sir Chaloner Ogle) |
| 1733 | Commissioned to HMS Wolf, a 14-gun sloop (promoted fast through staff sickness)[6] |
| 1734 | Mar 20th: Captain of the Flamborough, West Indies station, appointed by Sir Chaloner Ogle |
| 1735 | Back to England, on half pay |
| 1737 | Rented a house at Dartmouth Street St Margaret's parish, Westminster (near St. James Park)[7] |
| 1737 | Married Catherine Brooke (1720-1756) on 3 Oct 1737 at Somerset House/St Mary le Strand, Westminster |

---

[1] An album of original drawings, engravings and lithographs relating to Cassiobury Park, the Hertfordshire house of the Earls of Essex

[2] Charles Mosley, editor Burke's Peerage, Baronetage & Knightage, 107th Edition, 3 Vols

[3] TNA: PROB 11/1642/9, Will of the Rt Hon. Harriot Countess of Essex, date 3rd April 1821

[4] CTB Vol 30. Declared Accounts Mint, Warden's Accounts 1st Jan 1715 to 31st Dec 1716

[5] Oxford DNB and Clement Markham's Life of Robert Fairfax of Steeton have birth date 1705

[6] TNA: ADM 106/859/15 Captain Edward Hawke, the Wolf sloop, Port Antonio is sending his monthly books with 6 deadmen's tickets. 17th March 1734/35

[7] Westminster Archives, census and land survey

# Early Yorkshire Bladens

**Elizabeth's Son - Edward Hawke (Guardian Martin Bladen) (Cont/...)**

|  |  |
|---|---|
| 1737 | Inherited wife's properties at Scarthingwell, Towton and Saxton |
| 1739 | Daughter Frances Isabella Hawke born at Barking (Martin Bladen's home), daughter died infant[1] |
| 1739 | War with Spain and a general European War over Austrian Succession |
| 1739 | Captain of the Portland (West Indies, to protect trade), took his wife |
| 1740 | Captain of the Berwick (Mediterranean) under the poor command of Matthews and Le Stock |
| 1740 | Another daughter, Isabella, born at Barking, also died in infancy. (Living with Martin) |
| 1742 | Sailed for Barbados (took wife Catherine with him) for 6 months at least[2] 1st son Edward Hawke was born at St Michael's Barbados in June 1742, died as an infant |
| 1743 | The Portland got paid off, following storm-damage (dismasted) |
| 1743 | Jun: command of Berwick and joined the Mediterranean Fleet |
| 1744 | 2nd son Martin Bladen Hawke (1744-1805) was born (later, Barrister, Lincoln's Inn) |
| 1744 | Battle of Toulon - Hawke gained distinction against Franco/Spanish fleets |
| 1745 | Captain of the Neptune |
| 1746 | Present at the death at Hanover Square and funeral of Martin Bladen at Stepney |
| 1746 | Succeeded to Martin Bladen's safe Admiralty seat MP for Portsmouth as a Whig (to 1776) |
| 1746 | Following Martin Bladen's death, he was given a sapphire ring[3], probably a mourning ring |
| 1746 | Birth of son Edward |
| 1747 | May 3rd: Battle of Cape Finisterre |
| 1747 | May 14th: Articles of Agreement regarding a creditors' Memorandum of Agreement regarding Martin Bladen's estate |
| 1747 | Returned to Spithead on 31 Oct 1747, Prince of Wales honoured him with a visit on board Hawke's flagship, The Monarch[4] |
| 1747 | Appointed to command the Mars and Gloucester |
| 1747 | Jul 15th: promoted to Rear-Admiral of the White |
| 1747 | In command of the Devonshire, engaged the French at La Rochelle |
| 1747 | Attained Flag Rank. 2nd in command of the Channel Fleet. Defeated the French (Finisterre) and was made Knight of the Bath for his service on 15th November |
| 1748 | On constant active service and in command |
| 1748 | May 26th: promoted to Vice-Admiral of the Blue |
| 1749 | 3rd Son, Hon Chaloner Hawke was born[5] (named for Sir Chaloner Ogle, Admiral of the Fleet) |
| 1750 | Royal Visit on board Hawke's ship at Spithead to honour him (Prince Fred & Princess of Wales) |
| 1752 | Back on half pay |
| 1752 | Daughter Catherine was born |
| 1755 | Admiral in command of the Western Squadron |
| 1755 | Command of HMS St George flagship |
| 1755 | Apr: went to sea and took wife Kitty with him |
| 1756 | Hawke took over the Mediterranean Fleet command after Byng was 'ill', commanding Antelope |
| 1756 | At the Bay of Biscay blockaded and attacked French vessels at Rochefort |
| 1756 | Jul 4th: hoisted his flag in the Ramillies (Minorca had fallen to the French) |
| 1756 | Oct 29th: death of his wife Catherine at Lymington,[6] Hawke was in the Mediterranean at the time |
| 1757 | Applied for leave, to go to The Grange in Swaythling, nr Southampton to be with his family |
| 1757 | Feb 24th: appointed Admiral. July-Oct commanded vessels to capture Rochefort |
| 1758 | Combined operations, under the Command of Howe, but Hawke briefly resigned in indignation, he was persuaded to resume his duties but health problems forced his repatriation |
| 1759 | In command of the Western squadron and blockaded the French at Brest |
| 1759 | Part of the French fleet, during gales, slipped out of the port and Hawke gave chase |
| 1759 | Quiberon Bay. Hawke destroyed part of the French fleet and ended fears of invasion |
| 1760 | Jan 21st: returned to England a hero and to a Reception by the King |
| 1760 | House of Commons granted a pension of £2,000[7] p.a. for two lives (but no peerage) |
| 1761 | Commander of the Royal George, largest warship in the world. Nephew Capt Bladen Tinker was appointed to the same ship (probably at Hawke's request) |
| 1761 | Given the Freedom of the City of Dublin[8] |

---

[1] Barking Parish Records, Essex; one daughter died 13 September 1739 and another other on 3rd April 1740
[2] Newcastle Courant Sat 16 Jan 1742 reports Hawke's ship (Portland) setting sail for Barbados, and by July he and his wife are still there, as his son Edward is recorded as being born and baptised there
[3] TNA: PROB 11/1086/21. In his Will he bequeathed this ring (plus Chaloner Ogle's snuff box) to his grandson Edward Hawke
[4] A Guide to the Coasts of Hants and Dorset, p300 by Mackenzie Edward C. Walcott
[5] Saxton-in-Elmet Parish Register
[6] The Hawke Papers: A Selection 1743-71, p138, Ruddock F Mackay, 1990
[7] TNA: PROB 11/1086/21 Will of Rt Hon Edward Lord Hawke of South Stoneham, Hampshire
[8] The Gentleman's and London Magazine for January 1761, Vol. 30

# Appendices

**Elizabeth's Son - Edward Hawke (Guardian Martin Bladen) (Cont/...)**

|  |  |
|---|---|
| 1761 | Elder brother of Trinity House, a naval charity, (to 1781) |
| 1762 | Rear-Admiral (to 1765) |
| 1763 | Onwards, began to suffer health problems |
| 1765 | Vice-Admiral of Great Britain (to 1781) |
| 1766 | Privy Councillor |
| 1766 | First Lord of the Admiralty - in the Duke of Grafton's cabinet (to 1771) |
| 1766 | 20,000 acres of land in Florida was granted to Hawke by the Governor Sir Richard Russell (who renamed it Hawke's River)[1] |
| 1767 | Applied for Land Grant at Cape Breton, Nova Scotia, Canada (with 2 sons)[2] |
| 1767 | Member of the Admiralty Board, attended 118 out of 131 meetings |
| 1767 | Jan 15th: Admiral of the Fleet |
| 1768 | Member of the Admiralty Board, attended 126 out of 144 meetings |
| 1768 | Succeeded Sir William Rowley as Admiral of the Fleet (to 1781) |
| 1769 | Member of the Admiralty Board attended 118 out of 146 meetings |
| 1769 | Captain James Cooke named Hawke's Bay New Zealand in honour of him |
| 1770 | Member of the Admiralty Board attended 156 out of 186 meetings |
| 1770 | His son, Martin (barrister) married Cassandra Turner |
| 1771 | Hawke resigned to King George III as First Lord |
| 1772 | Retired from sea-going service, lived in Sunbury-on-Thames |
| 1773 | Hawke's second son Lieut.Col Edward (aged 27) died in a hunting accident |
| 1776 | May 20th: elevated to the peerage as Baron Hawke of Towton, Yorks |
| 1777 | Hawke living at Sunbury, son Chaloner either visiting or living at Scarthingwell |
| 1777 | Death of his son Hon Chaloner Hawke, knocked down by a post chaise |
| 1780 | Wrote his Will |
| 1781 | Oct 17th: died at Sunbury; Oct 31st, buried Church of St Nicholas, North Stoneham, near Swaythling |
| 1782 | Jan 7th: Will proved |
| 1782 | Publication of Hawke's: 'A Seamans Remarks on the British Ships of the Line' |

**Admiral Edward Hawke's Son - Martin Bladen Hawke (2nd Baron)**

|  |  |
|---|---|
| 1744 | Apr 20th: born |
| 1754-6 | Aug 1st: attended Eton School |
| 1760 | Inherited Glastonbury Abbey and estate from his Uncle (Gov) Thomas Bladen |
| 1760 | Mar 7th: received pension of £2,000 p.a. (part of his father's annuity from the government) |
| 1764 | Jul: attended Queens College, Oxford University[3] |
| 1766 | Nov 18th: admitted to Lincoln's Inn |
| 1768 | Whig MP for Saltash (to 1774) |
| 1769 | Rented a house in France, near Lisle (learning the French language) |
| 1770 | Jan 9th: spoke on the House of Commons on the "State of the Nation" |
| 1771 | Feb 6th: married at St George's Hanover Square London Cassandra Turner (youngest dau of Sir Edward Turner of Ambrosden, Oxford) |
| 1771 | Lived at Bloomsbury Square, his father's Admiralty residence |
| 1771 | Feb 21st: presented at Court |
| 1771 | Presented with the Honorary Degree of Doctor in Civil Law (as a Benefactor of Oxford University)[4] |
| 1772 | Jan 16th: daughter Cassandra Julia was born |
| 1773 | Speech in the Commons regarding Naval matters |
| 1774 | 1st son Edward Henry Hawke was born (later 3rd Baron) |
| 1774 | Feb 25th: voted against Administration on Grenville's Act |
| 1774 | Won the candidacy for MP, but was defeated in the election as MP for York Magistrate |
| 1775 | Old Bailey case regarding theft[5] |
| 1777 | Apr 1st: son Martin Bladen Edward Hawke was born |
| 1779 | Dec 10th: daughter Catherine born but died within 12 weeks of convulsion fits[6] |
| 1781 | Rev. Robert English licensed Chaplain to the Hawke family |

---

[1] TNA: PROB 11/1086/21 - Bequeathed 23,000 acres in East Florida to his only surviving son Martin Bladen Hawke, but says the land was "granted to him by the King". So the grant by Governor Russell was clearly by direction from King George III

[2] A History of the Island of Cape Breton by Richard Brown. 1869, p366

[3] Oxford University Alumni 1500-1886

[4] Bath Chronicle and Weekly Gazette, Thursday 11th July 1771

[5] Constantine Molloy indicted at the Old Bailey for stealing a cloth great coat from Bladen Hawke at Bloomsbury. Prosecutor, however, did not appear and so Molloy was acquitted

[6] Saxton-in-Elmet parish register. Catherine Hawke was buried in the chancel at Saxton Church

# Early Yorkshire Bladens

**Admiral Edward Hawke's Son - Martin Bladen Hawke (2nd Baron)**

| | |
|---|---|
| 1781 | Oct 17th: succeeded father as 2nd Baron Hawke (inherited 23,000 acres of land in Florida)[1] |
| 1782 | Joint Executor (with 3 others including Jeremiah Tinker) of his father's Will |
| 1783 | Chairman of East Florida Claims Committee (fought the Committee's cause in the Lords) |
| 1783 | Mar 13th: daughter Catherine Isabella was born, died 10 August 1786 |
| 1783 | Jun 21st: living at Scarthingwell Hall, first visit to them by Philippa Brooksbank |
| 1783 | Oct: social gathering: York Races, a Hunt Ball, with Brooksbank friends |
| 1784 | Slaves from his father's plantation of 20,000 acres[2] in Florida were repatriated to Dominica, some died en route and he wrote 3 letters to William Pitt Jnr TNA: PRO 30/8/143 complaining about the deaths |
| 1784 | Jul 29th: death of daughter Isabella Hawke[3] |
| 1785 | Smallpox in nearby Harrogate |
| | Admiral Hawke left Martin £11,000 to improve the Scarthingwell property |
| 1790 | Jan 18th: Lord & Lady Hawke dined with the Brooksbanks, they were Godparents to their new-born baby, called Edward Hawke Brooksbank[4] |
| 1790 | Jun 1st: Lord & Lady Hawke are at their London residence, Portland Place (where Philippa Brooksbank dined with them) |
| 1792 | Jul: Duel between Benedict Arnold and the Earl of Lauderdale, Hawke was Arnold's second |
| 1795 | Purchased a Game Duty Licence for himself and his son Edward |
| 1796 | Dec 1st: Mr Brooksbank (family friend) painted Lady Hawke's favourite lapdog |
| 1796 | Still at Portland Place: accepted a position on Sir John Sinclair's new Board of Agriculture |
| 1798 | Lord & Lady Hawke dined with the Brooksbanks at Healaugh Hall at Tadcaster |
| 1798 | Resigned as Vice-Captain of the Northern Regiment of West Yorkshire Cavalry in favour of his son |
| 1798 | JP at Wakefield Quarter Sessions |
| 1803 | Corresponded with Joseph Banks, Botanist on Capt Cooke's voyage to Brazil and Tahiti |
| 1805 | Mar 27th: died at Portland Place, Westminster |

**Admiral Edward Hawke's Son - Edward Hawke**

| | |
|---|---|
| 1746 | Born in Swaythling, Hampshire |
| | Lieutenant-Colonel in the Army |
| 1762 | 29th March. Ensign Coldstream Guards along with friend William Bosvile |
| 1765 | 13th September, promoted to Captain in 5th Foot[5] |
| 1769 | Rank of Major. Served in France and Africa |
| 1770 | Went to Morocco on a short visit with Capt William Bosvile |
| 1773 | 5th October - Married in Dublin |
| 1773 | Killed in a duel in Ireland before 15th October |

**Admiral Edward Hawke's Son - Hon. Chaloner Hawke**

| | |
|---|---|
| 1749 | Born, named after Sir Chaloner Ogle 1681-1750 |
| 1756 | Attended Eton School, arriving 18 Jan 1756[6] |
| 1765 | 14th August, entered into an apprenticeship indenture with Andrew Thompson, Merchant of London |
| 1767 | Applied for grant of land at Cape Breton, Nova Scotia, Canada (with father and brother Martin)[7] |
| 1775 | Admitted fellow commoner at Trinity College, Cambridge in March |
| 1775 | Cornet - Royal Regiment, North British Dragoons August (in Captain Ramsay's Troop)[8] |
| 1777 | Died 17th September, unmarried - killed on the road by a post chaise[9] |

---

[1] TNA: PROB 11/1086/21 Will of Rt Hon Edward Lord Hawke of South Stoneham, Hampshire

[2] The estate abutted that of Richard Russell who had 10,000 acres

[3] Saxton-in-Elmet parish register - 1784 DEATH The Honourable Miss Isabella Hawke the third daughter of the Right Honourable the Lord Hawke of Scarthingwell Hall by Cassandra his Lady, dau of Sir Edward Turner of Ambrosden Park, Oxfordshire, Bart. Died 29th July, buried in Saxton Chancel, aged 3 years. Died of water of the head

[4] Rev. Edward Hawke Brooksbank, M.A., J.P. born 19 December 1789 - died 1883

[5] Origin and Services of the Coldstream Guards, Vol. 2, Danniel MacKinnon, p489

[6] Eton College Records

[7] A History of the Island of Cape Breton, p366

[8] The History of the 2nd Dragoons, Royal Scots Greys

[9] Killed at Knightsbridge by his horse running against the pole of the post chaise. The Scots Magazine, Vol. 44. There was an unsupported theory that Chaloner was living with a woman and went by the name Mr Smith and when he died, the lady he resided with was called to the scene

# Appendices

**Admiral Edward Hawke's Daughter - Catherine Hawke (Kitty)**
Last of the children born to Admiral Hawke who survived and outlived him was Kitty:
- 1752 Born
- 1773 Reports that she may not have been sane
- 1824 Died

**Martin Bladen Hawke's Daughter - Cassandra Julia Hawke**
- 1772 Born 16th January
- 1793 Married 15 July 1793 to Samuel Estwick (MP) 1770-97 from Barbados (he died in Madeira)
- 1797 Husband died after a long, lingering illness in Madeira (buried Marylebone Old Church) where Cassandra erected a monument to his memory. Went to Madeira for his health
- 1800 Married secondly to Rev. Stephen Sloane, (son of Hans Sloane)
- 1812 Death of husband Rev Sloane, who died at Upper Harley Street in London[1]
- 1821 Third marriage to Thomas Green at Park Street, Grosvenor Square, London[2]
- 1825 Wrote her Will 15th December 1825
- 1825/6 Added two Codicils to her Will revoking previous bequests
- 1826 Probate, 1st July 1826

**Martin Bladen Hawke's Son - Edward Henry Hawke (Harvey-Hawke from 1798)**
*Earl of Rosse Line of Descent*
3rd Lord Hawke
- 1774 Born 3rd May, St George's Parish, Bloomsbury
- 1793 Queen's College, Oxford
- 1798 Aug 29th: married Frances Anne Harvey (*Debrett says 28th*) co-heir of Stanhope Harvey
- 1798 Legally changed surname to Harvey-Hawke by Royal Licence
- 1799 Birth of son Edward William Harvey-Hawke 4th Lord Hawke
- 1804 Birth of son Stanhope Harvey-Hawke 5th Lord Hawke on 18th January, Baron of Towton
- 1805 Succeeded to the title Baron Hawke of Towton upon the death of his father 27th March
- 1806 Birth of son Martin Bladen Harvey-Hawke
- 1809 Lady Hawke met her cousin Jane Austen
- 1810 Aug 19th: wife died
- 1824 Nov 29th: died

**Martin Bladen Hawke's Son - Martin Bladen Edward Hawke**
*Lord Hawke Line of Descent*
- 1777 Born
    Attended school at Hammersmith (fished in the Thames - for chad)[3]
- 1781 Grandfather died, bequeathed him diamond ring, gold watch, his best pistols made by Hodges, mathematical instruments, his best gun and best sword, emerald ring and a guilt uniform sword[4]
- 1795 Wrote 'The Ranger, a Collection of Periodical Essays, inscribed to Rev Thomas Atwood M.A. by the Hon. M.B.E. Hawke and Sir R Vincent'
- 1796 8th June - Dined with Lord & Lady Hawke and Philippa Brooksbank[5] and others (including 6 officers, Surrey Regiment) (at Scarthingwell)
- 1796 9th July - Dined at Scarthingwell with Lord and Lady Hawke and Philippa Brooksbank, followed by a play with the actress Mrs Siddons, play called "The Gamester"(violent thunderstorm that night)[6]
- 1798 Lord Hawke and family dined with their Brooksbank neighbours
- 1798 Captain of Troop, Northern Regiment, West Riding Yeomanry Cavalry
- 1797 Entered St John's College, Cambridge 23rd June[7]
- 1799 M.A.
- 1803 Wrote a poem about the Raby Hunt in Yorkshire
- 1805 Resigned as Army Captain

---

[1] The Literary Panorama, 1812
[2] Dod's Peerage, Baronetage and Knightage of Great Britain and Ireland
[3] The Sporting Review by Craven: The Late Hon. Martin Bladen: A Sketch of his Sporting Career by Nimrod (Charles James Applerley 1777-1843)
[4] TNA: PROB 11/1086/21 Will of Rt Hon. Edward Lord Hawke of South Stoneham, Hampshire
[5] Diary of Philippa Brooksbank 1781
[6] Diary of Philippa Brooksbank 1781
[7] Cambridge University Alumni 1261-1900

**Martin Bladen Hawke's Son - Martin Bladen Edward Hawke (Cont/...)**
*Lord Hawke Line of Descent*

| | |
|---|---|
| 1805 | May have been a House of Commons Whip[1] |
| 1806 | Wrote another poem "Trafalgar: or Nelson's Last Triumph"[2] |
| 1807 | Jun 6th: fought a duel with Colonel Mellish, Hawke unhurt[3] |
| 1809 | Friend Thomas Gascoigne accidentally killed whilst hunting with Hawke[4] |
| 1815 | Fishing on the River Tweed (caught 11 salmon in one day) |
| 1815 | Fishing on the River Tay (caught fish weighing 20-40 pounds-one 48" long) |
| 1815 | Mar 8th: married Hannah Nisbet (daughter of Thomas Nisbet of Mersington, Scotland) |
| 1815 | Wife Hannah was in Brussels where she "rides close to the Battle of Quatra Bras 'Out of Curiosity'"[5] |
| 1815 | Hannah attended Lady Richmond's Ball[6] on the Eve of Waterloo.[7] Not known if MBEH is with her, though as she was three months pregnant, then probably he was[8] |
| 1815 | Dec 25th: birth of son Edward Henry Julius (later 6th Baron Hawke) who was born in Brussels[9] |
| 1816 | Birth of daughter, who predeceased her father |
| 1818 | Birth of Thomas Edward Nisbet Hawke, born in Cologne, France |
| 1818 | Friend of Lord Byron |
| 1820 | Birth of a son Bladen Edward Martin Hawke |
| 1820 | Feb 13th: Paris. Invited to a Shooting Party with the Duc de Berri |
| 1824 | Attended a hunt in Yorkshire with Lord Hawke (Ed.Wlm Harvey-Hawke) and his brother Captain Stanhope Harvey-Hawke, both were his nephews |
| 1824 | Wife died |
| 1826 | Living at Towton Hall, Yorkshire (part of Lord Hawke's estate near to Scarthingwell) |
| 1833 | Living in Tours, France in a large chateaux in Calais (on the road to Guines)[10] |
| 1837 | Death of daughter, after a long illness |
| 1838 | Visited nephew, then current Lord Hawke (Edward) |
| 1838 | Ayg 17th: raced his horse 'The Flea' at St Omer - lost |
| 1838 | Badsworth Hunt Ball, Pontefract (attended by Martin and nephew Lord Hawke) |
| 1839 | Died in Tours, France, from angina pectoris[11] |

---

[1] Duel with Col. Mellish - they were rival whips with opposing politics returning from a Yorkshire election
[2] The Monthly Review, or Literary Journal, Vol 4, original copy CUL Zz.17.37
[3] Hull Packet (Yorkshire) 9 June 1807
[4] Parlington papers
[5] Lord Hawke, a cricketing legend by James P. Coldham
[6] The ball was given for her son, Lord William Lennox 1799-1881 - the 4th son of the Duke of Richmond, William was on Wellington's staff as an aide-de-camp. Love, Sex, Death and Words: Surprising Tales from a Year in Literature by John Sutherland
[7] Ibid
[8] Lady de Lancey's Narrative (and others) confirms the ball took place on the eve of the Battle of Quatra Bras, two days before Waterloo. She said "Some soldiers were killed the next day still wearing their shoes and silk stockings worn at the [Quatra Bras] ball, they had not had time to change before the march to battle commenced
[9] Complete Peerage
[10] The Late Lord Hawke, The York Herald, Saturday January 23, 1869
[11] Ibid

# Appendices

## WILLS

### Will of John Lacy, 1582

"Sept 2. 1582. John Lacye of Leventhorpe, esquire, I do nominate and appointe my dearlie beloved children and sones in lawe James Stansfeld, Thomas Leighe, and Dorathie Watterhouse, wedowe, exores of this my laste will. Loving frendes Richard Tempest of the Tonge, Robert Grenwood of Westerton, John Wilkinson of Hallyfax and William Currer of Marley, supervisors. To Marye, the doughter of Walter Hartley which he begot of my doughter Elizabeth, 3li. At 16. To Ellen Watterhouse, dougher to the saide Dorathie towards her marriage 6 li. 13s 4d at 16 and also one cowe which I had of her heartofore. To every childe that I am grandfather unto as hereafter followethe: to Anne Lacye and Hellen Lacye, daughters of my sone Richard, either of them 10s. To Thomas Wood his children, begotten of my doughter Rosamonde, every of them 6s 8d. To the children of my sone in lawe Walter Paslew as ensewethe, viz to Francys his son 40s and to either of his two daughters begotten of Ellen, my daughter, late his wife, 6s 8d. To my sone Nicholas Lacye his thre daughters, every of them 6s 8d. To my sone in lawe James Stansfield his thre children, begotten of my daughter Margaret, to every one of them, 6s 8d. To John Lacye, sone to Richard, my eldest sone, theis parcelles of armarie followeinge, one corslet which the furniture thereunto belonging, two plate cote which sleves, one tente, two billes or leade males, one speare, one bowe and a sheaffe of arrows, one gune cauled a calever. Also I bequithe one longe chiste standing in a newe chamber with three lockes which all the evidences in yt to the kepinge of Martyn Birkhead, esquire, Richard Lacye and John Lacye his sone, and every of them sevallie to kepe his key, and if anie occasion shall fortune to be that there the thre above named persons shalbe present at the opening thereof. To my cosen John Lacye of Brearley esquire, the elder, one fishing nett caulled the ould (ascaue). To Martyne Birkhead esquire one graie gelding which is comenlie cauled Foerdaies. To Walter Tempest one gelding which I had of hym called Grayface. To every dalie man servant and maide servant which shall dwell within my house at the daie of my deathe, every one of them 6s 8d. To Dorathie Watterhouse in respect of her service 3li. 6s 8d. To every of my said supervisares towards theire charges 40s. Resedewe of goods (after payment of debts, etc) to my said executors equallie. Witnesses Walter Tempest, John Haryson and Henrie Currier. Proved Nov 10, 1582 by the Exors (Reg. Test, xxii, 284)"
End

### Will of Sir William Savile (Written 18$^{TH}$ July 1642, Codicil 1$^{st}$ Jan 1644, died 24$^{th}$ Jan 1644, Proved 27$^{th}$ Jan 1744, buried 15$^{th}$ Feb 1644)

To be buried (if with conveniency it may be) at Thornhill amongst my ancestors. Whereas on the 20 Nov 1634 I being then by reason of fines and other assurances seized of an estate in fee simple of and in divers manors lands etc in counties York, Nottm, Lincoln, Derby, Stafford, Oxon, Salop, Wilts and Co. of City of York, did by indenture of that date grant two-thirds thereof to my brothers-in-law John Coventry of Barton, Co. Somerset, Esquire and Sir John Hare of Stow Co. Norf, knt, and my friends Sir John Ramsden of Longley Co. York, knt, Sir Rd Hutton of Hutton Pannell Co. York, knt., Fran Nevile of Chivete Co. York Esq., Wm Walter of Sarsden Co. Oxford Esq., Chas. Greenwood, Clk Rector of Thornhill aforesaid and Henry Cooksonne gent, my servant. To hold to them for 20 years upon the trusts therein declared. My will is that the said lease be for payment of my debts, and if it and my personalty be insufficient for that purpose, my land and tithes in Craven to be sold, and my Exors to have power to demise for 21 years (reserving £5 rent per ann.) my manor in Hunsworth and all my lands in Birstall Co. York. My most deare and loving wife £500, and the best bed I have, and such a suit of hangings as she shall choose, and all the plate and jewels she commonly keepeth in her chamber or closet. Eldest son George all my arms, both horse and foot. Daurs Anne and Margt £5,000 each at 18. Son Wm. £500 at 21. Son Henry £200 yearly for life out of my lands in Alton Co. Stafford and £1,000 at 21. If my wife shall have a child before I make provision for it, I give it, if a son, £200 a year for life out of my lands in Co. Derby and £500 at 21; and if a daughter £4,000 at 18. Each of my daurs £120 per ann till they have their portions, out of my lands in Co. Derby. All my children to be bred in such places as my Exors shall think fit. John Coventry Esqr and the rest of my friends named with me in this my Will as parties to lease of 20 November 1634 (living at my death) £30 each. Servants 2 years' wages each, except those to whom I leave annuities. List of annuities set down in a separate paper, to be paid out of my lands and milnes in Derby, Claiton and Inburchworth during the several lives of the persons to whom I give same. Henry Allen to have the land he now is in possession of, part of my demesne of Thornhill, until my son Geo. is 21, paing for the same £200 per ann., and not ploughing any part of the ground the last 3 years of his term (Margin note: Md, that I doe not meane he shall by this bargaine have the 20 loades of hay I now pay him, but I meane that he enjoy the closes knowen by the name of Britan Closes and Gelder Closes"). I give my wards their marriages, except His Majesty's ward Wm Savile, "to whom I entreat my executors to be very kind, and if he doe well to give him the least halfe of his wife's portion". Friends: Sir Thos. Danby, Sir Ingram Hopton, John Vaughan of the Inner Temple Esq and Captaine Tho. Beamont £20 each and a horse out of my stable. My honourable kinswoman the Countess of Kent £50. My faithful friend John Selden Esq £50. £100 to be bestowed in rings and given to my friends in remembrance of me. Wife and friends Sir John Ramsden, Sr Rd Hutton, Fran. Nevill Esq Exors. My Exors to take (if the Mr. of the Wardes be so pleased) the wardship of my son. To each of my Exors £40, and the running of 6 horses in any of my parks until my son shall attain 21.

Witnesses Chas. Grenewoode, W. Armitage, George Cartwright, Willm Denison, Tho. Beaumont, John Batte and Joseph Sill. Proved 21 Jan 1643 in the house of John Savile in York, before Philip Broome, M.A. surrogate by Lady Anne Savill, Sir John Ramsden, Sir Rd Hutton, power being reserved for Francis Nevile.

List of annuities to be paid out of my lands and milnes in Denby, Claiton and Inburchworth, Co. York.

John Batt of Okwell Esq £20

Thos. Farran, gent, my servant £20

Joseph Sill of Thornhill, gent £20

**Robt. Bladen, my servant 20 marks**

Geo. Cartwright, Tho. Colbrand, Tho. Raulines, my servants, 20 nobles each

Tho. Addy, my servant and his wife, and the survivor 20 nobles

Joseph Sikes, John Milner, my servants, 5 marks each

CODICIL: 1$^{st}$ Jan 1643/4

"Upon perusal of my Will made the 18$^{th}$ of July 1643, finding that I have made noe provision for the maintenance of my sonne Wm. during his minority" and I have settled the inheritance of Barroby and the rest of my lands in Co. Linc on him. I hereby give to him the Manor and advowson of Barroby and all other my lands in Co. Linc. And because this cannot take effect during my wife's life in case she stand to her jointure, therefore I give my said son Wm. £100 yearly during his mother's life out of all my Manors., in Co. Salop with power of distress in default of payment. But if my wife do take to her thirds and waive her jointure, then this rent charge to cease, Sir Paul Nele to have as I have devised to Sr. Ingram Hopton, Mr Robt. Butler £10. Witnesses Jo. Cosin, Robert Butler, Tho. Ferrand, Sam Jackson, Paul Neile, J. Monckton.

**Will of Nathaniel Birkhead of East Hague, South Kirkby  TNA: PROB 11/211/845 and PROB 11/214/608**
**Wrote his Will on 12th February 1649, died 20th February 1649, Probate 24th April 1650**
Probate to Alice Rogers and, after her decease, letters of administration to Edmund Watson 24th June 1656 **(Pembroke, 48; Brent, 56)** "In the name of God Amen, The twelfth day of February in the year of our Lord God one thousand six hundred and forty-nine, I Nathaniel Birkhead of East Heage [Hague] in the parish of South Kirbee [Kirkby] in the county of York Esquire being weak in body but of perfect remembrance (praise be God) therefore do constitute and make this my Last Will and Testament in manner and form following. That is to say first and principally I commit and commend my soul to Almighty God my creator and redeemer hoping assuredly through the onlie merittous death and passion of Jesus Christ my Lord and sufficient Saviour to have forgiveness of all my sins and after this life ended to enjoy life everlasting among the elect in the kingdom of Heaven, and my body I commit to decent buryall where it shall please God to dispose of the same. Item, I will devise give and bequeath to my daughter Alice Rogers, widow, late wife of Edmund Rogers and to her heirs and assigns for ever, all that my capital messuage and tenement called Eastheage [East Hague] in South Kirbee [Kirkby] with the appurtenances wherein I now dwell situate lying and being in South Kirbee [Kirkby] in the aforesaid county of York. And all the houses edifices buildings barns stables dovecoates milnes barksides foulds orchard gardenscrofts and closes meadows pasture land tenement profits rents commodities hereditaments and appurtenances whatsoever to my said capital messuage or tenement belonging or appertaining on to or with the same with or common lee hereto for use demised occupied or enjoyed or reputed taken or known as part and parcel or member thereof with all and singular their appurtenances lying and being in South Kirbee [Kirkby] aforesaid, North Emsall, South Emsall in the aforesaid county of York. And the reversion thereof and all other my lands tenements and hereditaments whatsoever situate lying and being in South Kirbee [Kirkby], North Emsall and South Emsall aforesaid or elsewhere within the parish of South Kirbee [Kirkby] with the appurtenance. Item, I devise will and give and bequeath to my said daughter Alice Rogers and her heirs and assigns for ever the reversion when it shall fall immediately after my decease of Alice Birkhead, widow, late wife of Daniel Birkhead, Doctor of Divinity my brother, deceased, of my lands tenements and hereditaments with their appurtenances lying and being in Aselby [Aislaby] within the parish of Eglecliffe [Eaglescliffe] within the bishopric of the County Palatine of Durham also Dureme in Essenham within the said County Palatine of Durham which said premises the said Alice Birkhead hath and holdesth for the term of her natural life. Item, I give devise will and bequeath to my <u>grandchild Nathaniel Bladen</u>, <u>sonne of John Bladen</u>, deceased, and to his heirs and assigns forever, all those my manors or lordships of Harden and Haworth with all and singular their rights rents member and appurtenances lying and being in the aforesaid county of York and to the said manors or lordships belonging or appertaining. And also that my messuage and tenement containing one burgage and a half situate lying and being in Wakefield in the aforesaid county of York, in one street there called Westgate now in the hands and occupation of Thomas Norton or his assigns and all houses edifices buildings barns, stables barksides foulds gardens orchards and crofts to the said messuage or tenements belonging or appertaining. And also one close of land arable meadow and pasture called Burman Croft lying in and being in Wakefield aforesaid now also in the tenure and occupation of the said Thomas Norton or his assigns. Item, I give devise will and bequeath to my nephew Robert Thompson and his heirs and assigns for ever that messuage half Burbage or tenement situate lying and being in Wakefield as aforesaid in the said street called Westgate wherein the said Robert Thompson now dwelleth, all edifices buildings garden and crofts to the said messuage half Burbage or tenement belonging or appertaining. Item, I give and bequeath to my daughter Elizabeth Lindsey wife of Robert Lindsey Esq fifty pounds, to be paid to her within one year after my decease in full satisfaction to her child's part and portion of all my goods cattels chattels having heretofor given her £1,500 for her preferment. All the rest of my goods cattels and chattels credits and debts I give and bequeath to my said daughter Alice Rogers. I do make the said Alice Rogers my said daughter sole executor of this my last will and testament, I the said Nathaniel Birkhead These being witnesses: Robert Arnold, Daniel Barber, William Tontell, his mark and Richard Bevitt.

**Will of Lady Frances Fairfax, 1692/3**
In the name of God Amen, I Lady Dame Frances Fairfax of Steeton in the Countie of the City of York doe make and ordain This is My Last Will and Testament, revoking all former Wills. First I bequeath my soul to God that gave it; and to Jesus Christ My Redeemer By Whose Merits I hope to be saved: And my Body to be decently buried at the discretion of my Executors hereafter to be named. And as to that Temporal Estate which God hath given me I bequeath as followeth. After my Debts and Funeral Expenses be paid and Discharged. First My Will and Mind is, that my debt to Mr Christopher Jackson of four hundred pounds be paid out of my estate for which I have given him my bond; and also my debt to William Topham, clerke, as it was given in upon account <u>to Mr Nathaniel Bladen</u>. Item, I give to my son Thomas Fairfax his father's picture set in gold: and the Great Bible in the Chappell. I give to my Daughter Catherine Fairfax[1] her late husband's picture and My Chariot. I give to my grandson William Fairfax my husband's picture at large: and Sir William Fairfax his mother's picture and all the goods in the Great Hall. I give to Mr Robert Fairfax my grandson three pounds and to Mrs Frances Fairfax and Mrs Elizabeth and Mrs Allathea three pounds each one. <u>I give to my grand children Wm Bladen and Martin his brother and also to Mrs</u>

---

[1] The fact that Lady Fairfax mentioned daughter Catherine in her will, which was written on 4th October 1692, shows Catherine survived, which is contrary to Markham's claim, in Admiral Robert Fairfax, p32, when he said, "Lady Lister's husband died very soon after the date of this last letter [1660] and soon afterwards she was married to Sir Charles Lyttleton of Hagley. Her second husband was appointed Deputy-Governor of Jamaica in 1662; and he went out to the West Indies, accompanied by his wife. She died there, with her infant son Henry on January 26, 1663. She was buried under a monument in a church which was entirely destroyed by an earthquake in 1692"

# Appendices

Isabella, Catharine, Frances and Elizabeth Bladen all my plate, linen, beddings and hangings and all the rest of my household goods to be equally divided amongst them. I give to my niece(?) Mrs Elizabeth Jackson Sir Edward Challoner's picture. I give to my nephew Mr Christopher Jackson a young black Filly. I give to Mr William Topham Junior and to Christopher Topham his brother ten shillings each one.[1] I give to the poor of the parish of Bolton Percy the sum of five pounds. I Make and Appoint my son Thomas Fairfax and my son Nathaniel Bladen sole executors of this My Last Will and Testament. In witness whereof I doe hereunto set my hand and seal this twenty ninth day of October in the fourth year of the reign of William and Mary King and Queen Anno Domini one thousand Six Hundred and Ninety Two. Witnessed by: Brian(?) Spence, Hayford Brown, Frances Fairfax.

## Will of Dr Richard Berry, Written 8th May 1651; 1st Codicil 29th May 1651, 2nd Codicil 4th June 1651, 3rd Codicil 8th June 1651; Probate 4th July 1651. TNA: PROB 11/217/545 - Abstract

Daughter Mary to have £100 per quarter whilst debts are settled then £300 per annum annuity.

Her husband to take the Berry surname and, if he does, they would have his lands in Hemsworth, Kinsey, Hodroyd and Havercroft. Other bequests to nephews and friends. Principal beneficiary to be his faithful and true friend John Fountaine. £20 annuity to nephew Marmaduke Monckton. Burial to be at night-time, with no Clerk or ceremony. 3 codicils added, one concerning Levetts.

## William's Branch:
### Will of Gerret van Sweringen of St Mary's, St Mary's County, Maryland- Abstract

Dated 25th October 1698, proved February 1698/9

To two sons viz Joseph and Charles equally and heirs, dwelling house, also the 'Council Rooms' and 'Coffee House' and lands thereto belonging. In the event of both sons aforesaid dying without issue, said estate to pass to daughters (un-named) by present wife. Wife (un-named) to have estate during widowhood, and she is not to be disturbed by child (un-named) or son-in-law (un-named). To daughters aforesaid personalty; son Joseph appointed Guardian of Daughters. To priests of Roman Catholic Church personalty. Execs: Wife aforesaid together with son Joseph aforesaid. Charles Carroll mentioned ref care of younger children. Test: Nich Croutch, Wm Asquith, Thos Grunwin, Thos. Sinnodd

### Will of Mary van Sweringen of St Mary's, St Mary's County, Maryland - Abstract

Written 17th February 1712/13, probate 5th September 1713

To daughters Dorothy and Tereshea van Sweringen personalty.

To son-in-law Wm Bladen and daughter Bladen and to dau Elinor Carroll personal estate.

To son Joseph, ex., residue of estate real and personal, including 200 a.,

"The Point" nr St Mary's to maintain daus Dorothy and Tereshea aforesaid

Test: Ann Maloni, Hannah Bantom, Wm Asquith.[2]

### Will of Benjamin Tasker (husband of Anne Bladen), written 15th February 1766, proved 30th December 1768

[The Hon'ble] Benjamin Tasker of the City of Annapolis Esq. Will 15 February 1766: proved 30 December 1768. To my wife Ann the dwelling house and lots adjoining and all plate and personal estate, she to be executrix. Land and negroes, to be sold and produce divided between her and my children. To my daughter Anna Ogle £2,500. To daughter Rebecca Dulany £2,500. To daughter Elizabeth Lowndes, wife of Mr Christopher Lowndes £2,500 to be used in trust for her during her husband's lifetime. To daughter Frances Carter, wife of Robert Carter in Virginia £2,500. Whereas the late Governor Ogle left me one of his executors, and each of his daughters £1,000, already paid his eldest daughter, to his youngest daughter to be paid as on my Book of Accounts marked S.O. fol 40. To my four grandsons which are my godsons viz Benjamin Ogle, son of the late Governor Ogle, Daniel son of Daniel Dulany, Benjamin son of Christopher Lowndes and Benjamin son of Robert Carter of Virginia £1,000 each. To my daughter Ann Ogle, Mr Christopher Lowndes and Robert Carter £1,000 in Bank of England for use of Benjamin Benson when 21, meanwhile the interest for his education in some public school in Great Britain. As my son Benjamin Tasker deceased by his Will desired me to sell his real estate I make the aforesaid three his executors or any two of them. As two tracts of land in Frederick County one called Vine containing ___, the other the Will, containing 100 acres, belonging to late Governor Ogle were patented to Mr William Steuart and by him conveyed to me I give them to Benjamin Ogle heir at law to the said Governor. Witnesses: Joseph Galloway, Sam'l Galloway, And'w Buchanan. Before Walter Dulany, Commissary General 4 July 1768 Ann the widow swears to above will. Administration with will annexed to Osgood Hanbury and William Anderson attorneys for Anne Tasker, relict in Prerogative Court of Canterbury for receiving dues and transferring £10,000 in capital stock of Bank of England, except £1,000 thereof etc. Second grant 20 November 1770 to James Anderson of Great Tower Hill in parish of St Olave Hart Street London, merchant, as one of attorneys for Ann Tasker, widow, residing in Annapolis, on transferring £5,000 part of £9,950 in Bank of England to Anne Ogle of Annapolis, widow and Benjamin Ogle of ditto gentleman, also £3,950 to said Benjamin Ogle, also £1,000 to said Ann Ogle of said Annapolis, Royal and Christopher Lowndes and Robert Carter Esquires. Administration of goods in Kingdom of England 3 November 1772 to said James Anderson of Great Tower Hill, St Olave Hart Street, London, Merchant, attorney for Anne Tasker, relict and executrix.[3]

---

[1] One of the young Topham youths was referred to by Admiral Robert Fairfax ... "My Aunt Bladen tells me that young Topham is at Steeton and very often drunk and rides with his groom, but when she comes down, she will make him ride alone"

[2] Maryland Calendar of Wills, Vols. II and III

[3] Virginia Gleanings in England: Abstracts of 17th and 18th Century English Wills and Administrations Relating to Virginia and Virginians: a Consolidation of Articles from The Virginia Magazine of History and Biography. By Lothrop Withington. 1903

# Early Yorkshire Bladens

**Will of Thomas Bladen, written 26<sup>th</sup> July 1777, codicil 5<sup>th</sup> March 1780, probate 26<sup>th</sup> August 1780**

I Thomas Bladen, late of Albemarle Street in the parish of St George Hanover Square in the county of Middlesex but of The Grange in the parish of Low Leyton in the county of Essex Esquire do make this my Last Will and Testament in manner following. I give unto my dear wife, Barbara Bladen, the annuity I have on the life of a Robert Colebrook Esquire for the life of my said wife. If the said Robert Colebrook shall so long live and from and after the decease of my said wife if the said Robert Colebrook shall her survive then the said annuity shall fall into and be considered as part of the residue of my personal estate, also I give unto my said wife all the rents of my Glastonbury Estate and of my house in Albemarle Street that shall be due to me at my decease and up to the next general quarter day after my death, also all the interest or dividends of my East India stock that shall be due to me at my decease and up to the next half yearly day after my decease when the rent interest or dividends shall become due and likewise all arrears of the said Robert Colebrook's annuity which shall be due at my decease and up to the next quarter day of payment thereof after my decease. Also I give unto my said wife all my household goods, furniture, plate, coaches, chaise, horses, stock goods and things whatsoever which shall be in or about my houses either in town or country at the time of my decease except money or securities for money and my pictures which pictures I direct to be sold with the residue of my personal estate as after mentioned to and for my said wife's own use and except I give unto my servant Richard Birk, if he shall be living with me at my death but not otherwise, one hundred pounds. I give unto my cook Skinner and to my laundry maid Sarah twenty five pounds each if they shall be respectively living with me at the time of my demise but not otherwise. I give and devise unto Martin Bladen Hawke esq, son of the Right Honourable Lord Hawke his heirs executors or administrators and assigns all my manors, messuages, farms, lands, tenements and hereditaments whatsoever at Glastonbury in the county of Somerset, also my house in Albemarle Street wherein I lately dwelt and all my real estates whatsoever in the kingdom of Great Britain and in America with their and every of their appurtenances and likewise all the rest and residue of my personal estate and effects whatsoever and wheresoever and of what nature or kind save In trust that he the said Martin Bladen Hawke his heirs executors administrators and assigns shall and do sell and dispose of the same to the best advantage and out of this money to be raised by the sale thereof pay or cause to be paid the sum of ten thousand pounds part thereof pursuant to my covenant in the Settlement made on the marriage of my daughter Harriet with the Earl of Essex and whereas on the marriage of my said daughter Harriet with the said Earl of Essex I advanced and paid as part of her marriage portion the sum of ten thousand pounds and by her said marriage settlement I have, as above mentioned, covenanted to pay the sum of ten thousand pounds more as the farther portion or fortune and whereas by the settlement made on the marriage of my daughter Barbara with the Honourable Henry Saint John I have committed to pay the sum of ten thousand pounds as a further part of this my said daughter Barbara's marriage portion. Now therefore in order to make her my said daughter Barbara equal in fortune with her said sister, Lady Essex and as it is my express will and desire that they may have and receive from me equally one with the other as my affection is equally divided between them. I give and bequeath unto the said Martin Bladen Hawke, his executors administrators and assigns from and after the decease of my wife Barbara the sum of ten thousand pounds upon trust to invest and place the same out for interest in his or their name or names in or upon good government or real security and to pay or to permit and suffer my said daughter Barbara and her assigns during her life to receive the interest dividends and produce thereof to and for her own separate and private use notwithstanding her said coverture it being my will that the same shall not be subject to the certain debts or encumbrances of her said husband and from and after the decease of my said daughter Barbara then, upon trust to pay and divide the same sum of ten thousand pounds and the stocks funds and securities wherever and whenever the same shall be then placed out and invested into and among all the children of my said daughter Barbara as well as sons and daughters in such shares and proportions as she my said daughter notwithstanding the said coverture shall either by her last Will and Testament to be executed in the presence of and attested by two more creditable witnesses or by any deed or other instrument in writing to be signed and sealed by her in the presence of and attested by the like number of witnesses give direct or appoint and for want of such gift direction order or appointment then unto and among all the said children equally share and share alike and if but one such child then to such child the share of a son to be paid and payable to him at his age of twenty one years or day of marriage which shall happen first and in the mean time I direct the entrust of the said children's respective shares or so much thereof as the said Martin Bladen Hawke his executors administrators or assigns shall think proper to be applied for and towards their respective maintenance and education but in case my said daughter Barbara shall dye without leaving issue such all of them shall die before they shall become entitled to the said ten thousand pounds as aforesaid, then upon trust to pay and apply the sum of five thousand pounds part of the said sum of ten thousand pounds unto such person or persons and to and for such uses intents and purposes as she my said daughter Barbara, notwithstanding her said coverture by her Last Will and Testament in writing or any other deed or instrument in writing to be signed and sealed by her in the presence of and attested by two or more credible witnesses shall give direct order or appoint and in default of such gift direction order or appointment with respect to the said sum of five thousand pounds and also as to the remaining five thousand pounds other part of the said ten thousand pounds upon trust to pay and apply the interest or dividends and produce thereof respectively unto and for the sole and separate use and benefit of my said daughter the Countess of Essex for her life notwithstanding her said coverture it being my will that this same shall not be subject to the certain debts or incumbances of the said Earl her husband and from and after her demise then upon trust to pay and apply the said last mentioned sums of five thousand pounds and the stocks funds and securities whenever and wherever the same shall be then placed out or invested into and among all the children of my said daughter the Countess of Essex as well sons as daughters in such shares and proportions as my said daughter the Countess of Essex notwithstanding her said coverture by her last will and testament in writing or any other deed or instrument in writing to be signed and sealed by her in the presence of and attested by two or more credible witnesses shall give direct order or appoint and for want of such direction order or appointment then unto and among all the said children equally share and share alike and if but one such child then unto such only child the share of a son to be paid and payable unto him at his age of twenty one years and the share of a daughter at her age of twenty one years or day of marriage which shall first happen and in the mean time I direct the interest of the said children's respective shares or so much thereof as the said Martin Bladen Hawke his executors administrators or assigns shall think proper to be applied for and towards their maintenance and education but in case my said daughter the Countess of Essex shall dye without leaving any issue or leaving such all of them shall dye before they shall become entitled to the said last mentioned sums of five thousand pounds and five thousand pounds as aforesaid then upon trust to pay and apply the same sums of five thousand pounds and five thousand pounds unto such person or persons and to and for such uses intents and purposes as my said daughter the Countess of Essex notwithstanding her said coverture by her last will and testament in writing or any other deed or instrument in writing to be signed and sealed by her in the presence of and attested by two or more credible witnesses shall give direct order or appoint and with regard to all

the rest and residue of the moneys that may arise by sale of my said real and personal estates upon trust that he the said Martin Bladen Hawke his heirs executors administrators and assigns shall and do place out and invest the same at interest in or upon good government or real security in his or their name or names and from and after the same shall be so placed out and invested upon trust to pay to or permit and suffer my said daughter Harriet Countess of Essex and her assigns to receive the interest dividends and produce of one equal moiety or half part thereof to and for her own separate and private use notwithstanding her said coverture. And also upon trust to pay to or permit and suffer my said daughter Barbara and her assigns to receive the interest dividends and produce of the other moiety or half part thereof to and for her my said daughter Barbara's own separate and private use notwithstanding her said coverture it being my express will that the same respective monies shall not be subject to the certain debts or incumbrances of the respective husbands of my said daughters and from and after the respective deceases of my said daughters said respective husbands or in case my said daughters shall respectively dye in their said husbands respective life times then and in either of the said cases upon trust to transfer assign pay and apply all and every the said last mentioned trust moneys to such person or persons and for such use and uses as they my said daughters notwithstanding their said covertures either by their respective last wills and testaments to be executed by each of them in the presence of and attested by two or more credible witnesses or by any other deed or instrument in writing to be respectively signed and sealed by each of them in the presence of and attested by the like number of witnesses shall give direct order or appoint and my will is and I do hereby declare that upon sale of all every or any of my said estates the money arising thereby shall be paid into the hands of the said Martin Bladen Hawke his heirs executors administrators or assigns and his or their receipt or receipts shall be a sufficient a discharge or discharges to the purchaser or purchasers thereof for the money which shall be paid by him her or them for the purchase or purchases of the same and that such purchaser or purchasers shall not be obliged to see to the application of such purchase money or any part thereof and my will is and I do hereby direct that until my said estates are disposed of the said Martin Bladen Hawke his heirs executors administrators and assigns shall pay and apply the rents issues profits and produce thereof in manner following, that is to say one moiety or half part thereof unto my daughter Barbara or her assigns and the other moiety or half part thereof unto my said daughter the Countess of Essex or her assigns for their respective sole and separate uses as aforesaid and I do appoint my said dear wife Barbara Bladen and daughters the said Countess of Essex and Barbara Saint John executrixes of this my Will and revoke all other Wills and Codicils by me at any time or heretofore made. In witness whereof I the said testator Thomas Bladen have to this my said Last Will and Testament contained in six sheets of paper affixed together at the top with my seal to the five first sheets hereof set my hand and to this the sixth and last sheet my hand and seal this twenty sixth day of July One Thousand Seven Hundred and Seventy Seven. Thomas Bladen, signed sealed published and declared by the said testator Thomas Bladen as and for his Last Will and Testament in the presence of us who in his presence at his request and in the presence of each other have hereunto subscribed our names as witnesses: Bateman Robson, Chris Norris of Lincolns Inn, Richard Hopkins, clerk to Messrs Robson and Norris.
5th March 1779
CODICIL I leave to my servant Richard Birk £50 in addition to what I have left him in the body of my Will and also I leave to his daughter Harriett Birk £50, Thomas Bladen.
Proved 26th February 1780 by the oaths of Harriet Countess of Essex and Barbara Saint John........

**Will of Barbara Bladen** London February 19, 1780 (wife of above)
I, Barbara Bladen of the parish of Saint George's do make this as my Last Will and Testament, I desire to be buried in the same vault with my dear husband and as privately as possible at one of the clock in the forenoon and only a hearst and one coach with my servants to attend me as pall bearers nor rings. I desire not to be nail'd up in my coffin under a week after I am dead. I leave each of the alms women of Low Leyton half a guinea a piece to buy them a Black Stuff Gown. I leave my daughter Barbara St John three thousand pounds for her own separate and private use notwithstanding her coverture it being my Will that the same shall not be liable to the certain debts or encumbrances of her husband General St John and, after her death (in case she has no children) to Lady Essex's children to be divided as Mrs St John thinks proper. I leave the two thousand pounds Lord Essex owes me to be divided between my four grandchildren to be paid them at the age of 21 years. I leave Thomas Bladen Capell two hundred pounds, I leave Lord Essex one hundred guineas for mourning. I leave General St John one hundred guineas for mourning. I leave my cousins Janssens, those that are Protestants, of Angoulême, one hundred guineas to be equally divided between the females but nothing to the males. I leave Thomas Bourdellou, my Godson, 20 guineas. I leave Hannah Skywar £20 a year for her life. I leave Mary Horseman 40 guineas and what clothes my daughters choose to give her, I leave Lady Essex the moiety of what I die possessed of for her own private and separate use notwithstanding her coverture. It being my Will that she shall not be liable to the control debts or encumbrances of her husband Lord Essex. I leave my daughter Barbara St John the other moiety of what I die possessed of (besides the three thousand pounds mentioned) for her own private and separate use and notwithstanding her coverture it being my Will that the same shall not be liable to the control debts or encumbrances of her husband. I leave my two daughters Barbara St John and Henrietta Countess of Essex my joint and sole executrixes, signed my hand and seal this present 18th of February 1780, Barbara Bladen.
20 April 1780 As I find by leaving laid out a good deal of my £6,000 and having given Mrs St John £2,000, that my stock will not procure as much as I intended to leave her which was £4,000.
4th February 1784 In the Prerogative Court of Canterbury appeared personally Barbara St John (wife of Honourable Henry St John) one of the Executors of the Will and Henrietta Countess of Essex - administration granted to both.

**Will of Barbara St John (née Bladen) - Abstract**
**PROB 11/1647, written 5th April 1821, proved 3rd August 1821**
The Hon. Barbara St John, widow of the Hon Henry St John, General of His Majesty's Forces being of sound mind memory and understanding do make this my Last Will and Testament as follows. Bequests to Capel cousins: Edward, William and Bladen Capel, great nephew Arthur Capel (son of John Thomas Capel), to Mary Ann Douglas now residing with me as a testimony of my sincere love and affection and as a reward for her kind and affectionate behaviour to my late husband and myself and also as a testimony of the comfort she has been to me her whole life in my affliction and bad health the sum of £3,000, plus an annuity of £100. To great-nephew Arthur Capel a picture. Executors Edward, William and Bladen Capel.

**Henry St John (husband of above) TNA: PROB 11/1604/134  Abstract**
Written 29th June 1816, proved on 8th May 1818
To be buried in the family vault at Lyddiard in Wiltshire.  Wife Barbara main beneficiary, along with his widowed sister Lady Louisa Bagot, sister-in-law Harriet, Countess of Essex and various St John nephews.

**Frances's Branch:**
**Will of Gervase Hamond, written 1706, probate 1707, PROB 11/496**
In the Name of God Amen I Gervas Hamond of Scarthingwell of the county of York Esq being in good health of body and of sound disposing mind and memory praise be therefore given to Almighty God do make and ordain this my Last Will and Testament in manner and form following.  That is to say, first and principally, I recommend my soul into the hands of Almighty God hoping assuredly through the meritorious death and passion of my Saviour Jesus Christ to have full and free pardon and forgiveness of all my sins and to inherit everlasting life and my body I commit to the ground to be decently buried in Saxton besides and as near as can be to my late dear wife.  If I shall happen to die within 20 miles of the said place my executors hereafter named not exceeding £40 in my funeral expenses and as touching the disposition of such temporal estate as it hath pleased Almighty God to bestow upon me I give and dispose thereof as followeth. Imprimis, whereas by a certain Deed of Settlement quadripartite made upon my marriage bearing date the 18th day of September in the four and twentieth year of the reign of our late Sovereign Lord King Charles II, I have full and good power and authority in case I should have any younger son or sons begotten on the body of Katherine, my said late wife deceased by any deed or deeds or by my Last Will and Testament in writing to be my me subscribed and sealed in the presence of two or more credible witnesses to grant limit or appoint to be going and issuing out of all and singular the manors messuages lands tenements and premises not thereby limited to the said Katherine my late wife for her life or her jointure now to me the said Gervase Hamond and my heirs immediately after the death of Joan Hamond my late mother deceased any annuity or annuities yearly rent charge or rent charges to any such younger son or sons for his or their life or lives so as no such annuity exceed the sum of £30 apiece by the year with clause of distress for non-payment thereof, the said annuities to take effect at any time I should appoint after the death of William Hamond Esquire my late father deceased and the said Joan Hamond my late mother, anything in the said Deed of Settlement to the contrary notwithstanding and by the said Deed of Settlement may more fully appear.  And whereas I have only one younger son Gervase Hamond begotten on the body of Katherine my said late wife, she my said late wife and also my said father and mother being all since deceased as aforesaid, now my will and mind is and according to and in pursuance of the said  recited power to me given as aforesaid I do hereby devise limit and appoint to my said younger son Gervase Hamond one clear annuity, or yearly rent charge of £30 per annum lawful English money every year and from and immediately after my decease for and during the tenure of his natural life to be going and issuing that all and singular the said manors, messuages, lands, tenements and premises charged and chargeable the same as aforesaid.  The said annuity to take effect immediately from and after my decease and in as large and ample manner as the said Deed of Settlement will allow.  And if it shall happen that my said annuity or yearly rent charge, or any part thereof, shall be behind unpaid in part or in all by the space of ten days next after the day or times whereon the same ought to be paid as aforesaid that then, and so often it may be lawful to and for the said younger son Gervase Hamond and his assigns into and upon my said manors lands and premises so charged and chargeable with the same as aforesaid and into every or any part thereof to enter and distraint and the distress and distressed then and there found to take lead drive and carry away and same in impound detain and keep until the said annuity or yearly rent charge and every part thereof with all arrearages thereof (if any be) be fully satisfied and paid unto my said younger son or his assigns.
Item, I give and devise unto my brother William Hungate (if he be living at the time of my death) £10 to buy him mourning with.  Item I give unto Miss Mary Anderton of Scarthingwell aforesaid the full sum of £300 and I also give unto her my own bed wherein I usually lie along with the bedding and other furniture thereunto belonging and also the silver spoon, cup and Knife and fork that my brother gave to me.  And I hereby discharge her of all accounts betwixt us and order my executors to seal her a general release.  Item I give and bequeath unto Katherine Treadaway £10.  Item I give and bequeath unto my steward Mr Richard Smith 20 guineas and all my wearing clothes and apparel whatsoever.  Item I give unto Christopher Baily my late servant £10.  Item I give and bequeath unto my eldest son William Hamond Esq the sum of 20 shillings in full of what he can or may claim or demand out of any part of my real or personal estate (except the entailed estate).  Item, I will and order that all my just debts be duly paid except such debts as I have as I and my eldest son stand bound for or have given security for which he, having been the occasion of borrowing, and they having been expended upon his account I think it but reasonable and equitable that he pay the same and accordingly I leave him charged therewith.
And I charge all my lands tenements and hereditaments which I have lately conveyed to Reginald Graham of Norton Conyers and Thomas Gill of Ripon both in the said county of York Esq upon certain trust therein mentioned and also my whole personal estate whatsoever with the payment of all my said debts (except before excepted).  And with the payment of all my legacies herein bequeathed and my funeral expenses and after the payment thereof I give all the rest residue both of my real and personal estate whatsoever unto the said younger son Gervase Hamond, his heirs executors and administrators forever and I make and appoint the said Reginald Graham and Thomas Gill joint executors of this my Last Will and Testament.  And I give unto the said Reginald Graham 5 broad pieces of gold and unto the said Thomas Gill 10 guineas for their care and pains in performing and executing this my last will, hereby revoking all former last wills by me heretofore made.  In witness whereof I have here unto set my hand and seal this 22nd day of July in the year of our Lord God 1706, Gervase Hamond. Presence: Philip Simpson, Sarah Calversy, James Ellershaw.

**Will of William Hamond, written 7th April 1711; Probate April 1713  PROB 11/532/279**
In the Name of God Amen, I William Hamond of Scarthingwell in the County of York being in sound mind and memory, praised be God but very weak do make this my last Will and Testament in manner and form following.  Imprimis, I recommend my soul to my maker and redeemer and my body to be decently but not costly buried at Saxton Church at the discretion of my Executrix hereafter named.  I being very sensible that my debts amount to a very great sum over and above what my personal estate will pay and satisfy, I therefore do hereby Will and fully empower my Executrix hereafter named to sell and dispose of such parts only of my lands tenements and hereditaments in Kirk Fenton, Little Fenton and Biggin in the county aforesaid as will pay and fully discharge all my debts, funeral expenses and legacies hereafter mentioned.  Item I give and bequeath to my dear brother Gervase Hamond the sum of £50 for mourning.  Item I give and bequeath to my dear cousin George Middleton the sum of 40 guineas.  Item I give and bequeath to Dr Johnson of Pontefract £10

for mourning. Item I give and bequeath unto Anthony Pratt the sum of £6 per annum during his natural life. Item I give and bequeath unto Elizabeth Banford the sum of £12 per annum during her natural life. Item I do Will and bequeath the guardianship of my children to my dear wife till they attain the age of 21 years and further do will and require they shall not marry till they attain the age of 21 years without the consent and approbation of my dear wife, but in case either of my said daughters should marry without her consent before they arrive at the age of 21 years, then I do leave it in the power of my said wife (excepting a sufficient recompense for their maintenance) to receive all the rents issues and profits of the remainder of my estate after my debts, funeral expenses and legacies are paid and satisfied to her only use and behoof during her natural life without being accountable to any person or persons whatsoever for the same. Lastly I do will and bequeath all my personal estate to my dear wife and do make and ordain her my executrix of this my Last Will and Testament. In witness whereof I have hereunto set my hand and seal this 7th day of April in 1711. William Hamond. Signed, sealed, published and declared to be my Last Will and Testament. In the presence of William Topham, Brian Kirk and Elizabeth Easterby.

**Will of Gervas Hamond (younger son of above and brother-in-law to Frances Bladen)**
**Will written 1737; proved 27th April 1757**
IN the Name of God Amen, I Gervas Hamond of Parlington in the County of York Esquire recommending my soul to the mercys of God Almighty and my body to be decently interred at Saxton in the Church there as near my dear father and mother as can be - if I shall dye within twelve miles of that place and that not above forty pounds shall be spent in my funeral do make and ordain this my Last Will and Testament of for and concerning such real and personal estate as God has blessed me with in manner following hereby revoking and annulling all former Will and Wills by me at any time heretofore made and published. Whereas Gervas Hamond late of Scarthingwell in the said County of York Esquire my late father deceased did in his life time by indentures of lease and release duly executed bearing date respectively the 19th and 20th days of July which were in the year of our Lord one thousand seven hundred and six grant and convey unto and to the use of Reginald Graham of Norton Conyers and Thomas Gill of Ripon in the said county of York esquires and their heirs and assigns all the messuages lands tenements and hereditaments whatsoever settled and limited to him his heirs and assigns in and by a certain Deed of Settlement made upon his Marriage being in all about the yearly value of £100 or so upwards and therein particularly mentioned and also all other the messuages lands tenements and hereditaments whereof he was seized in fee simple situate and being within the said county of York or elsewhere within the Kingdom of England together with their and every of their rights royalties members and appurtenances whatsoever upon Trust after his death out of the rents issues and profits of the said premises or by sale or devise thereof or any part thereof as to them should seem meet to raise levy and pay all such just debts of the said Gervas Hamond deceased and all such legacies as he should in and by his Last Will and Testament in writing particularly and expressly charge upon the said lands and premises and no other and after payment thereof and of the Trustees and charges upon trust and to the sole benefit and advantage of me, my heirs and assigns, forever and to and for no other use trust intent or purpose whatsoever and whereas the said Gervas Hamond, my said late father deceased, in and by his Last Will and Testament in writing duly made and published bearing date on or about the two and twentieth day of the same July did charge all the said lands and premises and all his personal estate whatsoever with the payment of all his debts except therein excepted and with the payment of all his legacies therein bequeathed and his funeral expenses and after payment thereof did give all the rest and residue both of his real and personal estate whatsoever unto me, my heirs executors and administrators forever and of his said Will made the said Reginald Graham and Thomas Gill his joint executors who in due form of law proved the same. And whereas several suits have been moved and carried on between the said Reginald Graham then Sir Reginald Graham baronet plaintiff from Frances Hamond widow and relict of William Hamond my elder brother deceased, Catherine Mary Hamond and Frances Hamond infants by their Guardian, daughters of the said William Hamond, Joseph Blake gentleman administrator of the said William Hamond and others defendants and between me the said Gervase Hamond plaintiff and the said Catherine Mary Hamond, Frances Hamond infants and Frances Hamond widow and the said Joseph Blake and others defendants touching the said premises which were afterwards on or about 6th June in the 13th year of the reign of her late majesty Queen Anne determined by the decree of the High Court of Chancery and the said premises directed to be sold and two thirds of the money arising by such sale after several reciprocal deductions and allowances to be made by each party to the other to be paid to me the said Gervase Hamond and the other third part thereof to the said infants Catherine Maria Hamond and Frances Hamond the which said decree was afterwards to wit on or about 14th day of May in the year of the reign of the late King George on a Rehearing of the said Causes on the petition of the said infants confirmed by the Lord Chancellor at least during the minority of the said infants. But he directed that the said estate should not be sold without the further direction of the court as by the said several Indentures last Will of the said Gervase Hamond my father deceased and the probate thereof and the said several certain orders relation being thereunto respectively had more at large may appear. And whereas the said Catherine Mary Hamond afterwards intermarried with Walter Brooke Esquire who together with the said Catherine Mary his wife, since deceased, on receipt of a moiety of the payment appointed to be paid to the said infants by the said certain order or satisfaction for the same did ratify and confirm the agreement proposed and approved by the High Court of Chancery and the said Frances Hamond, the daughter is also since dead having left Pullein her only daughter an infant of tender years so that the said lands and premises remain still subject to her claim of her mother's sixth part of the money to arise from the sale of the said premises after a proportionable deduction and allowance according to the directions of the said certain order with intent therefore to dispose of the said lands and premises and all my estate therein as hereinafter is mentioned, I do hereby give and bequeath all and singular the said lands tenements hereditaments and premises comprised or intended to be comprised in the said recited indentures of lease and release and Last Will of my father and all my estate right title trust interest property claim and demand therein and thereunto or in or to any part and parcel thereof and all and singular other my messuages land tenements and hereditaments and real estate whatsoever and where so ever unto my worthy friend Sir Walter Wagstaff Bagot of Blythfield in the county of Stafford Baronet and to his heirs and assigns forever, he paying the rent and out of the personal estate herein bequeathed to him all my just debts funeral expenses and legacies and I give to my three nieces Mary Gascoigne, Elizabeth Plumpton widow and Catherine Gascoigne the sum of £5 a piece and to my niece and god-daughter Ellen Gascoigne I give the sum of £10. Item I give to Dame Mary Gascoigne wife of my nephew Sir Edward Gascoigne Baronet the sum of 20 guineas to buy mourning with and to my god-daughter Mrs Gascoigne, eldest daughter of my said nephew Sir Edward Gascoigne I give the sum of £10 and to Mrs Elizabeth Gascoigne younger daughter of the said Sir Edward Gascoigne I give the sum of £5. Item I give to my two nieces Catherine Mary Brooke and Pulleyn to each of them one guinea to buy rings and I give to my nephew Robert Plompton Esquire two

guineas to buy a mourning ring and I do give to Henry Patrick my late servant £20 and to John Cheatham my now servant I give the like sum of £20 and I give to him who shall be my servant at the time of my death all my wearing apparel whatsoever.

I give to the poor of Saxton aforesaid cum Scarthingwell the sum of £5 and to the poor of Parlington I give the like sum of £5 and I give to the poor of Little Fenton cum Biggin the sum of £3 and my Will is and I do hereby order and direct that the said three last mentioned legacies to the poor shall be distributed in such proportions as my executor hereinafter named shall order and think fit all the rest residue and remainder of my goods cattle chattels rights credits and personal estate whatsoever after payment of my debts the said legacies and funeral expenses I give and bequeath unto the said Sir Walter Wagstaff Bagot whom I may constitute and appoint sole executor of this my last will and testament. In witness whereof I have hereunto put my hand and seal this 11th day of April in the year of our Lord 1737, G. Hamond, signed sealed published and declared by the said testator as his last will and testament in the presence of us who subscribed our names as witnesses thereunto at his request and in the presence of the said testator: Robert Hartley, James Catton, John Varley.

A Memorial of the above and within written Will was registered at Wakefield the 27th day of April 1757 near twelve at noon in Book A.V. page 562 and November 756. Ris. Bent Deputy Register.

THIS WILL was proved at London before the Worshipful Arthur Collier Doctor of Laws Surrogate of the Right honourable Sir George Lee Knight Doctor of Law, master Keeper or Commissary of the Prerogative Court of Canterbury lawfully constituted on the 25th day of May 1757 by the oath of Sir Walter Wagstaff Bagot Baronet sole executor named in the said Will to whom administration was granted of all and singular the goods chattels and credits of the deceased having been first sworn duly to administer.

**Elizabeth's Branch:**
**Will of James Ruthven, written 1st November 1698. Probate 9th December 1699. TNA: PROB 11/453/310**
In the Name of God Amen I James Ruthven in His Majesty's Regiment of Foot in the command of Colonel Francis Collingwood being sound in mind and body and of perfect memory praised be Almighty God for it but being bound by His Majesty's command for Antigua or some other of the Leeward or Caribbean islands and having [seen] before mine eyes the frailty and uncertainty of human life do make constitute ordain and declare and publish this my Last Will and Testament in manner and form following. In the first place I commend myself soul body and estate to the protection and disposal of Almighty God resting upon his mercy and the merits of my saviour Jesus Christ for the forgiveness of my sins and the salvation of my soul. And as to the temporal estate wherewith it hath pleased God to bless me whatsoever or wheresoever it shall be at the time of my death together with all my outstanding debts rights goods and chattels I give and bequeath them all and singular to my dear and loving wife Mrs Elizabeth Ruthven whom I make sole executor and legatee of this my Last Will and Testament. In witness whereof I have signed sealed published and declared this my Last Will and Testament this first day of November in the 10th year of the sovereign reign of our Lord King William 1698 in the presence of Cavendish Wooden Esq., Martin Bladen gent, and Robert Hawdy servant to Mr Wooden. Signed Ja. Ruthven.

**Isaac Sharpe (Last Husband of Elizabeth Bladen) - Will 1735 - Abstract TNA: PROB 11/675/329**
**Written 1735, probate 14th February 1736**
I, Isaac Sharpe, of the parish of Stepney, otherwise Stebbon-heath in the county of Middlesex, Clerk, do make and constitute this my Last Will and Testament in manner and form following....

£50 to son James Sharpe; £5 to grandson Branfill Sharpe; £5 to grandson Isaac Sharpe; £20 to wife Elizabeth for mourning; silver cup to son Thomas Sharpe (with his coat of arms engraven thereon); silver pint mug to son James; to grandson Lancelot Sharpe a silver half-pint mug. To sister Dorothy Sharpe £5 for mourning. Library books to be sold to pay debts; remainder to wife Elizabeth plus household goods, wife Elizabeth to be Supervisor of Will.

**Last Will and Testament[1] of the Right Honourable Edward Lord Hawke - Abstract TNA: PROB 11/1086/21**
**Written 25th September 1780, proved 2nd January 1782**
To be buried near his late wife in North Stoneham, Southampton and a monument to be erected. Principal beneficiaries: son Martin Bladen Hawke and daughter Catherine. Martin to receive pension of £2,000 p.a. (charged upon the Irish Establishment) granted by George II. Also Hawke's house in Hart Street, Bloomsbury Square and coach houses and stables in Southampton Street, Bloomsbury, 23,000 acres in East Florida. Daughter Catherine to have household goods, including and china from Goa in India given to the Admiral by Captain John Tinker. Sarah and Mary Birt to be carers for Catherine (until she regains her sanity)...... but in case it shall please God that she shall not be restored to a good and full sanity of mind before her death then I do hereby give and do bequeath to my dear grand-daughter Cassandra Hawke the only daughter now living of my said son Martin Bladen Hawke all the said several goods and things hereinbefore by me given to my said daughter.... And I give and bequeath to my grandson Edward Hawke an infant the eldest son of my said son Martin Bladen Hawke my diamond ring and my late uncle Colonel Martin Bladen's sapphire ring set round with brilliants and also my gold repeating watch with a large gold chain and the gold seals thereto belonging with my arms and crest on them respectively as likewise my gold snuff box that was Sir Chaloner Ogle's and my small gold ended cane with my crest and coronet on it.

Also I give and bequeath unto Jeremiah Tinker of Weybridge in the county of Surrey Esquire, James Brown and Thomas Collinson ... the sum of eight hundred pounds a year. ....... And I do hereby appoint the said Martin Bladen Hawke my son, Jeremiah Tinker, James Brown, Thomas Collinson and Sarah Birt and the survivor and survivors of them the Trustees for my said daughter during such time as long as she may continue in her present unhappy and melancholy condition...... I do hereby make ordain nominate constitute and appoint my said son Martin Bladen Hawke and the said Jeremiah Tinker, James Brown and Thomas Collinson executors of this my will and hereby revoke and make void all wills by me made and do declare this to be my last will and testament ....... In witness whereof ...... this twentieth fifth day of September in the year of our Lord One thousand seven hundred and eighty (Hawke) signed sealed published declared by the right honourable Edward Lord Hawke the testator as and for his last will and testament in the presence of us who in his presence and the presence of each other have subscribed our names as witnesses: James Shergold, Anthony Baker, Thomas Barnard.

---

[1] TNA: PROB 11/1086/21 Will of Rt Hon Edward Lord Hawke, 2nd January 1782

I Edward Lord Hawke, do declare that this writing shall be taken and considered as a codicil to my last will and testament and I do hereby give and bequest to my grandson Edward Hawke the eldest son of the Honourable Martin Bladen Hawke my son over and above the several legacies sums of money and items I have given to him by my said Will the sum of four thousand pounds seven hundred pounds owe and owing to me upon an assignment of a mortgage made to me by the Reverend Mr Thomas Mosley and others upon an estate late belonging to John Atkinson Esquire deceased situate lying and being in the Town and parish of Leeds in the county of York and secured to be paid to me with interest at four pounds per cent per annum and all my estate and interest in and benefit for the said mortgage to be paid and assigned to my said grandson Edward Hawke when and as soon as he shall attain his age of twenty one years. This will was proved at London with a codicil the seventh day of January in the year of our Lord one thousand seven hundred and eighty two.

**Will of Rt Hon. Martin Bladen Lord Hawke Baron of Towton TNA: PROB 11/1427/127**
**Written 15th March 1805, Proved 14th June 1805**

This is the Last Will and Testament of the Right Honourable Martin Bladen Lord Hawke Baron of Towton in the West Riding of the County of York this 15th day of March 1805, my eldest son the Hon. Edward Harvey Hawke being brought to my bed side by my particular desire, I do hereby make this my Last Will and Testament and appoint him the said Hon. Edward Harvey Hawke sole executor and residuary legatee of this Will and Testament hereby cancelling revoking and setting aside any other Will or Wills Codicil or Codicils that may have been made by me. I recommend to him my good and worthy friend John Fenton Tritton Esquire to assist him in carrying this my Last Will and Testament into execution. And I do so give, whether in law or equity, any power or powers to him the said Hon. Edward Harvey Hawke which I may have had at any time in law or equity for carrying this Will into effect and commend it to him to appoint the said John Fenton Tritton Esquire an assistant executor to him in the performance of this trust with £300 for a ring for a remembrance of the friendship between the two families and to make the value of the ring equal to £500 should the trouble undertaken by the said John Fenton Tritton Esquire require it. And I do hereby in pursuance of the powers and appointment given under the Will of the late Edward Lord Hawke my father bequeath to the Hon. Edward Harvey Hawke all the money and monies coming to me under such bequest under such Will or Wills or Codicils that from and out of the same recommend him to assign two third parts to his sister the Hon. Arabella Elizabeth Cassandra Hawke and the rest to dispose of as he thinks proper. I direct my legal debts may be paid and that I may be buried in Hampshire in the parish church of North Stoneham near my dear father and mother and ask my executor to give Mrs Sarah Birt, spinster, ten guineas for a ring, and I recommend her particularly to the countenance and protection of my executor. I leave my clothes to my servant John Rooks and ten guineas to each of my servants for mourning and two guineas more to those who attended my room except A. Culverwell and Nathaniel Storbitt whom I recommend to my executor and to give them each twenty guineas from and out of any money or moneys as reference being there was will appear hither to undisposed of - Hawke. Signed sealed and delivered in our presence by the testator whom before each other and in each other's presence have witnessed our and the testator's signature. A Culverwell, John Rooks, Nathaniel Storbitt. This Will was proved at London 14th day of June 1805.

**GENEALOGY**

The following is a part-genealogy from the Early Yorkshire Bladen family for information but is not intended to be comprehensive.

**Descendants of William Bladen**

1  William Bladen 1672-1718
+ Anne van Sweringen     1680 - 1727
   2  **Anne Bladen   1697 - 1775**
   +  Benjamin Tasker   1691 - 1768
      3  Benjamin Tasker  1720 - 1760
      +  Anne Kingdom (a Quaker) mar'd 1750
         Represented Maryland at Albany Conference with Benjamin Franklin (Pennsylvania). He was also an importer of thoroughbred horses. Lived at Belair (set in 2177 acres in Prince Georges County), inherited from brother-in-law Sam Ogle
      3  Anne Tasker 1723 -1817
      +  Governor Samuel Ogle      1694 - 1752 mar'd 1741
         4  Benjamin Ogle    1749 - 1808
         +  Rebecca Stilley
         Benjamin Ogle became the 9th Governor of Maryland and lived in the Belair Mansion that his father had built. Sam Ogle died in 1752 when his son Benjamin was a small infant and so, grandfather, Benjamin Tasker Senior stepped into assist and became a guardian for Benjamin. When Benjamin reached the age of 10 years he was sent, like many of the elite in Maryland, to be educated in England. Returning some ten years later in 1770 he found his family home, the Belair Mansion, to be occupied by his Tasker Aunts who showed no sign of relinquishing the property and he had to sue them to get possession. Benjamin had become great friends with George Washington and, in 1773, he hosted a dinner for Washington at Belair. Ogle married twice, firstly to Rebecca Stilley and they had one daughter, then secondly he married Henrietta Margaret Hill on 13th September 1770 at All Hallow's Church and by her he had son Benjamin Ogle II 1775-1844 and three other children: Ann, Samuel and Mary
         5  Elizabeth Ogle
      +  2nd Wife of Benjamin Ogle: Henrietta Margaret Hill  mar'd 1770
         5  Benjamin Ogle    1775 - 1844
         +  Anna Maria Cooke     1777 - 1856
         Benjamin married Anna Maria Cooke and had many children, some of whom married (like Benjamin's sister Anne) into the wealthy Tayloe family in 1792. The family at some time lived in the Octagonal House in Washington and two of their daughters died in that house - in fact, both daughters died in remarkably similar ways. Both had liaisons with men that their father didn't approve of, both got into an argument with him on the stairway or landing of the house and both either fell down the stairs or somehow fell over the balcony of the three story building and died. Their ghosts are said to still haunt the building.[1]
            6  Benjamin Ogle  1796 - 1839
            +  Julia Maria Dickinson mar'd 8th November 1824
            6  Elizabeth Ogle
            +  William Woodville of Baltimore
            Children: Richard Caton Woodville, William, Middleton, Anne and Elizabeth Woodville
            6  Mary Ogle
            +  Edward T. Tayloe of King George's County Virginia
            Children:  Edward, Poinsett, Bladen, William Ogle, George Ogle, Julia, Imogen and Catherine Tayloe
            6  Henrietta Ogle
            +  William H. Tayloe of Virginia
            Children: Henry A Tayloe, Sophia Tayloe and Emma Tayloe
            6  Susan Ogle
            +  John Hodges of Prince Georges County, Maryland
            Children:  John, Richard, Lewis, Upton, Maria, Carolina, Mary, Susan, Anna and Ellen Hodges
            6  Ellen Ogle
            +  Richard B. Mullikin
            Children: Richard, William, Walter, Arthur, Edward, Louisa, Ellen, Elizabeth, Emily, Susan, Annie Ogle and Mary Mullikin
            6  Louise Ogle
            +  Rev. Upton Beall
               7  Edward Sinclair Beall
               7  Brook Beall
               7  Ellen Louisa Beall
                  8  Amelia Beall
            6  Sophia Ogle
            +  Julius Forrest

---

[1] Floyd Randall. In the Realm of Ghosts and Hauntings. 2002

# Genealogy

- 7 Anna Maria Forrest
- 7 David Crawford Forrest
- 6 Catherine Ogle
- + Rev. Chas. Goodrich
- 6 William Cooke Ogle  1801 - 1868
- 6 Ann Ogle     1803 - 1820
- + Robert Neilson
  - 7 Emily Neilson
  - + Dr Blackburn of Virginia
- 6 Dr George Cooke Ogle     1817 - 1899
- + Anne Maria Cooke    Mar'd 1853
  - 7 Benjamin Ogle    1854 -
  - 7 George Cooke Ogle  1857 -
- 6 Richard Lowdnes Cooke Ogle  1819 - 1895
- + Priscilla Bowie
  - Children: Catherine, Fanny, Caroline, Louisa, Susan, Mary, Rosalie, Randolph, Henry Ogle
  - 7 Richard Lowndes Ogle
  - + Fanny Knight of Vermont
- 6 Rosalie Ogle 1821 - 1914
- + William Tayloe

5 Ann Ogle     1775 -1855
+ John Tayloe III  1771-1828  mar'd 1792
John Tayloe III owned 13 plantations and was a wealthy man and also a friend of George Washington. The couple had 16 children:
- 6 Children: Edward, Charles, William Henry, John, Henry Augustine, George, Lloyd, Robert Carter, Henrietta, Catherine Rebecca, Ann, Virginia, Ann Ogle, Elizabeth Tayloe, and
- 6 Benjamin Ogle Tayloe 1796-1868
- + Julia Dickinson
- + Phoebe Warren
  Plantation owner who had graduated from Harvard. Studied law in London and was presented to the Prince Regent. Returned to American Benjamin never held an elected office but was highly influential in politics behind the scenes. Married Phoebe Warren and toured Europe during the American Civil War.
  Children: John Tayloe b1826, Edward b1829, Estelle b1833, Anna 1834-36, Eugenie b1835 and Julia Taylor b1838

4 Meliora Ogle b1750
+ James Anderson d1785.
James was from Hertford, England, son of William Anderson, merchant and Rebecca Lloyd Anderson of Talbot County. He was in financial difficulties by August 1773 and his business affairs were taken over by his creditors
- 5 Rebecca Maria Harriet Anderson

4 Anne Ogle
4 Samuel Ogle
4 Mary Ogle

3 Rebecca Tasker   1724 - 1822  mar'd 1749
+ Daniel Dulany II  1722 - 1797 - the Younger (son of Daniel Dulany the Elder 1685-1753)
Daniel's brother Walter was Mayor of Annapolis. Sent from America to England for his education in the 1740s, became a lawyer. Appointed to Maryland's General Assembly to represent Frederick County.
- 4 Daniel Dulany    III - 1750 - 1824
  Sent from America to England for his education in 1761 and attended Eton School. Did not return to America, except for a short visit in 1785 when General Washington recorded him attending a fox hunt with Daniel and others. Daniel lived at 11 Downing Street, Westminster. Lost much land in Western Maryland because he was out of the country
- 4 Ann Dulany d.1828 at Brighton, England
- + William de la Serre
  - 5 Rebecca de la Serre (took the Dulany name) was adopted by her uncle Daniel Dulany III.
  - + Sir Richard Hunter
    She inherited a fortune from her uncle when he died in 1824. In 1829 she married Sir Richard Hunter - a doctor. She died in 1835 childless and half her fortune went to her husband Hunter (who remarried in 1836 to Frederica Bishop); the other half of Rebecca's fortune went to her cousin Rebecca Ann Dulany of Virginia
- 4 Benjamin Tasker Dulany (1752-1819).
- + Elizabeth French
  Before the American Revolution Benjamin lived at Prospect Hall, near Frederick Town. He married Elizabeth French, daughter of Daniel French of "Claremont" in Fairfax County, Virginia. As her guardian, George Washington attended their marriage in 1773. Benjamin was Aide-de-Camp to George Washington and gave him a beautiful white horse called 'Blueskin' which Washington rode during the American Revolution. Benjamin had married in 1773 to Elizabeth French (ward of Washington) and they had twelve children (6 boys and 6 girls). Washington would dine with the Dulanys but had a particular interest in a piece of land that Elizabeth French's family owned. For years Elizabeth's mother Penelope Marley French refused to sell the land to him but eventually agreement was reached.

- 5 Benjamin Tasker Dulany   1774 -
- + Elizabeth Rozier, daughter of Benjamin Rozier of Notley Hall, Maryland
    - 6 Major Rozier Dulany  - US Army
    - + Frances Carter   (Fannie) of Sabine Hall, Virginia
- 5 Elizabeth French Dulany
- + Major Joseph Forrest of Maryland
    - 6 Dulany Forrest - Lieutenant in US Navy
    - 6 French Forrest - Flag Officer in US Navy
        - 7 Rev. Douglas French Forrest
    - 6 Sophia Forrest
    - + John de Butts
        - 7 Richard Earl de Butts
        - + Sarah Hall
            - 8 Mary Welby de Butts
            - + Major Richard H Carter of Glen Welby, Virginia
- 5 Julia Dulany
- + Thomas Clagett
- 5 David French Dulany
- + Sarah Tingey, dau of Commodore Thomas Tingey, US Navy
    - 6 Daniel French Dulany - Lieutenant in the US Navy
    - + Miss Gault of Maryland
    - 6 Nancy Dulany
    - + Dr John Hunter of Virginia
    - 6 Sarah Dulany
    - + Major John Chichester - US Army
    - 6 Mary Dulany
    - + Spencer Mottram Ball of Virginia
- 5 Rebecca Dulany
- + Timothy Winn - Purser US Navy
    - 6 Elizabeth Winn
    - + Hon. Powhaten Ellis (Senator) of Mississippi
    - 6 William Winn
    - + Sophia Gault - daughter of Hon. James Carroll of Maryland
    - 6 Mary Winn
    - + William Dunlop - Charge d'Affaires
    - + Col. William Henry Dangerfield of Virginia
- 5 Ann Bladen Dulany
- + Commodore Thomas Tingey - US Navy/British Navy
- 5 John Peyton Dulany
- + Mary Ann de Butts
  English, daughter of Samuel de Butts and Mary Welby of Grantham, Lincolnshire
    - 6 Julia Dulany - married her cousin, 1st marriage
    - + Welby de Butts
    - + Rev. Samuel Rozell
    - 6 Mary Dulany
    - + George William Carlyle Whiting of Virginia, son of Carlyle Fairfax Whiting great-grandson of Hon. William Fairfax of Belvoir, Virginia
    - 6 Richard Henry Dulany 1820-1906 - married his cousin
    - + Rebecca Dulany, daughter of Major Rozier Dulany (heiress to Lady Hunter) Richard was born in Unison, Loudoun County, Virginia and was Capt/Colonel in the American Civil War (7th Virginia Cavalry).  He founded the Piedmont Fox Hunt  and the Upperville Colt and Horse Show - America's oldest horse show
      Children: Mary, Fannie, John, Hal and Richard Dulany
- 5 Louisa Dulany
- + Richard de Butts of Mount Welby, Virginia, son of Samuel de Butts
- + James Hall of Virginia
- 5 James Heath Dulany, M.D.
- 5 Bladen Dulany - Commodore in the US Navy
- + Mary Walker Carter of Virginia
- + Caroline Nourse, daughter of Major James Nourse of the District of Colombia
- 5 Henrietta Marie Dulany
- + William Herbert of Alexandria, Virginia.  Son of William Herbert and great-great-grandson of Hon. William Fairfax of Belvoir, Virginia
- 5 William Dulany - Colonel in the US Marine Corps

## Genealogy

- + Susan Wade, widow of Lt. Nelson Wade, US Army[1]
- 3 Elizabeth Tasker 1725/26 - 1789, mar'd 1747
- + Christopher Lowndes of 'Blenheim' 1713 - 1789
  Son of Richard Lowndes and Margaret Poole, emigrated to America 1738
  - 4 Harriett Lowndes
  - + Levi Gantt (soldier in the Revolutionary War)
    - 5 Margaret Lowndes Gantt d. 1880
    - + John Bowie 1799 - 1871 Provost Marshall in Civil War
  - 4 Ann Margaret Lowndes 1748 - 1822 - unmarried
  - 4 Benjamin Lowndes 1749 - 1808 - eldest son, lived at Bostwick
  - + Dorothy Buchanan - dau of General Andrew Buchanan of Baltimore
    - 5 Elizabeth Lowndes
    - 5 Andrew Lowndes
    - 5 Benjamin Lowndes
    - 5 Susan Lowndes
    - 5 Eleanor Lowndes
    - 5 Christopher Lowndes 1799 -
      - 6 Francis Lowndes 1751 - 1815
      - + Jane Maddox
    - 5 Francis Lowndes 1784 - 1867
    - + Angeletta Craighill
  - 4 Samuel Lowndes 1753 -
  - 4 Elizabeth Lowndes 1755 -
  - 4 Sarah Lowndes 1755 -
  - 4 Rebecca Lowndes 1757 - 1802
  - + Benjamin Stoddert 1751 - 1813 - 1st Secretary US Navy
  - 4 Charles Lowndes 1765 - 1846 - youngest son. Of Georgetown, later Jefferson Co. VA
  - + Frances Whiting
    - 5 Frances Lowndes
    - 5 Beverly Bladen Lowndes 1813 -
    - 5 Francis Whiting Lowndes 1815 -
    - 5 Francis Perrin Lowndes
  - + 2nd Wife of Charles Lowndes: Eleanor Lloyd 1776-1805 dau of Col. Edward Lloyd IV of Wye
    - 5 Harriet Lowndes 1795 - 1835
    - + Samuel (Dr) Scollay
      - 6 Charles Scollay
      - 6 Anne Lloyd Scollay
      - + Mr Beckwith of Virginia
      - 6 Samuel Scollay
      - 6 Eleanor Scollay
      - + Mr Moore of Virginia
      - 6 Elizabeth Scollay
      - + Mr Page
    - 5 Edward Lowndes 1797 - 1797
    - 5 Commander Charles Lowndes 1798 - 1885, mar'd 1824
    - + Sally Scott Lloyd (dau of General Edward Lloyd d.1834 and Sally Scott Murray 1775-1854). Edward Lloyd was Governor of Maryland 1809-11 and a Senator 1819-26.[2]
      - 6 Sally Lloyd Lowndes b1827
      - + John W Bennett (US Navy)
      - 6 Ellen Lowndes 1831-45
      - 6 Charles Lowndes 1832-
      - + Catherine Tilghman
      - 6 Harriet Lowndes 1836-37
      - 6 Edward Lloyd Lowndes 1843-5
      - 6 Richard Tasker Lowndes 1843-45
      - 6 Elizabeth Tayloe Lowndes 1844
      - + Dr Julius A. Johnson
    - 5 Lloyd Lowndes 1800 - 1879
    - + Marie Moore
      - 6 Richard Tasker Lowndes (1803-44) succeeded father

---

[1] Maryland Historical Magazine Vol. 13, No. 2, pp155-157. Also 'Something about the Dulaney (Dulany) Family and a sketch of the Southern Cobb family.

[2] Lowndes genealogy sourced from Old Kent: The Eastern Shore of Maryland. Notes illustrative of the most Ancient Records of Kent County by George A Hanson. 1876

- + Mary Goff
- + Louisa Black of Cumberland MD
  - 7 Eloise Lowndes
  - + Phillip Roman
  - 7 Elizabeth Tasker Lowndes, married cousin
  - + Hon. Lloyd Lowndes (Governor of Maryland)
- 6 Dr Charles Lowndes d.1865 Assistant Surgeon
- 6 Lloyd (Jnr) Lowndes  1845 - 1905
- + Elizabeth Tasker Lowndes 1842 - 1922
  Lloyd Lowndes was born at 'Blenheim' near Bladensburg and attended Washington College before going to law school where he graduated in 1872. He became a member of congress and in 1879 attended the Republican National Convention at Chicago. In 1895 he was elected Governor. He later retired and became President of Cumberland National Bank.
  - 7 Lloyd Lowndes  1871 - 1928
  - 7 Richard Tasker Lowndes  1871 - 1905
  - + Elizabeth Mc Dowell
    - 8 Richard Tasker Lowndes III (twin)
    - 8 Lloyd Lowndes (twin)
    - 8 Charles Tasker Lowndes 1874 - 1922, Colorado
    - 8 William Bladen Lowndes 1875 - 1941 President of the First National Bank, MD.[1]
  - 7 Elizabeth Lloyd Lowndes  1881 - 1963
  - 7 Tasker Lowndes  1883 -
- 6 Clarence Moore Lowndes d.1847
- 5 Elizabeth Ann Lowndes  1805 -
- + Horace Leeds Edmonson
  - 6 John Edmonson
  - 6 Horace Edmonson
  - 6 Leeds Edmonson
  - 6 Maria Lloyd Edmonson
  - 6 Charles Lowndes Edmonson
- 5 Richard Tasker Lowndes  1808 - 1844
  - 6 Elouisa Lowndes
  - 6 Elizabeth Tasker Lowndes 1842-1922
    Elizabeth Tasker Lowndes was described as a brilliant conversationalist and entertained President Benjamin Harrison (the 23rd President - that is to say, this President was the grandson of the 9th President William Henry Harrison who was cousin to Robert 'Councillor' Carter husband of Frances Tasker).
- 4 Richard Tasker Lowndes 1763 of Blenheim, Bladensburg and Bostock House
- + Ann Lloyd 1769-1841
  - 5 Elizabeth Tayloe Lowndes - 1878
  - + William (Rev) Pinkney (Bishop of Maryland)
  - 5 Anne Lloyd Lowndes  -d. 1850 unmarried
  - 5 Edward Lloyd Lowndes d.young
  - 5 Richard Tasker Lowndes  1804 - 1815
  - 5 Edward Lloyd Lowndes  1807 - 1832, unmarried
  - 5 Benjamin Ogle Lowndes  1810 - 1897, unmarried
- 3 Frances Ann Tasker  1738 - 1787
- + Robert "Councillor" Carter III  1726/27 - 1804
  - 4 Benjamin Carter  1756 -79 - unmarried
    Fithian, tutor to the Carter children, recorded in his diary rumours that Benjamin had taken a Negro girl about 16 years" into the stable and stayed there with her a long time.[2] He also called him a 'youth of genius ... fond of horses'
  - 4 Robert Bladen Carter 1759 ->1786 - unmarried. A tutor called him 'volatile and unsettled in his temper'. Source above
    Robert Bladen Carter was given control of his father's Billingsgate Plantation[3] in September 1780 which, unfortunately, he squandered by the age of 26 years. Robert ran up debts and fled to England in 1784 leaving his father to sort out the mess, which he did by selling Billingsgate. Robert returned some time later and, his trepidation at then having to approach his father for employment is clear from the following letter he wrote to him on 9th June 1786: *"This morning I waited on you in your library with an intention of asking you for some employment. It has, and ever will be the case I am afraid, when before you; in any serious reflections, I have observed a stoppage in my throat and intellect vastly confused: what it proceeds from God only knows - It is my wish if you would choose to be imployed by you. Every exertion of body*

---

[1] Maryland Historical Magazine, Dr Christopher Johnson
[2] Journals and Letters of Philip Vickers Fithian 1773-74: A Plantation Tutor by Philip Vickers Fithian. Several quotes on the disposition of the Carter children are from this same source
[3] Ibid

# Genealogy

*and mind will I exert in your behalf*".[1] Robert died unmarried, though it is known that his father blocked one attempt for him to marry.[2]

- 4 Priscilla Carter   1760 - 1823. Tutor described as 'steady, studious, docile ... and first Class of the female Sex'. *Fithian*
- \+ Robert Mitchell   mar'd abt 1778
  Priscilla Carter inherited part of the Bull Run tract (comprising farms Leo and Cancer) from her father, some 2,860 acres. Lawrence, brother of General George Washington, had proposed a marriage between his son George and Priscilla Carter, but she married Robert Mitchell who was her father's Clerk/Overseer.[3] Their property was 'Grove Mount', a colonial mansion on a high ridge overlooking the Rappahannock River. Robert and Priscilla had 8 children, including:
  - 5 Richard Tasker Mitchell
  - 5 Harriet Bladen Mitchell 1793-1841
  - \+ William James Weir 1792-1867
  - 5 Fannie Mitchell
- 4 Ann Tasker Carter (Nancy) 1762 - aft 1776  Fithian called her 'not constant in her disposition ... but cheerful'
- \+ John Peck
  Ann eloped with her tutor John Peck about 1776. (Peck being successor to Vickers Fithian) Although initially angry, her father relented and gave them 'Bladensfield' as a wedding present. Bladensfield (part of Nomini Hall estate) was an estate of 1,000 acres with a *"large frame house on a brick basement. The rear door, with peep-hole, is fastened by the hard-timbered bar that held it secure against the Indians in the 1690s"*[4]
- \+ Mr Quinlan (2nd husband)
- 4 Rebecca Carter   1762 -
- 4 Frances Tasker Lewis Carter   1764 -
- \+ Colonel Thomas Jones of Bathurst (married in 1781)
- 4 Elizabeth (Betsy) Landon Carter   1768 - 1842. Fithian described her as 'young, quiet and obedient'
- \+ Spencer Mottrom Ball 1762 - 1832
  Elizabeth Landon Carter was born 15 October 1768 at Nomini Hall in Westmoreland County, Virginia. Elizabeth was married by Rev. Henry Tasker, to Captain Henry Mottrom Ball on 27th March 1788 and the couple moved to Pohoke on 760 acres bought from her brother George. She died 3rd January 1842 at Portici, Prince William County Virginia. Their daughter Elizabeth Lucy Ball 1791-1855 married William Fitzhugh Carter in 1807. The couple lived at Mountain View, Fairfax County, Virginia.
  - 5 Fanny Tasker Lewis Ball 1792-1853
  - \+ Rev. John Taliaferro Lewis 1785-1862
  - 5 Alfred Ball d.1853
  - 5 Louisa
  - 5 Adeline
  - 5 Elizabeth Lucy Ball   1791 - 1855
  - \+ William Fitzhugh Carter   1782 - 1836
    Elizabeth acquired 250 acres of land when her brother died.
    - 6 Mary Adeline Carter   1831 - 1876
    - \+ William Henry Thornton   1824 - 1890
      - 7 Adeline Stuart Thornton   1857 - 1893
      - \+ George Richard Lee Turberville III 1845 - 1921 (John Turberville of Hickory Hill living less than 1 mile from Nomini Hall)
        - 8 Harriotte Lee Turberville   1881-1962
        - \+ Pinckney Lee McWhorter   1875-1949
- 4 Mary Carter   1767 -
- 4 Harriet Lucy Carter   1768 - Fithian described as 'bold, fearless, noisy and lawless .... always merry'
- \+ John James Maunt (an Agent for Lord Fairfax)
- 4 Amelia Churchill Carter   1769 -
- 4 Rebecca Dulany Carter   1770 -
- 4 John Tasker Carter   1772
- \+ dau. of Henry "Light Horse Harry" Lee
- 4 Sarah Fairfax Carter (Sally) 1773 -1829 (Proposed to by Hon. Richard Bland Lee - uncle of Robert E Lee, commander of the Confederate Army of North Virginia in the American Civil War, Richard was the brother of Henry 'Light Horse Harry' Lee, but refused)
- \+ Dr John Yates Chinn   1770-1830
  Sarah inherited part of the Bull Run tract (comprising farms Leo and Cancer) from her father.

---

[1] Letter 9th June 1786 'Robert Carter of Nomini hall: A Virginia Tobacco Planter of the Eighteenth Century' by Louis Morton, Charlottesville, Virginia, 1941, p225

[2] Accommodating Revolutions: Virginia's Northern Neck in an Era of Transformations 1760-1810 by Alfred H. Tillson Jnr

[3] The McCartys of the Northern Neck: 350 years of a Virginian family by William M McCarty, Kathleen Much, 2005

[4] Virginia: A Guide to the Old Dominion by Federal Writers' Project. 1956

- 5 Bartholomew Carter Chinn
- 5 Sarah Chinn
- + Lovel Marders (a Baptist Minister)
- 5 Priscilla Chinn 1825
- 5 Benjamin Tasker Chinn 1807-66
- + Edmonia Randolph Carter 1813-95
    - 6 Courtney Norton Chinn 1838
    - + Henry Augustine Tayloe 1836-1908
        - 7 Henrietta Ogle Tayloe
        - 7 Benjamin Tasker Taylor 1862
            plus 11 others (not all survive)
    - 6 Sarah Sophia Chinn 1839
    - + Robert Horner Tyler 1838-1902
        - 7 Robert Carter Tyler 1864
        - 7 Bailey Tyler 1865-1933
        - + Anner Moss Alrich 1871-1914
            Eight other children
        - + Mary Love Alrich 1870 (1st wife's older sister)
        - 7 Benjamin Chinn Tyler 1867
            Nine others
- 5 Sophia Elizabeth Chinn 1807-51
- 4 Judith Carter 1775 -
- 4 George Carter 1777 -
- + Betty Lewis
- + Elizabeth Grayson
    George Carter - youngest son lived with his family at 'Oatlands Plantation'. He Inherited 1,000 acres of a tract called Goose Creek (part of his father's Leo Plantation) in Loudoun County.[1]
- 4 Sophia Carter 1778 - unmarried
- 4 Julia Carter 1783 -
- + Dr Robert Berkeley

**2 Thomas Bladen 1698 - 1780**
- + Barbara Janssen, mar'd 1731
    - 3 Barbara Bladen 1733 -1821
    - + General Henry St John 1738 - 1818
    - 3 Harriet Bladen 1735 - 1821
    - + William Anne Holles Capel 1732 - 1799
        - 4 John Thomas Capel 1769 - 1819
        - + Caroline (Lady) Paget 1773 - 1847 mar'd 1792
            - 5 Harriet Jane Capel 1793 - 1819 mar'd 1817 in Lausanne
            - + David Okeden Parry-Okeden of More Critchell 1774 - 1833
                Harriet had, at one time, fallen for the dashing Baron Ernst Trip (a friend of Lady Caroline's Paget brother), a serial ladies-man but the passion was one-way and Harriet's letters to him were full of unrequited love. Unfortunately one such long letter seems to have been intercepted by her father John. A duel took place between Capel and Trip with Capel having the Duke of Richmond as his second. The duel passed off without bloodshed, both men apparently missing each other (Feb 1815). Then a short time later, to everyone's shock, Baron Trip committed suicide by shooting himself but left a letter for Harriet's uncle, which the family concealed knowledge about from her. In time, Harriet got over this episode and, by 1817, married David Okeden Parry Okeden of More Critchill and Turnworth, Dorset.
                - 6 Fitzmaurice Parry-Okeden d.1869
                - + Caroline Rees Horton
                    - 7 Algernon Fitzmaurice Parry Okeden
                    - 7 Grace Harriet Parry Okeden mar'd 1880
                    - + Ernest King of Wimbledon
            - 5 Caroline Capel b1794-d.young
            - 5 Georgina Capel 1795 - 1835 (aka Georgy or Dordy) mar'd 1821
            - + Ralph Smyth of Gaybrook, Westmeath, Ireland - d.bef 1831
            - + Pierce O'Brien Butler of Dunboyne Castle in County Meath
            - 5 Maria Capel 1797-1856, mar'd 1821 Lausanne
            - + Marqius Marius d'Espinassy de Fontanelle
            - 5 Louisa Ann Capel 1799-1842 mar'd 1827
            - + Count Auguste d'Espinassy de Fontanelle
            - 5 Horatia Capel 1800-1864, mar'd age 47, died Cassiobury (burnt)
            - + Count de Septeuil

---

[1] http:/benlomondmanorhouse.org/history/carterchinnhistory.htm

# Genealogy

5     Arthur Algenon Capel 1803-92 - 6th Earl of Essex mar'd x3
+     1st wife: Caroline Jeanetta Beauclerk 1804 - 1862 (g/dau 8th E. of Cork) mar'd1825
     6     Adela (Lady) Capel     1828 - 1860
     +     Archibald William Montgomerie     1812 - 1861
        7     Sybil Amelia Adela Montgomerie   - 1932
        7     Hilda Rose Montgomerie   - 1928
        +     Tonman Mosley
     6     Arthur de Vere Capel 1826 - 1879
     +     Emma Martha Meux   - 1905
        7     George Devereux de Vere Capel     1857 - 1916
        +     Eleanor Harriet Maria Harford 1860 - 1885
        +     Adela Grant   - 1922
        7     Randolph de Vere Capel     1865 - 1912
        7     Maud de Vere Capel   - 1921
        7     Evelyn de Vere Capel 1850 - 1939
        +     Eustace Henry Dawnay     1850 - 1928
        7     Sybil de Vere Capel     1858 - 1934
        +     Thomas Brassey   1836 - 1918
     6     Reginald Algernon Capel     1830 - 1906 mar'd 1858
     +     Mary Eliza Fazakerley - 1911
        Reginald attended Harrow School, Trinity College, Oxford. JP for Hertfordshire
     6     Randolph Alfred Capel     1831 - 1857
*     2nd wife of Arthur Algenon Capel:   Louisa Caroline Elizabeth Boyle   1833-1876   mar'd 1863
     6     Arthur Algernon Capell     1864 - 1940
     +     Louisa Elizabeth Paget     - 1914
     *     2nd Wife of Arthur Algernon Capell:
     +     Isabel Anne Watson   - 1939
        7     Constance Audrey Capell   1891 - 1953
        +     Harold Lister Farquhar     1894 - 1953
        7     Rachel Julia Capell     1894 - 1949
     6     Beatrice Mary Capell   1870 - 1954
     +     Edmund Banbury 1853 - 1938
        7     John Edmund Banbury     1914 - 1978
        +     Leila Elizabeth Russell
     6     Jane Capel     1805 - 1849, mar'd 1833
     +     Dr D Macloughlin
+     3rd wife: Louisa Elizabeth Heneage - d.1914 (dau 8th Duke of St Albans) widow of Lord George Paget
5     Jane (Mary) Capel 1805-49 (aka Janey) mar'd 1833
+     D Macloughlin, M.D.
5     Algernon Henry Campagne Capel     1807 - 1886 mar'd cousin in 1832
+     Caroline Paget     d1880 (dau of Adm Sir Charles Paget)
     6     Arthur Algenon Bladen Capel     1837 - 1847
     6     Brownlow Algernon Adolphus Capel     1838 - 1860
     6     Edward Charles Algernon Capel     1840 - 1899
     6     Reginald Randolph Algernon Capel 1841 -
     +     Marion Struthers - 1937
        7     Caroline Capell     1880 -
        +     Thomas Alexander Clapperton
        7     Milicent Florence Capell     1892 -
        +     Henry Knox Paul
     6     Etheldred Marmaduke Algernon Capel 1844 - 1873
     6     Charles Horatio Capel 1845 - 1924 mar'd 1868
     +     Alice Peel Bellairs     - 1936
        7     Arthur Algernon de Vere Capel     1869 - 1924
        +     Alice Anne Pine   - 1913
        *     2nd Wife of Arthur Algernon de Vere Capel:
        +     Alice Mabel Currie   - 1951
        7     Gertrude Blance Constance Capel
        7     Beatrice Alice Georgina Capel   d.1939
        +     Charles Bonneau
        *     2nd Husband of Beatrice Alice Georgina Capel:
        +     Tudor George Trevor - 1921
        7     Edith Florence Caroline Capel   Unknown - 1960
        7     Evelyn Maud Mary Capel   Unknown - 1943
        +     George Ernest Richards

- - 7 Henry Addison Devereux Capel 1873 - 1925
  - + Olive Mary Richardson-Bunbury - 1937
  - 7 Arthur Charles Lloyd Capell 1876 - 1895
  - 7 Mary Kathleen Capel Unknown -
  - + William Frederick Ullathorne Cosens
  - * 2nd Husband of Mary Kathleen Capel:
  - + Francis George West - 1900
  - * 3rd Husband of Mary Kathleen Capel:
  - + Edward Aubrey Courtauld Lowe
  - 7 Mabel Lillian Capel - 1974
- 6 George Marie Capel 1845 - 1915
- + Annie Lowe - 1928
- 6 Harriet Mary Capel Unknown - 1868
- + George Henry C F Malcolm Drummond 1834 - 1861
- 6 Florence Louisa Amelia Capel Unknown - 1924
- + Francis Nevil Reade - 1882
- * 2nd Husband of Florence Louisa Amelia Capel:
- + Francis Maurice Drummond
- 6 Millicent Florence Evelyn Capel b1852
- + Richard Cole

5 Mary Capel 1808-c18
5 Amelia (Katherine) Capel (aka Meeny or Menii) 1815 - 1892 mar'd 1857
+ Hon. Henry Stevenson Blackwood 1819 - 1865
5 Mary Capel Unknown - 1876, unmarried
5 Adolphus Frederick Charles Molyneux Capel (aka Dolly or Nam) 1813-1899 mar'd 1834
+ Charlotte Mary Maynard - 1871 (dau of Viscount Maynard)
- 6 Arthur Algernon Adolphus Fred Capel 1837 - 1870
- + Elizabeth Owen - 1882
- 6 Horatio Bladen Capel 1839 - 1933
- + Violet Annie Frost

  Rev. Horatio Bladen Capel - The 'Fighting Parson', served in the navy - where he had been a champion boxer. In 1877 he became Rector at Great Easton, Dunmow, Essex. It was reported that, during his time as rector at Great Easton, he practised high church rituals at a church where low church was, in fact, the norm and this led to many heated disputes locally, including specifically with the blacksmith. Rector and blacksmith decided to settle their differences with a fight in the churchyard - where no doubt Horatio's history as a champion boxer in the navy came in very handy. After differences were settled, the two became good friends.[1]
  - 7 Beatrix Violet de Vere Capel
  - + Raymond Smith
  - * 2nd Husband of Beatrix Violet de Vere Capel:
  - + Edward Reginald Tranter
  - * 2nd Wife of Horatio Bladen Capel:
  - + Ada Augusta Howkins 1842- 1916 b.Warks (dau of Theophilous Howkins b.1802,
      gent of Surrey and wife Marian b.1812 at sea
  - 7 Algernon Essex Capell CBE, DSO 1869-1952.
  - + Lois Ethel Slatter 1877-1944

    Rank Major, born at Tattenhall Wood, Staffs. Algernon and his brother Horace (see below) were living with their Howkins grandparents in 1871 and at Felsted Grammar School in Essex on the 1881 census. In 1887 he sailed round the Horn to South America. An eye injury (caused by fencing) meant he was unable to join the army but he joined the Capte Mounted Riders in 1889 and he saw action during the Boer War where he was present at the Relief of Ladysmith. He was taken captured whilst trying to rescue a comrade and held prisoner for four months. As part of Bethune's Mounted Infantry, he was a Captain and had been awarded the DSO and promoted to Major in 1902. In 1903 he married Lois Ethel Slatter and in 1906 he was Kenya's Assistant District Commissioner. By 1908 he was Commandant of Colonial Forces. In 1911 the King appointed him Official Member of the legislative council of the island of Grenada and Chief of Police in the West Indies. The family returned to England on 7th July 1913, sailing from (Trinidad) via New York to Southampton by first class on "Oruba" of the Royal Mail Steam Packet Company. Algernon re-joined the South African British Police force in Southern Rhodesia (now Zimbabwe) in 1913 and began his War service in 1914 as Commandeer of BSAP. He was mentioned in despatches by General Smutts. On 15th March 1915 he was the commanding officer of the Rhodesia Native Regiment fighting in British East Africa (Kenya) against the German East African front and he wrote a journal of the activities of 2RR regiment. *The 2nd Rhodesia Regiment in East Africa* by Lieutenant Colonel A.E. Capell. Made Commander of the British Empire in 1924 and was also awarded the Croix de Guerre. His wife and two sons died during his lifetime. He was cited for distinguished service in 1916: *"for conspicuous gallantry on several occasions during the*

---

[1] http://www.visitoruk.com/historydetail.php?id=29906&f=Braintree

*campaign"* and was awarded the Victory, British and Star Medals. By 1923 he had risen to Commissioner of Police in Southern Rhodesia. He died in Rhodesia and had three children:

- 8    Algernon Capell b. 1904-<1952
- 8    Joan Capell b. 1906
- +    W.J. Evans (farmer in Bindura district)
  - 9    Two sons and one daughter
- 8    Robert Devereux Capell 1909-<52 at Kikuyu, Ukamba in Kenya
- 7   Horace Charles George Arthur Capel 1868 - 1953 at Newton Bushel, Devon. As for brother Algernon above, lived with Howkins grandparents in 1871, Felsted Grammar School in 1881
- +   Clara Isabel Reade   - 1939
- 7   Henry A Capel b1874, Bristol
- 7   Mary Capel b1875
- 7   Arthur C S b.1877
- 6  George Marie (Rev) Capel 1845 - 1915
- +  Annie Lowe
  - 7   Arthur George Coningsby Capel 1879 - 1915
  - +   Phyllis Deacon
  - 7   Dora Amy Isabel Capel   - 1949
  - 7   Marie Kathleen Capel - 1970
  - +   Rudolph Keane Franks   - 1970
  - *   2nd Husband of Marie Kathleen Capel:
  - +   D'Arcy Mackinnon Dawes
  - 7   Leonie Annie Capel   - 1958
  - 7   Hilda Amalie Violet Capel - 1960
  - 7   Bertha Sybil Capel   - 1969
- 6  Harriet Mary Capel   - 1868
- +  George Drummond   1834 - 1861
  - 7  George Essex Montifex Drummond   1856 - 1887
  - *   2nd Husband of Harriet Mary Capel:
  - +   E C Dering
- 6  Florence Louisa Amelia Capel
- +  Francis Nevil Reade   - 1882
- *  2nd Husband of Florence Louisa Amelia Capel:
- +  Francis Maurice Drummond
- 5  Priscilla Elizabeth Capel 1815-d.young
- 4  Thomas Edward Capel    1770 - 1855
- +  Dona Maretti
- 4  William Robert (Rev) Capel    1774 - 1854
- +  Sarah Salter - 1874
  - 5  William Capel    1804 - 1876
  - +  Jane Anne Clutterbuck
  - 5  Jane Capel    1806 -
  - +  Thomas Truesdale Clarke
  - 5  Henry Robert Capel    1807 -
  - 5  Louisa Capel 1808 - 1908
  - +  James (Rev) Charles Clutterbuck
  - 5  Georgina Capel    1809 -
  - +  Nathaniel F Wodehouse    1802 - 1870
    - 6  Capel Wodehouse    1841 - 1906
    - +  Portia Maria Rashleigh    - 1912
      - 7  Edmond Wodehouse 1894 - 1959
      - +  Persis Joan Mary Rooper
      - 7  Dulcibella Wodehouse    1891 - 1971
      - +  Edward H Burton
      - 7  Alice Wodehouse    1892 - 1957
    - 6  Alice Jane Wodehouse   - 1901
      - +  Bevil Granville    1834 - 1909
      - 7  Bernard Granville    1873 -
      - +  Edith Halsey - 1952
        - 7  Violet Granville
        - +  Walter Henry Maudslay   - 1937
        - 7  Mary Olive Granville   - 1951
        - +  Arthur Herbert Edward Wood - 1934
        - 7  Muriel Granville
        - +  Frederick Blomfield
        - 7  Grace Granville

```
                    +    Harold McCorquodale      1865 - 1943
                    7    Morwenna Granville
                    +    Lionel Halsey     1872 - 1949
                6   Louisa Clara Wodehouse
                +   Edmond Henry Wodehouse    1837 - 1923
            5   Edward Samuel Capel 1811 - 1896
            +   Elizabeth Binnie  - 1851
                6   Arthur William Capel
                    7    Terence William Capel    1891 - 1962
                    +    Florence Penelope Whitham    - 1963
                6   Ada Capel    - 1922
                +   John Reginald Thomas Fullerton
                    7    Alan Edward Weston Fullerton    1877 -
                    +    Alice Ogston Marquand
                    7    Eric John Arthur Fullerton 1878 - 1962
                    +    Dorothy Sibyl Fisher   1873 - 1962
            5   Isabel Capel  1812 -
            +   A (Rev) Hawkes
        4   Thomas Bladen (Admiral) Capel    1776 - 1853
        +   Harriet Catherine Smythe - 1866
2   Christopher Bladen   1702 - 1732
```

It had been thought Christopher died young but he lived to at least 29 years of age from the following military record: 1731 *"Christopher Bladen, nephew to Col. Bladen, was appointed Ensign in Colonel Fielding's Regiment of Foot"*.[1] Hon. Lt-Colonel Charles Fielding c1717-46 was brother to the Earl of Denbigh and had been Captain of Pembroke's Horse. From the time of his marriage to Ann Bridges (née Palmer) in 1737 he resided at 14 Burlington Street on the Burlington Estate, Mayfair in Westminster from 1737-42 in the same house that was to later be occupied by Horace Walpole in 1788-1811.[2] Just a short distance round the corner from Fielding was Thomas Bladen (Christopher's older brother) was living on Grosvenor Square and the two (Fielding and Thomas Bladen) were no doubt were well acquainted.[3]

```
2   William Bladen    1704 -
2   Martin Bladen     1704 - 1749
+   Miss Wheatley
```

The following marriage in 1741 which cannot positively be stated to be William's son Martin but seems likely due to the size of estate both he and the lady had: *"Mr Bladen, a Cheshire gentleman of a fine estate was married at Ormskirk in Lancashire to Mrs Wheatley of that place, an agreeable Lady with a fortune of 10,000 l. fortune"*. Obituary: Martin Bladen of Wigan, Lancashire d. 5 April 1749.[4] It is not known if the couple had any children.

```
2   Priscilla Bladen   1708 -d.young
```

Presumed to have died young because sister Anne was referred to as the *"only daughter of the Hon. William Bladen of Annapolis"*.[5]

## Descendants of Frances Bladen
```
1   Frances Bladen   c1675 - 1731
+   William Hamond 1676 - 1711
    2   Catherine Hamond     1698 - 1721
    +   Walter Brooke    1694 - 1722
        3   Catherine Brooke     1720 - 1756  mar'd 1737
        +   Edward (Admiral) Hawke   1705 - 1781  1st Baron Hawke of Towton
        For descendants see Elizabeth Bladen's genealogy below (lines converge when descendants of Frances and Elizabeth marry)
        3   Frances Brooke   1720 - 1720
    2   William Hamond 1701 - 1701
    2   Martin Hamond 1702 - 1702
    2   Frances Hamond 1703 - 1729
    +   Thomas Pulleyne 1701 - 1759
        3   Frances Pulleyne 1726 - 1784
        +   Thomas (Rev) Mosley 1724 - 1784
            4   Frances Mosley   1754 - 1814
            +   J (Rev) Bindloss
```

---

[1] Sometimes spelt Feilding. The Granite Monthly, Vol. 4. 1881. Page 263
[2] Survey of London, Vols 31 and 32, part 2 (1963) pp566-72 (Burlington estate, Mayfair, north of Piccadilly, in the West End)
[3] Gentleman's Magazine 1732, vol 2, page 587 and Ipswich Journal 15 April 1749 (G.M. 188)
[4] London Magazine and Monthly Chronologer, Vol. 10, 1741, p309
[5] Something about Dulaney (Dulany) Family and a Sketch of the Southern Cobb family by Benjamin Dulany 1815-59, Washington

- 4 Elizabeth Mosley 1755 - 1756
- 4 Thomas Mosley 1757 - 1757
- 4 Catherine Maria Mosley 1759 - 1840
- + John Perfect
- 4 Thomas Pulleyne Mosley 1760 - 1813
- + Anne Babington
  - 5 Elizabeth Pulleyn Mosley 1790 - 1851
  - + John Crowder 1791 - 1838
    - 6 Anne Julia Crowder 1820 - 1890
    - + Matthew (Sir) Smith-Dodsworth 1819 - 1858
      - 7 Henrietta Smith-Dodsworth 1851 -
      - + Henry (Sir) Monson de la Poer Beresford
      - 7 Charles (Sir) Smith-Dodsworth 1853 - 1891
      - 7 Matthew (Sir) Blaney Smith-Dodsworth 1856 - 1931
      - + Agnes E Crowder
      - 7 Fred Cadwallader Smith-Dodsworth 1858 -
    - 6 John St Vincent Crowder 1856-1925
  - 5 Frances Mosley 1792 -
  - + Fred (Rev) Dodsworth  * 2nd Husband of Frances Mosley:
  - + Edward (Rev) Wyvill
  - 5 Anne Mosley 1800 -
  - + Montagu (Rev) Wynyard
- 4 Richard Mosley 1763 -
- 4 Anne Mosley 1765 -
- + E Robinson
- 4 Elizabeth Mosley 1766 - 1767
- 3 Thomas Pulleyne 1728 - 1728

## Descendants of Elizabeth Bladen
**1 Elizabeth Bladen 1677 - 1748**
- + Colonel Ruthven d1699 mar'd 1698 - no children
- + Edward Hawke 1682-1718, 2nd Husband of Elizabeth Bladen:
  - 2 Edward (Admiral) Hawke 1705 - 1781  1st Baron Hawke of Towton
  - + Catherine Brooke 1720 - 1756 mar'd 1737
    - 3 Frances Hawke 1738 - 1739
    - 3 Isabella Hawke 1739 - 1740
    - 3 Edward Hawke 1742 - 1742
    - 3 Martin Bladen Hawke 1744 - 1805  2nd Baron Hawke of Towton
    - + Cassandra Turner 1746 - 1813, mar'd 1771
      - 4 Cassandra Julia Hawke 1772 - 1826 - no children from all 3 marriages
      - + Samuel Estwick 1770 - 1797 (1st husband of Cassandra Julia)
      - + Stephen (Rev) Sloane d1812 (2nd husband of Cassandra Julia)
      - + Thomas Green d>1826 (3rd husband of Cassandra Julia)
      - 4 Edward Harvey-Hawke 1774 - 1824 died 29th Nov 1824 at Regents Park, London - 3rd Baron Hawke of Towton
      - + Frances Anne Harvey 1771 - 1810, mar'd 1798. Lady of the Manor of Womersley
        - 5 Hon. Edward William Harvey-Hawke 1799 - 1869 4th Baron Hawke of Towton
        - + Elizabeth Frances Ramsden d1824 (no children) mar'd 1821
        - + Frances Featherstonhaugh d1903 (2nd wife) mar'd 1848

        After Eton went to the Continent (no vacancy at Christ Church College, Oxford); 1821 Married Elizabeth Frances Ramsden 2nd August, daughter of Sir John Ramsden; 1824 Wife died (no children); 1824 Inherited title 4th Lord Hawke, Baron of Towton 1st December[1]; 1825; 1848 Married Frances Featherstonhaugh; (died 1903) - daughter of Walker Featherstonhaugh.
          - 6 Frances Cassandra Harvey-Hawke 1851 - 1921 mar'd 1870
          - + Lawrence Parsons 1840 - 1908 - 4th Earl of Rosse

          Hon. Frances Cassandra Harvey-Hawke - The only child of Edward 4th Lord Hawke, Frances married Lawrence Parsons on 1st September 1870. Lawrence Parsons K.P., F.R.S., D.C.L., LL.D, J.P., came from a family of academics; his father had graduated with first class honours in mathematics in 1822. He had erected the largest, at the time, telescope in the world on his estate which was called the 'Leviathan'. His mother was an accomplished photographer in the early days of photography with Fox-Talbot. Like his father, Lawrence was President of the Royal Dublin Society 1887-92, Chancellor of the University of Dublin and had been President of the Royal Irish Academy 1895-1900. He had attended Trinity College Dublin, had been a JP for the West Riding of Yorkshire, JP for Co. Tipperary and King's County, High Sheriff of King's County since 1867 and Lord

---

[1] Stockdale's Peerage of England, Scotland and Ireland, Vol. 1, by Barak Longmate

Lieutenant since 1892. Property held by this family included Birr Castle (70m south west of Dublin), Womersley Park near Pontefract in Yorkshire and Heaton Hall near Bradford.

    7    William Edward Parsons   1873 - 1918 - 5th Earl of Rosse
    +    Frances Louis Lister-Kay

William Edward Parsons 5th Earl of Rosse 1896 Commissioned into West Yorkshire Regiment; 1896 Promoted to Lieutenant ; 1897 Regular Officer in the Coldstream Guards; 1899-90 Served in the South African War[1]; 1900 Captain in the Irish Guards; 1905 Married Frances Louis Lister-Kaye b.1882; 1906 Appointed Major; 1908 Resigned from the military; 1914-18 - Rejoined the Army during WWI. William Parsons - otherwise Lord Oxmantown - was born in 1873. He was a professional soldier and married in 1905 on 19th October to Frances Louis Lister-Kaye the daughter of Sir Cecil Lister-Kaye 4th Bt and Lady Beatrice Adeline Pelham-Clinton. He resigned from the army in 1908 but when the First World War broke out he returned to service. He died from wounds received during that service. William and Frances had three children: Lawrence, Lady Bridget b.1907 and Hon. Desmond Edward Parsons 1910-37. Frances was a descendant (7x great-granddaughter) of Sir William Lister 1613-42 who was slain at Tadcaster fighting the parliamentary cause in the English Civil War and her 9x great-grandmother was Ursula Fairfax, sister to 1st Lord Fairfax.

    8    Lawrence Michael Harvey Parsons K.B.E. - 1906 - 1979, 6th Earl of Rosse
    +    Anne Messel 1902 - 1992, mar'd 1935

1918 succeeded to the title when his father died; Eton; Christ Church, Oxford; 1935 married Anne Messel; Chancellor of Dublin University; Active with the National Trust; 1939-45 Captain in the Irish Guards; 1945 M.B.E.; 1947-68 Chairman, Georgian Group; 1949-64 Vice-Chairman, University of Dublin; 1974 K .B.E.; 1979 died. He married Anne Messel in 1935 - this was Anne's second marriage as she had previously been married to Ronald Owen Lloyd Armstrong-Jones and the couple had divorced in 1934. Son from that first marriage was Anthony Armstrong-Jones who married Princess Margaret, sister to Queen Elizabeth II.

    9    William Clere Leonard Brendan Wilmer Parsons b.1936 - 7th Earl of Rosse
    +    Alison Margaret Cooke-Hurle, mar'd 1966

Born 21st October 1936; Attended Eton; Aiglon College, Grenoble University and Christ Church Oxford; 1955-57 Officer in the Irish Guards; 1963-80 Worked for the United Nations; 1963-65 UNTAB Ghana, Administration Officer; 1965-68 Assistant Resident Representative at Dahomey; 1966 Married Alison Margaret Cooke-Hurle, daughter of Major John Davey Cooke-Hurle; 1968-70 Area Officer, Mid-West Africa; 1969 Birth of son Hon. Lawrence Patrick Parsons, Lord Oxmantown (now married since 2004 to Anna Lin Xiaojing) with two children: Hon. William Charles Parsons born 2008, and Hon. Olivia Rose Xuewei Parsons born 2006; 1970-75; Assistant Resident Representative in Iran; 1971 Birth of daughter Lady Alicia Siobhan Margaret Nasreen Parsons (now married since 2007 to Nathaniel Clements); 1975-78 Deputy Resident Representative in Bangladesh 1978-80 Deputy Resident Representative in Algeria; 1979 Succeeded to the title 7th Earl of Rosse - previously known as Lord Oxmantown; 1980-91 Director, Historic Irish Houses and Gardens Association; 1981 Birth of son Michael John Finn Parsons; 1984-89 Member of the Irish Government's Council of Development and Co-operation; 1985+ Birr Scientific and Heritage Foundation; 1986-90 Agency for Personal Service Overseas; 1993+ Lorne House Trust

    9    Desmond Oliver Martin Parsons 1938-2010
    +    Aline Edwina MacDonald

7    Hon. Geoffrey Lawrence Parsons 1874 - 1956
+    Margaret Betty Gladstone mar'd 1911
7    Lady Muriel Frances Mary Parsons  1876 - 1927 mar'd 1906
+    Brig.Gen. Harold Maxwell Grenfell
    8    Elizabeth Mary Grenfell b1908
    +    Philip Tyson-Woodcock mar'd 1929
    +    John Davies, mar'd 1938
    8    Joan Sophie Grenfell b1912
    +    Maj. Douglas James Bailey mar'd 1935
    +    Capt. John de Moraville mar'd 1950
    8    Cassandra Lorna Grenfell b1915

5    Stanhope Harvey-Hawke  1804 - 1870 - 5th Baron Hawke of Towton

Capt. Hon. Stanhope Harvey-Hawke; 1823 entered the army at a young age; 1831 Retired from the army on half-pay; Won the Oaks with 'The Marchioness' - a celebrated horse; Won the Two Thousand Guineas and the St Leger in the same year with 'The Marquis'; 2nd at The Derby with 'Caractacus'; 1869 Inherited title 5th Lord Hawke but nothing else - the estate went to the daughter; 1870 Died. Stanhope entered the army at a young age and retired as a Captain in 1831 on half pay. He was not a wealthy man but, like his brother, he was a keen sportsman and his horses won the leading races of the day. When his brother the 4th Lord Hawke died in 1869 Stanhope was horrified to discover that he had been left nothing, that all of his brother's estate had been devised to his daughter Cassandra who later married the 4th Earl of Rosse. Stanhope was unmarried and the title passed over to his cousin Rev. Edward

---

[1] Yorkshire Leaders: Social and Political

# Genealogy

       Hawke 1815-87 when he died. Residence: Park House, Pontefract. In the sporting world he was known as "Stanhope Hawke".

   5   Martin Bladen Harvey-Hawke  1806 - 1857. Hon. Martin Bladen Harvey-Hawke. Predeceased his brothers. Unmarried and killed in a fox-hunting accident. Lord Scarborough's hound - accident close to Bramwith Hall.

4   Martin Bladen Edward Hawke 1777 - 1839

+   Hannah Nisbet

   5   Edward Henry Julius Hawke     1815 - 1887 - 6th Baron Hawke

   +   Joan Dowker 1840 - 1911

       Rev. Edward Henry Julius Hawke - 6th Lord Hawke-Early education at Tours, France (spoke perfect French); 1839 B.A. from St John's College, Cambridge; 1843 M.A. Cambridge; 1854 Rector of Willingham to 1875; 1857 Married Joan Dowker - 3rd daughter of Henry Dowker, Laysthorpe, Yorkshire mar'd 9th July 1857; 1840-aft 1911 and had 10 children; 1870 Succeeded to the title when his cousin Stanhope died; 1874 Retired from the Ministry and worked in the City in his later years;[1] 1874 Moved to Wighill Park, near Tadcaster in Yorkshire with his family; 1881 Member of the Carlton Club; 1887 Died at Midland Hotel, St Pancras, London. Buried All Saints, Wighill, Yorkshire. Broke his leg at an early age which was not set well and he was left with a stiff leg permanently. Was passionate about cricket and played for Willingham village cricket club. When his cousin Stanhope died in 1870 having only held the title Baron Hawke himself for a year, Edward succeeded to the title of Baron Hawke but not the estate. The Will of his cousin Edward William Harvey-Hawke had been drawn up to leave his estate to his daughter Frances who married Lawrence Parsons, the 4th Earl of Rosse. Rev. Edward and his family had lived quite modestly in a rectory but a member of the family who felt sorry for their circumstances provided a house at Wighill at a reduced rate for their benefit. Wighill had been associated for centuries with the Stapleton family and was located close to Tadcaster and Scarthingwell. One source quotes the compassionate relative as being a Walter Brooke (descendants of Elizabeth's sister Frances).

6   Edward Hawke   1859 - 1871  Commanded HMS Irresistible which was sunk after hitting a mine in the Dardanelles, Turkish Straits

6   Martin Bladen Hawke 1860 - 1938 - 7th Baron Hawke

+   Maude Edwards  - 1936

**Martin Bladen Hawke- 7th Baron[2]**

Martin Bladen Hawke, 7th Lord Hawke born Gainsborough, Lincs; 1870-4 St Michael's, Aldin House, Slough. Prep School; 1874-9 Eton School (19 appearances for Eton Cricket Club); 1875 Family moved to Wighill Park, near Tadcaster; 1878. Played in an Eton v Harrow cricket match; 1879-81. Privately tutored at home; 1879 Lieutenant in the 5th West Yorkshire Militia; 1881 Made his Debut for Yorkshire Gentleman's Cricket Club; 1881 Member of the Carlton Club (his father arranged); 1882-5 Magdalene College, Cambridge; 1882. Played for Cambridge County Cricket Club; 1883 Became Captain of Yorkshire County Cricket Club (held till 1910); Justice of the Peace.

1887 Succeeded to his father's title whilst he was on a cricket tour of Australia; 1887 Appointed as Magistrate, North-West Riding; 1889 Cricket tour to India and Ceylon; 1891 Cricket tour to USA; 1892 5th West Yorkshire Militia - Captain 3rd Btn Prince of Wales Own Yorkshire Regiment; Honorary Major; Colonel of the West Riding Volunteer Regiment; 1893 Cricket tour of India and Ceylon; 1893 Honorary Major; Chairman of Oxo Limited; 1894 Cricket tour of USA; 1894 Executor of J M Dawson's Will (of Brooke Hall, Wighill);[3] 1896 Captained England in South Africa (3 times); 1898 Elected President of Yorkshire County Cricket Club; 1899 Captained England in South Africa (2 times); 1908 last cricket season. Retired as Chairman of Selectors 1909; 1909 Cricketer of the Year 'Wisden'; 1912 Went to Argentina with an MCC cricket team; 1914 MCC President 1914-18; 1916 Married Maude Edwards (she died 1936); 1916 Went to live at 10 Belgrave Square - his wife's former marital home; 1924 Moved to North Berwick (wife's family home); 1925 Caused a storm over his comment "Pray God, no professional shall ever captain England"; 1927 Executor of Emily Dunning's Will; 1932 Treasurer MCC Cricket; 1938 died. Martin Bladen Hawke was best known for his cricketing skills. In 1892 the Taunton Courier and Western Advertiser wrote of him "*he is a good looking, pleasant, modest fellow and though as yet not a great statesman he is a good conservative. He is a light-hearted bachelor*". Born in 1860, he did not marry until age 56 when he wed the widowed Maude Edwards, a wealthy widow and through her he acquired property. Maude's former marital home at 10 Belgrave Square, London was where the couple lived immediately after marriage. Maude's late husband had been a wealthy businessman. Hawke also retained the lease on his family

---

[1] Sat on the Board of Buenos Aires Great Southern Railway, the Direct United States Cable and the Taital Railways. Cited in 'Lord Hawke: A Cricketing Legend' by James P. Coldham, 2003

[2] Portrait in possession of the Hawke family

[3] Tadcaster Gazette 22nd June 1895

home at Wighill Park at Tadcaster in Yorkshire until the lease expired in 1925. Then the couple were to live at Huttons Ambottall in Yorkshire.  Another property Hawke acquired through his wife was Glasclune in North Berwick, about 20 miles away from Edinburgh, Scotland which the couple used as a holiday home and it is thought that this is where Hawke spent his final days - dying at a nearby nursing home.  Martin Bladen Hawke played for the Yorkshire Gentlemen's Cricket Club and became Captain of the Yorkshire County Cricket Club at just 22 years of age and during his tenure eight County Championships were won.  His experiences in the cricket world were captured in his book "Recollections and Reminiscences" and he remained of amateur status throughout his career.  Brother Stanhope went into the Navy and his brother Henry went into the Army.  He was on a cricket tour in Australia in 1887 when news of his father's death reached him.  He died without heirs and the title passed to his younger brother Edward Julian Hawke.

- 6  Stanhope Hawke 1863 - 1875 Admiral Hon. Stanhope Hawke.  Promoted to Lt in 1899, Captain in 1905, then by 1911 was an Admiral in command of HMS Hampshire (ship lost in WWI)
- 6  Bladen Edward Hawke    1865 -
- 6  Harold Brooke Hawke 1867 - 1913
- 6  Mary Catherine Hawke    1869 - 1948
- 6  Eleanor Jane Emily Hawke 1871 - 1940
- +  Arthur Gordon Watney d.1927 mar'd 1921
- 6  Edward Julian Hawke 1873 - 1939 - 8th Baron Hawke of Towton
- +  Frances Alice Wilmer 1876 - 1959

    Edward Julian Hawke - 8th Lord Hawke -1887 Eton School; 1900 Married Frances Alice Wilmer (1876-1959); Managing Director of Bombay Trading Company; Director of the National Bank of India; Lived at Kiplongton Grange, Sevenoaks, Kent; both Edward and wife Frances were buried at All Saints Church, Wighill, Yorkshire

- 7  Veronica Margery Hawke 1915 - 1997
- +  Jack Briscoe Masefield, Assistant Commissioner of Police in Malaysia d.1993
- 7  Bladen Wilmer Hawke    1901 - 1985 - 9th Baron Hawke of Towton
- +  Ina Mary Faure Walker

    Bladen Wilmer Hawke - 9th Lord Hawke; 1901 Born in Karachi, India; 1911 Living with grandmother Jane on 1911 census; Winchester College; 1923 King's College, Cambridge, B.A.; Manager - Bombay-Burma Company; 1934 Mar'd Ina Mary Faure Walker 1913-2002 - daughter of Henry Faure Walker of Highley Manor, Balcombe, Sussex; succeeded to title in 1939 when his father died; 1939-45 served in the Ministry of Economic Warfare in the War Office; 1946 M.A.; 1953-7 Lord-in-Waiting; 1955-85 Member of Church Assembly and 1958-85 Church Commissioner

- 7  Julian Stanhope Theodore Hawke 1904 - 1992 - 10th Baron Hawke
- +  Georgette Margaret Davison

    Julian was buried All Saints Church, Wighill, Yorkshire. 11th and 12th Lords Hawke descend.

- 6  Alice Cassandra Hawke    1875 - 1957
- 6  Catherine Isabel Hawke    1877 - 1942
- 5  daughter Hawke 1816 - 1837
- 5  Thomas Edward Nisbet Hawke 1818 -
- 5  Chaloner Hawke 1819 -
- 5  Bladen Edward Martin Hawke 1820 - 1877

    Commander Bladen Edward Martin Hawke; 1839 Appointed Mate, Royal Naval College for Instruction;[1] 1844 Appointed Lieutenant;[2] Commander in the Royal Navy;[3] 1852+ Broke his back falling from rigging whilst serving on the China Station, lived his whole life with his brother Edward and his family; 1852+ Pensioned from the Navy by 6th July 1852;[4] 1877 Died 13th September (reported in the Illustrated London News)

- 4  Catherine Hawke 1779 - 1780
- 4  Isabella Hawke    1783 - 1786
- 4  Annabella Elizabeth Cass. Hawke    1788 - 1818
- 3  Edward Hawke    1746 - 1773
- 3  Chaloner Hawke    1750 - 1777
- 3  Catherine Hawke 1751 - 1824
- 3  William Hawke    1753 - 1753
- 2  Thomas Hawke    1707 - 1707
- 2  Frances Hawke 1716 - 1742
- +  Thomas Maule
- * 3rd Husband of Elizabeth Bladen:
- + Isaac Sharpe    1659 - 1735 mar'd 1723

---

[1] United Service Magazine Vol. 35.  Also TNA: ADM 196/4/501, 19th November 1839 enrolled as Lieutenant in Navy
[2] United Service Magazine p406
[3] Illustrated London News
[4] The Navy List 1852

# Name Index

## ADDITIONAL SOURCES

In addition to sources quoted within the book, the following have been consulted:
The Visitation of the County of York (Volume 36) - Surtees Society, Durham, Eng 26
The Visitation of Yorkshire in the years 1563 and 1564 made by William Flower, esquire, Norroy king of arms v 16, 18
The visitation of the county of York begun in MDCLXV. and finished a Dni MDCLXVI - Dugdale, William, Sir, 1605-1686
Hemsworth Parish Registers 1654-1812
Saxton-in-Elmet Parish Registers 1538-1812

YORKSHIRE PARISH RECORD SOCIETY:

Volume 1  St Michael le Belfrey 1565-1653
Volume 2  Burton Fleming 153 8-1812
Volume 3  Horbury 1508-1812
Volume 5  Monk Fryston 1538-1678
Volume 6  Patrington 1570-1731
Volume 8  Blacktoft 1700-1812
Volume 10 Kippax, 1539-1812
Volume 11 St Michael le Belfrey 1653-1772
Volume 12 Brantingham 1658-1812
Volume 13 Hampsthwaite 1603-1794
Volume 14 Wath-upon-Dearne 1598-1778
Volume 15 Cherry Burton 1561-1740
Volume 16 Marske-in-Cleveland 1570-1812
Volume 17 Hartshead 1612-1812
Volume 18 Linton-in-Craven 1562-1812
Volume 19 Bolton-by-Bolland 1558-1724
Volume 20 Pickhill-cum-Roxby 1567-1812
Volume 21 Howden 1543-1659
Volume 22 Bolton-by-Colland 1725-1812
Volume 23 Grinton-in-Swindale 1640-1802
Volume 24 Howden 1543-1702
Volume 25 Hackness 1557-1783
Volume 26 Aldborough 1538-1711
Volume 27 Rothwell 1538-1689
Volume 28 Gargrave 1558-1812
Volume 29 Terrington 1599-1812
Volume 30 Thornhill, part 1, 1580-1678
Volume 31 Allerton Mauleverer 1557-1812
Volume 32 Howden, 1543-1659
Volume 33 Otley 1562-1672
Volume 34 Rothwell 1538-1689

Volume 35 Kirklington 1568-1812
Volume 36 St Martin, Coney Street, York  1557-1812
Volume 37 Halifax 1538-1593
Volume 38 Settringham 1559-1812
Volume 39 Austerfield 1559-1812
Volume 40 Thornhill, part 2, 1743-1812
Volume 41 Goodramgate Holy Trinity 1573-1812
Volume 42 Thirsk, 1556-1721
Volume 43 Danby-in-Cleveland 1585-1812
Volume 44 Otley Pt II 1632-1753
Volume 45 Halifax 1536-1593
Volume 46 Garforth 1631-1812
Volume 47 St Andrew's Kildwick in Craven
Volume 48 Howden, 1543-1659
Volume 49 Darrington 1567-1812
Volume 50 Harewood 1614-1812
Volume 51 Rothwell, part 2 1690-1763
Volume 52 Bishophill, St Mary 1602-1812
Volume 53 Thornhill part 3, 1754-1812
Volume 54 East Rounton 1595-1837
Volume 56 Farnham 1569-1812
Volume 57 Snaith 1558-1657
Volume 58 Sheffield 1560-1634
Volume 60 Sheffield 1560-1634
Volume 61 Kilburn, York  1600-1812
Volume 68 Sheffield 1560-1634
Volume 70 St Crux, York, 1539-1716
Volume 71 Winteringham 1558-1812
Volume 72 Kildwick-in-Craven
Volume 80 Ripon I 1574-1628
Volume 90 Great ayton 1600-1812
Volume 117 Rillington 1638-1812

Plus, parish records of Marske, Holderness, Snaith 1537-1657, Hackness, Kirkleatham 1559-1812, Bolton, Coniston, Farnham 1569-1812, Monk Fryston 1538-1678, Rillington, Ledsham 1539-1812, Allerton Malverer, Horbury in Wakefield 1598-1812, Wath-upon-Dearn 1598-1778,

| | | | |
|---|---|---|---|
| Halifax St John the Baptist | 1517-1847 | Southowram | 1723-1846 |
| Haworth | 1645-1812 | Sowerby | 1651-1812 |
| Hemsworth St Helen's | 1538-1876 | Sowerby Bridge, Christ Church | 1709-1812 |
| Luddenden St Mary | 1653-1812 | Tadcaster | 1570-1859 |
| Pontefract | 1544-1812 | Thornhill | 1580-1812 |
| Saxton-in-Elmet | 1539-1994 | Wakefield | 1795-1832 |
| South Kirkby, All Saints | 1620-1853 | St Martin, Coney St., York | 1557-1812 |

Whitby Parish Registers 1600-76, Oughtibridge, Norton Lees, Ecclesfield, Ecclesal, everthorpe, Attercliffe and Hampswaite.
Calderdale Family History Society's Full Transcription Index. Yorkshire Assizes Rolls: 3 volumes - King John and King Henry III - 1199-1271
YORKSHIRE DEEDS:  12$^{th}$ to 17$^{th}$ Centuries, Volumes 1 to 10
Early Yorkshire Charters, Volumes 1-3, 6, 8 and 11
West Riding Session Records: Orders 1611-42; Indictments 1637-42 Ed. John Lister

## Name Index

| | |
|---|---|
| Abbot, Richard | 42 |
| Addison, Joseph | 194 |
| Allanson, Sir William | 63 |
| Anderson, James | 127 |
| Andsley, Robert | 44 |
| Anglesey, 1st Marquis (Paget) | 149 |
| Arnold, Benedict | 184-185 |
| Ash, Dame Mary | 104-105, 110-111 |
| Atkinson, Anne | 17, 27 |
| Atkinson, Sir Robert | 17, 27 |
| Atkinson, Mary | 17, 27 |
| Audley, Lord | 52 |
| Austen, Cassandra | 184, 188 |
| Austen, Jane | 183-184, 188 |
| Austen, Francis | 184 |
| Ayscough, Elizabeth (Savile) | 22 |
| Bacon, Francis | 55 |
| Bacon, Sir Francis | 55 |
| Bacon, Nathaniel | 55 |
| Bagot, Sir Walter Wagstaff | 168 |
| Bairstowe, Michael | 26 |
| Baker, John | 186 |
| Baker, Walter | 43, 103 |
| Baker, William (Windsor) | 43-44, 103 |
| Baltimore, Ld (Calvert) | 114, 131 |
| Barrette, Barbara de | 115 |
| Barnaby, Eustace | 86-87 |
| Barnard, Alderman Henry | 64 |
| Barnard, Alderman John | 64 |
| Barry, Mary | 27, 46 |
| Barwick, Lady (Toulston) | 74 |
| Bath, Earl of | 79, 82, 90, 193 |
| Batt, John | 41 |
| Bedford, Dukes of | 130, 142 |
| Bedloe, William | 78-79, 82 |
| Belasyse, Ursula (Fairfax) | 110 |
| Bellasis, Mr (Fairfax cousin) | 51 |
| Bentinck, Henry William | 146 |
| Bentinck, William Cavendish-Scott | 150 |
| Berkley | 34 |
| Berrie, Duc de | 190 |
| Berry, Dr Richard | 5, 27-29, 32, 36, 41-48, 58, 69, 71-72, 84-85, 98, 102-103, 106, 156, 197, 227 |
| Berry, Prudence (Gargrave) | 27-28, 43 |
| Berry, Susannah (Fountain) | 46 |
| Bess of Hardwick | 18, 21, 33 |
| Birkenhead, Sir John | 71 |
| Birkhead, Alice (Lacy) c1530 | 11, 15, 24, 59 |
| Birkhead, Alice (Lacy) c1560 | 24, 46, 58-59 |
| Birkhead, Alice (Rogers/Watson) | 67-68 |
| Birkhead, Elizabeth (Lindsey) | 67-68, 70-71 |
| Birkhead, George Salvin | 58 |
| Birkhead, Gilbert | 59 |
| Birkhead, John | 59-60 |
| Birkhead, Margaret (Bladen) | 51, 56, 58, 60, 67-68, 71 |
| Birkhead, Martin | 15, 24, 51, 58-60 |
| Birkhead, Nathaniel | 19, 28, 42, 46-47, 51, 56-61, 65, 67-69, 72, 206, 226 |
| Birkhead, Richard | 24, 59-60 |
| Birt, Sarah | 187 |
| Bixxon, Robert | 26 |
| Black, William | 132 |
| Bladen, Anne (Sweringen) | 121 |
| Bladen, Anne (Tasker) | 115, 123, 125-128, 131, 217, 227 |
| Bladen, Barbara (Janssen) | 130, 133, 136, 140, 143, 228, 229 |

# Name Index

| | |
|---|---|
| Bladen, Barbara (St John) | 125, 130, 135, 136, 138-140, 143, 218, 229 |
| Bladen, Catherine (Fowke) | 8-9, 96, 99-101, 104-105, 109-113, 155, 164, 166, 178, 193, 209-210, 227 |
| Bladen, Charles | 109 |
| Bladen, Charles (s.o. Dr Thomas) | 115 |
| Bladen, Christopher | 125-126 |
| Bladen, Elizabeth (Clarke) | 10, 17, 48, 67, 69 |
| Bladen, Elizabeth (Hawke) | 8, 96, 101, 104-105, 109-110, 128, 155, 174-175, 178-180, 213, 227, 232 |
| Bladen, Elizabeth (Lacy) | 9, 11, 15, 17-20, 22-24, 28-29, 41, 43-47, 59-60, 68, 96, 102-103 |
| Bladen, Frances (Ham'd/Har.) | 8, 92, 96, 101, 104-107, 109-110, 112, 127, 155-159, 163-173, 180, 211-213, 227, 231 |
| Bladen, Harriet (Essex) | 2, 125, 130, 135-136, 140-144, 149-151, 178, 218-219, 228-230 |
| Bladen, Isabella (Fairfax) | 74, 78, 95-96, 98, 100, 104, 107-109, 114, 174 |
| Bladen, Isabella (Tinker) | 8, 96, 193-195 |
| Bladen, Isabella (Vavasour) | 8, 96, 101, 104-105, 109-110, 155-156, 209, 227 |
| Bladen, John | 8, 10, 12, 17, 40, 42, 47-56, 59-67, 69, 197, 207-208, 226 |
| Bladen, Margaret (Birkhead) | 56, 58, 60, 67-68, 71 |
| Bladen, Martin (Colonel) | 7-8, 57, 60, 63, 85, 94, 99, 101, 104-107, 113, 122, 126, 128-131, 133-134, 158, 163, 168, 172, 177-178, 180-181, 193-197, 199-201, 213-217, 226 |
| Bladen, Martin (Wlm's son) | 125-126 |
| Bladen, Nathaniel | 8, 10, 31, 42-43, 47-48, 56, 58-60, 67-110, 119, 114, 126, 156, 159-161, 164, 174, 168, 193, 197, 199-201, 208-209, 226 |
| Bladen, Priscilla | 125-126 |
| Bladen, Ralph | 18 |
| Bladen, Robert | 8-12, 15-44, 47-50, 56-60, 62, 67-69, 72, 84, 98, 103, 106, 156, 197, 206-207, 225 |
| Bladen, Thomas | 2, 115, 123-140, 142, 144, 178, 180-181, 217-218, 228-229 |
| Bladen, William (Maryland) | 8, 99-101, 105, 111, 114-123, 125-128, 132, 155, 197-198, 202-205, 210-211, 226-227 |
| Bladon, John McKno | 138 |
| Bladiston, John | 119 |
| Blakiston, Nathaniel | 116-117, 119 |
| Blathwayt, William | 99, 114 |
| Blount, George | 194 |
| Bolton, Duke of | 104 |
| Bonaparte, Napoleon | 146-148 |
| Bonnet, Stede | 130 |
| Bordiers, Claude | 87 |
| Bosvile, Jane | 24 |
| Bosvile, Thomas (Newhall) | 35, 51 |
| Bosvile, William | 185 |
| Boughton, Elizabeth (Wortley/Cavendish) | 17-19, 21-22, 26, 33-35, 40 |
| Bouchier, Sir John | 63 |
| Bouncker, Grace | 21, 24 |
| Boyne, Thomas | 32 |
| Boynton, Catherine (Fairfax) | 62 |
| Boynton, Matthew | 62-63 |
| Braithwaite, Mariane | 96, 127 |
| Braithwaite, Richard | 172 |
| Briscoe, John | 87 |
| Brockett, Margaret | 28 |
| Brodrick, Alan | 194 |
| Brontë, Anne | 11 |
| Brontë, Charlotte | 11 |
| Brontë, Emily | 11, 25 |
| Brontë, Patrick | 11 |
| Brooke, Catherine | 128, 156, 168, 179-192 |
| Brooke, Humphrey | 172 |
| Brooke, Walter | 156, 168, 170, 172, 186 |
| Bryant, James | 88 |
| Brydges, James (Chandos) | 102, 113, 129, 158, 194 |
| Buccleuch, Duchess of (Montagu) | 143 |
| Buckingham, Duke | 5, 77, 94-96 |
| Buckingham, Duchess (Fairfax) | 5, 77, 87, 91, 94-96, 104-105, 111, 155 |
| Bull, John | 68 |
| Burney, Fanny | 183 |
| Byng, Admiral | 131, 139, 181, 220 |
| Byng, John | 139 |
| Byng, Frances Penelope | 139 |
| Byng, Robert | 139 |

| | |
|---|---|
| Byron, Lord | 149, 190 |
| Caitlin, Agnes | 35 |
| Calvert, Benedict | 138 |
| Calvert, Caroline | 123 |
| Calvert, Charles | 124, 131, 135 |
| Calvert, Frederick (6th Ld) | 123 |
| Capel, Adela Caroline | 125, 154 |
| Capel, John Thomas | 125, 144-150 |
| Capel, Adm. Thomas Bladen | 125, 143, 150-154 |
| Capel, Thomas Edward | 125, 144, 148-149 |
| Capel, William Robert | 125, 142, 150 |
| Capel, William Anne (4th) | 142 |
| Capel-Coningsby, George | 125, 144-145 |
| Capell, Adolphus | 125 |
| Capell, Algernon | 125, 147 |
| Capell, Algernon, Henry | 125 |
| Capell, Arthur | 125 |
| Capell, Arthur Algernon | 125, 144-145 |
| Capell, Arthur de Vere | 125 |
| Capell, Bladen Horace | 125 |
| Capell, Bladen Ozro | 125 |
| Capell, Charles | 125 |
| Capell, George | 125 |
| Capell, Horace | 125 |
| Capell, Horatio Bladen | 125 |
| Capell, Reginald | 125 |
| Capell, Robert de Vere | 125 |
| Cardonnel, Adam de | 87 |
| Carroll, Charles (Settler) | 116-118, 120, 123, 128, 132, 186 |
| Carroll, Margaret | 118 |
| Carroll, Thomas King | 116 |
| Carter, Robert | 123, 125, 127 |
| Cauldwell, John | 35 |
| Cavendish, Arabella | 130 |
| Cavendish, Elizabeth (Boughton/Wortley) | 17-19, 21-22, 26, 33-35, 40 |
| Cavendish, Lord Henry | 144 |
| Cavendish, Lord James | 130 |
| Cavendish, Lord John | 184 |
| Cavendish, William | 17-18, 21, 33, 129 |
| Chaloner, Lady Frances (Fairfax) | 70, 73-75, 77, 83-85, 94-95, 98, 100-101, 107, 109, 226-227 |
| Chaloner, James | 74 |
| Chaloner, Sir Thomas | 100 |
| Chapman, Stephen Rev. | 31, 70-71, 75 |
| Chetwynd, Walter | 81 |
| Churchill, Anne | 130 |
| Clarges, Sir Walter | 97, 158 |
| Clarke, Elizabeth (Bladen) | 10, 17, 48, 67 |
| Coke, Lady Mary | 142 |
| Coleman, Sarah | 88-89 |
| Coleman, Thomas | 88-89 |
| Colles, Francis | 104 |
| Collingwood, Admiral | 151 |
| Collingwood, Col. Francis | 174 |
| Colson, John | 92 |
| Coney, George | 33, 35 |
| Coney, Nathaniel | 97 |
| Coney, Richard | 33 |
| Coney, Sir Sutton | 33-34 |
| Coney, Thomas | 33-34 |
| Coney, Sir Thomas | 19, 26, 32-34 |
| Copley, Capt | 64 |
| Copley, Lionel | 99, 114 |
| Cornelys, Madam Teresa | 142 |
| Cornforth (Bladen tenant) | 43-46 |
| Cornwallis, Charles, 1st Earl | 103 |
| Cornwallis, Gen. Charles | 103 |

# Name Index

| | |
|---|---|
| Cottington, Lord | 55 |
| Couldwell, Nicholas | 35 |
| Corri, Augusta Elizabeth | 189 |
| Cresap, Col. | 137 |
| Crofts, Anthony | 33, 35 |
| Crofts, Sir Henry | 33 |
| Cromwell, Oliver | 28, 46, 66, 87 |
| Cromwell, Thomas | 14 |
| Dale, Elizabeth | 67 |
| Dale, Margaret | 47 |
| Dale, Roger | 28, 61, 68 |
| Damer, Hon. Lionel | 143 |
| Danby, Earl - see Osborne) | |
| Dandy, Edmund | 37 |
| Dangerfield, Thomas | 81 |
| Danvers, Henry | 30 |
| Darley, Henry | 63 |
| Darley, Sir Richard | 63 |
| Darnall, Henry | 105 |
| Delafaye, Charles | 194 |
| Denman, Alderman Nicholas | 64 |
| Dent, Maj. William | 116, 118 |
| Denton, John | 24 |
| Dodsworth, Roger | 45 |
| Dorsey, Edward | 120 |
| Dorsey, Samuel | 120 |
| Downing, Mrs | 81 |
| Duffet, Mr | 88-89 |
| Dulany, Benjamin Tasker | 123 |
| Dulany, Daniel Snr | 125, 127 |
| Dulany, Daniel Jnr | 123-125, 129, 134 |
| Dunblane, Lord | 79-80 |
| Dunston, John | 87 |
| Duplin, Nicholas | 87 |
| Duplin, Paul | 87 |
| Eden, Sir Robert | 123-124 |
| Ellison, Godfrey | 35 |
| Embreys, Joseph | 86 |
| Emmet, Sir Alexander | 14 |
| Essex, Harriet (Bladen) | 2, 125, 135-136, 140-144, 149-151, 218-219, 228-230 |
| Essex, Earl of | 125, 129, 135-136, 144-145, 153 |
| Estwick, Samuel | 188 |
| Fairfax, Anne (Wentworth) | 53 |
| Fairfax, Anne (wife 3$^{rd}$ Ld) | 95 |
| Fairfax, Brian (1633-1711-author) | 77-78, 94 |
| Fairfax, Brian (s.o. above) | 85, 138 |
| Fairfax, Brian (s.o. above) | 94, 159, 161, 166 |
| Fairfax, Bridget (Gargrave) | 27, 29 |
| Fairfax, Catherine (Boynton) | 62-63 |
| Fairfax, Catherine (Lister) | 74 |
| Fairfax, Catherine (d.of Rbt) | 111 |
| Fairfax, Charles (s.o. Brian) | 94 |
| Fairfax, Elizabeth (sist. Rbt) | 93 |
| Fairfax, Ferdinando (2$^{nd}$ Ld) | 62-64 |
| Fairfax, Ferdinando (s.o. Brian) | 94, 138 |
| Fairfax, Lady Frances (Chaloner) | 70, 73-75, 77, 83-85, 87, 94-95, 98, 100-101, 107, 109, 226-227 |
| Fairfax, Henry (4$^{th}$ Ld) | 77-78, 159, 166 |
| Fairfax, Isabella (Bladen) | 74, 78, 95-96, 98, 100-101, 104, 107-109 |
| Fairfax, Margaret (Hotham) | 62 |
| Fairfax, Mary (d.o. 3$^{rd}$ Lord) | 5, 77, 87, 91-92, 94-97, 104-105, 111, 155, 163 |
| Fairfax, Admiral Robert | 74, 92-93, 111, 152, 161, 163-165, 169 |
| Fairfax, Thomas (1$^{st}$ Visc. Gilling) | 62, 159 |
| Fairfax, Sir Thomas (1$^{st}$ Ld) | 49-53, 78, 138, 197 |
| Fairfax, Sir Thomas (3$^{rd}$ Ld) | 40, 45, 50, 62-63, 65, 77, 87, 197 |
| Fairfax, Thomas (5$^{th}$ Ld) | 166 |
| Fairfax, Thomas (s.o. Steeton) | 74 |

| | |
|---|---|
| Fairfax, Thomas (d. of Rbt) | 111-112 |
| Fairfax, Brig.Gen. Thomas (Dublin) | 100-101, 111-112, 163, 166, 193 |
| Fairfax, Ursula | 110 |
| Fairfax, Sir William (Steeton) | 27, 63, 73-74, 77, 107 |
| Fairfax, William (s.o. above) | 74 |
| Fanshaw, Henry | 86 |
| Fanshaw, Thomas | 86 |
| Farrar, Brian | 13 |
| Farrer, Henry (Ewood) | 13, 75 |
| Farrer, John (s.o. above) | 75 |
| Farrar, Thomas | 41 |
| Farrar, William (Virginia) | 41, 107 |
| Favell, Thomas | 27 |
| Field, William | 35 |
| Fielding, Charles | 126 |
| Foche, Frances | 195 |
| Foche, Mary | 195 |
| Fogg, Mrs Mary | 119 |
| Forbes, Thomas | 122 |
| Forrest, Richard | 42 |
| Fountain, Elizabeth | 156 |
| Fountain, John (Melton) | 27, 44, 46, 98, 156 |
| Fountain, Thomas | 27, 43-44, 47, 98 |
| Fowke, Capt | 112-113 |
| Fowke, Martha | 113 |
| Fowke, Roger | 113 |
| Fowke, Sydenham | 113 |
| Fowke, Thomas | 113 |
| Fowlis, Sir Henry | 63 |
| Fox, Charles James | 185 |
| Foxcroft, Anthony | 26 |
| Franklin, Benjamin | 127, 195 |
| Galway, Earl of | 193-194 |
| Gargrave, Bridget (Fairfax) | 27, 29 |
| Gargrave, Catherine(Wentworth) | 27, 29, 36, 47 |
| Gargrave, Sir Cotton | 24, 27-30, 36, 44 |
| Gargrave, Elizabeth (Levett) | 28 |
| Gargrave, Francis | 29-31, 44 |
| Gargrave, Prudence (Berry) | 27-29, 43 |
| Gargrave, Sir Richard | 29-31, 36, 84 |
| Gargrave, Thomas | 27, 29, 34, 36, 68 |
| Gargrave, Sir Thomas (Speaker) | 29 |
| Gascoigne, Sir Edward | 167 |
| Gascoigne, Sir John | 158, 167 |
| Gascoigne, Thomas | 158, 186 |
| Gawnt, Thomas | 35 |
| Gawthorpe, George | 35 |
| Gibbs, Elizabeth | 193 |
| Gibbs, Mary | 193 |
| Gifford, Major John | 65-66 |
| Gill, Thomas | 162, 167 |
| Gledhill, Thomas | 15 |
| Gleurie, Louise | 87 |
| Godfrey, Sir Edmund Berry | 82, 97, 101-102 |
| Gore, Thomas | 130 |
| Gould, Elizabeth | 97 |
| Graham, Sir Bellingham | 173 |
| Graham, Sir Reginald | 162-163, 166-167 |
| Grafton, Duke of | 96, 194 |
| Grafton, Duchess of | 143 |
| Grantham, Col Thomas | 61 |
| Green, Thomas Frederick | 188 |
| Green, Rev Henry | 57 |
| Green, Richard | 42 |
| Grundy, Elias de | 87 |
| Gunning, Maria | 139 |

# Name Index

| | |
|---|---|
| Hamilton, James | 52 |
| Hamilton, Lady | 151 |
| Hamilton, William | 151 |
| Hamond, Anthony | 113, 158 |
| Hamond, Catherine Maria | 155-156, 159, 164, 167, 170, 172 |
| Hamond, Frances (Bladen) | 8, 96, 104-105, 110, 127, 155-164, 167-173, 180, 211-213, 227, 231 |
| Hamond, Frances (dau of above) | 156, 164, 167 |
| Hamond, Gervase (Snr) | 155-163, 165, 168, 230 |
| Hamond, Gervase (Jnr) | 155-156, 162, 165-171, 173, 231-232 |
| Hamond, William | 34, 104, 110, 155-167, 169, 173, 230-231 |
| Hamond, William (grandfather) | 156 |
| Hanbury, Osgood | 127 |
| Hanbury-Williams, Fraces | 142 |
| Harman, George | 106, 126, 156, 168-173 |
| Harper, Thomas | 85 |
| Harpur, Sir John | 18 |
| Harvey, Frances | 189 |
| Harvey, Henry (Gawthorpe) | 68 |
| Harvey, Stanhope | 189 |
| Hatton, 1st Viscount | 98 |
| Hawke, Annabella | 179, 192 |
| Hawke, Bladen Edward Martin | 179 |
| Hawke, Bladen Wilmer | 179 |
| Hawke, Cassandra Julia | 179, 187-189, 223 |
| Hawke, Catherine (Brooke) | 128, 156, 168, 179-192 |
| Hawke, Catherine (d.of above) | 179, 182, 187, 223 |
| Hawke, Chaloner | 179, 186, 222 |
| Hawke, Edward (Snr) | 104, 174-177, 179, 219 |
| Hawke, Edward Admiral | 128, 131, 136, 139, 151, 156, 168, 172-175, 177-192, 219-221 |
| Hawke, Edward (s.of above) | 179, 185-186, 222 |
| Hawke, Edward George | 179 |
| Hawke, Edward Harvey | 173, 179, 189 |
| Hawke, Edward Henry Julius | 179, 223 |
| Hawke, Edward Julian | 179 |
| Hawke, Edward Wlm Harvey | 179, 189 |
| Hawke, Elizabeth (Bladen) | 8, 96, 104-105, 110, 155, 174-175, 178-179, 213, 227, 232 |
| Hawke, Frances Cassandra Harvey | 179, 189 |
| Hawke, Frances Harvey | 104 |
| Hawke, Frances (d. of Ed) | 177-178 |
| Hawke, Julian Stanhope Theodore | 179 |
| Hawke, Martin Bladen b1744 | 136, 173, 179, 182-185, 187-188, 221-222, 233 |
| Hawke, Martin Bladen b1860 | 179 |
| Hawke, Martin Bladen Edward | 148, 158, 179, 182, 190-191, 223-224 |
| Hawke, Martin Bladen Harvey | 179 |
| Hawke, Stanhope Harvey | 179, 189, 192 |
| Hawke, Thomas | 175 |
| Hawke, Veronica | 179 |
| Hawke, William Martin Theodore | 179 |
| Hawkesworth, Richard | 35 |
| Haye, Richard | 35 |
| Herbert, Jane | 158 |
| Hicks, Thomas | 118 |
| Hill, Robert | 87 |
| Hillary, Joseph | 65 |
| Holdsworth, Edward | 26 |
| Holdsworth, Rev Robert | 13-15 |
| Holgate, Mary | 37-38 |
| Holgate, Robert | 32 |
| Holgate, Thomas | 37-38 |
| Hollis, Grace | 130 |
| Hollis, John (1st Duke Newcastle) | 135 |
| Holme, Thomas | 35 |
| Hopper, Andrew | 65 |
| Horne, Cotton | 29-30 |
| Hotham, Sir John | 62 |
| Hotham, John Jnr | 62-63 |

| | |
|---|---|
| Hotham, Margaret (Fairfax) | 62 |
| Houghton, Henry | 33, 35 |
| How, Mrs | 71 |
| Hoyle, Samuel | 26 |
| Hungate, Sir Francis | 155, 167 |
| Hungate, Joan | 157 |
| Hungate, Dame Mary | 167 |
| Hunt, Rev Thomas | 18, 20-21 |
| Hurst, Rev Thomas | 68 |
| Ibotson, Christopher | 35 |
| Illingworth, Richard | 26 |
| Inchiquin, Earl of | 96 |
| Ivy, Lady Theodosia (Stepkins) | 87-90 |
| Ivy, Thomas | 87-88 |
| Jackson, Charles | 159 |
| Jackson, Christopher | 87, 94 |
| Janssen, Abraham | 135, 143 |
| Janssen, Barbara (Bladen) | 123, 125, 129-130, 133, 135-136, 140, 143, 228, 229 |
| Janssen, Catherine Anne | 143 |
| Janssen, Henrietta | 143 |
| Janssen, Mary | 123 |
| Janssen, Theodore | 123, 129 |
| Janssen, William | 143 |
| Jeffreys, Hanging Judge | 89, 92 |
| Jeffreys, John | 134 |
| Johnson, Mr | 64 |
| Joyne, John | 81 |
| Kaye, Richard | 35 |
| Kerr, Lord Mark | 153 |
| Knox, Thomas | 79-82 |
| Lacy, Alice | 15, 24 |
| Lacy, Elizabeth (Bladen) | 9, 11, 15, 17-20, 22-23, 28-29, 41, 43-47, 59-60, 68, 96, 102-103 |
| Lacy, Ellen (Lister) | 15 |
| Lacy, Ellen (Paslew) | 59 |
| Lacy, Helen (Waterhouse) | 19-20, 22-24, 26, 39, 51 |
| Lacy, John 1507-82 | 11-15, 59, 225 |
| Lacy, John 1561-1638 | 15, 24, 58-59, 206 |
| Lacy, Margaret | 13 |
| Lacy, Richard (Cromwellbothom) | 23-24, 59 |
| Lacy, Sarah (Waterhouse) | 15 |
| Lacy, Thomas | 14, 72 |
| Lambert, Colonel John | 63 |
| Lamplugh, William | 75 |
| Lane, John | 79-81 |
| Lanney, Peter de | 87 |
| Laud, William | 55 |
| Laurence, Thomas | 117 |
| Laurence, Sir Thomas | 117-119 |
| Leeds, Mrs | 156, 164 |
| Leigh, Dr Theophilus | 183-184 |
| Leigh, Rev Thomas | 184 |
| Leventhorpe, Alice | 15 |
| Levett, Elizabeth (Gargrave) | 28-29 |
| Levett, Dr John | 47-48, 96 |
| Levett, Thomas | 28, 45, 47-48, 96 |
| Lindsey, Elizabeth (Birkhead) | 67-68, 70-71 |
| Lindsey, Robert | 46, 67-68 |
| Lister, Ellen (Lacy) | 15, 72 |
| Lister, Michael (Frerehead) | 16 |
| Lloyd, Maj. Gen. Edward | 119, 124, 127 |
| Lloyd, Elizabeth | 127 |
| Lloyd, Philemon | 122, 127 |
| Lloyd, Sampson | 127 |
| Locker, Edward Hawke | 181 |
| Locker, William | 181 |
| Loftus, Letitia | 115 |

# Name Index

| | |
|---|---|
| Longueville, Henry | 87 |
| Loudon, Lord | 140 |
| Lowndes, Christopher | 124-125 |
| Lowndes, Lloyd | 124 |
| Lowndes, Rebecca | 124 |
| Lowther, Sir John | 64 |
| Lowther, Sir William | 161 |
| Ludlam, Stephen Rev | 75 |
| Lynes, Philip | 120, 122 |
| Macnemara, Thomas | 118-119, 121-122, 128 |
| Marlborough, Duke of | 105, 130 |
| Mason, George | 128, 136-138 |
| Maule, Henry | 177-178 |
| Mauleverer, SirThomas | 63 |
| Mawson, Edward Rev. | 71, 75 |
| Mellish, Colonel | 191, 224 |
| Metcalfe, Thomas | 65 |
| Middleton, Joan | 155 |
| Midgley, John | 35 |
| Midgley, Joseph | 59 |
| Midgley, William | 60 |
| Million, Henry | 87 |
| Milner, Alderman (Leeds) | 95, 97 |
| Mokeston, Nicholas | 35 |
| Monckton, Elizabeth | 27, 44 |
| Monck, Christopher | 193 |
| Monck, Gen. George | 63, 94-95, 193 |
| Monckton, Elizabeth | 156 |
| Monckton, John | 27, 98 |
| Monckton-Berry, Marmaduke | 27, 44-47 |
| Monckton Robert | 85 |
| Mond, Richard | 44 |
| Monson, Sir Thomas | 36 |
| Montagu, Elizabeth | 141 |
| Moore, Ogle Capel Theodore | 143 |
| Morrice, Colonel | 61 |
| Morton, Mr | 69 |
| Mosley, Rev Thomas | 168, 173 |
| Nash, Beau | 142 |
| Neale, Thomas | 87-89, 102 |
| Nelson, Admiral Lord | 151, 153 |
| Newcastle, Duke of | 196 |
| Newton, Sir Isaac | 177 |
| Neville, Henry | 86 |
| Newcastle, Duke of | 64 |
| Nicholls, Mary | 59 |
| Nicholson, Francis | 114, 116 |
| Norfolk, Duke of | 13-14 |
| Nuthead, Dinah | 115 |
| Oates, Titus | 78-79, 81-82, 101 |
| Ogle, Anne | 125, 127 |
| Ogle, Benjamin I | 123-125 |
| Ogle, Benjamin II | 125 |
| Ogle, Benjamin III | 125 |
| Ogle, Sir Chaloner | 180, 186 |
| Ogle, Meliora | 127 |
| Ogle, Samuel | 123-125, 129, 131-132, 134, 138 |
| Ord, Mr | 159 |
| Osborne, Anne (Walpole) | 90 |
| Osborne, Bridget (Plymouth) | 77, 86, 90-93, 97 |
| Osborne, Catherine (Herbert) | 97 |
| Osborne, Charles | 73, 75, 77, 85 |
| Osborne, Dorothy | 99 |
| Osborne, Edward (Latimer) | 76-80, 82, 90-91, 197 |
| Osborne, Francis | 101 |
| Osborne, Martha (Granville) | 90 |

| | |
|---|---|
| Osborne, Thomas (E. Danby) | 30, 76-83, 90-91, 97, 99, 101, 114, 197 |
| Osborne, William | 79, 81 |
| Oscliffe, John | 42 |
| Ostercliffe, John | 44 |
| Paget, Lady Caroline | 144, 146-149 |
| Parkin, James | 37 |
| Parkin, John | 32 |
| Parkin, Thomas | 32 |
| Parry-Okeden, David Okeden | 149 |
| Parsons, Laurence (6th E. Rosse) | 179, 189 |
| Parsons, Richard (1st E. Rosse) | 103-104 |
| Parsons (4th E. of Rosse) | 104, 179 |
| Parsons, William (5th E. Rosse) | 179 |
| Parsons, William (7th E. Rosse) | 127, 168, 179 |
| Paslew, Francis | 59 |
| Paslew, Sir John | 59 |
| Paslew, Walter d1545 | 59 |
| Paslew, Walter d1573 | 59 |
| Pelham, Elizabeth | 103, 130 |
| Pelham, Henry (Prime Minister) | 130 |
| Pelham, Thomas (Newcastle) | 130 |
| Pembroke, 7th Earl | 97-98, 101 |
| Penrose, Mr | 64 |
| Perry, Micajah | 105 |
| Pierrepont, Grace | 130 |
| Pierrepont, Frances | 130 |
| Plymouth, Earl of | 79, 86, 90 |
| Popple, Alderman William | 64 |
| Potter, Henry | 33-34 |
| Potts, Mr | 69 |
| Potts, Thomas | 122 |
| Powlett, Henrietta | 103 |
| Powlett, Mary | 103-104 |
| Powlett, Ld William | 103-104, 113 |
| Prather, Thomas | 137 |
| Pride, Elizabeth | 193 |
| Pride, Thomas | 193 |
| Pringle, Thomas | 115 |
| Pue, Rev | 157, 159 |
| Pulleyne, Frances | 156, 173 |
| Pulleyne, Thomas | 156, 168, 172-173 |
| Queensbury, Duke of (4th) | 139, 142 |
| Radcliffe, Edward | 17, 27, 119 |
| Radcliffe, Sir George | 5, 17-24, 27, 39-40, 50-53, 60, 66 |
| Radcliffe, Thomas | 60 |
| Raikes, Mayor Thomas | 63-64 |
| Ramsey, John | 122 |
| Randolph, Edward | 99, 111, 114, 120 |
| Randolph, Sarah | 99 |
| Rawson, Matthew | 42, 44 |
| Reading, Thomas | 115 |
| Redhead, Arthur | 36 |
| Redhead, Elizabeth | 36 |
| Reind, Alexander | 122 |
| Rennison, John (Bilborough) | 92 |
| Richmond, Duchess of | 147 |
| Richmond, Duke of | 147 |
| Robinson, Arthur | 103 |
| Robinson, Thomas | 131, 139 |
| Rogers, Edmund | 67 |
| Rookes, William | 15 |
| Rosland, John | 42 |
| Ross, Dr David | 137-138 |
| Rumbold, Sir Thomas | 128 |
| Rumbold, William | 128 |
| Russell, Elizabeth (Bedford) | 142 |

# Name Index

| | |
|---|---|
| Ruthven, Capt James | 104, 174, 179, 232 |
| St George, Sir Richard | 51 |
| St John, Barbara (Bladen) | 125, 135, 138-140, 143, 218, 228-239 |
| St John, Frederick | 139 |
| St John, Henry | 125, 129, 136, 138-139, 230 |
| St Quintin, Sir William | 63 |
| Saltonstall, Mary | 25 |
| Savile, Anne (Wentworth) | 17, 27, 39-40 |
| Savile, Anne (Coventry) | 39-41 |
| Savile, Elizabeth (Ayscough) | 22 |
| Savile, Sir George (Thornhill) | 17, 19, 22, 27, 34, 39-40, 50 |
| Savile, Sir Henry (Thornhill) | 12-13, 34 |
| Savile, Margaret | 33 |
| Savile, Sibyl (Shibden Hall) | 24 |
| Savile, Thomas (Exley) | 12 |
| Savile, Thomas (Clifton) | 24, 40 |
| Savile, Sir William (Thornhill) | 17, 27, 34, 39-41, 54, 60, 62, 225-226 |
| Saye & Sele, Lady Elizabeth | 183-184 |
| Scholey, Henry | 41 |
| Scuthwell, Sir Robert | 81 |
| Selwyn, George | 139-140 |
| Seward, Ann | 118 |
| Seymour, Gov. Col. | 117-119 |
| Shales, Robert | 87 |
| Sharpe, Horatio | 138 |
| Sharpe, Isaac | 177, 179, 232-233 |
| Shelley, Mary | 149 |
| Sherrard, George | 34 |
| Sill, Joseph (Thornhill) | 41 |
| Sloane, Hans | 188 |
| Sloane, Rev Stephen | 188 |
| Smythe, Agnes | 30-31 |
| Shillito, Thomas | 27 |
| Shrewsbury, Earl of | 94 |
| Smith, Hugh | 115 |
| Smith, Mary | 115 |
| Smythe, Harriet | 152 |
| Sotwell, Richard | 35 |
| Sotwell, Robert (Hoylandswaine) | 35 |
| Spencer, Charles (Sunderland) | 130 |
| Spencer, Diana | 130 |
| Sprigg, Richard | 87 |
| Squibb, John | 175 |
| Stapleton, Robert (Wighill) | 63 |
| Stewart, Lady Susan (Galloway) | 143 |
| Strafford, 1st Earl (see Wentworth) | |
| Strafford, 2nd Earl | 72 |
| Stansfield, John | 12 |
| Stepkins, John (elder) | 88 |
| Steuart, George | 138 |
| Stoddert, Benjamin | 124 |
| Strudwick, Edward | 105 |
| Style, Alderman William | 64 |
| Sunderland, Duke of | 194 |
| Sunderland, Richard | 19, 25-26, 34 |
| Sweringen, Anne van (Bladen) | 115, 121, 125, 155 |
| Sweringen, Eleanor van | 116 |
| Sweringen, Gerret van | 115-116, 122, 227 |
| Sweringen, Mary | 116, 122, 227 |
| Swift, William | 35 |
| Swift, Jonathan | 113 |
| Swift, Richard | 113 |
| Swinburne, Henry | 186 |
| Swyft, Mary | 33 |
| Syms, James | 86 |
| Talbot, George | 120 |

| | |
|---|---|
| Talbot, Gilbert (Shrewsbury) | 18 |
| Talbot, Margaret | 18 |
| Tarrant, Thomas | 180 |
| Tasker, Anne (Bladen) | 125-126, 217, 227 |
| Tasker, Anne (Ogle) | 123 |
| Tasker, Benjamin | 122-123, 125-128, 227 |
| Tasker, Benjamin (Jnr) | 123-125, 135-136 |
| Tasker, Elizabeth | 124-125 |
| Tasker, Frances | 123, 125 |
| Tasker, Rebecca | 123, 125 |
| Tayloe, Ben Ogle | 125, 127 |
| Tayloe, John III | 125 |
| Taylor, Francis (attorney) | 85, 106, 169-171 |
| Taylor, John | 127 |
| Taylor, John Bladen | 127-128, 165 |
| Tempest, Nicholas | 13 |
| Tempest, Sir Richard | 11-15, 22 |
| Tempest, Thomas | 58 |
| Thornton, Thomas | 42, 90 |
| Tinker, Isabella (Bladen/Blount) | 8, 96, 193-195 |
| Tinker, Jeremiah | 187 |
| Tinker, John | 194-195 |
| Tinker, John Bladen | 128 |
| Toft, Elizabeth | 59 |
| Tomlinson, Thomas | 57 |
| Thompson, George | 122 |
| Tonge, Israel | 79, 81 |
| Topham, William | 73-75, 83, 165 |
| Townshend, Charles | 103-104, 130 |
| Townshend, Elizabeth | 103 |
| Townshend, William | 103 |
| Trappes, Anne | 17, 20, 27 |
| Trappes, Sir Francis | 17, 21, 27 |
| Trengrouse, Thomas | 175 |
| Turner, Cassandra (Lady Hawke) | 183, 183-184 |
| Turner, Sir Edward | 183 |
| Vavasour, Isabella (Bladen) | 96, 104-105, 109-110, 155-156, 209, 227 |
| Vavasour, Peter | 110, 155-156 |
| Vavasour, Sir Walter | 110, 158 |
| Vezey, Capt Theodore | 113 |
| Villeneuve Admiral | 153 |
| Wainwright, Thomas | 30-31 |
| Wales, Princess Dowager | 182 |
| Waller, Sir William | 79 |
| Wales, Prince of (Hen Stuart) | 22 |
| Walker, Richard | 42 |
| Walpole, Dorothy | 103, 130 |
| Walpole, Horace | 139 |
| Walpole, Sir Robert | 103, 130-131, 135, 181, 194, 196, 198 |
| Wandesford, Sir Christopher | 53 |
| Warcup, Edmund | 79, 81 |
| Waterhouse, John | 14 |
| Waterhouse Helen (Lacy) | 19-20, 22-24, 26, 39, 51 |
| Waterhouse, Jane (Bosvile) | 22 |
| Waterhouse, John | 24, 51 |
| Waterhouse, Philip | 19-20, 22-24, 29, 39 |
| Waterhouse, Robert | 24, 29, 60 |
| Waterhouse, Sarah (Lacy) | 15 |
| Waters, Capt | 64 |
| Waterton, Jane | 24, 29 |
| Waterton, Thomas | 24 |
| Waterton, Sir Robert (Agincourt) | 29 |
| Watson, Alice (Birkhead, Rogers) | 67-68 |
| Watson, Edmund | 67-68, 72 |
| Wellington, Duke of | 147-148 |
| Wentworth, Anne (Savile) | 17, 27, 39 |

# Name Index

| | |
|---|---|
| Wentworth, Anne (Fairfax) | 53 |
| Wentworth, Catherine (Gargrave) | 27, 29 |
| Wentworth, Sir George (Woolley) | 53 |
| Wentworth, Hugh | 71-72 |
| Wentworth, Margaret | 19 |
| Wentworth, Sir Thomas (Strafford) | 17, 19-20, 27, 39-40, 50, 52-54, 66 |
| Wentworth, Thomas (Watson) | 72 |
| Wentworth, Sir William | 17, 27, 85 |
| Wessell, Abraham | 87 |
| West, Gilbert | 141 |
| West, Mr (attorney) | 160 |
| Whitehall, Gilbert | 76 |
| Widdrington, Catherine | 158 |
| Widdrington, Mary | 158, 167 |
| Widdrington, Roger | 158 |
| Wood, Henry | 35 |
| Wood, Richard | 64 |
| Woodford, William | 128, 136-137 |
| Wortley, Edward | 35 |
| Wortley, Eleanor | 17, 27 |
| Wortley, Elizabeth (Boughton) - later Cavendish | 17-19, 21-22, 26, 33-35, 40 |
| Wortley, Elizabeth (dau of abv) | 33 |
| Wortley, Sir Francis | 18-22, 24-27, 32-42, 50, 197 |
| Wortley, Sir Francis (son of abv) | 33, 35 |
| Wortley, Grace (Brouncker) | 21, 24 |
| Wortley, Mary | 11 |
| Wortley, Sir Richard | 17-18, 24, 27, 33 |
| Wortley, Sarah | 33-34 |
| Wortley, Thomas | 33 |
| Wright, Dick | 158 |
| Wrightson, John Battie | 31 |
| Wrightson, Robert | 17, 31, 68-75, 83-85, 98, 102, 106 |
| Wrightson, Thomas | 75 |
| York, Edward Duke of | 139-140 |
| Young, Sir William | 130-131 |

www.ingramcontent.com/pod-product-compliance
Lightning Source LLC
Chambersburg PA
CBHW080552090426
42735CB00016B/3214